I0816144
MADE IN
HACKNEY
MADE IN
HACKNEY
COMMUNITY
COOKERY SCHOOL
MADE IN
HACKNEY

MADE IN HACKNEY
Ian
Henry
THE COMMONERS

Sarah Bentley
& the Made In Hackney chefs

100+ Global Recipes

WE COOK PLANTS

For people.
For the planet.
With joy.

NOURISH
EAT WELL, LIVE WELL

WE COOK PLANTS
Sarah Bentley & the Made in Hackney Chefs

First published in the UK and USA in 2025 by
Nourish, an imprint of Watkins Media Limited
Unit 11, Shepperton House, 83–93 Shepperton Road,
London N1 3DF

enquiries@nourishbooks.com

Editorial Director: Ella Chappell
Copyeditor: Anne Sheasby
Proofreader: Emma Hill
Head of Design & Art Direction: Karen Smith
Design Concept: Abi Hartshorne
Typesetting: Eleri Stanton
Production: Uzma Taj
Commissioned food photography: Sarah Doig
Food Stylist: Bianca Nice
Prop Stylist: Megan Rose Thomson
Portraits & Reportage Photography: Marcus Duran
Additional Food Stills: Photography: Tom Skelton;
Styling: Amy Hiller

Additional photography with thanks to:
Marcus Duran, Casey Lazonick, Rebecca Zephyr Thomas, Tara Rudd, Emel Ernalbant, Tom Hains, Nadia Bruney, Nick David, Nadia Bruney, Tanya Harris, Issy Croker, Emily Grant, Lauren Anders Brown, Tom Skelton, Kuba Nowark, Simon Way, Jonathan Perugia, Gary Manhine, Dom Dorin, Sophie Verhagen, Lucy Young, Pasco Ashton, Daniella Maiorana, Nicola Bushnell, Thomas Mattey, Kate Beatty, Katja Lumezi

A CIP record for this book is available from the British Library
ISBN: 978-1-84899-445-4 (Hardback)
ISBN: 978-1-84899-446-1 (eBook)

10 9 8 7 6 5 4 3 2 1

Typeset in Natom Pro & Brother 1816
Printed in China

The manufacturer's authorised representative in the EU for product safety is: *eucomply OÜ - Pärnu mnt 139b-14, 11317 Tallinn, Estonia, hello@eucompliancepartner.com, www.eucompliancepartner.com*

Publisher's note
While every care has been taken in compiling the recipes for this book, Watkins Media Limited, or any other persons who have been involved in working on this publication, cannot accept responsibility for any errors or omissions, inadvertent or not, that may be found in the recipes or text, nor for any problems that may arise as a result of preparing one of these recipes. If you are pregnant or breastfeeding or have any special dietary requirements or medical conditions, it is advisable to consult a medical professional before following any of the recipes contained in this book.

Notes on the recipes
Unless otherwise stated:
Use medium fruit and vegetables
Use fresh herbs, spices and chillies
Do not mix metric, imperial and US cup measurements:
1 tsp = 5ml 1 tbsp = 15ml 1 cup = 240ml

MADE IN HACKNEY
COMMUNITY COOKERY SCHOOL

nourishbooks.com

* CONTENTS

Dedication

* To my mum Margaret and dad Gordon. I wish so much you could hold and read this book. You might not be here to do that, but your energy, spirit and love run through every word. I know you'd be chuffed to bits with it.

* To all the people that have been part of, participated in, supported or believed in Made In Hackney's work and mission, we extend the deepest love and gratitude. Without you all, none of this would have been possible.

* To everyone involved in the food justice and food system transition movement, ancestors and present activists, we link arms and bow down. It takes a movement, and it's a privilege being part of this with you all.

OUR SUPPORTERS

This book would not be possible without the support of these independent UK brands – Clearspring, Viridian and Mr Organic. All are long-time supporters of Made In Hackney and are the real deal when it comes to doing business differently. We acknowledge they're not the most budget brands, but their high quality, commitment to organic, clean labels and traceable sourcing from artisan producers means we think they're well worth the price. It's always a privilege to use their products. You'll see them recommended throughout this book. This endorsement comes from years of our chefs and community members telling us how much they enjoy these products, and appreciation for the support these brands and the people behind them give our work.

Clearspring

Founded in 1993 by Christopher Dawson, this independent family business has pioneered authentic Japanese specialities and organic fine foods, crafted without compromise.

We first met Maria, Clearspring's Managing Director and Christopher's daughter, back in 2013. She drank tea with us in our tiny basement kitchen. We had an instant connection through our shared passion for plant-based, organic, ethically sourced foods that are good for people and the planet.

Clearspring have supported us ever since – donating products to our classes, meal service, community parties, supper clubs and emergency food hampers. During their 30-year celebrations in 2023, we were their official charity partner, and they helped us to provide 30,000 plant-based meals to households in need of food support.

Clearspring is the go-to brand for many of our chefs who love their uncompromising dedication to clean, high quality plant-based wholefood ingredients, unique artisanal products and great flavour. This includes favourites Clearspring Organic Japanese Yaemon Tamari, Miso, Silken Tofu, Matcha and their Sushi range, alongside wonderful international ranges such as their Organic Italian Cold Pressed Oils and Vinegars, a Sri Lankan Coconut range and a growing Organic Thai range.

Viridian Nutrition

Viridian Nutrition was founded by Cheryl Thallon in 1999. She wanted to create a line of pure supplements she was happy to give to her daughter Holly. Fast track to now, and Holly is the company MD and has recently restated the company's commitment to being "indie-forever" to ensure the quality of their food supplements can't be compromised by shareholders. Viridian specialise in nutritionist-formulated "no junk" capsules, liquids and powders. Their products are free of artificial fillers and additives. There are no sweeteners, flavourings, colours, artificial preservatives or binders, which are often found in so many other supplements.

They have product lines dedicated to all life stages, including menopause, men's and women's health, pregnancy and fertility, vegan support and kids. Many MIH folk, including our naturopaths and nutritionists, use their Vegan Essential, EPA & DHA Oil, magnesium, prostate support and super food powders and give them excellent ratings. Every year Viridian make donations to ethical charities nominated by their independent health store stockists. They've supported our work since 2014 with financial and product donations, the creation of a community recipe book, and collaborating on shared content.

Mr Organic

Founder and MD of Mr Organic, Valerio Simonetti, a third generation Italian organic producer, heard about us and asked his team to get in touch to support our work – a rare event in the charity world! We were chuffed as we had already started using Mr Organic products in our classes due to their superior quality and commitment to artisan produced, organic staples with clean labels. The North London-based company is bonded by "farming, family and friendship", which resonated with us deeply, and for Italian staple products we don't look anywhere else as the quality is unrivalled.

In 2022 Mr Organic launched their own charity – The Organic Family Foundation – to whom they donate 5% of all their profits. We're one of four founding charities to be supported by the foundation and we've collaborated with the brand on community food pantry days, community parties, emergency food hampers and have hosted the team for West African and Caribbean cookery classes. Once you've tried their olive oils and vinegars, tomato purée, tinned cherry tomatoes, passata and tagliatelle pasta, you'll be hooked.

WELCOME!

Want to eat nutritious, delicious, budget-conscious food that's good for you and the planet? Know you need to get more plants on your plate but not sure how? Love exploring different cultural cuisines? Interested in discussing some of the big issues surrounding our broken food system? If you answered yes to any of those – or all of those - welcome! You've found your new foodie community.

Hello, I'm Sarah, founder of Made In Hackney (MIH), a plant-based eating revolution disguised as a community cookery school and charity. Our mission is to use the power of plants to end health inequalities, hunger, the climate crisis and bring together and celebrate diverse communities. Since we fired up our hobs in 2012, we've upskilled and inspired thousands of people to grow, cook and eat more plants for the sake of planetary and human health. Now we're joining you in your kitchen to help you do the same.

So why cook with us?

The thousands of beautiful souls we've had the pleasure to cook with are just like you. They want to do the right thing food-wise for themselves, their families and the planet. Most of our class participants are not veggie or vegan, and plant-based eating is a new, sometimes daunting change. When we opened, veganism and plant-based eating was viewed with scepticism, so we made sure people didn't know what our food policy was before they arrived. We had a hunch that the satisfaction of learning new skills, the good vibes and the tasty, interesting food would win people over. And by and large it did, people returning class after class for "More of that delicious and surprisingly filling rabbit food". True quote!

For some people the experience was a lot. Food is emotional and cultural, part of our hard wiring and identity. Walking into a kitchen and being met by piles of unfamiliar seeds, grains and herbs can be unsettling. And we thank everyone who felt this but opened up their hearts, minds and stomachs to give a new way of eating a go.

Our approach at MIH is to offer planet-friendly, inclusive, unpretentious, flavour-packed, multicultural plant-based cuisine with wide appeal. We've cooked with pensioners, corporate executives, school students, carers, toddlers, teenagers, hospital patients, hostel residents, care leavers – almost none of them vegan – but who with just a bit of encouragement found a new love of plant-based eating.

This book contains over 100 recipes from thirteen years-plus of community cooking. So when we say these recipes are tried and tested, we mean it. When you're cooking in a pensioners' luncheon club, or at a youth centre, you've gotta have your flavour profile on point and be prepared to take some frank feedback. The occasional "Egh what's that?" comments were tough, yes, but it only made us – and our recipes – stronger. And it makes the moments folk describe our food as, "peng", "utterly delicious" and "very surprising, in a good way" all the more worthwhile.

As MIH founder turned ambassador, aka chief storyteller and eater, I will be your culinary guide through this book. A few recipes are mine, but most are by our amazing chefs who bring their unique foodways, cultures and culinary personalities to the table. These chefs have dedicated thousands of hours inspiring, upskilling, feeding and collaborating with communities to experience the benefits of plant-based food. And we celebrate and appreciate them here.

Everyone that attends a MIH class is on a different journey, and consequently their lives are enriched in unique and beautiful ways (see just some of those stories in the box on the right), just as yours will be with this book.

And these are just the stories from our cooking classes. The over 250,000 free meals we've provided since 2020 have supported households during times of crisis. In the sixth richest city in the world – London – the fact people are going hungry is an outrage and an indictment of our dysfunctional political and economic system. Each meal is an act of defiant love and a challenge to the status quo.

It's not just us. We're part of a global movement of disruptive community collectives striving for a juster, healthier, happier world. These groups do incredible things in challenging circumstances with very few resources. We appreciate you and bow down.

Our food is not just fuel, but nourishment, connection, empowerment and – if you want it to be – a political statement. A statement that centres an inclusive approach to life grounded in local and global equity and an anti-racist outlook.

This book is peppered with information about big themes such as land justice, the climate

- **Seema** learned to cook healthier, more affordable meals for her family and kids, upping their vegetable intake easily once she had more recipes up her sleeve.

- For **Rachel** the cooking classes were her first act of self-care after being a full-time carer for her partner for ten years.

- **Margaret** learned to cook her preferred West African cultural foods in a way that lowered her Type 2 diabetes insulin needs. She also made new friends, which helped with the stress of caring for two adult sons with learning difficulties.

- **Aged 83, Patrick** learned to cook for the first time after his wife passed away, turning up for class with a glint in his eye and an apron that said BIG SAUSAGE with an arrow pointing downward.

- **Joan** learnt to bake and decorate a birthday cake for her vegan granddaughter and was delighted to evolve her skills so she could keep showing her love with delicious cakes.

- By making the diet and lifestyle changes recommended in our classes, **9-year-old Maisy,** with the support of her mum, healed a debilitating bowel complaint that was preventing her from enjoying her childhood.

- **Chantal,** who was living in a women's shelter, felt so inspired after doing our cooking course she set up a vegan brownie business.

- After taking our course a group of over **55 men** living alone in Poplar formed the Men's Vegan Café, a pop-up where they cook for their community whenever there's an event on their estate. We never saw that one coming!

Young women on You Make It's holistic mentoring scheme cooking with us.

crisis, body inclusivity, health inequalities and decolonizing the food system. This provides a grounding for the why behind MIH.

Most of our dishes use widely available plant-based ingredients but a few may be new to you. These recipes are an opportunity for a new cultural and culinary adventure. We'll advise you how to find ingredients and tell you how to prepare them (see p 272 for Tips & Tricks), so don't avoid these recipes, embrace them. For what is life without new experiences?

Many recipes are grouped into whole meals because that's how we structure our cookery classes, but many dishes can be made on their own and plonked on toast or a baked potato. If you want to go all out, you can make the whole meal. If you're short of time, just make an element of it. It's all good.

We've got some simple dishes to get going with, and trickier recipes to elevate your kitchen skills. If you're a newish plant-based cook, a huge welcome hug to you. Everyone can grow, cook, ferment and eat more plants. It's just a case of access, practice, familiarity and evolving your palette. Don't be disheartened if things don't grow, ferment or taste amazing the first time. They rarely do. Growing and cooking are muscles that build every time you use them. So keep going, you've totally got this.

And finally a little reveal. I'm not the most organized, skilled or precise of cooks. I'm a feeder, eater, enthusiastic learner and daughter of a fierce and highly skilled home economics teacher – but unlike many of our teachers, I'm no pro chef. So if I can make these recipes, so can you. Don't take things too seriously in the garden and kitchen. In our classes we always say the most important ingredient is joy. Thanks for cooking plants with us. You're gonna love it.

Sarah & the MIH chefs x

P.S. By purchasing this book you are helping us to deliver more life-changing plant-based cookery classes and to provide plant-based food support to households experiencing food insecurity. THANK YOU for supporting our work.

***DISCLAIMER** The MIH chefs and supporters are a diverse bunch with differing perspectives. The views expressed in this book do not necessarily reflect all our collaborators' views. But what unites us all is a belief in food justice, that everyone has the right to access nutritious, delicious, climate-friendly food; and that to reduce health inequalities and tackle the climate crisis, we all need to eat more plants.*

CHAPTER 1

WHO ARE MADE IN HACKNEY?

Made In Hackney fired up its hobs for its first community class on a chilly October evening in 2012. The kitchen buzzed with people bearing jars ready to fill with chutneys and jams. Fruit from local orchards was chopped. Spices added. Laughter and stories shared. Hearts, stomachs and jars were filled.

But before this joyful debut things had been, shall we say, eventful.

The builder tasked with turning the basement of health food store Food For All (F4A) in Stoke Newington into our community kitchen went rogue. At the time of his exit and "good luck" leaving note, the kitchen units weren't installed, there weren't any sinks, tiles, fire doors, flooring or shelves. It looked like something from "Britain's Worst Builders" TV show. We threatened legal action. He replied, by text, "Do your worst lassie".

After sobbing in a crumpled heap, what came next was beautiful. My co-founder Joshna Lovage and her dad, F4A director Govinda, shop customers, parents of kids who attended Sunrise Nursery next door, yoga and meditation students from Ananda Marga located above the shop, my husband Baba and his practical pals – all descended to complete what the builder couldn't. Many a night me, Baba and super volunteer Vinayaka were there until 2am tiling, sawing and finishing. It was an incredible testimony to people power and we opened just two weeks later than originally planned.

Although we haven't experienced a calamity of such magnitude again (but umpteen smaller scale ones like when I double-booked the kitchen, and when we got shut out a venue due to a misunderstanding about an unpaid energy bill), the spirit in which the kitchen was made was indicative of how many wonderful things at MIH would happen over the coming years. With love, hope and the power of community.

In our first year we ran 174 cookery classes. We cooked with the London Gypsy Traveller Unit under 12s, Action For Children's young carers, Mums from Ihsan, the local Islamic children's centre, people from the hearing- and sight-impaired community, type 2 diabetic patients, young people not in education or training, new parents in addiction recovery, over-50s men living alone, families with young children and so many other wonderful community members. We cooked in nurseries, schools, hostels, community centres, pensioners lunch clubs and shelters. It was an amazing year, tweaking and adapting to meet the needs of the diverse people that walked through the kitchen door every day. This learning and evolving has never stopped.

The vegan food, as long as the recipes turned out well, was generally well received. There were plenty of quips about a dish being better with a sausage on top or a glug of cream, but even these folk came back week after week to try new things and have a joyful time. I'll always remember a nutritionist who attended with a youth group who made chili non-carne with lentils and veg served with brown rice and locally grown organic salad. The young people yammed it down – result! – but on their way out the nutritionist handed out ham sandwiches, crisps and chocolate saying they were concerned the meal we made was nutritionally inadequate. I'm hard to fluster, but my jaw must have hit the floor.

Over time and with growing acceptance about plant-based diets, incidents like these became less frequent. Sure, people still asked in lesson two or three, so when are we going to cook chicken? But by and large people embraced learning something new for the sake of their health and the planet. And the mix of international cuisines, different core skills (fermenting, baking, food growing) and challenge-solving class themes – Feed Four For £3s, Healthy Pack Lunches, Invisible Veg Kids' Food, One Pot Wonders, Zero-Waste Cooking – kept people coming back for more. Jamie Oliver even paid us a visit and featured us on his Channel 4 TV show "Meat-Free Meals". Regular attendee Lynn told us, "What I like about what you do is you don't proselytize and tub thump." (What a phrase!) "You let the food do the talking. You change us without telling us to change. You make us want to do it. It's very clever."

Our first eight years were spent spreading the plant-based love and cooking, cooking, cooking. In 2019 we delivered 355 classes – nearly one for every day of the year. Then the pandemic hit and the steam we'd been building up abruptly halted, and everything changed. Three weeks before the first national lockdown we could see our community was being hit hard. People were losing their jobs, were isolating due to ill health or were scared to go out. At this time there was no support or direction from the government. But for the sake of public health, we decided to pause all in-person gatherings. The hobs fell silent.

Big smiles in chef Raha's Persian cookery class with participants and volunteer Alma.

A few sleepless nights followed and in that time we decided to respond to what our community needed most – food and connection. And if no one could come to the kitchen – we would bring it to their front door. What came next was the most industrious period of our lives. In just two weeks we developed, fundraised for and launched our Community Meal Service in partnership with Angelina's restaurant. Their chefs did the cooking, and we did the fundraising, food surplus donation securing, outreach, volunteer management and delivery.

Being one of the first community responses in the country, our campaign went viral and featured on BBC, Sky and French M1 news. We raised £30K in three days (not usual for us; fundraising is an uphill grind) and within a week of lockdown we were delivering meals to 500 residents every day. I'll never forget our first shift, cycling through a deserted Hackney and arriving at Dalston Lane to see 30 cycle couriers wearing MIH high-vis jackets stood two metres apart stretching down the street waiting to pick up meals. It was surreal. But it proved to me yet again the power a small group of people could have to make change.

For many months our cycle couriers were the only people many residents saw – our riders providing smiles, chat and in some cases 999 calls when they found people collapsed on their kitchen floors. The response from our community ranged from the emotional to the comical. People shared gratitude after our meals were the first food in their household for days; requested simpler child-friendly dishes (we made these); and asked jokingly if we could deliver extra toilet paper as their tummies weren't used to quite so much fibre!

The service was planned for three months, but due to the pandemic being followed by the cost of living crisis we kept it going for three years – making and delivering a whopping 250,000 meals by then all being cooked in-house by our own team of chefs. We got to a point though where the cost and capacity to run it was going to sink us, so we made the heart-breaking decision to scale back. As hard as this was it was the right call and resulted in the fantastic Community Made programme being developed, a twice weekly collaborative cooking session where community members batch cook a few hundred meals – which are delivered to local food projects for distribution and directly to housebound residents. We still do the community cooking classes, the ticketed masterclasses, team building events, outreach stalls and community feasts – so we keep ourselves busy!

By the time we'd been operating for ten years we had a fair bit of knowledge and experience – mostly learned the hard way! Our masterclass programme saw some of the first classes in the UK to focus on vegan phish, meats, cheeses, aquafaba and plant-based dairy made from wholefood ingredients, and our amazing team of chefs meant we offered some of the most culturally diverse vegan food in the country.

So we banished our imposter syndrome and developed two programmes to share this knowledge: Plant Prospects – to upskill, influence and inspire civil society to go more plant-based; and Global Plant Kitchens – a course and mentoring scheme to accelerate a movement of worldwide plant-based community cookery schools. PP saw us do a ten-city tour of the UK inspiring and upskilling food power players to go more plant-based. At the time of writing, the Global Plant Kitchens training platform had sign-ups from over 30 countries and has mentored groups in Macao (China), Peru, South Africa and five groups in cities across the UK.

All the joy in chef Sareta's Cooking On A Budget class

When I think about our hands, hearts and hobs stretching out to other souls around the globe who, like us, believe in the healing and transformative power of plants, I find it hard to believe the little community cookery school that almost didn't get built has come this far. We couldn't have done it without all the thousands of people that believed in us along the way. And that includes you. So welcome aboard. Now let's cook some seriously delicious plants.

PLANTS FOR ALL

Millions of people go hungry in so called "developed" wealthy nations, the UK and USA, every day. This is a gross injustice. A range of projects exist to support people to access enough nourishing, plant-based food. To find out more, visit the MIH website where we have created a Plants For All guide of these support projects.

SARAH'S STORY

“Hi, I'm Sarah Bentley, founder of Made In Hackney, chief eater, culinary guide and storyteller.

Sharing the inspiring work of the MIH community in book form has long been a dream, so I'm pinching myself to finally find myself writing these words. Before we proceed, a little about me.

I grew up in a village outside the rural market town of Grantham in Lincolnshire, UK. My mum was a home economics teacher, sensational host and home cook. My dad was a sales person for a steeplejack business and was a master storyteller and deep empath. They were both active in the local community. They supported people and helped make things happen.

Food was our household's love language. Mum baked, cooked and preserved her care for us into hedgehog-shaped bread rolls, epic Sunday spreads and batches of damson chutneys and vinegars. Dad hoovered it up with relish – supporting by peeling spuds and taking us out to eat to give Mum a break and for us to experience international cuisines at a time when diverse cultural foods weren't prevalent in the 'shires.

I was a sensitive child, questioning things about the world I didn't think made sense – something my mum encouraged. I now know I'm neurodiverse, ADHD and highly sensitive, but in the 80s we didn't talk about that – so I learned to mask and keep my mouth shut in school when ideas about the world and people were presented in ways I sensed were wrong, but didn't have the language to unpick.

Grantham is surrounded by non-organic crop, animal and dairy farming. Sausage baps, bacon butties, Sunday roasts and cheese are local staples. So when I went veggie age nine, it was quite a thing.

I was a sensitive child, questioning things about the world I didn't think made sense – something my mum encouraged.

Sarah and her Mum Margaret aka Nana B – who'd just led a brilliant jam and chutney making workshop age 75.

Age 18 I couldn't beat a path quick enough to London, where I forged a career as a music journalist. I was drawn to scenes with a rebel heart, a thumping bass and a deep social context. I loved how being a journalist you learned new things every day and I regarded the trust people placed in me to share their stories as the deepest privilege.

A trip to Jamaica as a young journo changed my life. I was introduced to Rastafarian Ital cuisine and within two weeks of eating like this my IBS cleared up and my erratic period regulated. I went wholefoods, plant-based vegan and never looked back.

I began hosting Skank and Grill parties in my Hackney garden – vegan BBQs with banging tunes. Inspired by my mum's party catering and a desire to share the benefits of plant-based eating, I made huge vegan feasts. People asked what ingredients were and scribbled down recipes. I could see sharing food in this joyful way was a powerful vehicle for change.

After 15 years documenting other people's efforts to create culture and change, I wanted to do something myself. I volunteered on Growing Communities patchwork farms and learned to grow organic food. This lit a fire in me I hadn't felt for years. Hands in the soil, sun on face, I learned to raise and care for plants with beautiful folk hungry to return to the source and stick two fingers up to the corporate control of our food. This experience combined with a life-changing interview with Indian food sovereignty activist Vandana Shiva and I knew: my path was food. It always had been.

Sarah at MIH's Veg Dash fun run awarding chef Sareta a prize for best costume! What a lovely spud she made.

And so next came Made In Hackney, a 12-year journey of steep learning and deep collaboration. When we started I had no idea that the little community cookery school would become the global community and vehicle for change it is today. It's been a wild ride. I may have got the party started, but it's the amazing people – chefs, volunteers, team and community members – that came next and believed in a kinder, more equitable, and joyful way of living, eating and being together that made MIH what it is today.

And although I no longer work in the charity's operational side, I'll always remain a proud ambassador and regard my time leading MIH as one of the deepest honours of my life. ”

* WHY PLANTS?

When it comes to human and planetary health, nothing else on Earth has the transformative and healing powers of plants. We're being stretchy with the term "plants" and including the fungus kingdom too. Cheeky.

Growing, cooking and eating more plants has the potential to reduce chronic illness, reduce the catastrophic environmental impact of our relatively recent cheap-meat heavy diet, reduce animal suffering and bring communities together through an inclusive and compassionate approach to food.

If you're reading this book, you're probably onboard with this. But just in case you need a motivation injection, here's the most persuasive data to get more plants on your plate.

▶ PEOPLE

Up until now, in the world's economically wealthiest nations, each generation's life expectancy has steadily increased. However a combination of poverty wages; escalating living costs; nutrient-poor, high salt, fat and sugar foods; the global obesity epidemic; rising rates of chronic disease; pollution; sedentary lifestyles and jobs; and environmental degradation mean that the life expectancy trend for millennials is expected to reduce. This makes this generation the first in modern history to potentially have shorter lifespans than their parents.

Health Benefits Of Adopting A Plant-Based Diet

Cardiovascular disease
25–30% reduction in risk

Type 2 diabetes
30–40% reduction in risk

High blood pressure
50% reduction in risk

Cancer
19% reduction in risk

Stroke
Reduced risk

Source: Plant-Based Health Professionals, 2024

If the British population ate a plant-based diet

NHS expenditure would reduce by £6.7 billion per year

A potential 2.1 million fewer cases of disease

A gain of 170K quality adjusted life years across the population

Source: The Vegan Society, Study by the Office of Health Economics, 2024

The World Health Organization's first step to healthy eating:

"Eat a nutritious diet based on a variety of foods originating mainly from plants, rather than animals."

A global move to a vegan diet would avert 8.1 million plus premature deaths per year by 2050.

Source: Oxford Martin School, PNAS, 2016PLANET

▶ PLANET

It's impossible to talk about the climate crisis without sounding like an overdramatic harbinger of doom because, well, that's just the truth about where we're headed. And it's scary as hell.

If temperatures keep rising at present rates, a combination of extreme weather causing floods, droughts, hurricanes and forest fires – plus rising sea levels – will put whole nations' homelands and thousands of communities under water or make them untenable for life. Mass migration, famine and war will no doubt follow. Sorry, there just isn't a way to inject joy into this.

But as apocalyptic as all this sounds, we still have a small window to abate the worst version of this scenario (we're too late to avert it altogether) and begin a new era of planetary healing and regeneration. A mass transition to plant-centred diets by people who source sustenance from the global food system (as opposed to, say, nomadic hunter gatherers) is a leading solution in our tool belt of responses. Here's why.

Animal agriculture is the leading cause of climate change.

Dr Sailesh Rao, Climate Healers, Vegan World Position Paper, 2020

Vegan diets have 70% less environmental impact than high-meat diets.

Vegan diets produce 75% less greenhouse gas emissions than high-meat diets.

Source: University Of Oxford, Medical Science Division, 2023

Planetary Benefits Of Adopting A Plant-Based/Vegan Diet

- 75% Reduction In Land Use
- 54% Reduction In Water Use
- (Up to) 66% Reduction In Biodiversity Loss

Source: University Of Oxford, Medical Science Division, 2023

Humans use 31% of the land area of the planet for grazing farmed animals.

Fifth Assessment Report of the UN, IPCC

Humans extract five times as much food from the earth for farmed animals than for themselves.

Fifth Assessment Report of the UN, IPCC

A sustainable diet of more plant-based foods could reduce risk of death from chronic illness by 25%

Source: Planetary Health Diet Index (PHDI), Harvard University, 2023

▶ COMMUNITY

We've seen first-hand the power of nutritious, culturally varied food to build community.

Growing, cooking and eating food together creates bonds unmatched by many other activities. Whether you have your hands in the soil, or stirring a pot – creating nourishment together opens up space for care, connection and truth-sharing, including uncomfortable and difficult ones.

We all need to eat. Making sure no one in your community goes hungry is a defiant act of collective care that builds a foundation for a different way of being on this Earth.

We've seen it. And it's beautiful.

Inclusion In diverse communities plant-based diets are the most inclusive. It accommodates the widest range of cultural and religious requirements, ensuring no one is left behind in the transition to climate-friendly food.

Connection Wholefood plant-based diets provide an opportunity for exploration, connection and storytelling through shared ingredients, spices and techniques.

Safety Cooking plant-based foods with communities including children is the safest diet in terms of food preparation and hygiene.

Lower cost A global study found in high-income countries a vegan or vegetarian diet based on wholefood ingredients being cooked from scratch at home costs up to one third less than other diets.

Source: University Of Oxford, Medical Science Division, The Lancet Planetary Health, 2021

COMPASSION

Choosing a diet free of meat, fish, eggs, dairy, honey and other animal products is the most compassionate dietary choice you can make.

You're stepping outside the current social norm where killing or coopting a sentient creature for sensory pleasure has been distorted and sold to us as essential sustenance. It's also presented to us as a fair exchange: the farmer feeds and looks after the animals for a period of time, and in turn, they're milked, "egged" (what would you call that?) or killed (many years before their natural life cycle) in horrific killing houses and then turned into cuts of meat or fish. Have animals really signed up for this?

Once you've looked these myths in the eye, it's hard to turn your back on the billions of creatures killed every year for food. And don't forget the marginalized labourers working in abattoirs and on trawlers who have the sordid job of killing day after day, so we can eat flesh. There's got to be another way.

ANIMALS

80 billion animals are killed every year for food. *Source: Viva!*

FISH

2 trillion wild fish are killed every year.

124 billion farm fish are slaughtered annually.

4.4 billion shellfish are killed a year.

Source: Fish Count

WORKERS

Slaughterhouse workers experience significantly higher levels of PTSD (Post-Traumatic Stress Disorder), PITS (Perpetration-Induced Traumatic Stress) and other psychological distress (SPD) disorders than the general population. The occupation is also associated with higher levels of substance abuse, addiction and causing harm to others.

Source: Michigan State University, 2009 Study

ABUSIVE CONDITIONS

One out of every five fish caught is through illegal, unreported and unregulated fishing in conditions where abuses of workers are common. 128,000 workers are thought to be trapped in forced labour on remote fishing vessels around the world.

United Nations & International Labour Organisation

IN CONVERSATION WITH…

Exploring the Transformative Power of Community

A conversation with poet, community builder and activist Yazzie Min of Stand For Humanity

Why is it important to build community in a world of activism and change-making?
Yazzie: We're not meant to do life alone! There are nearly eight billion people on this planet. If we were meant to do anything alone, why are there so many of us?! Humans have this hilarious obsession with thinking we're separate to nature. There's nowhere in nature that survives on its own. So why do we think we can? We need to have people of different backgrounds, cultures and ways of thinking, different hearts and souls; part of whatever we need to change. And that's not going to come from one person's worldview. That's going to come from multiple people's worldview, and the beautiful feedback loop of the magic experienced when you do these things with others and make memories together.

Because change-making and activism – it's more than a job, right. It's a vocation, a way of life.
It is your life. Sometimes people ask me, so when did you start? And I'm like, I don't know, age three, when my memories start. It's not anything other than being a human that cares. Doing that in life, having company to do that with, and the joy, support, not burning out, having sustenance from each other in community, not only feels good, but it's also logically the only way we're going to improve the world.

How does community sustain a movement?
It's having joy alongside the hard parts. I wish I remember where I heard what I'm about to say but it was something like: whatever it is you're fighting for, you have to also make it part of the fight. So for example if joy isn't part of what you're doing to get there, how do you expect it to be on the other side in this imagined utopia, freedom or liberation? Give yourself freedom, give yourself joy wherever you can, however it looks. Because that has to be part of the fight. It's not something to save for last. It has to be alongside you, and when you've got a community that you can dance with, protest with, take action with, cook with, go on play dates with – then it becomes achievable.

Striving for change can feel hopeless if you're doing it alone.
There's a billion different ways we could be living. The toxic systems we're in now, we give them license to exist because of the belief and energy we put in them. So if that's true, then we can create different systems, we just need to put our energy and belief into them instead. The current holders of power who want to keep things the way they are will inevitably come down on anyone creating a different way. So ultimately, doing it on our own, we get burnt out. If we have community, we can tend to each other, care for each other, and still unite as a force for change. On our own we're vulnerable. If we haven't got community, a person's work can be taken down, and just like that it ceases to exist or continue.

Visions for new ways don't feel so audacious when other people are imagining them with you.
Exactly. If we all gave a different system energy and belief, we could all live freely off the land on this beautiful planet. We could just be here. Eating good food, dancing and making music. Building families and taking care of each other. It didn't have to get to the chaos of now. The beautiful part is, no matter how horrific things have been, when you have community, hope finds a way.

It has to, or we'd submit to the worst parts of life and never try to change anything.
And that's why hope always finds a way. Ten years ago, I didn't know the power of hope. Then I started to spend time with displaced people in refugee camps across Europe and saw where their hope had carried them. That's when I realised hope is massive. And it doesn't die; no matter what, it finds a way to rise. And when that happens in community, it catches like wildfire. Like, if one person's got it, another person will get it. And trying to do that on your own when things are so bleak and there's lots of reasons not to have hope, community is a solid backer.

What forces are at play to make communities less powerful?
In the UK we could talk about the fourteen years of austerity implemented by the Tory government. Where in the sixth richest country in the world people go hungry and die of cold because they can't pay their energy bill. When you bring scarcity into people's lives on a sociopathic level, actively create poverty, this stops people from rising up as they're consumed by survival. This scarcity mindset turns people against each other and breeds the idea that we just need to take care of ourselves. That we can't afford to be hospitable or take care of anything or anyone outside of just me.

And this mindset is a fertile breeding ground for racism.
The othering, blame and racism is the bandwagon people jump on next. The media fuels the fire to continue building separation. So much is drip fed down by the media, because with racism, even if you're at the bottom of the class ladder as a white person, at least you're not Black or brown, Muslim, Arab, Asian etc. That still serves as a way to have power over your brothers and sisters. But we're right here next to you. Doing the same thing, being trolled by the same people. Keeping us fighting and separate is their goal. To not allow unity across groups. We all know coalition is the only way. So not just a community, but a coalition of communities. That's where my heart is. Nothing gets me going more than seeing different groups of people coming together with the same mission, and that's also what absolutely petrifies the establishment.

If we have community, we can tend to each other, care for each other, and still unite as a force for change.

How might being in community help you achieve goals?
Having people rooting for you, supporting you, and sharing your conviction to make change keeps me on track. You need to actively seek these people out. They might not be your family or oldest friends. Sometimes those people drag you the most. Having community is a sanity saver. You may find there are people in your life whose views no longer resonate with you. It doesn't mean you have to cut them off, but it does mean you need to get sustenance and resource yourself with other friendships and spaces that support your growth.

Being in a community doesn't always mean it's harmonious and easy. It's not all brown rice and tofu as is said in some activist circles when things get bumpy.
We don't need to pretend community should always be easy. In some ways community is your chosen family. In all spaces there are people, or situations that arise, which can be hard work. It's how you deal with these moments that matters. It's all an opportunity to help us grow, understand each other better and ourselves. Over the last ten to fifteen years I've been part of some incredible movements that ended badly because of human dynamics, but many relationships were sustained beyond that. The bonds that you get from that kind of community, I don't think there's an English word for it. It's an incredibly special thing. And there's so much power that lies in it. Power to make change. Power to dream up the world we want to see. Power to make it happen. Without community, we wouldn't have that.

THRIVE ON PLANTS

Most of us don't have a background in health or nutrition, and so getting a handle on what it takes to thrive on a plant-based diet can feel like a lot. Not because it's particularly complex, but because of the amount of biased misinformation flying around. Someone says supplements are useless, someone else says they're essential. Someone says soy is to be avoided, someone else says it's an excellent addition to a plant-based diet (it is!). It's very confusing. And people tell us this in our cookery classes again and again.

To cut through all the noise, we got together with Dr Shireen Kassam, Consultant Haematologist and Founder of Plant-Based Health Professionals UK (PBHP) and Rohini Bajekal, nutritionist, author and longtime Made In Hackney supporter and teacher to bring you the knowledge. You're welcome.

TOP PLANT-BASED HEALTH MYTHS BUSTED

Plant-Based Diets Are Extreme And Unhealthy

Wrong. We know from decades of research that a diet of mostly or exclusively plants is associated with great health. You can reduce your risk of chronic disease and you can exceed at high performance sports. There's nothing extreme about a diet that's good for you and the planet. As it's radically different to the current mainstream food culture, people like to suggest it's extreme. But there is nothing extreme about a way of eating based around fruit, vegetables, whole grains, legumes, nuts and seeds..

Humans Were Not Designed to Be Plant-Based

Since the start of humanity we've mainly been foragers as opposed to hunters. We've been eating plants, nuts, seeds and berries wherever we can find them. Prehistoric humans were consuming 100g of fibre a day. The average daily intake in the UK now is around 18g. A 100% plant-based diet is probably relatively new, but that doesn't mean we shouldn't adopt it in order to thrive, end animal suffering and look after the planet with a growing population.

Dairy is Essential For Calcium

This is an industry-generated myth. The benefits of milk are hard-wired into modern Western culture. Calcium is a mineral in the soil and cows get it from eating calcium-rich sources like grass or as an added supplement in their feeds, so there's nothing essential about getting calcium from milk, which is for calves. Greens, beans, calcium-set tofu, dried fruit, nuts and seeds, fortified plant milks and yogurts are excellent sources of calcium for adults and children.

Vegan Diets Are Full of Ultra-Processed Foods

This is a popular attack on plant-based diets at the moment perpetuated by the meat and dairy industry. Most people are omnivores in the UK, with 57% of our diet consisting of ultra processed food, compared to 14% in France and between 60% to 90% in America. For British kids it's as high as 66%. So this isn't a vegan issue but a wider food culture issue. A wholefood plant-based diet is one of the healthiest choices you can make, and including a few meat and cheese plant-based alternatives is fine. It all comes down to making mostly healthy choices.

Volunteers Juliana and Lynn having a laugh after class.

Older Vegans/Plant-Based Eaters Have Weaker Bones

Despite some sensational headlines there is no solid evidence for this. It all comes down to making sure you're consuming relevant nutrients for bone health – protein, calcium, vitamin D, zinc and selenium – and avoiding excess alcohol and smoking. Virtually all nutrients are important for bone health, but the main activity that promotes it is weight-bearing exercise and resistance training. As we increasingly follow sedentary lifestyles, more people are going to suffer with weaker bones.

You Cannot Be Plant-Based When Pregnant

Most dietetic associations around the world state a healthy, varied vegan diet is suitable for all stages of life, including pregnancy. Again, it needs a little bit of knowledge and some basic culinary skills but there's no reason why you can't have a healthy vegan pregnancy if you're going to ensure you're consuming a wide variety of fruit, vegetables, whole grains, legumes, nuts and seeds.

Vegan Diets Are Dangerously Low in Iron

Plant-based diets do often have a slightly lower iron content and vegans may have slightly lower iron stores than meat eaters, but that's not necessarily a bad thing as it can be advantageous for reducing risk of certain chronic diseases such as liver disease, diabetes and heart problems. You can easily meet your iron requirements on a varied wholefoods plant-based diet. The recommended daily amount of iron is 8.7mg for men aged 19 and over, 14.8mg a day for women and people who menstruate aged 19 to 49, and 8.7mg a day for women over 50 or whose periods have stopped. Iron is the most prevalent nutrient deficiency in the world, and most people are currently not plant-based.

Children Will Not Thrive If Raised Plant-Based

Simply untrue. We've seen some horrific headlines over the years about malnourished children supposedly being vegan when in fact it turned out they were being neglected, grossly underfed or being fed only fruit. It's very sad and only serves to create clickbait headlines and feed the culture wars. A well-planned, varied, mainly wholefoods plant-based diet provides all the essential vitamins and minerals children need to thrive.

Chef Bruna's children thriving on a plant-based diet and enjoying a MIH summer community party.

* 12 TIPS TO THRIVE ON A PLANT-BASED DIET

1: Eat 9-10 Portions of Different Fruits and Veg a Day

We know this sounds like a lot at first, but if you're vegan or eating a predominantly plant-based diet, consuming a wide variety of whole plant foods is key. 80g is a portion – typically an adult handful. Five-a-day isn't enough to truly thrive, and ideally (budget and access allowing) you'd cover five with breakfast and a mid-morning snack alone. Many experts are now recommending a minimum of 30 different plants a week – which may sound like a lot, but once you get into plant-based shopping and cooking you'll appreciate what a huge abundance of fruit and veg is out there (20,000 worldwide, apparently). Remember: dried, canned and frozen fruit and veg count as well.

2: Count Colours, Not Calories

Different vitamins, minerals, polyphenols, antioxidants and other wondrous things are found in different plant-based ingredients. Without becoming an ingredient geek, an easy way to get what you need is to ensure you eat a wide variety of different coloured whole plant foods a day/each week – greens, reds, purples, orange, yellow – you get the picture. And sorry, rainbow cake doesn't count. I mean, we love rainbow cake, but that's not what we're talking about here!

3: Supplements – Take Them!

If you're vegan or eating a plant-centered diet, PBHP recommends taking vitamin B12 and vitamin D3 supplements and if budget allows an algae-derived EPA/DHA supplement is good to add in. Something like the Vegan Society's Veg 1 multivitamin or the Viridian Vegan Essential multivitamin will cover all your bases, except the EPA/DHA.

4: Experiment With Your Carbs

Wheat and potatoes are the most common sources of carbohydrate consumed in the UK, USA and across much of Europe. Our gut microbiome is much happier when we eat a wide variety of foods. So diversify your carb intake by bringing in sweet potatoes, yam, brown rice, wild rice, quinoa, oats, millet, legume-based pasta, spelt flour, gram flour (chickpea/garbanzo flour), buckwheat, teff, barley, oatmeal, lentils and beans to your diet.

5: Don't Skip Breakfast

Breakfast eaters are shown to have better health outcomes and lower rates of disease. It doesn't have to be complicated. Make porridge/oatmeal or muesli by mixing a variety of seeds, nuts, ground flaxseed and dried fruit with oats and decant into a tub for the week. Top with fruit such as banana, apple, blueberries or whatever takes your fancy.

6: Up the Iron Absorption

To up your iron intake, you can pair vitamin C-containing foods – citrus fruit, berries, red and green peppers, broccoli, Brussel-sprouts, cauliflower – with iron-rich foods such as lentils, nuts, tofu, spinach, kale, quinoa and oats. This doesn't need to be anything fancy. It might look like a snack of tangerine and cashew nuts, porridge with strawberries or a squeeze of lemon on greens. Clever hey.

Sarah, Tara, Roshni, Adam, Carla (back). Ruth and Daphne representing at the Veg Dash fundraising fun run.

7: Go Large

A wholefood vegan meal will generally need to be a bigger portion than a non-vegan meal, because a healthy vegan meal tends to be lower in fat and higher in high-water content ingredients than non-vegan meals. So to fill up, feel sustained and be well nourished, you will find you need to eat more at meal times. If you're doing a lot of exercise you'll probably need more nutrient dense snacks on hand like trail mix (a blend of tasty nuts, seeds and dried fruit) or edamame. Alas, the going large recommendation doesn't apply to high sugar-, fat- and salt-containing vegan comfort food.

8: Get That Protein

People tend to get very panicky about not getting enough protein but there's really no need. Soya (tempeh, tofu, edamame), beans and peas (black beans, kidney beans, chickpeas), lentils, oats, nuts and seeds, tahini, nutritional yeast and mushrooms are all good sources of plant-based protein. If you're training seriously or you're at an older age, you might want to consider a good quality protein powder made from pea, hemp, brown rice, soya or pumpkin seed to add to smoothies or your morning porridge.

9: Daily Ferments

Try to work a serving or two of fermented foods into your daily diet to improve the health of your gut microbiome. Fermented foods can seem scary at first but they've been eaten for thousands of years so this isn't a new food fad! Try sauerkraut, kimchi, fermented nut or seed cheese, garri (a West African dish of fermented cassava), homemade idli or dosa, or drinks like kefir and kombucha. Store-bought versions of these products can be pricey, so why not try making them yourself. Head to p 336 for our Ferments section.

10: Read the Label

When buying pre-made items (no shade here – we all need to from time to time) do read the label. Look out for high levels of salt, sugar and trans-fat (as opposed to the healthy fats in nuts and seeds) as well as industrially produced ingredients such as high-fructose corn syrup, flavour enhancers, artificial colours and sweeteners – as you should keep consumption of these types of ingredients to a minimum. Non-vegan ingredients such as whey powder and eggs find their way into cereal bars, curry pastes, muesli and crackers, so do check.

11: Remember Your Why

If you've decided to eat more plants for the planet, for the animals or your own personal health goals – remind yourself of this when you go off course. And don't beat yourself up if you fall off the wagon – you're a wonderfully imperfect human just like all of us. It can take a few weeks for your palate to change – so as time goes on you'll crave animal products less and plants more.

12: Enjoy Your Food

This is a guilt-free/diet-free zone, unless to support a specific medical condition. Eating is a sensual act. Pleasurable. Satisfying. Comforting. It can conjure up memories of home, family, friends, culture and more. Try not to eat food on the go or in front of a laptop. Sit down, take your time, and truly enjoy. Food can be such an enriching interest – so try out new recipes and ingredients from different cultures. And don't forget to chew your food properly rather than bolt it down! Your digestion will thank you.

NN You'll find more nutrition nuggets from Shireen, Rohini and other MIH experts throughout the book. You're welcome!

DIVE DEEPER

If you want to dive deeper we highly recommend you check out the Plant Based Health Professionals UK website. Created by expert doctors, dietitians and nutritionists they offer evidenced information on plant-based diets and everything from pregnancy to children's diets, budget-friendly cooking, bloating, high blood pressure, iron, healthy swaps and more.

* To Supplement or Not to Supplement

We recommend a food first approach whereby you are sourcing all your key nutrients – omega-3 fatty acids, calcium, iron, selenium and zinc – from the food you eat. However, if you are vegan or predominantly plant-based it's important to take B12 and D3 from September to early April. The Vegan Society's Veg 1 supplement is a great low cost catch all and we love Viridian Nutrition's Vegan Essential and single vitamin B12 and D3 products.

Vitamin B12 is needed to make red blood cells and for nerve function. The recommended daily intake for adults is 1.5µg. The ability to absorb B12 varies, particularly with age, so taking a 25-100µg daily or 2000µg weekly supplement is recommended. Higher doses of at least 50mcg may be advisable if you are over the age of 50 or if you have other health conditions such as coeliac disease. If you choose to obtain B12 from enriched foods, like yeast extract or nutritional yeast, eat 3 servings every day – but due to some brands' high levels of salt, we don't recommend you get this all from yeast extract. A supplement is the most reliable way of meeting your body's needs for B12.

When it comes to iodine, a daily supplement containing up to 150 micrograms in the form of potassium iodide or potassium iodate may be advisable – especially for when you're trying to get pregnant, during pregnancy and when breastfeeding as iodine plays a critical role in early brain development. Dulse, nori or certain plant-based drinks/yogurts fortified with iodine are good options.

In order to meet calcium needs, fortified foods and drinks such as plant-based milks, yogurt and calcium-set tofu can help (it says whether it contains calcium on the label), along with an intake of leafy greens, beans, whole grains, nuts and seeds.

Some supplements, such as vitamin A supplements, can actually have negative health effects, acting very differently when they are isolated. Always consult your doctor or nutritionist, especially if you are taking other medications.

* Going Plant-Based Trouble Shooting

Even if you're informed about plant-based eating, clarifications and common concerns may still arise. Over the years we've heard them all. So let's unpick some of the things that crop up for new plant-based eaters.

I've Gone Plant-Based And I'm Not Feeling Good. What's Happened?

There are three areas where people new to plant-based eating often fall short. These are: not increasing portion sizes because they're not aware of the high water content in fruits and vegetables. Not having a culinary repertoire built around a variety of fruit, vegetables, whole grains, beans, nuts and seeds so they're not getting the variety of nutrients. And not taking a vitamin B12 and vitamin D3 supplement, which can affect energy levels. If you don't feel well, it is worth seeing a specialist plant-based nutritionist or dietitian. Plant-Based Health Professionals UK has a free directory of plant-based health professionals on their website, as does Plantitician.org in the US.

Is it True that Nutrients Are More Bio-available in Animal Products?

It's true some nutrients are more bioavailable in animal products. However bioavailability of a specific nutrient does not tell you anything about the wider impact of a food on health, which is the important bit. Zinc and iron are more bioavailable in animal meat because, unlike in plant-based sources, they don't come in a package that also contains fibre or nutrients like phytates that inhibit their absorption. But does this mean we can't get enough of these nutrients to thrive on a plant-based diet? Not at all. Plants have so many other benefits such as being low in unhealthy fats, low in sodium and high in antioxidants, minerals and vitamins that this is more important than the bioavailability of single nutrients.

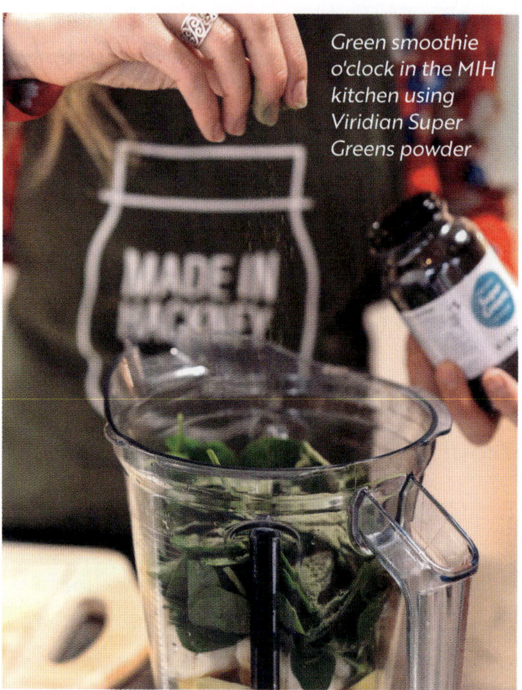

Green smoothie o'clock in the MIH kitchen using Viridian Super Greens powder

I've Heard About Calcium & Iron Thieves – What's That?

Food very high in sodium (salt), caffeine (teas, coffee, etc.) and alcohol can all negatively impact bone health as they reduce your body's ability to absorb calcium. The same applies to iron absorption – the polyphenols in tea, coffee and red wine inhibit iron absorption. We're not saying never consume these things, but it's good to not have too much of them or during meals.

Should I Really Soak my Nuts?!

Soaking nuts, seeds, grains, pulses and legumes for a few hours prior to cooking is recommended. It reduces the amount of cooking time (so saves on fuel costs), makes these ingredients more easily digestible and the nutrients in them – particularly zinc – become more bioavailable. Soaking nuts and seeds prior to eating or cooking also reduces the amount of phytates or phytic acid in them. Phytic acid is referred to as an anti-nutrient, as the crafty blighter can reduce the absorption of iron, zinc and calcium. But, as with all food, it's not a case of them being 'bad', because phytic acid can also protect against oxidative damage and insulin resistance.

▶ Why Do People Think Gluten is Bad?

There's no need to avoid gluten unless you have coeliac disease, which affects around 1% of the global population. Gluten sensitivity is a thing – but it's still being researched. It typically affects the gut and causes digestive issues such as bloating. You might have tried going gluten-free and felt better, more energetic. But you have to ask yourself: is this because you have a gluten sensitivity? Or because you stopped eating white bread, cakes, pastries, biscuits and endless pasta and replaced it with a variety of different grains and plant-based wholefoods?

▶ I've Heard Soya is Bad For Our Health and the Environment

Our ambassador Dr Nitu Bajekal is a women's hormone health expert and gynaecologist and has written and spoken a lot on this topic, so we'll hand over to her. "Soya gets a terrible rep thanks to a lot of misinformation and disinformation often from vested industries and from people who don't really understand how soya works. I don't have a view on soya. It is scientific fact that soya is safe and beneficial. It's not my opinion. The science is clear. Soya is rich in high quality protein, and also contains fibre, micronutrients and vitamins. High quality soya products in the form of soya milk, organic, calcium-fortified tofu, tempeh, edamame beans, soya chunks and mince are all excellent additions to a healthy diet. The soya farms displacing the Amazon rainforest are growing soya for animal feed for animals being reared for meat - not for vegans. If budget allows, buy organic soya grown without pesticides and herbicides and aim to have one portion a day for children, two for adults and up to four if you're working out a lot."

▶ I'm Sure I've Read Soya is Bad For Women's Health

From a health perspective, soya gets a bad rep due to its oestrogen content, which is actually beneficial for all people of all ages and gender identities. Plant oestrogens are present in many health-supporting plant-based foods – blueberries, chickpeas, beans, pistachios. Soya contains a particularly good amount of plant oestrogens, which are beneficial in reducing breast cancer risk and lots of other cancers like liver, ovarian, womb and prostate cancer. Plant oestrogens actually block mammalian oestrogens (found in animal and human tissue) from creating mischief. Plant oestrogens also promote a healthy heart, help to keep weight down and to lower cholesterol. The latest review of all studies published in 2024 have shown that women with breast cancer who consume soya regularly have a significantly lower risk of death and recurrence.

▶ I've Been Advised a Vegan Diet Doesn't Support Perimenopause/Menopause

This is a biased and misinformed opinion potentially based on a concern around not being able to access enough B vitamins, but most likely it's down to inexperience in plant-based nutrition. Although some women are lucky and have a smooth hormonal transition, perimenopause symptoms, if unexpected, unsupported and untreated, can wreak havoc on your life and overall health and happiness. Contrary to what many people understand, perimenopause symptoms start anywhere from 2–8 years before menopause (when you have your last period), and although common are often misdiagnosed, particularly in younger women. Having a doctor well informed about perimenopause and menopause is like a lottery win, as many out-dated patriarchal ideas about caring for women's health during this stage of life abound and prevent you from receiving the care you need. If your doctor or healthcare professional can't support your perimenopause/menopause journey ask to see a menopause specialist or consultant.

Changing your lifestyle can have a hugely positive impact on your experience of perimenopause/ menopause. Reducing your stress levels (we know, easier said than done), not smoking, limiting alcohol, exercising regularly – particularly resistance and weight training – and eating a healthy, plant-based diet can all play a key role. You could do all this but still experience unpleasant symptoms (racing heartbeat, insomnia, anxiety, joint pain, brain fog, UTIs, loss of libido to list just some) and therefore should receive medical help. After a medical assessment it may be concluded other treatments might be needed, but often what would most benefit women is Hormone Replacement Therapy (HRT) and lifestyle advice.

Only around 14% of women in the UK experiencing perimenopause/menopause symptoms take HRT. This is partly due to a misinterpretation by the media of a US study (WHI) that claimed HRT caused increased rates of breast cancer. The headlines went wild reporting this, but then didn't bother to run later stories to clarify the findings in more detail so both the public and many health professionals to this day believe HRT significantly increases a woman's chance of getting breast cancer. This is not the case when used in the right age group (women in perimenopause and within ten years of menopause). There is free reliable information available online about managing the perimenopause/menopause with our top choices being the British Menopause Society, the NHS and Dr Nitu's website. In the UK, you can download an HRT certificate that for £20 covers HRT costs for a year.

MIH ambassador Dr Nitu and her daughter Rohini Bajekal, a MIH volunteer nutritionist, after delivering a Cooking For Hormone Health class

Dr Nitu and Rohini Bajekal (yes, they're mama and daughter) led some popular and empowering Cooking For Hormone Health classes at Made In Hackney. Their Edamame Lentil Khichadi recipe is delicious and you'll find it on p 132. They recommend a varied, wholefood plant-based diet rich in good quality soya and legumes as ideal to support you on your perimenopause/menopause journey and can reduce common symptoms like hot flashes. This way of eating also benefits other hormonal health conditions such as PCOS and fibroids. Recommended sources of soya include a calcium-fortified soya milk/yogurts, tofu, tempeh and edamame. Foods to avoid eating regularly if your hormones are lively include deep-fried foods, high-sugar foods like cakes and pastries, and foods high in sodium such as takeaways. We know. All the good stuff. But don't worry, there's still plenty of culinary deliciousness out there. And believe us, your hormones will thank you for it.

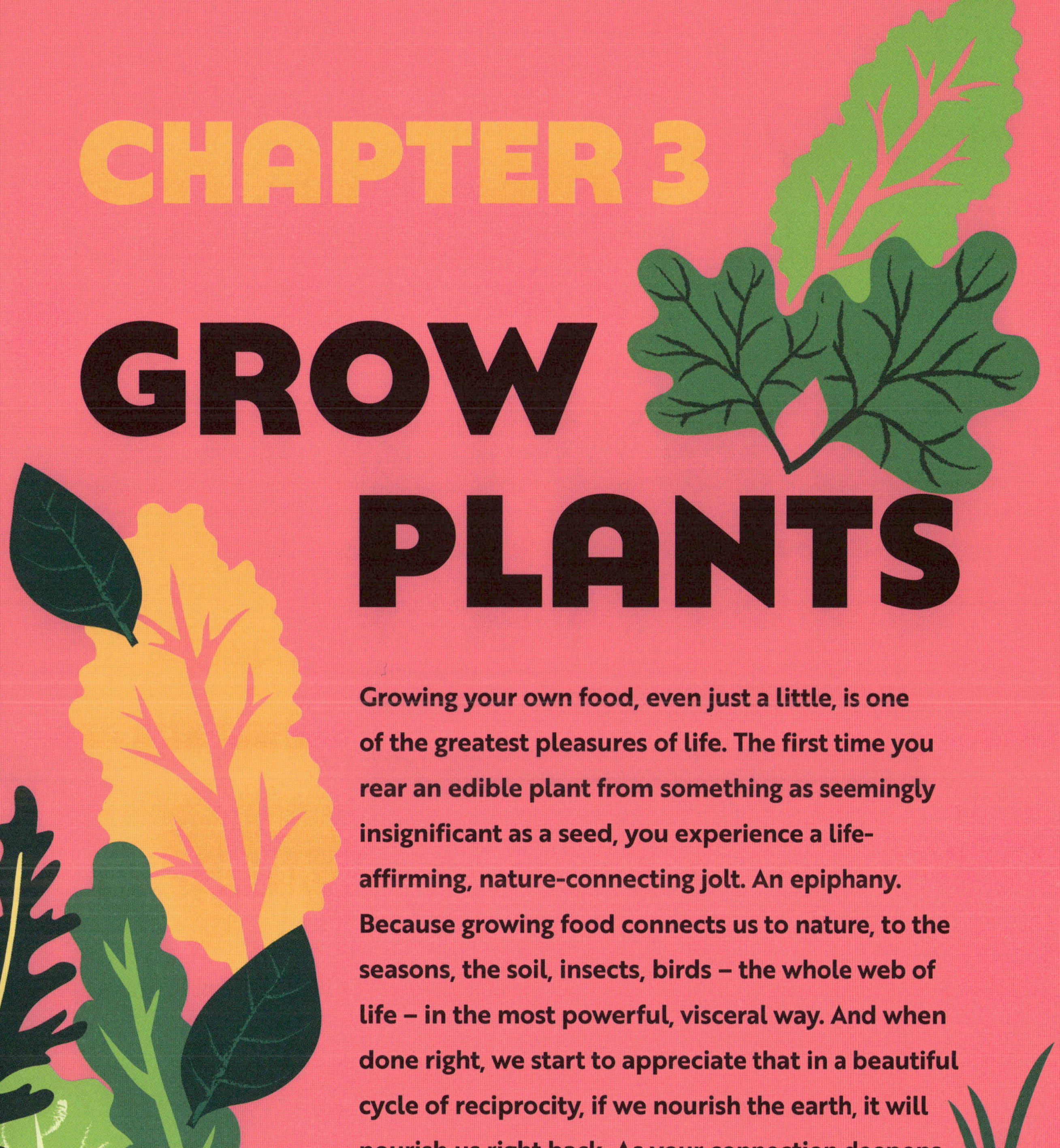

CHAPTER 3

GROW PLANTS

Growing your own food, even just a little, is one of the greatest pleasures of life. The first time you rear an edible plant from something as seemingly insignificant as a seed, you experience a life-affirming, nature-connecting jolt. An epiphany. Because growing food connects us to nature, to the seasons, the soil, insects, birds – the whole web of life – in the most powerful, visceral way. And when done right, we start to appreciate that in a beautiful cycle of reciprocity, if we nourish the earth, it will nourish us right back. As your connection deepens, you'll feel and see soil for the life-sustaining miracle it is and feel more and more outraged at the pollutants we pour onto it day after day. Yep, growing food, it's fun, but it's also deep.

Getting started with food growing can feel intimidating. Don't worry, we understand and we've got you. Like our food growing classes, this chapter is about getting started. Everything here can be grown in a micro-allotment – a window ledge, kitchen counter, balcony or patio – whatever space you have as long as it gets natural light. It might feel small scale, but you'll reap the benefits of tending and eating organic food without the effort of managing a garden or allotment.

For a more social experience, get involved in a CSA (community supported agriculture) farm or community garden. These are brilliant places to hone your skills and meet other folk seeking the mental and physical health benefits of getting out of our heads and into our hearts and hands.

Many new growers head to a garden centre or gardening aisle in a supermarket. Beware, the products sold here are often toxic with labels on the back featuring crossed out human skulls, frogs, bees and insects. The chemicals promoted as the key to a perfect lawn are almost always harmful. They perform the task at hand – getting rid of an aphid infestation or unwanted moss – while also bumping off lots of other plants, insect and amphibian life. They're damaging to human health too and are recommended to be used wearing protective masks. It's not good, is it? We won't be using any of these products. We'll be growing organically, and we'll cover why later.

Gardening is like cooking – everyone and every culture has developed their own ways, passed down through ancestors or learned from a friend or neighbour. Sometimes what works for you won't for someone else. My Aunty Joyce roots all her cuttings in glasses of water on her windowsill. When I've tried this my cuttings rot. That's the way gardening goes. Stay open to learning, but don't be afraid to be loyal to what you know works for you. Experience is key, and accepting there'll be many plant casualties along the way is part of the journey. Now let's get our hands in the soil.

* A Few Useful Terms

Annual
Plants that go through their life cycle in a year and therefore need sowing from seed every year.

Biennial
A biennial plant takes two years to complete its life cycle. If in its second year it flowers and goes to seed, food growers treat these plants like an annual.

Perennial
These are long-lived plants that come back year after year. They usually die back in the winter and burst back into life in the spring.

Herbaceous
Plants with soft, flexible green stems. Older growth can go woody, but new growth is soft, flexible and green.

Woody Trees and Shrubs
Have woody stems and trunks of varying degrees of flexibility and thickness.

Deciduous
Plants and trees that drop their leaves every year, usually early autumn to early winter.

Evergreen
Plants and trees that keep their leaves all year round.

Compost
Compost has been made by rotting down a mixture of nitrogen-rich (green alive stuff) and carbon-rich (brown dead stuff) organic matter to create a nutrient-rich growing medium. You can make your own in a compost bin (but you need an outdoor space) or buy it in bags from garden centres and online. Organic compost is more expensive than non-organic but if you've got the coin it's worth the investment. The Earth's soil is made from a mix of organic matter, sand, loam and clay, mineral particles and stones. The composition differs from area to area. Growers add more organic matter in the form of compost to soil to improve its nutrient density and structure. See p 51 for how to compost.

Soil Types
There are three main types of soil – sand, loam and clay. Loam is preferable as its particles are not too big (sand) or small (clay). Each soil type has a different pH, which means different plants like to grow in different soil types. Blueberries for example like a very acidic soil. Unless you're growing on the moors, which naturally have very acidic soil, you'll need to grow blueberries in a pot with added acid heavy, or ericaceous as it's called, soil. If you were setting up a new garden you'd test your soil's pH levels before planning what to grow. But for micro-allotment growing this is just background info to deepen your understanding. Or if you want to grow blueberries in pots! If you're buying compost and growing only in that you don't need to pH test it.

Free-Draining Soil
Soil that water soaks through quickly as opposed to pooling and taking a long time to soak through.

Seedling
A plant in its earlier stage when it has germinated from a seed and become a very small plant. They have a small root structure, a stem and their first few leaves.

Plug Plants
Small plants grown from seed that are robust and established enough to be moved from their initial position. They're larger and more established than a seedling but still usually no bigger than the palm of your hand.

Aphids
Small, sap-sucking insects that multiply very quickly and can soon destroy your crops and plants. They come in different colours and varieties, often but not always cleverly camouflaged with the colour of the plant they're gobbling up. See tips on how to naturally repel aphids on p 51.

Pollination
This is how flowering plants reproduce. Pollen travels from the anther, the flower's male part, to the stigma, its female part when a pollinator insect moves from flower to flower. Some plants pollinate thanks to the wind and rain while others cleverly

pollinate themselves. An amazing survival trait! In different parts of the world lizards, bats and birds even get involved with pollination. Most flowering plant species rely on pollinator insects to transfer the pollen from flower to flower.

Pollinators
Insects that fly from flower to flower spreading pollen and therefore allowing the plants to pollinate. Pollinators are not just honeybees, solitary bees, buff-tailed bumblebees (love that name!) but also hover flies, seven spotted ladybirds, butterflies, wasps, beetles and many flies. Yes, flies!

Green Manures
This is the collective name for amazing plants such as clover, lupins, alfalfa, phacelia, winter field beans and grazing rye, to name just a few, which suck nitrogen from the air then release it into the soil via their root nodules – replenishing the soil with one of the most important chemical elements needed for food growing. Organic growers use them to replenish their soils instead of agricultural chemicals, leaving an area covered in green manures for a whole growing season, then putting it back to use the following year after the soil has had a rest and has had time to replenish. Veganic growers that don't use animal manures rely on green manures and composting to add nutrients back into the soil – with great success.

Plant Positioning
FULL SUN – the plant needs to get sun for most of the day.
PART SUN – the plant needs to get sun for at least half of the day.
FULL SHADE – the plant needs to be almost completely in shade.
PART SHADE – the plant needs to be in shade for at least half the day.

EQUIPMENT HACKS

Setting yourself up with all the gardening kit at once can be pricey. Here are some DIY hacks for making your own equipment.

DIY WATERING CAN Using the end of a corkscrew puncture 10–15 small holes into the top of a plastic bottle. This makes a nifty DIY water sprinkler.

CRATES AND CARTONS Make your own seedling trays out of plastic crates or wooden crates sourced for free from grocery shops. Line them with strips of brown paper so they hold the soil in place. This will gradually rot down so if keeping them inside your house place the crates on a tray. Don't use cardboard to stand them on as this will rot and weld itself to your floor.

SEEDLING POTS Wash out yogurt pots and reuse as plant pots. Use a corkscrew to puncture five holes in the bottom for drainage.

PLANT LABELS Cut yogurt pots into strips to make plant labels. It might seem extra but labelling – name of plant, date of sowing – is a solid practice.

BROKEN CROCKERY/STONES To stop plants in pots getting waterlogged and their roots rotting, add a layer of broken crockery, stones or gravel to the bottom of the pots before adding the compost. I like to think of this as plants not wanting a soggy bottom!

DIY equipment hacks - a sprinkler and seedling tray made by Sarah's son Rowan from a bottle and Clearspring silken tofu cartons.

HOW TO FEED PLANTS

Stink Juice aka Comfrey Tea

I call plant feed made from comfrey Stink Juice. And yes, it does pong so it's not to be splashed onto a fresh pair of kicks. It's not toxic, it's just pungent. Plants love it.

Stink Juice is high in the golden trinity of nutrients, **NPK – Nitrogen, Phosphorus and Potassium**. The K is the letter that symbolizes Potassium in the periodic table. Oh science, how ye make no sense! Anyway, plants need nitrogen for healthy leafy growth, phosphorus for cell division and growth of the plant tip (important for your seedlings) and potassium helps flowers and fruit to form. Even if you're not growing flowers and fruit, your plants need potassium to stop them wilting on a dry, hot day. And we can make this incredible plant elixir for free entirely from natural, organic materials – no nasty chemicals needed! Result.

COMFREY PLANT FEED

1: Forage for comfrey in a wild space that has an abundance of it. Use a plant ID app, as a few wild plants look very similar, especially before flowering. Fill a plastic bag.

2: Decant your comfrey leaves into a large container with a lid located outside. (If you're based in the UK, a council food caddy makes a great vessel.)

3: Fill it up with water, and leave to stew for two to three months. You can use after one month but the longer you leave it the better.

4: Label your stink juice with a laminated label to prevent kind folk throwing away this smelly, dirty looking water.

5: Add one part feed to five parts water to a watering can and use it to water seedlings and mature plants located outdoors. And when planting out your seedlings put some in the hole before adding the plant.

You can make a plant feed out of nettles following the same process. It will be high in nitrogen, enzymes and lactic ferments and will be very good for your plants. It doesn't have the full NPK package like comfrey tea, but it's still great.

FAQS

Is it too pongy to use indoors?

In the above quantities. If you only have an indoor space stuff 3 large leaves into a one to two litre bottle then fill up with water. Due to the reduced amount of comfrey it won't smell as strongly as the bucket method.

Where to get comfrey leaves?

I grow some in my garden but also forage some. Its leaves are a little prickly to touch and its flowers are white or lilac. The leaves look very similar to alkanet plants, which have blue star-shaped flowers. Comfrey seeds for sale are usually the Bocking 14 variety, which have been bred to have dormant seeds so the plants don't take over your garden. They're perennial but won't spread like the wild variety.

When does comfrey grow?

Comfrey pops up from early spring and can stay around until the end of October.

If you're in a big city it's warmer due to pollution and so likely to appear earlier.

How to grow comfrey?
You can buy and grow comfrey from seeds, a plug plant (small plants already grown with roots) or grow it on from root cuttings. To take root cuttings, cut one of its long tap roots into roughly 5cm/2in pieces and plant them 3–5cm/1–2in deep.

Can I use comfrey for anything else?
Pollinator insects love it. You can cut the leaves and place them around the stem of high-nutrient loving crops like tomatoes. Some gardeners, when they're planting larger plants out, line the hole the plant root will go in with comfrey leaves. Each comfrey plant can give you three "flushes" of growth a year, meaning you can cut it back and let it grow again up to three times a year.

Anything else I need to know?
Comfrey can grow for up to 20 years. It's an amazing plant and a great friend and asset to organic gardeners.

BANANA PEEL JUICE

Banana peel feed is another great free-to-make plant food. It has high levels of potassium, calcium, magnesium, sulphur and phosphorus.

1: Soak the peels of three to five bananas in a bowl of water for three days.

2: Decant this water into a bottle or jug.

3: Like Stink Juice, dilute using one part banana peel juice to five parts water.

This feed contains potassium, phosphorus, magnesium and calcium – juicy minerals your salad and herb crops will enjoy.

SEAWEED MEAL AND LIQUID SEAWEED FEED

An organic fertilizer made entirely from seaweed that gives a steady, slow release of nutrients into the soil encouraging healthy plant growth. Unlike the above two feeds, you have to buy this unless you live near the coast where there's a long history of folk using foraged seaweed as fertilizer on the land.

1: Collect a small bucket of seaweed.

2: Rinse it thoroughly then leave it to dry out completely in the sun.

3: If you have a compost bin where you make your own compost, add the seaweed to boost your compost's nutrient profile.

4: If you don't, blend it into a powder or meal, store it in an airtight container and mix half a teaspoon into your soil when potting seedlings. You can also sprinkle it onto the surface of the soil near your plants.

LIQUID GOLD Another rad and free type of plant food is human urine! Yes, you read that right. This high in nitrogen liquid can be mixed with water and used near the area next to the stems of crops like tomatoes, aubergines, peppers – not sprinkled directly onto your leafy greens! Dilution rates vary but one part urine to ten parts water is commonly recommended. Alas if you're on strong medication it isn't recommend you use your own wee. Sorry. And best to only use it in your own garden rather than gadding off to a community garden with a pot full of your own pee. Not everyone will share your radical ways. Respect that.

* SEED SOWING 101

There are a few different ways of sowing seeds. Yes, the wind and animal fur may just chuck seeds willy-nilly about the landscape, but the success rate of those seeds is relatively low. When we're growing food we will be much more particular than the wind.

Shop bought seedling trays are often divided into multiple small modules. Sizes vary but I use seed trays with 40 cells.

Single Sowing
One seed per module. Got it. Just one.

Multi-Sowing
Two to four seeds per module sown together in the same hole. You do this for salad crops like spinach, kale, chard, rocket and other leafy greens where multiple plants can happily grow in a bunch.

Broadcast Sowing
This is usually done over a larger area, or in a seedling tray with no modules. Seeds are scattered or evenly sprinkled over the surface of where you want them to grow.

How Deep?
Seeds like to be planted twice the depth of their actual size. So if you're planting a large broad bean/fava bean that's 3cm/1in in size, you push it 6cm/2in down into the ground. You eyeball this – no need for rulers. Many seeds are tiny specs that you place on top of the soil and just lightly cover with soil. I like to say to the kids – tickle them in.

▲ *Single sown seeds in a tray with modules.*

Gravel is King
I recommend standing your seedling trays or pots on a shallow tray with 3–4cm/1–1½in-high sides filled with pea shingle-sized gravel. The roots of the plants will grow through at the bottom of their pot or tray and weave around the gravel to become long and strong. Fill the gravel tray with water and your plants suck this from the bottom, cleverly self-watering. Top growers water plants from the bottom, not from the top.

The Stuff on Top
After sowing, some growers cover the top of the soil with vermiculite, perlite or biochar. Vermiculite and perlite are finite resources that have to be mined so I don't use either. Biochar is made from burnt wood. There's a lot of discussion about how it can boost soil nutrients and is more environmentally sustainable, while other growers worry it could change your soil pH. I don't use this either and my seedlings grow fine.

LET'S GET GROWING

BOTTOMLESS SALAD BAR

For a constant supply of salad, sow a new tray every three weeks so when one is finished you have another to start harvesting. In the colder months it will take longer for your salad to grow and you'll need a warm house and a sunny window ledge for it to get enough light. Some people use heated mats, which you plug in and stand your seedling trays on to give them a boost of warmth. They're quite nice things to ask for as a present.

EQUIPMENT YOU'LL NEED:

Tray or crate with 3-4cm/1–1½in-high sides
Seedling tray with holes punctured in bottom and lid
Gravel (optional but nice to have)
Organic multi-purpose compost or seed compost
1 x packet mixed leaf salad seeds
Seedling tray lid or clingfilm
Small watering can or an upcycled bottle sprinkler (see p 34)
2-5 litre bag seedling compost or multipurpose compost

1: Line the high-sided tray with 2cm/¾in depth of gravel. If you don't have it, no biggie. The salad bar will still work.
2: Fill your seedling tray up to 1cm/½in from the top with compost.
3: Press the compost down firmly and top up with more soil. This is important for your little plants to grow strong. They need to push a bit.
4: Fill the tray containing the gravel with water, to 1cm/½in above the gravel. Stand the seedling tray in the water for five minutes.
5: Scatter the surface of your seedling tray evenly with the mixed leaf salad seeds.
6: Lightly cover with soil and leave in a warm, sunny position.
7: Now pop on the seedling tray lid or cover the with clingfilm/plastic wrap. This provides warmth so your seeds germinate quicker. If using clingfilm keep a close eye on them as once they germinate (tiny plant head has popped out of the soil) they can go mouldy unless you remove the clingfilm quickly.
8: Water whenever the soil looks dry. This could be daily during hot conditions or every three to four days in cooler temperatures. If your plant is standing on a gravel tray you should water the gravel, not the actual seedling tray. Weird I know. But the plants will suck up the water from the bottom and develop stronger roots. If you don't have the gravel tray, water very gently with a sprinkler head. Within six to eight weeks you should be joyfully harvesting your first mixed salad crop!
To harvest don't pick with your hands but cut the leaves at the base of the stem neatly with scissors (ripping damages the stem, which will make the plant less vigorous and susceptible to disease) and only take what you're going to eat right now. The different seeds take slightly different times to grow hence you can keep cutting the salad again and again. Organic salad is go!

TIPS & TRICKS... Be the Wind

In my food growing classes I always ask the kids what "weather" is missing from inside a green house. Light and warmth gets through the glass. Rainwater is emulated when they water the seedlings. What else do plants need weather-wise? It might sound surprising, but a little wind. Plants and trees that grow indoors are at risk of growing too thin, leggy and weak. They need to sway a little in the breeze to build a strong trunk or stem. To emulate the wind gently stroke your seedlings to imitate a breeze. Organic farmers are often seen walking through their greenhouse lightly running their hands along all the seedlings. They're not being overly affectionate – they're being the wind!

LET'S TALK ABOUT... ORGANIC

NEWSFLASH: Most agricultural chemicals used on non-organic farms today were developed around the time of World War I for use in warfare. Yes, the same products that today are sprayed on our food were designed to bump people off. These chemicals rarely discriminate. They kill all life, not just the aphid or insect currently causing an issue, but every pollinator, bug, beastie and creature the web of life depends on.

From a human health point of view this style of farming is catastrophic. When farm workers spray crops they're supposed to wear head-to-toe protective equipment including breathing masks. That's how toxic this stuff is. Unsurprisingly, incidents of certain types of cancer among farm workers, presumably from long-term exposure to these chemicals, is higher than in the general population. Research conducted by the American organization Beyond Pesticides has found an association between "pesticide use and increased incidence of leukaemia; non-Hodgkin's lymphoma; bladder, colon, lung, and pancreatic cancer; and all cancers combined that are comparable to smoking for some cancer types."

This is serious, hard-to-hear stuff, especially if buying all organic food isn't an option, which it isn't for most of us. And many people argue that without current conventional methods of agriculture we wouldn't have been able to produce the abundant and cheap food modern society is built on.

It's true, the "chemical age" has led to a huge growth in farm productivity and fed millions of people cheaply. But at what long-term cost? Depleted soils. Destroyed ecosystems. Collapsed pollinator populations. Polluted waterways. Sick people. High rates of farmer suicide. **And frustratingly, anyone with an appreciation of the delicate biological interconnectedness of life has long seen this coming and viewed this style of farming as the counterintuitive life-killing juggernaut it is.** And yet here we are with the bulk of our food grown this way, reliant on seeds and chemicals produced by a handful of global ag corporates – Bayer, Syngenta, Corteva, Adama, UPL, BASF, UPL, FSC – that make billions from a model of farming that's killing people and planet.

So we should all be demanding and seeking access to organic food as one of our basic human rights. Let's clarify what exactly organic means.

In the West, food labelled organic should have been certified by a governing body to ensure it's been grown using organic farming principles. In the UK this body is the **Soil Association**, in Europe it is the **International Federation of Organic Agriculture Movements** (IFOAM) and in **America it is US Department of Agriculture** (USDA Organic).

Organic food has been grown without the use of artificial pesticides and fertilizers, and in animal farming without growth regulators and with closely regulated, approved feed additives only. Instead farmers use techniques such as crop rotation, green manures, plant diversity and wild planted areas to support pollinators and other beneficial insects.

These farmscapes tend to be more resilient to extreme weather, build soil health and suffer less from mass infestations. But organic farms are hard work to run, are still susceptible to the usual challenges of farming (extreme weather, aphid infestations, cost and availability of skilled labour), require

Look out for the Soil Association logo on products in the UK

more human labour and in some ways more planning and vision than conventional farms.

WHY DOES ORGANIC TEND TO BE MORE EXPENSIVE?

Organic crop farms also receive fewer subsidies than non-organic meat and dairy farms. A study by the Environmental Change Institute found meat and dairy farming received more government subsidies globally than crops farmed for human consumption. Only a few countries such as China and Chile bucked this trend. In the UK arable farmers can apply for a countryside Stewardship subsidy for managing land in a more environmentally sustainable way. But it's a smaller pot than what meat and dairy farmers can access, and recent changes and limitations to this scheme have resulted in protests from the farming community.

So as a farmer, you've got to really believe in organic, and be able to see it working financially and practically, to have the confidence to convert to it, a process that takes a minimum of two years and requires a lot of headspace to tackle. And this is all while continuing to farm, a physically demanding and relentless job where 4am wakeups and 10.30pm clock-off times (particularly during harvest periods) are not uncommon.

With all this in mind, it's not surprising organic food is less readily available and comes at a higher price. But if more people demand it and farmers were offered training, financial support and incentives, more farmers would convert and the prices would come down. The same can be said about dairy farms wanting to convert to plant-milk production, or cattle farmers wanting to switch to mushroom growing. Financial incentives and training are crucial to make this a desirable and viable option.

WHAT ABOUT REGENERATIVE FARMING?

Isn't regenerative farming good enough or better than organic? Now that's a juicy question. The issue with regenerative farming is, unlike organic, there is no governing body or set of standards. Farms can describe themselves as regenerative when all they've done is dash a few wildflower seeds about. Of course many regenerative farms do much more than this and are committed to lowering their environmental impact despite not having a governing body assessing their practices, but there isn't the rigour and consistency organic certification has. It's easy for marketeers to use regenerative as a buzz phrase to greenwash a farming-as-usual approach. And that's never going to bring about the rapid changes people and planet urgently need in terms of the way food is farmed and produced.

✱ GROW YOUR OWN HERBS

Growing your own pot herbs is a brilliant addition to your pantry/micro allotment. Herbs are used to season food and make teas and tonics, ointments and tinctures. They're packed with antioxidants, vitamins and minerals and have been used for thousands of years to aid wellbeing and as part of rituals and celebrations.

There are hundreds of herbs you could grow from all over the world, and multiple varieties of each one. There are over 300 varieties of thyme and 30 different species of mint with 7,500 varieties – so don't be fooled into thinking there's just the one type that your local garden centre stocks. The herbal plant kingdom is so much deeper and richer than that.

For our first eight years MIH was based underneath Food For All health food shop, which contains one of the largest herbal apothecaries in London. We loved being surrounded by the jars of barks, roots, spices and tinctures and overhearing the different remedies exchanged by the customers and staff, most of whom were qualified medical herbalists. It's an amazing community service facility.

We're going to presume this is the start of your herb growing journey, so we'll start with the basics and only discuss the culinary uses. Learning about their medicinal uses is an adventure for another day.

All these herbs can be used fresh or dried. Fresh herbs have more antioxidants and other beneficial properties than dried, but dried are practical for long-term storage, especially during the colder months.

▶ TIPS & TRICKS...Where to Buy

Buy herb plants from reputable garden centres or specialist herb sellers online. Forget the herbs in pots in supermarkets; these are bred fast and furiously and usually conk out after a few days. You can also grow a herb plant from a cutting (more on that later).

BASIL

Grow: From seed each year.
Use: Delicious in pestos, pasta, salads, wraps, soups, quiche – dishes with a Mediterranean profile. Thai basil is purple and has a sweeter, stronger flavour and is used in cuisine across East Asia.
Likes: A full sun, very sheltered warm spot and nutrient-rich soil. Grows well indoors on a sunny window ledge as it doesn't like sudden and unexpected weather changes and storms. Also likes to be sown every few weeks to give your kitchen a constant supply.
Dislikes: Cold, damp conditions and any rough treatment from passing traffic (kids, dogs, cats, foxes, big boots).

CHIVES

Grow: From plug plants, from seed or divide an existing clump.
Use: They're usually eaten raw, chopped up finely in salads, dips and as a garnish. They're a staple herb in many cuisines including Northen European, East and South Asian, Middle Eastern, North and Southern American.
Likes: Full sun but they'll still grow in partial shade and nutrient rich, well-draining soil.
Dislikes: Being in very dry, poor soil. Excessive harvesting in its first year (restrict to three – four harvests a year, then in year two you can harvest monthly).

CORIANDER/CILANTRO

Grow: From seed each year. Calypso and slow bolt varieties are recommended for their longevity.
Use: In a base for many Indian and Sri Lankan curries, as part of Thai salads and summer rolls, as a garnish on many East Asian dishes, as part of Trinidadian green sauce. If you can buy it in a Middle Eastern store or produce market, it usually comes in much larger bunches than the scanty amounts in supermarkets.
Likes: Free-draining soil, a full sun, sheltered position. They like to be pruned regularly to create bushy growth and stop them bolting (going to seed). Once it reaches a height of 10–15cm/4–6in, pinch out the top 2–3cm/¾–1¼in of the plant to encourage bushy growth.
Dislikes: Not being harvested regularly, the cold, unexpected changes in weather, drought. At 85°C/185°F it will bolt and go to seed. This is less likely to happen if in peak summer it's located in partial shade.

MINT

Grow: From a young plug plant, root cuttings or divided clumps of established mint.
Use: In mocktails, cocktails and other drinks, salads, dips, teas, stews, curries. It's a truly global herb used across South and East Asia, Europe, the Middle East, North and South America and across Africa. It grows abundantly and needs very little caring for.
Likes: Full sun but will also grow in partial shade. It spreads rapidly so likes big pots for it to expand out into. It likes to be regularly picked and towards the end of the summer cut down to just above the soil and fed with a nitrogen-rich feed – then you'll get fresh new autumn growth. It likes nutrient-rich, loose, damp soil.
Dislikes: Small spaces, being grown next to

other varieties of mint (it can affect their unique scent and flavour) and being ignored. It likes to be picked, watered and separated into new plants.

OREGANO

Grow: From plug plants, a stem cutting or divide a large plant.
Use: It is very popular in Italian, Turkish, Mexican and Greek cuisine, used in sauces, pizzas, salad dressings, za'atar and chimichurri.
Likes: A warm, sunny position in dry soil. It is drought-tolerant and doesn't like heavy clay soil. It will thrive in a pot inside or outside during the warmer months and needs watering every one to two weeks. If it's growing in the ground it usually requires no watering.
Dislikes: Having wet roots, being cold and unsheltered. It doesn't like inconsistent temperatures, inconsistent light or high humidity. A sunny window ledge seems like a good idea.

PARSLEY

Grow: From seed each year.
Use: In tabouleh, salads, pestos, stews, phish dishes and as a garnish scattered on the top of dishes. It comes in flat leaf or curly leaf varieties and is famously enjoyed by Peter

Rabbit! Pick the leaves by cutting them off neatly with scissors or a harvesting knife so new growth can flourish.
Likes: Like basil, it will respond well to nutrient-rich soil, once to twice weekly watering (possibly more if it's very hot) and once weekly feeding. It likes a sunny, sheltered position.
Dislikes: Being overcrowded next to other plants so they have to compete for nutrients, having waterlogged roots, too shady a spot or being starved of water and feed.

ROSEMARY

Grow: Buy a plug plant or cuttings.
Use: The leaves add a deep aromatic flavour to fried potatoes, stews and soups. Can also be used in homemade cosmetics and teas. Its leaves are available all year round, but the plant only grows in the warmer months.
Likes: A full to mainly sunny position in free-draining soil. If growing in a pot choose the largest your space can manage and be sure to put lots of broken crockery, stones or gravel in the bottom of the pot for drainage.
Dislikes: Having wet roots. So if you have heavy clay soil in your back garden (like most Londoners do), consider planting it in a large container or raised bed instead.

SAGE

Grow: Buy a plug plant or take cuttings.
Use: Is delicious stirred into plant-based butter and used on pasta or gnocchi. Is a traditional part of stuffing – sage and onion stuffing – and works well in nut roasts, lentil bakes and vegan haggis.
Likes: Full sun and free-draining, poor quality soils similar to thyme. Water once to twice a week – it likes slightly damp soil.
Dislikes: Don't feed it too much plant-feed as the fast growth will potentially reduce its flavour. It also doesn't like being waterlogged and having wet roots.

THYME

Grow: From a plug plant or cuttings.
Use: The delicious leaves are used in a wide variety of global cuisines. In Caribbean cooking people often lob the whole stalk into a stew or soup then fish it out before serving and the leaves have come off.
Likes: Full sun and dry, free-draining soils. Only water it every 10–15 days. It will grow in fairly poor, stony soil, so is happier in potting compost, which has fewer nutrients than general multi-purpose compost.
Dislikes: Having wet roots and being waterlogged. So if you have heavy clay soil in your back garden (like most Londoners do), consider planting it in a large container or raised bed instead.

OTHER HERBS WE LOVE TO GROW

Lemon Balm, Lemon Verbena, Apple Mint, Chocolate Mint, Fennel, Tarragon, Curry Plant, Chamomile, Fever Few, Lavender, Borage, Echinacea, Cuban Thyme/ Broadleaf Thyme, Thai and African Basil

POT HERBS – DO'S & DON'TS

Flower Time

All pot herbs will eventually flower and go to seed. Their flowers can be very beautiful and loved by pollinator insects. After flowering and going to seed that's the end of the road for annual pot herbs. For perennial you prune them back and wait for next year's growth. Every herb likes slightly different pruning so look this up before you cut.

Always cut your herbs with scissors or a harvesting knife - never rip, pull or tear.

Clean Cut

When you harvest herbs it's best to make a neat, clean cut with secateurs or a harvesting knife. Raggedy cuts and hand pulls are more likely to allow infection and disease into the plant. Plus the plant will expel energy trying to repair the tear as opposed to making tasty leaves for you to eat.

Solo Players

You might see beautiful planters packed with a mixture of small herb plants in a garden centre or online. These look very nice and make great gifts but they won't last. The differing herb plants will compete for nutrients and there won't be enough space for them to grow. We recommend growing your herbs in their own pots and not mixing them. We know people do – but your plants will last longer if you don't.

Don't Over-Water

New gardeners often love their plants to death by over-watering them. Some want weekly watering and others every two to three weeks. Pop a little note on your herbs so you don't forget which likes which. Many people stand plants in a dish of water when they go away so they can self-water. This is great for some plants, but many drought-tolerant herbs hate constant wet roots.

Give Me Space

Once your plants have grown to a good size you'll need to pot them on to a bigger container, unless you planted your small plug plant into a big pot to begin with. You'll know to pot it on as it will look too big and top-heavy for its little pot.

Troubleshooting

Plants can experience all manner of issues from pests and diseases. As beginner growers we can't go into them all here – but we do recommend you use an ID app or pest and disease book to identify what's wrong and take appropriate organic action. The solution could be anything from hand-picking pests off, to spraying the plant in soapy water, to feeding the plant more regularly, to potting it on, to finding some ladybirds and popping them on your plants for them to eat the aphids. Fast action is often key to bringing a plant back from the brink.

> **TIPS & TRICKS...**
>
> **What's the Difference Between a Herb and a Spice?**
>
> **Spices are usually made from dried roots, barks, fruits, seeds and other non-leafy parts of plants. Herbs are usually the fresh leaves, stems or flowers of non-woody plants. Some plants are both a herb and a spice, like coriander/cilantro where you eat the fresh leaves and the dried seeds.**

PLANTS FOR FREE AKA TAKING CUTTINGS

My mum used to keep a pair of scissors and a clip seal bag with a wet tissue in it in her handbag so she could take cuttings from plants she saw about the place! Many a time as a child I saw her snipping away at a plant on a public wall, or she'd get chatting to someone gardening and they'd give her a cutting. Her brother used to joke she could make a chair leg grow. I think he was right.

She shared the cutting love with hundreds of people from her magnificent garden and when I visit my home village in Lincolnshire people often stop and tell me about the different plants Mum gave them and how she'd helped them to fill their gardens this way. Even the ambulance driver that took her to the hospice when she was very poorly surprised me by saying her garden was full of plants grown from cuttings my mum had given her when she used to drive her to chemo treatments.

I love teaching people how to take cuttings as you can see the spark of possibility in their eyes as they see how easy and straightforward it is. I recently did a Level 2 organic horticulture qualification, which had a whole module on cuttings. I'm not going to go into that much detail, just the highlights to get you going.

TAKING HERB CUTTINGS

Cuttings can be taken from almost any plant. The three main types of cuttings are softwood, semi-hardwood and hardwood cuttings. Softwood cuttings have the highest success rate so we'll focus on these.

Softwood cuttings are taken from the fleshy, usually green, non-woody section. This is the new growth of the plant, full of vitality and therefore most able to exert energy to both stay alive and establish a new root.

EQUIPMENT YOU'LL NEED

1–4 pots at least 15cm/6in high and 123m/5in wide
Cutting compost
Secateurs
Root hormone powder or your own spit if you're not on medication.

How to Take Cuttings

1: First get your pots ready. Select plant pots at least 15cm/6in in height, 12cm/5in plus in diameter so the cutting can establish good roots before needing to be potted on.

2: While you're taking cuttings do a few (then if some don't make it you've hedged your bets) so line up at least four pots and add a 2cm/¾in line of gravel in the bottom of each for drainage.

3: Next fill the pot with seedling or cutting compost. Press the compost firmly down with your hands then top up and firm down again. Stand the pots in a tray of water.

4: Using sharp scissors or secateurs cut three 10–15cm/4–6in lengths off your herb plant. Rosemary, sage, thyme all work well. Add three cuttings to each plant pot.

5: If you're removing from a very large, established plant you could take up to 12

cuttings. If it's a small to medium size plant, three to six is the most you should take.

6: Remove the lower sets of leaves from the cuttings until you're left with two layers of leaves at the top.

7: Each place on the stem where there was leaf growth is called a node. Reduce your cutting in size by cutting it at a diagonal angle just below a leaf node – this is where the most growth hormone is. The slanted cut increases the surface area for the root to grow out of.

8: Now sterilize the end of the cutting to stop bacteria getting into it. Dip it into root hormone inoculator powder, or into water that had willow twigs steeping in it for a few weeks, or by dipping it into your own spit in your hand – as long as you're not on any strong medications.

9: Insert the cutting into the soil in your pot so that its remaining leaves are about an inch above the soil surface. Add three cuttings to your pot in a triangle formation. The cuttings should root in three to six weeks. You'll know if they've worked as the cutting remains green and vibrant looking. If it hasn't rooted it will start to flag and eventually die.

10: After two months remove each cutting to its own pot to grow on into a larger plant. There you have it. Plants for free!

* PLANTS FOR FREE – SEED SAVING

Saving seed can seem like quite advanced gardening shenanigans, but it's pretty straightforward.

Save seeds from plants that are thriving and free of disease to ensure quality seedlings. As a general rule of thumb (but it does differ plant to plant) seeds are usually produced two months after a plant has flowered. There are a few different ways plants can store their seeds: mainly heads, pods, nuts, cones, catkins, winged seeds (like sycamores), berries, capsules and – my favourite – exploding seed heads. Collect seeds on a dry day once the seeds have "ripened" e.g. the seed has changed colour. In the edible plant world this is usually from green to brown. Pick the seed heads (pods or otherwise) and lay them out on a tray in the warmth to dry out for a few days. This makes it easier to extract the seed. Remove the chaff (plant material that isn't the seeds) and store the seeds in a labelled paper bag or envelope in a dry, warm place to use either straight away, later in the growing season or next year. This goes without saying but don't mix your seeds in the same bag! Some gardeners go all out and add things like silica gel to the paper bags to absorb moisture to stop the seeds rotting. I've never done this and my seeds have been fine. Savers of heritage or heirloom seeds often want the seeds to stay true to their variety, so they place bags over plants to stop pollinator insects from pollinating them (and potentially mixing them with another variety) and instead take pollen from one plant and transfer it to the next themselves by hand or using a small paint brush. Nifty hey.

✱ LET'S TALK ABOUT... The Politics of Seed

Like soil, seeds are the cornerstone of life. Many of us in the Global North, unless we're growers, have probably not considered how our existence depends on the information contained in these tiny, life-giving specks of information.

The fundamentals of food sovereignty – peoples', communities' and whole nations' right to control their own food supply without being beholden to global corporate entities or other nations – starts with seeds. Stories of historical migration, both forced and self-actualized, tell of seeds and tubers being carried with people in an attempt to preserve their foodways in new lands. During the horrors of the transatlantic slave trade, kidnapped people weaved seed and grain into their hair as a means of survival.

Today, in the face of unavoidable climate change, having a wide range of seed and crop varieties is crucial to human survival. And yet the UN Food and Agriculture Organization reports that between 1900 and 2000 75% of the world's crop varieties have disappeared and 50% of the global seed market is owned by just four corporations – Bayer, Corteva, BASF and Syngenta. It's not radical to regard this as seriously scary. It is even more scary that these corporations are legally obligated to be chiefly concerned with making their shareholders money, not taking care of people and the planet. And now they're holding the keys to the world's food stores.

Plants are amazing in that they evolve and adapt to their local environment. So as temperatures gradually rise, plants will adapt to cope with these changes. These adaptions are passed down in the seeds, generation to generation, plant ancestor to plant ancestor. Seeds developed in labs by big agriculture firms for specific strains – disease resistant, drought tolerant – although useful and clever, often have terminator technology built into them, meaning the plant will not produce seeds and farmers will have to repeat purchase every year, creating cycles of dependency, crushing debt and high levels of farmer suicides. In India between 2000 and 2018 the Punjab Agriculture University collected proof of 16,606 farmer suicides, most of them in the six districts of the Punjab cotton belt. Many hanged themselves. Others poisoned themselves with the chemical fertilizers that pushed them into debt.

And this is why peasant farmers, indigenous growers and seed savers/keepers are so vital and deserve deep respect and solidarity. They're not only resisting the mass corporate co-option of our global food supply and exercising our collective right to live off the land, but they're keeping alive thousands of crop varieties that would otherwise perish. Varieties with genetic codes that have the power to adapt, change and feed the world.

Today, in the face of unavoidable climate change, having a wide range of seed and crop varieties is crucial to human survival.

MICRO-GREENS

Micro-greens are immature shoots of salad crops fancy restaurants scatter on top of expensive meals. Like cress – but way posher! You eat them bigger than a seedling, but nowhere near as big as a mature plant. They pack a flavour punch and are more nutrient dense than when fully grown plants. You can grow them indoors in seedling trays or special elongated micro-green trays for longer roots. They're space-efficient and ready in 10–14 days. They're expensive to buy and only specialist places sell them, so growing your own is where it's at.

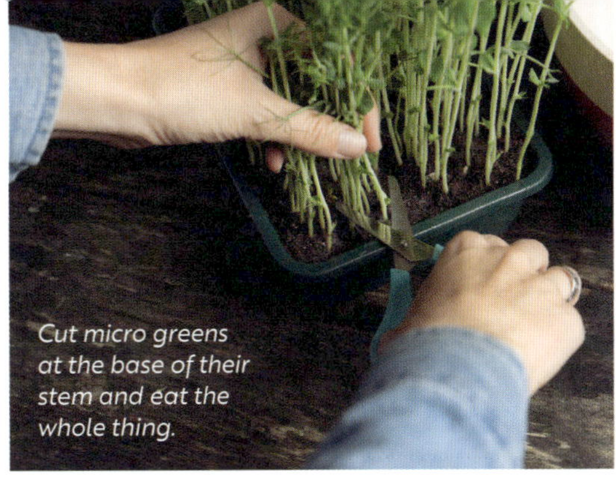

Cut micro greens at the base of their stem and eat the whole thing.

SUITABLE FOR MICRO-GREEN SOWING

Radish, rocket, lettuce, chicory, endive, leaf beet, pea shoots, spinach, pak choi/bok choy, kale, swiss chard, broccoli, mizuna, purple mustard, sunflowers.

To grow micro-greens follow the same process as your bottomless salad bar (see p 39) but sow the seeds much denser. For smaller speck-/dust-like seeds, aim for 21 seeds per square inch (2½cm by 2½cm square). For larger seeds like pea shoots, spinach and chard, cover the entire area with no gaps in between the seeds. Yes, you read that correctly. You want a dense crop of small plants which you harvest with sharp scissors when they're 5–7cm/2–2¾in high.

Soil-Free Growing

If you don't want to bring a bag of soil into your house or lifting is a challenge, you can grow microgreens on coconut matting/mesh. You buy it in sheets, cut it to the size of your seedling tray and press one layer into the tray instead of soil. The matting is light in nutrients so you'll need to use a liquid feed as well.

Sow trays of micro greens every 3 weeks for a constant supply of nutrient dense greens.

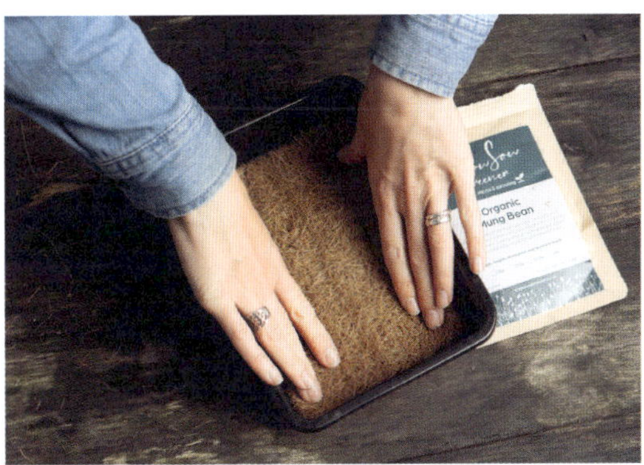

For soil free, indoor growing use easy to store and lift coconut matting.

SEED SPROUTING

I once fed one of my husband's heavy meat-eating friend a salad with sprouted mung beans in it and half an hour later he asked me what the crazy food was that was making him feel so perky and alive. I was impressed with his system's rapid response!

Sprouted seeds are exactly that: seeds, beans, legumes and lentils that have been soaked in water overnight then left to sprout in a jar or tray for a few days and given daily rinses with water. By day two to four (depending how hot it is) they grow little tails. Cute. At this point they're ready to eat raw in salads, as a garnish, or you can cook them if making a dhal or curry.

Commonly Sprouted Lentils, Beans and Legumes

Mung bean, green lentils, brown lentils, chickpeas, aduki beans and peas.

Commonly Sprouted Seeds

Alfalfa, broccoli, sunflower, radish, mustard, fenugreek, kale, clover

NN **HEALTH BENEFITS**

Small sprouts, big nutrition. Sprouting lentils and legumes prior to eating raw or cooked makes them easier to digest so reduces bloating and flatulence. Sprouting increases the bioavailability of nutrients such as vitamins B and C and protein, while also increasing their antioxidant load, which is good news. We want all the antioxidants.

HOW TO SPROUT SEEDS

Choosing Your Sprouting Vessel

There are loads of different seed sprouting jars and trays on the market. For alfalfa seeds I started using a 600ml/20fl oz glass jar with its lid loosely balanced on the top with a tiny gap. It worked! A fine mesh or breathable cloth cover would have been better. I then tried a terracotta stacking sprouter that looked beautiful but I didn't have much luck with it – the seeds dried out before sprouting. I don't think it got enough light. Then I was gifted a sprouting jar that sits diagonally on a metal frame sat on top of a square ceramic tray. I love the jar and get great results with it.

You can pick sprouters up second hand as people buy them with good intentions and then, well, we all know that one. If you do it a few times you'll be hooked and you get amazing nutrient-dense food for the price of the seeds, as sprouted seeds usually cost big money in independent stores.

EQUIPMENT YOU'LL NEED:

Sprouting seeds, beans, legumes or lentils of choice
Bowl for soaking
Sprouting jar or tray – a specialist one or a large glass jar will do
Room temperature water (ideally filtered) for soaking and rinsing

**In these instructions when I say seed I'm referring to seed, bean, legume or lentil.*

1: Put the seeds in a bowl and cover with water so the water sits 2cm/¾in above the line of seeds. Leave to soak for 10–12 hours.
2: The seeds will plump up and double in size.
3: Drain and rinse the seeds in a fine sieve.
4: Add the seeds to your sprouter tray or jar and spread them out evenly. Leave in a cool, dry place in the light but not on a windowsill as direct sunlight is too strong.
5: Rinse and drain every day for two to four days until little tails have formed on the beans or legumes, or long, thin tails (like cress) have grown from the seeds. These are ready to eat! Scatter on salads, use as a garnish or cook in a dhal, curry or other dish that calls for lentils/legumes. Store in the fridge and consume within a few days.

* GARDENING OUTSIDE

KIND PEST CONTROL

We recommend kind, compassionate ways of dealing with pests aiming for balanced deterrence as opposed to termination.

Barriers

Cloches, netting and plastic collars made from empty bottles can be used to create a physical barrier between a plant and things that might eat it.

Copper Tape

Can be applied around the diameter of a plant pot to deter slugs and snails from climbing up. The tape gives the mollusc a tiny electric shock encouraging them to about turn. I once saw a snail storming along a piece of copper tape with no desire to get off it. Must have enjoyed the tingle. Takes all sorts.

Hand-Picking

For small-scale gardens, hand-picking aphids, slugs and snails off your plants is effective.

Attract Hoverflies & Ladybirds/Ladybugs

Aphids are tiny, speck-like insects that will munch your plants. An infestation starts with just a few aphids, but if not dealt with swiftly you'll soon have dense communities of little black (green or purple) speck-like insects. Ladybirds and hoverflies are aphid-eating machines. Attract them with poached egg plants – which hoverflies love – and plants with flat-topped flowers such as calendula, sweet alyssum and marigold, which are enjoyed by ladybirds. Ladybirds need to hibernate – or "overwinter" – so set them up a bug hotel so they're ready for aphid-eating action come spring.

MAKING COMPOST

Like growing your own food, making compost is a joy. When you make compost, you make life and nourishment in a form that regenerates rather than depletes the earth. In a closed loop system fresh produce in the form of scraps, peelings and leftovers can be turned into a nutrient-rich growing medium – compost – that supports the growth of more fresh produce. Beautiful. In nature nothing is wasted, everything is reused.

If you're in the UK and you have no outdoor space to make your own compost, use your council's food waste collection service.

If you do have outdoor space, try making your own. Despite what you may read online, the correct ratio for home composting is 3 parts browns to 1 part green. Compost in: bays, compost bins, tumblers, heaps.

▸ TO MAKE COMPOST

Add 3 Buckets/Bowls/Cups of Browns (Carbon) For Every 1 Bucket/Bowl/Cup of Greens (Nitrogen)

BROWNS
- Dead leaves
- Dead plants
- Dried grass
- Straw/hay
- Small twigs
- Biodegradable tea bags
- Brown paper bags
- Cardboard
- Unbleached paper

GREENS
- Fresh grass
- All green plants
- Fresh produce scraps
- Fresh produce peelings
- Coffee grounds
- Weeds that haven't gone to seed
- Hair from your hairbrush
- Finger and toenail clippings

CHAPTER 4

PLANT STAPLES

Whether you've still got your L plates on in the kitchen, or you're a seasoned cook, you'll find tips and tricks in this chapter you'll definitely find useful. We'll take your through kitchen practices and cooking techniques for staples, grains, proteins and other hero/shero ingredients needed to develop a plant-based culinary repertoire.

You'll also learn how to create meaty, fishy, creamy, cheesy and eggy tastes and textures using nothing but wholefood plant-based ingredients. We don't have a pantry section, as you'll encounter all the ingredients your pantry needs as you learn about how to use them. From how to properly wash non-organic produce, to making a seriously fishy looking sushi filling from watermelon, and what cookware to use for a non-toxic kitchen – it's all here. You're welcome!

PLANT STAPLES

Herbs & Spices Starter Kit

One thing that's crucial to making plant-centred meals is seasoning – herbs and spices are the key to unlocking incredibly tasting all-plant meals.

Herbs and spices are packed with antioxidants and build flavour profiles to give you those rich, deep tastes our palates crave. If you're at ground zero of building up your herbs and spices, get started with our top 12 as voted for by the MIH team.

- **Smoked paprika**
- **Turmeric**
- **Garam masala**
- **Ground cumin**
- **Cinnamon**
- **Mixed herbs (rosemary, thyme, sage, oregano, basil)**
- **Ground ginger**
- **Chilli flakes**
- **Bay leaves**
- **Garlic powder**
- **Curry powder (Caribbean)**
- **Onion powder**

Herbs and spices that got an honorary mention include: ground coriander/cilantro, cardamom, Chinese 5 spice, allspice/pimento, mustard powder/seeds, star anise, Caribbean all purpose seasoning and the don of creating plant-based eggy flavours: kala namak, i.e. black salt – more on this on p 72.

WHAT'S BETTER – LOCAL, SEASONAL OR BOTH?

Both! Locally grown, seasonal food gets a gold star on the environment front as it has a lighter carbon footprint due to the short distance it travels. Also, as it's seasonal, it hasn't needed loads of inputs (fertilizers, heat lamps) and it tends to be more flavoursome and nutrient-dense. Confusingly, local food that isn't seasonal isn't always the most sustainable choice. Tomatoes grown in Spain in the sunshine then shipped to the UK, will have a lighter carbon load than locally grown British tomatoes that have grown in heated greenhouses. Produce packaging in supermarkets doesn't declare the farms' growing practices – it just says "Local" or something ambiguous like "Britain" or "America's Finest". That's why, if possible, shopping in farmers' markets or signing up to a sustainably focused fruit and veg box scheme is always the best environmental choice. It takes away the stress of trying to work out what's the best choice in a supermarket (Packaging free? Seasonal? Local? Organic?) as the farmer or kind folk at the veg box scheme have done all this for you! As we're now used to eating global food and flavours, many local veg box schemes supplement local produce with international fare, particularly during the hungry gap (when very limited seasonal produce is available), which in the UK is between April and early June.

HOW TO WASH NON-ORGANIC PRODUCE

We're big supporters of organic at MIH and you can read about why on p 40. We fully understand for many people it's financially out of reach and also, depending on where you live, it isn't always available. So, if you're using non-organic produce, wash produce properly to remove pesticide and herbicide residues that are damaging to human health. Here's how.

OPTION 1

Soak in a vinegar (white or malt – basically the cheapest) and water. Use one part vinegar to four parts water and soak for 20 minutes. Rinse thoroughly afterwards. Not recommended for berries.

OPTION 2

Soak in a bicarb/baking soda and water solution. Use one teaspoon of bicarbonate of soda/baking soda per 500ml/17½ fl oz of water and leave to soak for 20 minutes. Rinse thoroughly afterwards.

OPTION 3

Soak in a salt and water solution. Use one part salt to ten parts water. Ideally use Himalayan or sea salt and leave to soak for 20 minutes. Rinse thoroughly afterwards.

This intergenerational baking class was delivered in collaboration with Hackney Council to celebrate Windrush.

To Peel or Not To Peel?

For health reasons we recommend you peel all non-organic fruits and vegetables, including roots like ginger and turmeric, before use. This is because much (but not all) of the pesticide and herbicide residue will accumulate on the skin. To reduce exposure to these chemicals we recommend peeling and then soaking non-organic produce. For organic produce a quick wash to remove any leftover soil or bacteria is fine.

Waxed or Unwaxed?

Our preference for citrus fruit, especially if using the peel to zest or in a tea, is unwaxed. Many organic citrus fruits are also unwaxed but not always. Unwaxed can be hard to source – if this is the case just wash the citrus.

Choosing Plant Milks

We love plant milks at MIH and like to experiment with different ones whether oat, soy, almond, coconut, rice or some of the newer ones such as pea and potato. I was even interviewed by the *New York Times* about the possibilities of potato milk. All plant milks are not created equal and some are high in sugar and oils. We recommend unsweetened, fortified plant milks (they've had Vitamin D, calcium, B2 and B12 added) that are low in oil and salt for everyday use, or non-fortified, clean label plant milks (ones with very minimal ingredients, usually under four things) but as long as you keep a good supplement routine or you know you're getting these vitamins elsewhere in your diet. A 2024 study recently came out proving soy milk, even the sweetened varieties, are nutritionally superior to cow's milk. Read more about the benefits of soy on p 29 and why dairy is ethically problematic on p 92. For zero-waste cooks, making your own plant milks is simple and fun. You need a high-speed blender and a muslin or nut milk bag.

* HOW TO COOK PLANT-BASED STAPLES

To be a successful plant-based home cook you need to nail your staples. A mushy grain, some badly cooked tofu or undercooked legumes and your whole dinner game will be off. Get a handle on cooking these foundational ingredients as explained by top MIH chef Sareta Puri. Let's go.

* GRAINS

BROWN RICE

What you need to know Brown rice is a wholegrain that has a more earthy flavour than white and is more nutritionally dense – being higher in fibre and having a low GI (glycemic index).

Do

- Choose brown rice over white whenever you can.
- Check the instructions on the packet as many rice varieties will differ.
- Leave to cool fully before storing in the refrigerator for a maximum of 24 hours.
- If reheating, make sure it is heated through completely to remove any bacteria.

Don't

- Undercook brown rice. It will not turn to mush in the same way that white rice can.
- Use too small a saucepan or the rice will outgrow the pan!

How to Prepare

Rinse well to remove excess starches. Do this by putting it in a sieve and running cold water over it until clear or soaking in water and mixing it well then carefully draining the water off. Repeat until the water is clear.

If you have time, soak it overnight, or for at least four hours, to give a fluffier texture.

How to Cook

Cooking rice will vary from family to culture so if you find a way you like, stick with that.

Once rinsed, put the rice into a large enough saucepan for it to double in size. Add double the amount of water, so if you've used 100g/3½oz of rice it would be 200ml/6¾fl oz of water. Always use cold water and bring to a boil in the pan. Once boiling, reduce to a simmer and put a lid on the pan. Don't open or stir it during this time.

Simmer for approximately 30–35 minutes until the water has mostly absorbed and the rice is soft.

Turn off the heat and take the lid off. Leave it for 5–10 minutes for the steam to evaporate off and the remaining rice should be soft and fluffy with no bite.

Note, some easy cook varieties will cook in under 25 minutes.

BASMATI RICE

What you need to know Basmati rice can be white, brown or easy cook. It tends to be fluffier and more flavourful than regular rice and is touted as having more nutritional benefits than everyday rice.

Do

- Opt for brown rice over white whenever you can.
- Check the instructions on the packet as many rice varieties will differ.

- Leave to cool fully before storing in the refrigerator for a maximum of 24 hours.
- If reheating, make sure it is heated through completely to remove any bacteria.

Don't
- Overcook, or it will go very soft.
- Use too small a saucepan.

How to Prepare
Rinse well to remove excess starches. Do this by putting it in a sieve and running cold water over it until clear or soaking in water and mixing it well then carefully draining the water off. Repeat until the water is clear. If you have time, soak it overnight, or for at least four hours, to get a fluffier texture.

How to Cook
Cooking rice will vary from family to culture so if you find a way you like, stick with that!

Once rinsed, put the rice into a large enough saucepan for it to double in size. Add double the amount of water, so if you've used 100g/3½oz of rice it would be 200ml/6¾fl oz of water. Always use cold water and bring to a boil in the pan. Once boiling, reduce to a simmer and put a lid on the pan. Don't open or stir it during this time.

If cooking white basmati, cook for about 12 minutes. Brown or wholegrain will take approximately 25 minutes. Check that all the water has been absorbed. Remove from heat, keeping the lid on, and wait for at least five minutes. Fluff with a fork then serve.

WILD RICE

What you need to know Tends to be longer, firmer with a nuttier taste than regular rice.

Do
- Be aware that wild rice will increase in volume by 3 – 3½ times the raw volume.

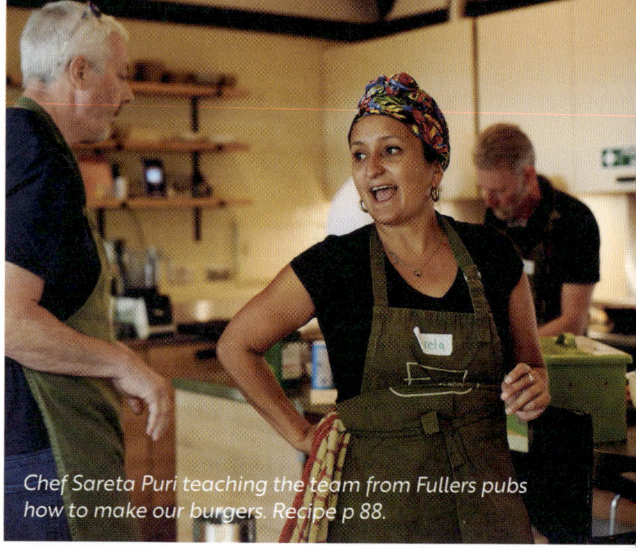

Chef Sareta Puri teaching the team from Fullers pubs how to make our burgers. Recipe p 88.

- Cook a pan of white rice for bulk, and a smaller pan of wild rice, then combine the two to increase the nutrient profile.

Don't
- Undercook it or it will be too hard.

How to Prepare
As with all rice, it's important to rinse before cooking. It also benefits from being soaked. Soak in a bowl for at least 2-3 hours.

How to Cook
Put the rinsed, drained rice in a large saucepan and cover with three times the amount of water. Bring to the boil then reduce to a simmer.

Cover and cook for approximately 20–25 minutes until most of the water has evaporated. If it hasn't you can drain it off. If you have not soaked the rice, cooking time will be approximately 40–45 minutes.

Cooking time will vary according to the variety of rice, which is why it's better to start with more water and drain off any excess.

SUSHI RICE

What you need to know Sushi rice is a short-grain, glutinous rice cultivated in Japan. It has a sticky texture making it perfect for sushi.

Do

- Substitute it for arborio rice in risottos or arancini recipes.
- Only cook it until it is al dente or it can become too soggy.
- If seasoning with rice vinegar or mirin add once the rice is cooked but still hot.

Don't

- Substitute arborio rice to make sushi, it's too sticky!
- Freestyle the amount of water you use – read the packet and follow instructions.

How to Prepare

Rinse the rice in a strainer until the water runs clear. There's no need to soak sushi rice.

How to Cook

Put the rinsed, drained rice in a large saucepan and cover with three times the amount of water.

Bring to the boil then reduce to a simmer for about 8–10 minutes.

Turn off the heat and let it stand for a further five minutes with the lid off. After it's cooked you can season it if using in sushi – usually with rice vinegar and salt.

BUCKWHEAT

What you need to know Despite its name, buckwheat is a seed not a grain and is therefore gluten-free.

Do

- Season it if the earthy flavour isn't for you.
- Grind it into flour (or buy it as a flour) to make delicious gluten-free pancakes.
- Look out for and try Japanese soba noodles, which are made from buckwheat.

Don't

- Overcook buckwheat or it will go mushy.

How to Prepare

Rinse well until the water runs clear.

How to Cook

To get the best texture you should toast the buckwheat groats in a dry pan until they release a nutty aroma and are lightly browned.

Transfer the buckwheat to a saucepan with 1½ times the amount of water and a pinch of salt. An option is to add a glug of olive oil or tablespoon of vegan butter at this stage. Bring it to the boil, cover and reduce to a simmer.

Cook until the water is absorbed and the grains have fluffed up – this should take about 12–14 minutes. Turn off the heat and leave for a few minutes before serving.

QUINOA

What you need to know Pronounced "keen-wah", quinoa is a gluten-free pseudo-grain made from a flower's seed. It has a mild nutty taste and is a great flavour sponge. It is a great source of protein, as well as fibre, lysine and amino acids.

Do

- Flavour it while you cook it – try boiling it in vegetable stock or miso. Or just use your fave blend of herbs and spices.
- Use a large enough pan as it will double in size when cooking.
- Use cooked quinoa to bulk out – and add protein – to homemade burgers.
- Try making savoury quinoa porridge/oatmeal!

Don't

- Use too much water. Some recipes suggest two times water to quinoa but that can easily end in soggy quinoa!

How to Prepare

Soak for 2–5 minutes in cold water before cooking then drain in a sieve.

How to Cook

To get perfectly fluffy quinoa use 1½ times water to quinoa.

Boil the water then add the quinoa and a pinch of salt. You can use vegetable stock or a teaspoon of miso mixed into the cooking water. Bring to a boil then reduce to a simmer and cover with a lid. Let it cook for 15 minutes before removing from the heat.

Leave for a minute before fluffing with a fork.

PEARL BARLEY

What you need to know Pearl barley is a barley grain with its husks removed and then polished. With the husks on, it is pot barley.

Do

- Use it to bulk out soups.
- Use it interchangeably in recipes that call for any type of barley.
- Use it in risotto as a substitute for rice.

Don't

- Soak pearl barley overnight, although pot barley benefits from being soaked.

How to Prepare

Give it a quick rinse to remove dust or stones.

How to Cook

Use three parts water to one part pearl barley. Boil the water and then add the grains.

Add a pinch of sea salt. Alternatively, you can boil it in vegetable stock.

Reduce to a simmer and cover with a lid. Simmer for about 25–30 minutes until most of the water is absorbed.

Turn off the heat and check after five minutes when all the water should have absorbed and the grains should be al dente.

BULGUR WHEAT

What you need to know Bulgur wheat is a nutrient-rich cracked wheat with a slightly earthy and nutty taste.

Do

- Use it in veggie chilli or meatballs to help bulk out the mix and give a meaty texture.
- Try it as an oat replacement in porridge.

Don't

- Use too much water or it will turn slushy.

How to Prepare

Rinse well.

How to Cook

Use one part bulgur to two parts water. Add a pinch of sea salt to a pan of boiling water then add the bulgur. Reduce to a simmer and cover with a lid. Simmer for 12–15 minutes until the water is absorbed.

Turn off the heat and leave for a few minutes then fluff with a fork. It should be soft but not soggy. If you prefer it al dente you can cook for 2–3 minutes less.

Alternatively, if you put it in a bowl with hot water, cover it and leave it for 25–30 minutes with no heat on, the grains should absorb the water and become soft enough.

MILLET

What you need to know Millet is a gluten-free ancient grain.

Do

- Use whole millet in salads or as a side dish to stews and curries.
- Toast and sprinkle over soups and salads.

Don't

- Overcook it or use too much water or it will go mushy.

How to Prepare
Toast dried millet lightly before cooking to enhance the nutty flavour.

How to Cook
For a firm millet, use two parts water to one part millet. For a softer result, use three parts water to one part millet.

Bring a pan of water to the boil, adding a pinch of sea salt. Add the millet and reduce to a simmer, covering with a lid.

Simmer for at least 15 minutes for a firmer finish. You can drain excess liquid off now. For a softer finish, cook for another ten minutes until all the water is absorbed.

PROTEINS & HERO INGREDIENTS

FIRM TOFU

What you need to know Tofu is an East Asian staple made from compressed soy beans. It's one of the highest forms of plant proteins with 8g/¼oz of protein per 100g/3½oz serving. It's low in fat and contains all essential amino acids. It's versatile and takes on flavour so can be used as a straight swap for chicken, fish and even mince.

Do

- Flavour or marinade – tofu is a flavour sponge.
- Experiment with different types of tofu (soft-firm, medium-firm, extra-firm, silken) as each has unique results.
- Freeze tofu to give it maximum flavour absorption qualities by increasing its sponginess. Defrost it and then use as normal.
- Check out your local Asian superstore for more affordable tofu and more variety.
- Tear your tofu instead of cutting it – the texture will create crispy bits once cooked.

Don't

- Give up on tofu if you don't like it the first time. Try a different preparation method or flavour profile.
- Don't get your tofu types mixed up. A cheesecake will use silken tofu and you won't get the same results with a firm type.
- Eat it un-marinated and raw unless you're a seasoned tofu eater as it can be bland.
- Use too low a heat to cook tofu or it will remain soft and may stick to the pan.

How to Prepare
As tofu is spongy it is best to press the water out of it before marinating or cooking to enhance flavour absorption. Place it on a plate with curved edges to catch the water. Add some weight to the top of it such as a chopping board with two tins on top and leave for 2–3 minutes. You can also buy a fancy tofu press, but you don't need one.

Once pressed, cut into cubes or chunks, marinade with your chosen flavours and cook accordingly.

How to Cook
To bake tofu put it on a non-stick baking tray in the oven at 200°C/390°F and bake for 25–30 minutes, giving it a shake after 10–15 minutes to ensure it gets crisp all over.

To fry tofu in a pan you can use one to two tablespoons of vegetable oil heated on a high, smoking heat. Be careful, as the oil can splash!

Air fryers produce fab results for tofu. If your marinade contains oil you likely don't need to oil your air fryer, otherwise a light spray of oil will do. Place the tofu pieces well-spaced out in the air fryer and cook at 200°C/390°F for ten minutes, shaking the basket halfway.

SILKEN TOFU

What you need to know Silken tofu is a smooth, soft, crumbly type of tofu. It is commonly used in sauces and desserts such as mayonnaise, yogurt and cheesecake.

Do

- Blend tofu as an alternative to cream, yogurt or milk.
- Make an egg substitute with silken tofu. Fry in a non-stick pan with some black salt, turmeric and pepper to get scrambled tofu.

Don't

- Press silken tofu or it will crumble into mush!
- Try to deep fry silken tofu. It has too high water content to go crispy and the oil will spit at you.
- Freeze silken tofu. You will not yield the same spongy results as regular tofu.
- Overstir when scrambling or it will fall apart.

How to Prepare

Drain the small amount of water from the carton and slowly slide the piece of silken tofu out. Handle it with care as it will crumble with ease! Use a sharp knife to cut into pieces, if required.

How to Cook

Many silken tofu recipes do not require cooking – for savoury dishes, you simply cut it into cubes and add to a sauce at the end of cooking or top it with garnishes.

Many sweet recipes will require it to be blended. Or you could mash it to a less smooth consistency.

We do not recommend deep frying tofu however it can be shallow fried. Coat it lightly in some rice flour or potato starch and cook in a small amount of hot oil. Be patient and careful when turning over once browned.

TEMPEH

What you need to know Tempeh is an Indonesian ingredient of fermented soy beans. It is made from whole soy beans pressed together with a bacterial culture (*rhizopus oligosporus*) that helps to hold it together. If you're not familiar with tempeh or fermented foods, you might think it has a funky taste – good funky, with a nutty or cheesy undertone. It also soaks up other flavour easily. As a wholefood, tempeh has even more nutritional goodness than tofu with 19g/¾oz of protein per 100g/3½oz and additional prebiotics because it is fermented.

Do

- Cut into thin slices, marinade with smoky flavours and fry for a bacon alternative.
- Try out different types of tempeh made from chickpeas or chana dal – or get creative and make your own.
- Boil or steam a block for ten minutes to reduce the strong flavour and bitterness.
- Marinade it liberally to soak up any flavours – the longer the better.
- Chop, crumble or grate it into recipes instead of mince.

Don't

- Eat it raw or unflavoured – it is best when used to soak up flavour or cooked so it takes on a crispy texture.

How to Prepare

Tempeh is quite sturdy so can be cut into slices or pieces of any thicknesses or size and also works well blitzed to a mince.

How to Cook

To bake, space out slices or pieces on a non-stick tray and cook at 180°C/355°F for 20 minutes until crisp around the edges.

To sauté, heat a tablespoon of vegetable oil or use a good non-stick pan and cook on each side until lightly golden, about four minutes per side.

To air fry, space out the tempeh in the air fryer and cook at 200°C/390°F for ten minutes, shaking the basket halfway.

JACKFRUIT

What you need to know Jackfruit is an Asian tree fruit with two popular cooking varieties. The young green jackfruit is used in savoury dishes and the sweet yellow variety is, unsurprisingly, used in desserts.

Do

- Use young green jackfruit for savoury dishes.
- Rinse it well, otherwise it will taste briney.
- Double cook it for maximum flavour retention – crisping it up with spices and then using it in a sauce.

Don't

- Expect to get your protein from jackfruit. It is a fruit and does not offer much nutritional value. Add other proteins to your jackfruit dishes e.g. nuts, soy yogurt or tahini.
- Eat jackfruit plain. It is fairly flavourless.

How to Prepare

Drain and rinse very well to remove any briny aftertaste. Pull the chunks apart with your fingers or forks. Any remaining tough core pieces can be cut into smaller slivers.

How to Cook

We recommend coating jackfruit chunks in your chosen spices first, laying on a non-stick baking tray – making sure to not overcrowd the tray – and bake at 200°C/390°F for around 20 minutes until crisp and brown. You can also pan-fry it for the same results.

From here, you can add it to any sauce, stew or curry as a meat substitute.

A smiling participant enjoying Duchess Nena's festive Nigerian feasts class.

BANANA BLOSSOM

What you need to know Banana blossom is a fleshy, pinky-purple flower that grows at the end of a banana stem. The texture means it is an ideal replacement for flaky fish dishes and is a great vehicle for flavour.

Do

- Rinse it well from any brine so it can take on the flavours you're using.
- Try it as a substitute for tofu or jackfruit when creating a battered phish and chips.

Don't

- Worry if you don't like bananas. It doesn't have a banana-y flavour at all!

How to Prepare

If using the canned variety, you only need to rinse well in water before preparing. You can use the blossoms whole or slice them thinly depending on the dish you are making.

If using fresh blossoms, peel off the purple layers and cut them off above the stems and wash well. Using fresh is quite a lengthy process.

How to Cook

The cooking method depends on the dish. They can easily be sautéed or lightly fried in a pan with a spoon or two of vegetable oil and your chosen spices, herbs or other flavours e.g. onions and garlic.

Otherwise, you can marinade the pieces then batter and fry – or breadcrumb and bake – for a fish replacement.

SHIITAKE MUSHROOMS

What you need to know Shiitake mushrooms give that rich, umami flavour that excites your tastebuds as well as having a meaty texture. As with all mushrooms, shiitake mushrooms are one of the few plant-based sources of vitamin D – plus they have plenty of immune-boosting properties.

Do

- Dust off mushrooms with a brush or a damp cloth so they don't get too wet.
- Soak dried shiitake mushrooms before cooking them, unless you are putting them straight into a broth.
- If using fresh, store in a paper bag in the main part of the fridge. This gives them more airflow than the vegetable drawer meaning they don't go damp.
- Blitz dried shiitakes into a mushroom powder to add a umami pop to any dish.

Don't

- Wash fresh shiitake mushrooms (or any mushrooms) as they retain water making it harder to go crispy or flavourful.
- Eat the stems raw as they are too tough and woody.

How to Prepare

The dried variety should be soaked in approximately twice the amount of warm water for at least 20 minutes until soft and expanded. Retain the water to use as stock.

Fresh shiitake mushrooms should be dusted off for dirt, as per all mushrooms, and then can be used whole or sliced.

How to Cook

To get the best meaty texture, heat a pan with some oil in and throw in the shiitakes. Use a pan lid smaller than the pan to press down on whole shiitakes until they are crisp and seared. Use tongs to turn and crisp the other side. Alternatively, pan fry the slices in oil until soft.

For stocks and soupy dishes, you can add fresh ones in directly without that step or throw in dried ones.

To make crispy shiitake pieces, cut the stems off and marinade the caps in a mixture of olive oil, smoked paprika and sea salt then bake for around 25 minutes at 180°C/355°F until crisp. This also works in an air fryer for about 16–18 minutes, shaking halfway.

OYSTER MUSHROOMS

What you need to know Oyster mushrooms come as a cluster as opposed to the long thick trumpet of the king oyster mushroom. We rate the oyster mushroom for its meaty, umami properties and ability to take on flavours.

Do

- Keep them whole or in half and press them into juicy mushrooms "steaks".
- Lightly brush or wipe with a damp cloth to clean.
- Shred them with a fork to create a pulled pork vibe.

Don't

- Forget to season them thoroughly as they're great flavour absorbers.

How to Prepare

If you have a cluster, pull them apart gently, either into single pieces or larger clumps.

How to Cook

Follow the press and sear technique detailed on the shiitake mushroom page. There's more water in oyster mushrooms so as you press water will release from the mushrooms. Press down hard to release the water for about 20–30 seconds. You can drain off the water if you don't want it in your dish.

To barbeque, press and sear first, then season and oil and put directly on to the barbeque, flipping after 3–4 minutes or when crisp. This method also works in the grill/broiler.

To air fry, marinade or season then coat in a little oil and air fry at 180°C/355°F for ten minutes until crispy.

ARTICHOKE HEARTS

What you need to know Artichoke hearts are the meaty centre of globe artichokes. They have an earthy, nutty flavour and can take on a soft, pulled texture making them an ideal fish or meat substitute. They are high in fibre, vitamins K and C and magnesium.

Do

- Opt for canned or jarred over fresh to get an instant flaky texture.
- Look for artichoke hearts in water or brine instead of oil.
- Rinse the pieces to remove brine or oil.

Don't

- Confuse it with Jerusalem artichoke, which is the edible tuber of a different plant.

How to Prepare

Canned or jarred hearts only need to be rinsed. If they're whole, cut them into quarters. For fresh globe artichokes, it is best to steam the head whole and then pull off the more fibrous outer leaves to access the softer heart, which can be cut into chunks.

How to Cook

To get a fishy or meaty alternative you need to flavour and prepare them according to a recipe. Quartered hearts can be battered and fried as fish pieces, or you can tear the hearts up and use them in Ocean Cakes (see p 126).

CHICKPEAS/GARBANZO BEANS

What you need to know Chickpeas are the queen of pulses – adaptable, affordable and accessible. With 19g/¾oz of protein per 100g/3½oz they are also a nutritional powerhouse.

Do

- Use a pinch of bicarbonate of soda/ baking soda when soaking dried chickpeas.
- Retain the liquid – the aquafaba – from canned chickpeas to use as an egg substitute in baking.
- Rinse canned chickpeas well or the aquafaba flavour lingers.
- Use a pinch of asafoetida to reduce the bloating or gassy effect of any pulse.
- Look out for black chickpeas (kala chana) – a more nutty and rich variety popular in South Asian cuisine.

Don't

- Add acidic ingredients e.g. tomatoes to chickpeas until they are cooked otherwise they will not soften.
- Add canned chickpeas too soon to a dish if there's other ingredients to cook for longer as they could get mushy.

How to Prepare

For dried chickpeas, soak them in a large pan or bowl with twice the amount of water for at least eight hours. They will still need to be cooked after that. Alternatively, slow cook them for three hours on a high heat or six hours on a low heat, until soft.

Canned chickpeas should be thoroughly rinsed before using in a recipe. They are already cooked so they only really need to be heated through in a dish.

How to Cook
Dried chickpeas should be cooked before adding to a dish – once soaked they will take about 60–90 minutes on a simmer. A pinch of salt enhances the flavour.

Canned chickpeas can be added to a dish at any stage.

For a tasty snack, roast cooked chickpeas – coated in your choice of spices or just lightly salted – on a non-stick baking tray at 210°C/410°F for 20–25 minutes until crispy. Or pop them in the air fryer for 12–15 minutes.

Sareta and volunteer Juliana sharing their skills. There's not much Juliana doesn't know about cooking and growing.

BROWN LENTILS

What you need to know The most commonly used lentils in meaty dishes, brown lentils have a richer, deeper, more umami flavour than other varieties.

Do

- Rinse well and make sure to sift dry lentils for small stones or debris.
- Use canned lentils in salads so there's no need to cook them first.
- Batch-cook dried lentils then freeze them into portions for quick protein additions to any dish.
- Use as mince in lasagna, burgers, meatballs and other recipes.
- Use a pinch of asafoetida to reduce the bloating or gassy effect of any lentil or pulse.

Don't

- Soak before cooking. They are soft enough to go straight to the cooking stage.
- Forget to season lentils – they can be rather bland otherwise.
- Expect them to hold their shape if cooked for a long time. If you want something with bite go for a puy or beluga lentil.

How to Prepare
Both dried and canned brown lentils should be rinsed well in a colander before cooking.

How to Cook
In any saucy dish like curry or stew add the brown lentils after the onions and garlic stage and cook down in stock or sauce until soft. Alternatively, you can cook lentils separately in double the amount of water, simmering for 25 minutes until soft. Then add to any dish.

* FLAVA FLAVA

We humans are creatures of habit. We might consciously want to eat more plants but still crave the meaty, fishy, cheesy, creamy, eggy flavours we've become used too.

Being able to create these tastes and textures with wholefood plant-based ingredients is a skill worth acquiring. How to do it is not rocket science. In fact, it's often just seasoning and ingredient pairings, but occasionally there's a technique that yields the most incredible and surprising results.

Whatever plant-based seasonings are used in meat, fish, egg or dairy recipes can be used to make plant-based versions of the same dish. If one of your favourite meat-containing meals is a dish with trimmings and condiments, try making these as well, and you'll find the "theatre of the dish" (the dipping, wrapping, eating with fingers) remains not only the same, but was one of the reasons you enjoyed it so much in the first place.

* MEATY

▸ Meaty Textures

MUSHROOMS

Mushrooms have an intense, meaty flavour and chewy texture if cooked and seasoned right. Shiitake are particularly rich, umami and flavoursome, oyster mushrooms work well shredded to emulate meat, and closed cup and button are good all-rounders. Use minced in Bolognese, in dumpling and taco fillings, and as part of burger patty mixes. Large mushrooms such as beefsteak and wild mushrooms like chicken of the woods work great barbequed. To create deep, meaty tastes and textures they need to be sauteed for twenty minutes plus to reduce their water content and be better able to absorb seasonings.

JACKFRUIT

In the West jackfruit is usually bought canned in brine or water. It comes in chunks, which need to be sliced and pulled apart to emulate pulled pork or chicken. You can sauté, fry or bake jackfruit. The thinner, less watery the jackfruit to begin with, the quicker it will cook and absorb other flavours. Canned jackfruit tastes quite bland, so seasoning and cooking well is crucial. Bland jackfruit is usually a result of too much liquid and it not being cooked for long enough or with enough seasoning. See p 61 for more.

AUBERGINE/EGGPLANT

Slice thinly and marinade for at least an hour (but ideally overnight) with soy sauce, liquid smoke, maple syrup and smoked paprika and use in dishes that usually call for bacon. Pan fry then cut into chunks to throw on top of a mac and cheese (like crispy bacon) or wrap it around vegan sausages "pigs in blanket" style.

COCONUT CHIPS

Marinade coconut chips in the same seasoning as the aubergines to create a crispy, crunchy bacon-like dish topper. Batch-make them and store in a jar to use on salads, on top of soups, mac and cheese and other dishes.

SOY CHUNKS AND MINCE

Also called TVP (textured soy protein), dried soy or soy meat. It is made from defatted soy flour and the soy paste leftover from making soybean oil. It comes in all shapes and sizes with East Asian grocery stores often having the widest variety of products, but you can buy it as chunks or mince in most supermarkets. It is ambient, meaning it doesn't need refrigerating, travels well and lasts for months. Before use, it needs to be soaked in boiling water for at least ten minutes. You then squeeze the excess water out of it to ensure it cooks nicely and absorbs the seasoning. Use in stir fries, as mince to make sausages and burger patties or as a pasta topping or wrap filling. It's meaty in texture but bland otherwise so you need to season it well.

VITAL WHEAT GLUTEN

This flour-like ingredient can be used to create a chewy, tasty meat replacement called seitan. It's a good option for people who are allergic to soy. It's been processed to remove almost all the starch, so it's close to pure gluten. If you have a gluten sensitivity or you're celiac seitan is not for you. You make the seitan by adding water, seasonings of your choice (bouillon and onion and garlic powders are good and a little plain (all-purpose) flour then mixing it into a dough. Break pieces off with your hands and steam for ten minutes. Use it in stir fries, stews and to make things like wings, burgers and steaks. It keeps for three days in the refrigerator and also freezes well.

TEMPEH

These fermented soy beans from Indonesia are high in protein and have a deep umami flavour and firm, chewy texture. You'll find how to cook it on p 60.

CAULIFLOWER

Cauliflower florets make fantastic veggie spicy wings. Coat in a batter of gram and plain (all-purpose) flour and then either air fry, oven roast or deep fry. We recommend air frying if you have one as results are similar to deep frying but it uses far less oil. Serve with a homemade spicy sauce for the full experience.

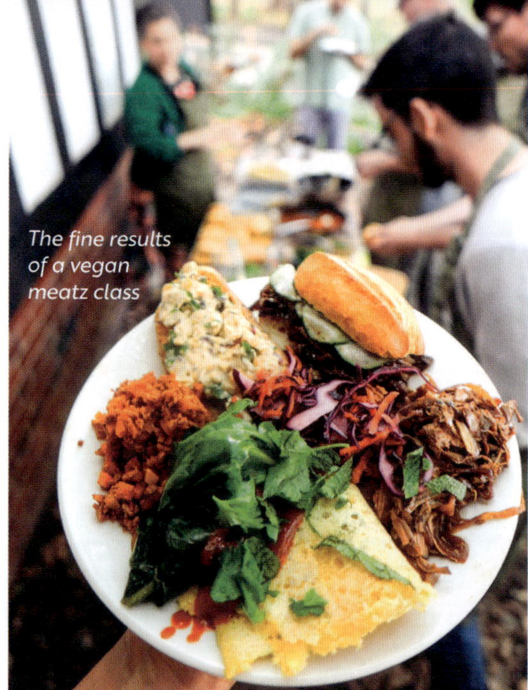

The fine results of a vegan meatz class

BANANA PEELS

Yes – you can use banana peels to make a potassium-packed pulled pork style meat replacer. Cool huh. See recipe p 240.

BROWN LENTILS

These lentils can be used in meals that call for mince. They have an earthy, nutty, chewy texture. You can cook them in stock/bouillon and they season well with miso, balsamic vinegar, chilli and tomato pastes. See p 64 for how to prepare them.

SUNDRIED TOMATOES & CHICKPEAS/ GARBANZO BEANS

Sometimes it's all in a pairing. When you mix together finely sliced sundried tomatoes with mashed chickpeas you get a chorizo-like experience. See p 210 for a banging recipe that uses this combination.

Meaty Flavours

Use these seasonings and ingredients to create deep, rich, smoky, umami flavours reminiscent of meaty dishes.

Vegan Worcester sauce – a delicious sauce that usually contains vinegar, molasses, soy or tamari sauce, onion powder, garlic powder, allspice, cloves, ginger, minced capers and tamarind paste. Non-vegan Worcester contains anchovies.

Liquid Smoke – a liquid seasoning that makes things taste like they've been smoked. Look for brands that use chicory and minimally processed ingredients.

Soy Sauce – a salty, liquid seasoning made from wheat and soy beans. Look for low sodium brands with no E numbers and minimally processed ingredients. Some soy sauces contain fish so check the label.

Tamari Sauce – a Japanese form of soy sauce made entirely from soy with no wheat. Slightly thicker, it has a deep flavour and is usually a bit less salty than soy sauce.

Yeast Extract – this is the unbranded name for Marmite! If you don't want to buy the Unilever-made product you can get yeast extract in health food stores made by smaller independent brands.

Jerk Seasoning – a traditional spicy Jamaican seasoning usually containing allspice, scotch bonnet, ginger, thyme, garlic, cinnamon, onions and spring onions. It's used as a rub on meat, poultry and fish.

Chipotle Seasoning – a spicy Mexican seasoning used in salsa, soups, marinades, rubs and adobo, a marinade usually used on meat.

Brown Rice Miso – a traditional Japanese seasoning made of fermented soybeans and brown rice with a deep, complex flavour. Source unpasteurised versions to get maximum gut health supporting qualities.

Gravy – this comforting sauce associated with roast dinners in British cuisine is traditionally made of onions, flour, vegetable stock and meat fat. Vegan gravy replaces the meat fat with mushrooms and miso.

Kimchi Paste – this delicious Korean seasoning is used to make the fermented dish kimchi (see p 354 for recipe) but is also in dishes such as kimchi pancakes or noodles. It's made of Korean red peppers, onions, garlic, ginger, rice vinegar and sometimes sugar. Traditionally it contains fish sauce so check the label.

BBQ Sauce – A condiment that originated in Carolina, USA in communities of enslaved Africans. It usually contains tomatoes, sugar, vinegars, mustard, paprika and chilli powder, with some chefs adding cola, Worcester sauce, liquid smoke, or even fruits. We have a recipe for Hedgerow BBQ sauce on p 244.

Spices for meaty flavours

These spices add a deep umami flavour often associated with eating meat.

- Smoked paprika/paprika
- Black pepper
- Szechuan peppercorns
- Chilli
- Tarragon
- Thyme
- Rosemary
- Smoked salt
- Iru (fermented locust bean)
- Mustard powder

FISHY

▶ Fishy Textures

BANANA BLOSSOM

These have a chunky, flaky texture that make them an ideal substitute for fish. In the West, banana blossoms are bought in tins and are quite a pricey, speciality ingredient. In East and South Asia you buy the flowers fresh and they're very cheap and take quite a bit of processing. See p 61 for how to cook.

FIRM TOFU

You can use firm tofu instead of white fish, like cod, haddock and pollock, to make phish & chips. Batter it along with a nori seaweed sheet for that crunchy, fishy deliciousness. Recipe on p 108.

JACKFRUIT

When shredded and seasoned green jackfruit can be used to create a canned tuna-like experience or as a substitute for saltfish in Jamaican national dish ackee and saltfish. See p 141 for recipe and 61 in cooking staples.

CHICKPEAS/GARBANZO BEANS

When mashed or blended to a chunky crumb chickpeas make a surprisingly good substitute for canned tuna. Once it's all seasoned up with chives, sweetcorn, mayo and capers, it really looks very similar and makes a great sandwich filling, jacket potato topper or cold buffet dish. See p 220 for a recipe.

CARROTS

Carrots can be cut wafer thin and used to make a clever smoked salmon equivalent known as carrot lox. Marinade overnight in liquid smoke, dill, chives, capers, lemon and olive oil. Serve on top of a cultured vegan cream cheese on a bagel or cracker and prepare to be wowed by the umami flavours.

WATERMELON

This is a really cool one. Roast chunks of watermelon in the oven at 190°C/375°F for one hour in a dressing of nori sprinkles (cut up seaweed sheets), soy sauce, apple cider vinegar, miso paste and garlic to create a delicious tuna steak-like experience. Serve as is or use to make sushi. A scatter of black and white sesame over the top adds to its visual appeal. Warning – it looks incredibly fishy when in a maki roll so you might need to reassure vegan guests.

TOMATOES

You can use fresh plum tomatoes (not canned) in a similar way to watermelon to create a tuna-like experience. You need to skin the tomatoes, boil them and then add straight away to a bowl of ice water. Once cooled you gently peel them, season like the watermelons (or close to) and serve.

ARTICHOKE HEARTS

The flaky texture of artichoke hearts is what makes them an excellent fish substitute. They absorb flavour well and are a great replacement for crab. In the West they're most commonly available in jars or tins in oil, water or brine. And yes, in case you're wondering, they are the centre of globe artichokes. See p 126 for a great Ocean Cakes recipe.

▶ Fishy Flavours

Use these seasonings and ingredients to create fishy tastes.

Seaweed – nori sheets, nori sprinkles, wakame, laverbread, kombu – these can all be used to add a deep, ocean taste to dishes. Most seaweed products are sold dried in air-tight packets. Wakame and kombu need hydrating before use. Nori sheets are pre-dried and ready to use – some need toasting first to enhance their flavour. Laverbread is a little known, canned Welsh delicacy made from laver seaweed, sea salt and water. Most seaweed comes from China, the Philippines and Indonesia but you can look for locally sourced seaweed from artisan companies such as The Cornish Seaweed company in the UK.

Lemon Pepper Seasoning – a tasty spice blend that usually contains a mixture of black pepper, lemon granules, turmeric, onion powder and salt. It is used in a variety of fish dishes to create an instant depth of flavour and you can use it in any plant-based version. Look for products with no added sugar or flavourings.

Kombu Dashi Granules – this is an excellent vegan alternative to dashi, which contains bonito (wafer thin smoked or fermented fish shavings). Kombu is a type of kelp seaweed most commonly grown in Japan, China and Korea. These granules are usually made of dried kelp powder, salt, sugar, kelp extract, dextrin and amino acid seasoning. They can be found in East Asian grocery stores.

Lemon – the juice and zest of lemons are used in fish dishes around the world.

Parsley – this tough green herb is grown across Europe, Asia and North Africa and used in various global cuisines. There are different types of parsley including curly-leaf parsley, flat-leaf parsley and root parsley. They are all relatively easy to grow at home on windowsills and in small spaces.

Dill – this beautiful feathery green herb is often used in fish and salad dishes. It has a strong, unique flavour like nothing else. It is harder to grow than parsley and we recommend you buy it in big bunches from Middle Eastern or Mediterranean grocers.

The Peng Patties young chefs making the most stunning sushi in one of their sessions.

Tarragon – this herb is native to Serbia, Europe and Central Asia. It has a sweet liquorice taste and is often paired with white-flesh fish dishes, alongside lemon and black pepper. Fresh tarragon is not always found in budget supermarkets but it is readily available dried.

Chives – this herb from the allium family has a strong onion taste. Chopped up fine it is often added to fish sauces, mayonnaise, salads and used as a garnish. It's easy to grow and because of its smell it's used in organic growing to deter aphids. Remember, if someone is allergic to or avoiding eating onions, then they also can't eat chives.

Liquid from jars of capers or gherkins – this tasty salt, water or vinegar combination has been gently infused with the flavours of the gherkins or capers. Many people discard it but we recommend you put it aside and use to season plant-based fishy dishes.

CHEESY

Cheesy Textures

NUTS

Cashew and almonds are the nuts most commonly used to craft vegan cheeses, but you can also use brazil nuts and macadamias (though they are expensive). Blended into a sauce they create a creamy, umami flavour, and if cultured/fermented for a soft or even hard cheese the flavour deepens still. Soak nuts in advance to release the nutrient blockers. See p 28 for more about soaking nuts, and see p 345 for a delicious fermented cashew cheese recipe.

SEEDS

Sunflower seeds and pine nuts are used to create cheeses and cheesy sauces. If making a pesto, pine nuts are expensive, so instead a mix of sunflower and pumpkin seeds with nutritional yeast works great. Pumpkin seeds are good to add as they contain zinc.

WHITE POTATOES

White, floury potatoes such as Maris Pipers, Desiree or King Edwards are an excellent low-cost ingredient to use in a cheesy sauce or bechamel. They bulk out dishes and are much cheaper than nuts.

BUTTERNUT SQUASH AND SQUASH

Roast in the oven and then blend into a cheesy sauce along with marmite, nutritional yeast, yeast extract, tomato paste/concentrate, plant milk and black pepper. They are a great way to add nutrition to a cheesy sauce and give it an orangey colour.

PLANT MILKS

You can use all types of plant milks in cheesy sauces and cheeses but our favourites are oat, soy and almond. Not all plant milks are created equal so look for those with minimal oil and preserving ingredients, that are organic (if this is a priority for you) or have added vitamins and nutrients like D3, B12 and calcium.

TOFU – SILKEN AND FIRM

Both silken and firm tofu can be used to make a variety of cheesy replacements such as a ricotta (see recipe on p 252) or a cheesecake. You would usually mash or blend the tofu to change its consistency.

Cheesy Flavours

Nutritional Yeast - Lovingly referred to as "nooch", this is the golden ingredient that delivers delicious cheesy, salty, umami flavours to plant-based meals. Pretty much all vegan cheeses and vegan cheese sauces use it and in the West it's a plant-based kitchen staple. We recommend you buy the B12-enriched vegan version.

Yeast Extract - (see p 67) used to give a salty, umami taste to cheesy sauces.

Chives – (see p 69) used in cheesy dishes to give a crisp contrast to a creamy cheese.

Tomato Paste/Concentrate – used in small amounts to add colour and a rich depth of flavour to cheesy sauces.

Dried Fruits (Cranberry, Apricot and Figs) – these are commonly found on cheese board pairings or are used inside cheeses in small chunks. Add them to your homemade cheeses or serve on a vegan cheese board.

Spices for cheesy flavours

- **Smoked paprika**
- **Mustard seeds/powder**
- **Black pepper**
- **Mixed Herbs**

* CREAMY

▸ Creamy Textures

NUTS

Like cheese, soaked then blended cashews and almonds are our favourite nuts for creating decadent creamy textures. Add a little water, a pinch of salt and sweetener of choice like date or maple syrup – and you have your own delicious nut-based cream.

OATS

You can make delicious homemade pourable oat cream by soaking oats in warm water for two hours (no longer or they go slimy) and then blending them with water, salt and sunflower or rapeseed oil. Pass through a sieve and there you have delicious oat cream. You can add a sweetener like maple or date syrup if you wish. Yum.

COCONUT

Canned coconut milk can be used to make a decadent whipped cream. Pop the can of coconut milk in the fridge to chill overnight. Remove and then add the thick coconut cream that's gathered at the top of the tin to a food processor ready to be whipped. Leave the liquid behind or your cream won't whip. You can buy coconut whipping cream but warning – it's pricey. To sweeten, sift in a little icing sugar; liquid sweeteners can make it sag. Whip with an electric whisk until thick peaks form. This is notoriously tricky and the brand you buy affects how easily your coconut cream whips.

SOY MILK

When combined with coconut oil you can make a stunning whipped cream that's much more budget-friendly than coconut whipped cream. We recommend using unsweetened soy milk and refined coconut oil, so the cream tastes more creamy than coconutty. The trick to success is that, before blending, the two ingredients need to be similar temperatures. This means waiting for your melted coconut oil to cool down and your refrigerated milk to warm up! Blend, refrigerate and once completely cooled, whip. Another tip is to cool your mixing bowl before use.

Chef Amandeep making golden milk/turmeric latte. Recipe p 332.

▸ Creamy Flavours

Vanilla extract, essence or pods – a hint of vanilla, apparently the most popular flavour in the world, can be used to elevate a cream or creamy sauce. The spice is native to Central and South America but Madagascan vanilla is rated for its exceptional quality. When cooking for people who are in recovery from addiction, extracts/essences must be avoided as they're a trigger ingredient, so opt for the pods instead. They are more expensive but offer a higher quality vanilla flavour.

EGGY

Eggy Textures

SILKEN & FILM TOFU

These can be used to create scrambled tofu (see p 266), mayonnaise, egg-fried rice dishes and even whole replica fried eggs and scotch eggs (this is advanced kitchen alchemy!). See p 60 for how to cook. Again seasoning is key.

FLAX SEEDS

Ground flax seeds (also called linseeds) are used to create a gelatinous texture to replace eggs in baking. Buy whole seeds and grind them yourself as this is cheaper than buying pre-ground. They come in brown or golden colours; both are great. To make one flax egg, combine one tablespoon of ground flax with 2½ tablespoons of water. Stir, and let rest for five minutes to go gooey. Use in recipes in place of one egg, but it isn't an exact science so we recommend using specifically vegan recipes to ensure success.

CHIA SEEDS

These work just like ground flax. No need to grind them first, use them as they are: one tablespoon of chia seeds plus 2½ tablespoons of water.

AQUAFABA

This is a fancy name for the liquid from canned or cooked chickpeas/garbanzo beans (or other legumes but chickpeas work best) whipped in a blender to create a frothy texture for baking, omelettes, mayonnaise and meringues. See p 376 for more.

MOONG DHAL

Moong dhal is the yellow centre of mung beans. It is not the same as yellow split peas so don't confuse the two. You can use it to make an excellent scrambled egg replacer as an alternative to tofu scramble. You soak then drain your moong dal then add it to a blender with your seasonings (see below) and tapioca starch. Next, pan fry the mixture into a scramble-like consistency. Cool, huh!

CORN OR TAPIOCA STARCH

Plant-based chefs use both of these starches (they're different ingredients) to bind, thicken and give a stretchy sense to plant-based egg yolks and scramble.

Eggy Flavours

Kala Namak – this pungent black salt hails from the Himalayas and the salt mines of India, Pakistan, Bangladesh, Nepal and other Himalayan nations. It has a strong sulphuric, eggy smell and should be used in small quantities. It gets its flavour from the trace minerals and iron.

Nutritional yeast – although more commonly used to create cheesy tastes, a small amount is useful when creating eggy dishes such as omelettes (see recipe p 204) and quiches.

Turmeric – mainly used for its colour, this creates a bright yellow like the yolk of an egg.

Mustard powder – used for both its colour and distinct flavour, mustard powder is made from ground mustard seeds. The seeds come in brown, black and yellow varieties. It is used in a variety of egg dishes such as devilled eggs, egg mayonnaise sandwiches and tofu scramble.

STORE-BOUGHT EGG REPLACERS

There are a range of pre-made egg replacers on the market made from all the above ingredients. These do work, but it's usually more cost-effective to make your own from scratch.

THINGS THAT MAKE YOU GO MMM MMM

Much of what we've just learned about cooking, seasoning and creating specific flavour profiles with plants can be described as the quest for umami! It's one of the five major tastes along with sweet, bitter, salty and sour. It is the flavour used to describe glutamate, and particularly monosodium glutamate, which occurs when you cook and season food in a certain way.

Whereas sweet, salt, bitter and sour have identifiable tastes, glutamate itself doesn't taste like anything, but it works in harmony to amplify other taste sensations. It has the synesthetic property of making food seem heartier, more satiating and tend to make you go mmmmmmmm.

Animal-derived foods tend to be high in the glutamate/umami flavour – either naturally or from their typical cooking processes. Dried, aged or processed meats have considerably more glutamic acid than fresh meats, as these processes break down complete proteins and release free glutamic acid.

You can create plant-based sources of umami with seasoning and cooking techniques such as roasting, browning, grilling, sautéing, and caramelizing – all of which increase the umami flavour by releasing glutamate from the plant-based proteins.

Foods with built-in umami include ferments, nutritional yeast, yeast extract, seaweed (wakame being the highest), toasted nuts and seeds, savoury spices, certain vegetables – onion, garlic, tomato, peas, sweetcorn, beans, carrots, sweet potatoes, soybeans, avocado, spinach, cabbage and in particular mushrooms.

Participant Amy gets stuck in to making saurekraut in our fermentation workshop.

* Cooking Terms

We try to avoid unnecessarily fancy terms at MIH but at the same time we're a cooking school and want to empower you with the lingo to go forth and cook from all kinds of books. Here are some phrases you might encounter in our recipes.

Julienne – to cut a fruit or vegetable into thin matchstick-length pieces.

Dice – to chop into tiny cubes.

Sauté – to fry quickly in a little hot oil.

Parboil – to partially cook an ingredient by boiling it for a short length of time until it's softened but not cooked all the way through.

Temper – a technique used in Southeast Asia where you gently fry spices in oil to release their flavours and fragrance then add to your chosen dish. You can do oil-free tempering by dry frying spices in a pan or dry roasting them in an oven.

Massage – using hands to rub a vegetable – usually kale – with a small amount (⅛ teaspoon) of either water, oil, lemon juice, or salt, to soften so the vegetable appears cooked but is still raw.

* Non-Toxic Kitchenware

Not all cookware is created equal. Many items you'll commonly find in the kitchen are made with materials that leech environmental pollutants into our food, potentially disrupting our hormones, immune system and our genes. Many pots and pans now claim to be "non-toxic" when in fact they're not. Follow our guide and you'll soon be free of toxic kitchenware. Look for cookware bargains in charity shops and online second hand.

✗ AVOID

Plastic
Plastic is lightweight and hardwearing, but if you can avoid using it in the kitchen do, especially if the cookware will come into contact with hot food or is being used to heat food up. Avoid plastic chopping boards as every time you cut into the board you're introducing microplastics to your food.

Aluminium
Aluminium is rife in cookware, packaging, foil and containers. We want to reduce exposure to aluminium, as it's been linked to neurological issues and bone disorders. Occasional usage is fine, but not daily, because consistent exposure could potentially cause harm. Aluminium is used in the centre of some pans to help distribute heat. This is fine as long as it's covered by stainless steel.

Teflon Pan Coatings
When exposed to high temperatures over 250°C/480°F Teflon coatings start to break down. Teflon is made from perfluoroalkyl and polyfluoroakyl substances (PFAS), which are linked to a range of health issues such as liver disease, low birth weight, certain cancers, fertility and other reproductive issues.

✔ USE

Food Grade Stainless Steel

Unlike aluminium or Teflon, stainless steel cookware doesn't contain chemicals that can leech into your food. It's a metal alloy usually made up of a combination of nickel, chromium and iron. Look for stainless steel pans, gastros, blender blades and knives.

Ceramic

Ceramics are inorganic non-metallic solids (yes, we're getting sciencey) usually made from clay minerals such as kaolinite. Modern ceramics are often made from silicon carbide and tungsten carbide. They don't leech chemicals into your food and are safe at all temperatures.

Glass

Hard as it is to believe, glass is made from liquid sand. Like ceramic it's inert in terms of toxicity and if you buy reinforced glass like Pyrex it makes for great hard-wearing cookware material.

Cast Iron

Although cast iron skillets tend to be very heavy, they're a great investment if you can lift one. They keep food warm longer, the heat distributes evenly and apparently they add iron to your food. Fantastic. Be careful of little chefs banging them down onto inductions as they could break the glass.

Wood and Bamboo

Wood and bamboo (a woody grass) are excellent materials for chopping boards, mixing spoons, spatulas, bowls and cups. In commercial kitchens you're not allowed to use wooden boards in case microbes lodge in the grooves, but at home and especially in a plant-based kitchen they're fine and can be cleaned with a wipe down and regular oiling.

Marble and Granite

This is pretty fancy but marble and granite make for excellent, sanitary heavyduty chopping boards, pestle and mortars and kitchen counter tops.

Unbleached Parchment Paper

Unless you're a zero-waste kitchen unbleached parchment is a useful swap for foil. If you have aluminium cookware or old baking trays, it's prudent to line them with parchment before putting the food on top. Bleached parchment contains dioxin and is linked to potential health issues such as certain types of cancer, hormone health, reproductive health and can negatively impact the immune system.

Food Grade Silicone

As silicone looks like plastic it's hard to believe it's benign, but apparently when used under 230°C/445°F it doesn't leech any harmful chemicals. Some people love silicone for reuseable cup cake liners, baking tray mats, air fryer mats and oil brushes.

▶ Don't Panic!

Avoiding all this stuff day in day out is impossible if you eat in other people's homes, in restaurants, buy any type of pre-made food or cook in kitchens in a holiday let. Using it a little is not going to cause any issues, it's long-term, frequent exposure we want to reduce.

Water

For ferment recipes we recommend you use filtered water due to the chlorine and other chemicals found in tap water that may hinder the fermentation process. For other recipes, tap water will work fine but we do recommend using filtered water if you have access to a filter. Tap water varies in quality around the world. Recent studies have found London mains tap water is polluted with "forever" chemicals such as perfluorooctanoic acid (PFOA) and perfluorooctane sulfonic acid (PFOS), which are linked to a range of ailments, including cancer, liver damage, reduced fertility and birth defects.

* IMPORTANT NOTE ABOUT OUR RECIPES

Our recipes are formatted differently to most cookbooks. Here's what we do, and why.

Prep

We write the prep of ingredients out in step one of the method rather than include it in the ingredients list. This is because some folk find it confusing to add the prep to the ingredients list. Plus, we like to be right there with you cooking from the get-go, including the prep stage.

Equipment

We list the equipment you need to have or get out to make the dish. The only pieces of equipment we don't list are chopping boards, ovens and hobs/stove tops, as you need those in 95% of recipes. When we say a piece of equipment is optional we mean it, but sometimes it can be more work.

Abbreviations

After hearing about many baking projects that have gone wrong due to this error, we always write out teaspoon and tablespoon in full to help cooks not get the two confused. G, oz, ml and fl oz are shortened as these can't be confused with anything else.

Descriptors

We include timings and descriptors in our recipes so you know what you're aiming for.

Precise

We try to avoid using unclear, non-specific phrases such as a glug, a little, a bit etc. as this just isn't specific enough for many folk. We have kept "a pinch" for salt and black pepper. This is less than a quarter of a teaspoon.

Numbered Method Steps

We number our method steps to help people stay on track and for those moments when you've got distracted and need to find your place in the recipe again.

Read First, Cook Next

Read the recipe before you cook. There's information that's vital. Get the equipment and ingredients out, weigh/measure, then cook. This way you can be more in the flow. Many meals have multiple elements as they were part of two hour classes. If you don't have two hours, just make one or two dishes. It's all good.

Health Vs Authenticity

Many recipes have been adjusted to be more health-conscious than their traditional versions. This is because we want to support our communities health and wellbeing.

Long Thing

Many ingredients lists look long. It's often spices, substitution suggestions and UK/US words - so don't be put off.

▸ Badges

Many of our recipes have badges directing you to other parts of the book for shopping and ingredient advice. This is so those who are familiar with the ingredients can get cracking, but those who aren't can get informed.

Wherever you see this **Nutrition Nuggets** icon, you can flick to the back of the book to find out more about nutritional benefits of the dish.

Wherever you see this **Tips & Tricks** icon, flick to the back of the book for hacks, shopping tips, storage tricks and more.

RECIPE CATEGORIES

We have given our recipes nifty abbreviated categories so you can choose what you need right now.

PAP-Pots & Pans
Require no fancy equipment such as blenders, food processors and the like.

BC – Budget Conscious
Describing something as low cost or affordable is inappropriate as this is dependent on everybody's unique circumstances. We apply this BC category to dishes where you can feed four people for under £6/$8, so about £1.50/$2 a portion or less. We have not costed in the price of storeroom staples.

HIP – High In Protein
For people seeking a high protein meal post work-out, because you're ageing, or because you haven't eaten anything else protein-dense that day – we've got you.

FF – Fast Food
Delicious homecooked meals that can be made in under 30 minutes.

1Pot – One Pot
This is for people who want to keep things simple and not end up with loads of washing up. One pot or pan meals.

GH – Gut Healthy
Taking care of our gut health is crucial for good health. We have highlighted dishes packed with lots of different fresh produce, pre- and probiotic ingredients, antioxidants and anti-inflammatory properties and cooking techniques.

GF – Gluten Free
Recipes that are gluten-free. Any gluten-free alternatives that could easily replace gluten-containing ingredients are listed at the top of these recipes.

We thought about adding the category "Over 7" to help people striving to eat over 30 different plants a week. But we realised we'd be slapping this on most of our recipes, so we've left it out. Cook with us, you'll get your 30 plants a week in.

IN CONVERSATION WITH...

Sukhin Tye, MIH's Volunteer Manager

Nothing would have been possible at MIH without the support of our incredible volunteers who've collectively given thousands of hours of their time, attention and love.

From the community-led rescue job of our first ever kitchen build, to every single cookery class we've hosted, to every emergency meal we've cooked and delivered, a volunteer has helped make it happen, and we could not appreciate them more.

In our founding days our first Volunteer Manager, Nynke Brett, built our volunteer programme, as a volunteer herself, before we could formalize it into a paid role. Not ideal at all, but we were new, funding short, and learning as we went, and thankfully Nynke was up for the ride.

Our current Volunteer Manager (there's only been two in thirteen years) Sukhin Tye joined us a week before the first lockdown, and instead of training volunteers for a cookery school she found herself managing a cycle courier service to despatch emergency meals. It wasn't in the job description, but it was what was needed, so she rolled up her sleeves and got stuck in. We chatted to Sukhin about why people volunteer and how it enriches their lives.

Why do people volunteer with MIH? What's their motivation?

Sukhin: People volunteer to give back to the community and to do something for wider society. They might like to make friends, meet new people and see life in a bigger way. Some people want to acquire new skills in cooking and/or knowledge specific to their health and the environment. Many volunteers say our ethos resonates with theirs, and they want to give their time to a cause where plant-based food empowers communities and diverse groups of people. Many say it's not just about making friends, but being opened up to a wide variety of people from different backgrounds that they wouldn't ordinarily meet in their own social networks. Personally I've found volunteering has been developmental.

There are thousands of volunteering opportunities out there. How do you choose what to do?

There are two ways you can go about it. Seek opportunities in something you know you'd enjoy and would develop you as a human being. Or take an opportunity that's totally different, off the edge from your usual work and life experiences. This can really expand you, but you need to be a bit brave.

We have some incredibly dedicated volunteers who've done over 100 hours of volunteering.

Yes, we have quite a few who have. They've made friends and are part of a volunteer community. They volunteer in other places too, but they come back to us, because I think there's something really bonding about cooking and eating together. Also we offer a variety of activities. Volunteers don't have to stick with cooking – they can be a class host, deliver meals by bicycle, do a community outreach stall or help with a corporate workshop.

So volunteers don't just do one role?

Some do, but many try different things and go on quite a journey with us. We had one volunteer who started off batch cooking meals, then she became a class host. She wanted more, so she became a project assistant, and got to know the behind the scenes workings of the charity. Ultimately, she found a job based on her experience. It's development from a skills and experience point of view, but also you become more human. You learn to be more empathetic, compassionate and integrate with different types of people.

So using volunteering as a pathway to employment is quite common?

Very common, and often

unintentionally. It is great when a volunteer starts on the path to give time and care to the wider community, but it leads to something for themselves too. Now we've been around 12 years, it's amazing seeing the legacy of volunteers working in the food or community food sector. They came to us when they were in recovery and needed to build themselves back up. Or just out of college or uni, or leaving a corporate job, or had one afternoon a week off to try something new. And they took the experience and built on it until they're working in the sector. It's really lovely to see. There are people at food organizations all over London who started off as volunteers for MIH.

Do these volunteers stay in touch or come back?
Yes people dip in and out over many years. Even after a volunteer leaves they're never disconnected, they'll always be part of us. I think it's like the root system of a forest; once you're embedded in fertile ground, you remain part of it. It's wonderful to see those shoots and people reaching out in different ways. It's not about the job, but something in the heart that wants to stay connected. I think that's very beautiful.

What's the line between paid roles and voluntary roles?
It's certainly something we had to get to grips with over the years as we grew and became more established. My view is people should be paid to do compulsory work, and organizations shouldn't be leaning too heavily on volunteers. But at the same time, people love to volunteer in a meaningful role. In a role that makes a real difference. You have to be mindful of not taking advantage of people. The way I've balanced it out with myself is to put flexibility in a role. If the activity needs six hours of somebody's time, but the volunteer has just two hours due to childcare needs or studying for exams, then you're grateful for those hours. The volunteer is always free to choose. This approach is appreciated because that care and flexibility should be in any organization that works with volunteers. Setting the expectation of a volunteer role very clearly is also important. And that any department who has a volunteer in it knows not to overreach or apply pressure.

How do you develop volunteers?
By offering opportunities to develop human potential and deepen their humanity. Whenever you can, invite volunteers to events, networking things, social events, festivals – offer potentially enriching experiences. It's a loss and sometimes a heartache when they leave, but in a way that's when you know you've provided a good experience for them to build on. You offered nurturing and fertilizing soil for them to grow in their own way. You're part of their journey.

Who are our volunteers? What are their life circumstances?
It's very mixed, which people really appreciate. 20% are retired or not working. There's people on flexi time, although a lot less now because of the cost of living. Some people have two to three jobs these days. We have a lot of freelancers, students, people who are in-between jobs, people on sabbaticals, people who want to try out a different career. Recently we had someone who was very senior in an accounting company. He took a sabbatical and joined us to cook community meals each week. He really enjoyed it. We have musicians, actors, comedians – people with flexible gigs. It's a lovely mix.

Some organizations are automating their volunteer management systems and removing the personal touch. What do you think about that?
It's great for admin but in terms of relationships, it can't replace the human touch. People like to feel seen and acknowledged. To be considered and have their life circumstances and personalities taken into account. I of course don't know what's happening in 500 volunteers' lives, but for volunteers I've had recent interactions with, I try to remember to check in on them and ask about big life events like surgeries, bereavements, new babies. To look after people and appreciate people, the human touch is essential.

Should everyone who can try volunteering?
I think everybody should volunteer in their life at least once if they're able to. It can change your life for the better. I'm not just saying that because I'm a volunteer manager. Many people have told me this. It's a human development journey. Wherever you start, you see how it deepens you, your connection with life and the community. With my own experiences volunteering has made me more empathetic and more connected. You develop relationships and skills, but you also develop the heart and spirit.

MEET THE CHEFS

Nothing would be possible at MIH without our talented, passionate and dedicated chefs. They're an incredible bunch who are passionate about the transformative power of cooking and eating planet friendly food in community.

They've cooked countless meals for our community support services, lugged equipment across London for pop up kitchens, and inspired and upskilled thousands of people to cook more plants in our classes. Their experience ranges from Michelin restaurants to cooking in schools, on wellbeing retreats, hosting supper clubs, running food social enterprises, workshops, market stalls and eating establishments. Some are famous cookbook authors, TV chefs and restaurateurs who support us when they can, or, are our official charity ambassadors. Lucky us! Thank you MIH chefs - we appreciate you!

* **Abdulkareem Lafene**
Aka Baba. Forest school leader, tree surgeon and founder Sarah's husband and consequently MIH's longest serving, most vital volunteer.

* **Amandeep Verdding**
Chef, caterer, practising nutritionist, founder of Biba Kitchen and MIH cookery teacher. Her style is influenced by her Punjabi mother's knowledge of Ayurveda.

* **Amy Hiller**
Teacher of MIH's Nourishing Sweet Treats and Vegan Baking classes, vegan snack business owner, qualified Healing Diets Coach, former music teacher and global traveller.

* **Andi Oliver**
TV presenter, trailblazer, author, podcast host, foodie powerhouse, national treasure and one of MIH's celebrity ambassadors.

* **Angela Chou**
Co-founder of pioneering vegan cheese brand I AM NUT OK and their Hackney-based deli café The Third Culture along with her partner Nivi Jasa and Cliff the dog.

* **Anna Jones**
Hackney local, renowned veggie chef, author of five acclaimed cookbooks and one of our celebrity chef supporters. Anna has delivered fundraising classes for MIH packed with techniques for elevating veg.

* **Asa Simonsson**
Our longest-serving fermentation teacher. She's a wholefoods plant-based chef, retreat chef, NHS district nurse, naturopath and author of a book about fermentation.

* **Betty Vandy**
Aka Bettylicious. Plant-based chef, former street food trader, founder of Liverpool community café Gather At The Table and soon to be book author.

* **Bruna Oliveira**
Naturopath, cheesemaker and wholefoods plant-based chef. She lives in Mexico and runs a health and wellbeing coaching business.

* **Eddie Garza**
Chef, cookbook author and leading figure in the movement to reform food systems in Hispanic Communities. The US-based chef's work has been featured on *CNN, Hola! TV* and *TV Venezuela*.

* **Ekowa and Zahira Paul**
Father and daughter duo who are co-founders of Peng Patties, a social enterprise that supports young adults to learn skills, vegan recipes and nurture their entrepreneurial flare.

* **Ellie Brown**
Creative plant-based culinary force and founder of Kinda Co. a trailblazing British vegan cheese company that sells over 8,000 plant-based cheeses a month.

* **Emel Ernalbant**
Vegan Chef School trained chef, photographer, teacher of MIH's Middle Eastern cuisine masterclasses and founder of vegan community cookery school Greens & Others.

* **Fiona McCallister**
With a background in community organising and environmental education Fi runs an intergenerational community project and works as a Health & Wellbeing Coach.

* **Flo Francis**
Acupuncturist, baker, boater and head chef of MIH's Community Made programme leading volunteers to cook hundreds of meals for households who need food support.

* **Fran Bernhardt**
Food policy specialist who supports governments in restricting unhealthy food adverts and celebrating fruit, veg and nuts.

* **Freddie Charles**
Hackney local, yoga, functional fitness and meditation teacher who has taught MIH gluten-free bread-making and yoga for our Retreat in the City events.

* **Hannah Walker**
Wild food enthusiast and forager, zero-waste chef, former NHS dietician, foraging teacher, MIH cookery class teacher specializing in diabetes support and nettle obsessive.

* **Jah Spirit (RIP)**
Jah Spirit was a much-loved and respected local community leader, reggae soundsystem emcee, Ital food chef and proprietor of a Caribbean grocery store on Broadway Market in East London.

* **James Lawrence & Lee Desai**
AKA Dr Legumes, a restaurant, cookery school and community interest company in Folkestone, southern England, and mentees of our Global Plant Kitchens programme.

* **Joel Bravette**
aka Jay Brave. MIH's youth ambassador, co-host of the Better Beings podcast, inspiring leader, speaker and author. Joel runs youth cooking classes for MIH – including our famous Wraps & Raps sessions.

* **Jordan Bourzig**
Classically trained French chef who worked in Michelin establishments. Now on an alternative cookery path, he is a College of Natural Nutrition-trained vegan nutritionist and cookery class teacher at MIH.

* **Karla Zazueta**
MIH cookery teacher, cookbook author, food writer and former secondary school teacher originally from Baja California in northern Mexico.

* **Linda North**
Czech-born fermentation enthusiast, nutritional therapist, health coach and founder of The Green Nut. Volunteered at MIH's Community Meal Service – and is now a cookery class teacher.

* **Mark Breen**
Classically trained chef who taught Italian, Sri Lankan and Gourmet Mushroom Masterclasses for MIH. Now a Senior Creative Partner at environmental charity Hubbub.

* **Mauro Strumendo**
Food scientist, plant-based chef, teacher of Italian Masterclasses, specializing in vegan, gluten-free versions of classic Italian dishes. Manager of our Plant Prospects Programme.

* **Melissa Saint Hill**
Former MIH teacher and trustee. Registered nutritionist, recipe developer, founder of the Diverse Nutrition Association, food stylist known on Insta as @the_bare_scientist.

* **Michael Ninvalle**
Former Trinidadian TV personality turned classically trained chef. Worked in Michelin-starred restaurants as a head chef and does private catering for celebrities.

* **Nena Ubani**
aka Duchess Nena. Self-taught vegan chef, TV personality, teacher, herbalist and author of many cookbooks including *Igbo Vegan*. She is a trailblazer in Nigeria for plant-based diets.

* **Niki Webster**
Niki is the recipe developer behind Rebel Recipes and author of six stellar vegan cookbooks that many MIH teachers and team love to cook from.

* **Nishma Shah**
Founder of Shambu, an award-winning vegan catering and food education business. Teacher of Gujarati and East African cuisine and host at international vegan food festivals.

* **Dr Nitu Bajekal**
Senior Consultant Obstetrician and Gynaecologist, author of the brilliant *Finding Me In Menopause* and one of our charity ambassadors.

* **Oliver Bragg**
Wholefood, plant-based chef and teacher for Goldster, the College Of Naturopathic Medicine and recipe developer for V For Life, an organisation that promotes vegetarianism for the over 50s.

* **Rachel de Thample**
Chef who has worked in the kitchens of Heston Blumenthal and Peter Gordon. Was Head Of Fantastic Food at Abel & Cole. Author of seven cookbooks.

* **Raha Eskafi**
MIH's former Community Programmes manager and Persian Cuisine teacher. Still Chill, her organisation set up with her sister, provides wellbeing support through mindfulness and self-compassion.

* **Rebecca Ghim**
Founder and CEO of The Ferm, a London-based vegan zero-waste Korean Fermentary company. Hailing from Gwangju, South Korea, she leads classes in Korean cuisine and ferments.

* **Rohini Bajekal**
Nutritionist and lifestyle medicine professional, former communications lead at Plant-Based Health Professionals and co-author with her mother, Dr Nitu Bajekal, of *Living PCOS Free*.

* **Roshni Shah**
Founder of supper club 8 Plates, MIH's enterprise manager and former manager of Plant Prospects, our consulting service. She now works at Sustain as the Diversity Outreach Lead.

* **Rowan Bentley-Lafene**
A neurodiverse young chef, mocktail and flavour enthusiast and Sarah's son.

* **Dr Rupy**
The culinary health legend behind The Doctor's Kitchen. He volunteered with MIH to learn about the challenges people faced around healthy eating, eventually becoming our charity ambassador.

Sami Tamimi
Palestinian chef, restaurateur, writer. Former business partner of Yotam Ottolenghi and co-author of three cookbooks. Made 600 meals as part of our community meal service and led fundraising classes for us.

Sandor Katz
Storyteller, international author of many books, teacher and fermentation icon. His 2003 book *Wild Fermentation* is a cult classic.

Sandra Farrell
Msc in Global Public Health Nutrition, BA in Food and Professional Cookery with certificates in Plant Based Nutrition and Practical Horticulture, Sandra is a treasured MIH volunteer and outreach stall leader.

Sara Kiyo Popowa
Plant-based chef, recipe creator, food stylist, photographer, leader of MIH's Japanese cookery classes and author of *The Opinionated Guide To Vegan London, and Bento Power.*

Sara Shah
Earth chef, cookery teacher, wellbeing retreat caterer, busy Mama and artisan raw cakes and chocolates business-owner.

Sareta Puri
Restaurant consultant, recipe developer, supper club host, and teacher and Former Head Chef of Community Meal Service at MIH. Now the Diversity & Outreach lead at Sustain.

Sharon Gardner
Wholefood plant-based chef, naturopath, nutritionist, pilates instructor and home fermentation enthusiast. Sharon has been teaching at MIH for over a decade.

Sonali Tailor
Chef, MIH's Cookery School Coordinator, Masterclass programmer and proud Mama, Sonali is the author of the eBook *Suppers By Sonali* and hosts events of the same name.

Steve Wilson
Founder of Mediterranean Food Journeys in Spain, chef, cookery teacher and founder of various food social enterprises.

Sukhin Tye
MIH's much-loved volunteer manager. Sukhin trains volunteers for the cookery school and co-manages the food support programme Community Made.

Dr Sunni Patel
Crohns warrior, holistic wellness and culinary medicine coach and founder of Dish Dash Deets – a health coaching and education platform that supports people with practical wellbeing tips.

Veryan Wilkie-Jones
aka Mama MIH. Former Community Programmes Manager for seven years, running the Masterclasses programme, renowned for her party planning and homemade treats.

Vivianne Pontes
Former Programmes Assistant & Enterprise Manager, and cookery teacher. A biochemist, there is little she doesn't know about food science.

Woin Tegegn
Proud vegan, Mum of three incredible girls and founder of Ethiopian catering business, Ethiopic Kitchen. Woin has taught Ethiopian cooking classes for MIH for years as well as for the brilliant charity Migrateful.

Ximena Ransom
Food grower, chef and MIH's first cookery class teacher. She's now a full time grower on a two acre farm supplying organic veg to seventy households in Greenwich.

Yasmin Khan
Award-winning cookbook author and broadcaster, Yasmin was MIH's project manager when we were tiny. She has since published three highly acclaimed cookbooks.

Zoe Marks
Plant-based chef and cookery teacher who has taught for MIH for many years, specializing in sustainable, conscious food for schools and community groups.

COOK PLANTS

Yes people, it's time to cook plants! These recipes make up a 'Greatest Hits' of our community cooking over the last twelve plus years created by over 60 different chefs and with the input (or brutal feedback!) of thousands of community members.

These dishes are a celebration of international plant-based cooking and are each small culinary adventures into different cuisines and plant-based cooking skills. Exploring cultural cuisines as a vegan or veggie can be challenging, the push and pull of authenticity versus cruelty-free, health-conscious eating a tough seesaw to balance. But that's why we've spent over a decade working with chefs to bring you authentic flavour profiles with 100% plant-based recipes that are good for you, the planet and all that dwell on it.

As a cookery school we're all about building skills and confidence so you can conjure up delicious meals from scratch using whatever you have in your cupboard.

Start by cooking from the recipes, and then with time, you'll instinctively know what goes with what and be able to wing it.

Coming up in these sections we've got The Main Event, where you'll find delicious main meals, Side Show, featuring snacks and side dishes, A Sweet Finale, showcasing nourishing sweet treats, Drink To That for hot and cold refreshments and finally It's Alive, where we bring you fermented foods, a skill we highly recommend you build into your plant-based culinary repertoire.

You will no doubt encounter ingredients you've never worked with before and that's OK. Where appropriate we offer tips, substitutions and DIY versions but sometimes only the real thing will do. It's worth the investment, if you can. As you cook more plant-based you'll build up your store-room staples, but if pay day is a long way away and a recipe requires a few specialist ingredients, make a note of it, choose another recipe for now, and come back to that when you can.

You'll also learn how to craft meaty textures, fishy flavours, eggy tastes and creamy textures from nothing but wholefood plant-based ingredients. These dishes provide familiarity, comfort and enjoyment. We're also going to start you off on your foraging slash wild food journey. Exciting!

And when things go wrong in the kitchen (as they will) don't be disheartened. Every chef has blips, in fact this is where your culinary understanding deepens so embrace these moments, learn from them, then move on. Don't take things too seriously, have fun and remember, the most important ingredient in all your food – is joy. Happy cooking.

THE MAIN EVENT

Ok friends, let's get ready to rumble. This section is packed with juicy recipes that will elevate your plant-based cooking skills while giving you a global tour of different cultural cuisines. Many meals in this section consist of multiple elements, carefully selected to create an incredible meal, teach a range of skills and not take longer than two hours to make an entire dinner party with multiple elements.

Of course there are many days and nights we need to cook in under 30 minutes (or less) – so pick out the main dish from these meals and come back to the whole thing another time. We've got everything from comfort classics like British phish and chips to Ethiopian feasts, Trinidadian Carnival street food, Japanese bento and Mexican cheesy chorizo. So crank up the tunes, put your pinny on and let's cook some delicious plant-based food.

   use gluten-free oats and tamari instead of soy sauce.

SERVES: 4 PATTIES | TIME: 30–40 MINUTES

SARAH AND SARETA'S BANGING BURGER PATTIES

"This is a delicious, nutrition-packed burger that looks surprisingly meaty. The foundation for this recipe comes from the burger chef Sareta Puri developed for MIH's collaboration with Fuller's pubs. I adapted it to use ingredients I usually have in and to boost the nutritional profile. My PDA autistic son, who can only give brutally honest food reviews, gives this burger patty top ratings. He's a big fan of faux meat so creating a wholefoods burger patty he enjoys was a big win. It creates a fair bit of washing up – but it's worth it if you make a quadruple batch to load up your freezer. Adding chutney or relish is optional. I've used my mum's homemade damson chutney and shop-bought tomato relish – both worked well."

EQUIPMENT

Saucepan, timer, sharp knife, sieve/fine-mesh strainer, grater, food processor or blender (but easier in a food processor), small bowl, large frying pan, wooden spoon, large mixing bowl

1. Let's start by cooking the quinoa in a medium saucepan of boiling water on a medium heat (see Cooking Staples on p 57). Set a timer so you don't forget about it. Drain.

2. While the quinoa is cooking, prep the rest of the ingredients.
- Slice the onion and mushrooms.
- Grate the beetroot/beets on the larger setting of a hand grater.
- Blend/process the oats into a flour.
- Blend the sunflower seeds down to a crumb (not a flour).
- Rinse the kidney beans.
- Measure out all the flavourings/seasonings (not the salt, you'll add that later) and pop in a bowl – they'll go in the patty mix at the same time.
- If eating now, slice your gherkins and tomatoes for the toppings.

3. Heat 2 teaspoons of the vegetable oil in a large frying pan on a medium heat for 1 minute. Add the onion and fry until it goes pink but not crispy.

4. Add the mushrooms and cook until they're soft – this should take about 6 minutes. Transfer the onion and mushrooms to a blender. If there is any liquid, drain it off first.

5. Add half the cooked quinoa, all the beetroot, the kidney beans and salt. Pulse until the mushrooms and beans are broken down to a chunky texture, not a smooth paste. Then add the sunflower seeds and pulse once to combine. >>

BURSTING
WITH
ITALIAN ORGANIC
TOMATOES!
Mr Organic
ITALIAN ORGANIC
TOMATO
KETCHUP

INGREDIENTS (next page)

INGREDIENTS

50g/1¾oz/scant ⅓ cup uncooked quinoa

1 red onion

100g/3½oz closed cup chestnut mushrooms

35g/1¼oz raw or cooked beetroot/beets

100g/3½oz/generous 1 cup gluten-free rolled oats

50g/1¾oz/⅓ cup sunflower seeds

200g/7oz (drained weight) cooked/canned kidney beans

1 tablespoon B12-enriched nutritional yeast (optional)

1½ teaspoons yeast extract

2 teaspoons tamari or dark soy sauce or brown rice miso paste

1 tablespoon your favourite chutney or relish (optional)

½ teaspoon smoked paprika

¼ teaspoon black pepper

¼ teaspoon garlic powder

½ teaspoon chopped fresh thyme leaves

4 teaspoons vegetable oil

½ teaspoon sea salt

To Serve

4 gherkins

2 tomatoes

4 vegan burger buns, halved and toasted, or have as naked burgers in a lettuce leaf

4 lettuce leaves or other salad leaves/greens of your choice (rocket is nice)

6. Transfer the mix into a large bowl and stir in the rest of the quinoa, the ground oats (add a bit, stir, add a bit, stir, until all is used) and the flavouring/seasoning mixture. Stir well to combine.

7. Heat the remaining oil in the same frying pan on a medium heat for 1 minute, then weigh out 150g/5½oz of mix per patty (you'll make 4 patties). You can eye-ball this if you don't mind different patty sizes.

8. Roll the mixture lightly in your hands to make a ball. Add to the frying pan and gently press down into a patty. Depending on your pan size, you can fry 2–4 at the same time.

9. On a medium heat, fry the patties for about 6 minutes on each side until browned and the surface is hard.

10. Serve each patty in a toasted vegan burger bun with slices of gherkin and tomato, lettuce leaves or salad leaves/greens of choice, or serve naked in a lettuce leaf.
We have great recipes for fermented ketchup on p 341, coleslaw on p 254 and potato wedges on p 111 to accompany your burger.

TIP *Take rings off your fingers before handling the burger patty mixture – this stuff is sticky!*

The MIH team at Fullers pubs who we developed a fundraising plant-based burger menu item for.

use gluten-free macaroni and swap the yeast extract for a gluten-free soy sauce or tamari.

SERVES: 4 GENEROUSLY | TIME: 1¼ HOURS LEISURELY COOKING, PLUS (OPTIONAL) 8 HOURS SOAKING

SARAH'S BUTTERNUT SQUASH MAC 'N' CHEESE

"This is a wholefoods plant-based do-over of a classic comfort dish. Mac 'n' cheese was created by African-American chef James Hemings while he was experiencing enslavement in the Thomas Jefferson household. For an alternative super-creamy nut-based mac 'n' cheese, use Angela's Nacho-Average Dip recipe on p 248 as the sauce. "

EQUIPMENT

Baking sheet, frying pan, blender, large bowl, saucepan, colander, sharp knife

INGREDIENTS

130g/4¾oz raw cashews (optional)
1 medium butternut squash (about 1kg/2lb 4oz)
1 clove garlic
1 teaspoon olive oil
Pinch of sea salt
500g/1lb 2oz dried macaroni
1 x 400g/14oz can butter/lima beans
700ml/24fl oz/3 cups oat milk
15g/½oz B12-enriched nutritional yeast
1 teaspoon mustard seeds
1 teaspoon yeast extract
1 teaspoon apple cider vinegar
½ teaspoon ground turmeric
Pinch of black pepper

(continues next page)

1. If using the cashews, soak them in cold water ideally 8 hours before making the dish. Anything over 3 hours is fine. If you forget to do this, you can always soak them in boiling water for 15 minutes just before you want to use them. But the cold soaking method is better. See Thrive on Plants on p 28 for more on this practice.

2. Preheat the oven to 200°C/400°F/gas 6.

3. Place the whole butternut squash in the oven and roast for 1 hour or until the skin has browned and you can poke a skewer easily into it. Alternatively, use 1 x 700g/1lb 9oz bag of pre-prepared frozen butternut squash cubes. Set a timer for 30 minutes. When it goes off, add the clove of garlic, coated in the olive oil, to the oven to roast.

4. While the squash is roasting, make your topping. To make the omega crunch, add the almonds and sunflower seeds to a dry frying pan on a medium heat and lightly toast for 3 minutes.

5. Add all the omega crunch ingredients to a blender and blitz until you get small chunks of almonds. Decant into a bowl and set aside.

6. Boil a pan of water and once bubbling, add the pinch of salt and the macaroni. Cook according to the package directions (see also Cooking Staples on p 55).

7. While the pasta is cooking, drain both the butter/lima beans and cashews of water and rinse. Add them and all the remaining ingredients to a blender – but don't blend just yet.

8. Once cooked, drain the pasta using a colander, return to the pan and pop the lid on to keep it warm.

9. When ready, take the squash and garlic out of the oven. Wear oven gloves to hold the squash and, using a sharp knife, cut it in half down its length. >>

For the Omega Crunch

75g/2¾oz/generous ½ cup whole (skin-on) almonds*

75g/2¾oz/½ cup sunflower seeds

40g/1½oz flaxseeds

3 tablespoons B12-enriched nutritional yeast

Handful of fresh basil or 1½ teaspoons dried basil (optional)

1 teaspoon olive oil

*To make this dish lower cost you can skip the almonds and use 150g/5½oz/1 cup of sunflower seeds instead. You can also skip the flaxseeds but these have a great nutritional profile so keep them in if you can.

10. Use a spoon to scoop out the middle seedy bit and set aside. You can make a roasted seed snack with these, if you like. Next, scoop the orange flesh out and add to your blender along with the roasted garlic.

11. Blend into a smooth cheesy-looking sauce. If you need to loosen it, add water ½ tablespoon at a time. You don't want it to be too runny.

12. Add your pasta to a large baking dish, then pour the sauce over the pasta and gently mix to combine. Sprinkle with the omega crunch topping.

13. Turn the oven down to 160°C/325°F/gas 3. Bake the pasta dish for 20–30 minutes, or until it has slightly hardened on the top and become darker in colour.

14. Serve with steamed greens such as cavolo nero or kale or a salad for a delicious, nutrition-dense, comforting meal.

Dairy Cheese & Health p 370

LET'S TALK ABOUT… DAIRY IS SCARY *by Sarah Bentley*

We need to talk about dairy farming. Contrary to what some people subconsciously believe, cows don't produce superfluous milk for human consumption. Like any other mammal (including humans), female cows produce milk to feed their babies. In order to ensure a continuous supply of milk, heifers living on dairy farms are kept in an endless cycle of pregnancy and lactation. A mother cow would usually raise and feed its calf for 7–14 months. In the UK, on industrialized dairy farms calves are removed within days. The boy calves are either shot in the head and killed straight away, or exported to Europe potentially to be eaten as veal, or reared in the UK to be killed for their beef aged 22–23 months. Girl babies are separated, fed by bottle and reared to be milking cows. As most mothers would, the heifer fights to keep her calf and cries for days after the separation. If you've ever heard this noise, it's utterly heartbreaking.

A heifer's natural life cycle is about 20 years, but such is the strain on her body (and no doubt psyche) a milking cow's average life on an industrial dairy farm is four to five years. Many suffer from horrendous mastitis, which any person who's breastfed and had will attest is a grim, painful condition.

True, not all dairy farms are the same. A few smaller, more conscious farms may let the calves stay with their mums longer, may not push the heifers to the same extremes as industrial farms, but it all amounts to the same thing in the end. Milk bought from a supermarket or grocery store is from an industrialized farming system. No matter how idyllic a scene the marketing depicts, remember what the cows have endured to produce that milk. People get misty eyed about the heritage of dairy farming in the UK, Europe and the US, but this is misplaced empathy, as what farmers really need is financial and technical support to adapt to climate-friendly, plant-centred farming. My grandfather was a dairy farmer in Dublin, Ireland in the 1900s. He lost the farm when the British colonizers did a compulsory purchase for 10% of its real value. The 10% Granddad received he spent trying – and failing – to fight the British government in court. This is a way of saying: times change (but alas not the behaviour of colonizing nations). But personally we can honour our past without living in it. I'd like to think that had Granddad kept his farm he would have been an early adopter of plant-based milk production, but I'll never know.

SERVES: 4 | TIME: 1 HOUR 20 MINUTES

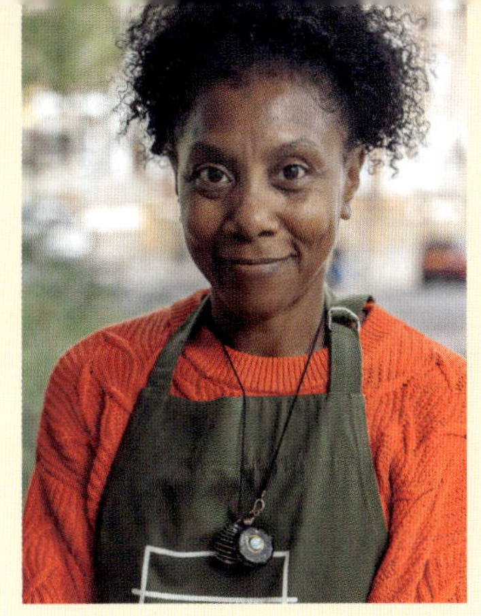

SHARON'S CARIBBEAN FUSION BRUNCH

"This is one of my go-to comfort dishes, as it transports me back to the Caribbean with its warm, nourishing flavours. I'm a big advocate for having enough fibre in the diet and kidney beans are a favourite of mine; it's one of the many reasons I love to teach this dish. There are loads of recipes out there for chickpea flour pancakes but the one I've shared is a great one to start with. You can add a variety of herbs to the mixture, even finely chopped veg, if you like. The mushrooms work as an open sandwich topper, jacket potato filling, served alongside some quinoa, or for this brunch on top of a chickpea/gram flour pancake. I recommend you batch-make the BBQ sauce so you can make it again but quicker. And try to find avocados, or pears as we call these large Caribbean-grown avocados, at an Afro-Caribbean market stall or shop."

TO MAKE THE WHOLE MEAL

1. Make up the chickpea pancake batter and store in the refrigerator.
2. Make the mushrooms.
3. While the mushrooms are in the oven, make the salsa, pear (avocado) salad and slice the plantain.
4. Fry the plantain in a pan or add to the oven.
5. Make the pancakes. Assemble everything.

SERVES: 4 (MAKES 4 LARGE OR 8 SMALLER PANCAKES) | TIME: 30 MINUTES

SAVOURY PANCAKES

EQUIPMENT

Sharp knife, large mixing bowl, frying pan, wooden spoon, flipper

INGREDIENTS (next page)

1. Finely chop the fresh herbs if using, then add all the ingredients – except the water and oil – into a large mixing bowl, adding black pepper to taste.

2. Add half the water and mix well – it should be quite thick. Slowly add more water, a little at a time, ensuring you mix as you do, so that it forms a not too thick or too thin batter. Batter is fickle, so you may not need to use all the water, or you may need to add a little more.

3. Leave to one side until ready to use – this can be made in advance (it will keep for 2 hours at room temperature or overnight in the refrigerator). When you are ready to make the pancakes, use a fork and beat the mixture again. >>

INGREDIENTS

- Small handful of fresh parsley or coriander/cilantro (optional)
- 200g/7oz/1½ cups chickpea/gram flour
- 1 teaspoon dried oregano
- ½ teaspoon ground turmeric
- ½ teaspoon sea salt
- ½ teaspoon baking powder or 2 tablespoons aquafaba
- Black pepper
- 400ml/14fl oz/1⅔ cups water (you may need more or less)
- Rapeseed/canola oil, for frying

4. Heat a frying pan on a medium-high heat, add a teaspoon of oil to coat the bottom, then when ready, pour around 60ml/2fl oz/¼ cup of the batter into the hot pan (depending on size of pan and how many pancakes you want to make), swirling it around to cover the pan surface.

5. Cook for 1–2 minutes until the edges begin to brown and curl up. Use a flipper to turn the pancake over, then cook for another minute until it is golden brown on the other side.

6. Remove to a plate and repeat to make the remaining pancakes, adding a teaspoon of oil to the pan to cook each pancake. You'll either make 4 large or 8 smaller pancakes. Keep the cooked pancakes warm in the oven, separated with baking parchment.

7. Top the pancakes with the BBQ mushrooms, avocado salad and tomato salsa and serve the plantain on the side. Enjoy.

use gluten free soy.

SERVES: 4 | TIME: 10 MINUTES

SPICY TOMATO SALSA

EQUIPMENT

Sharp knife, small frying pan, serving bowl

INGREDIENTS

- 1 medium-large onion
- 2–4 tomatoes
- 1–2 cloves garlic
- ½ red pepper
- 1–2 fresh red or green chillies, or ¼ teaspoon cayenne pepper or dried chilli/hot pepper flakes
- 15g/½oz fresh herbs of choice (such as parsley or coriander/cilantro), or 1 teaspoon dried herbs (optional)
- 2–4 tablespoons olive oil
- 1 teaspoon tamari or dark soy sauce
- 1 teaspoon sweetener (such as maple, date or rice syrup)
- ½ teaspoon black pepper
- ½ teaspoon sea salt

1. Let's prepare the ingredients.
- Slice or dice the onion.
- Chop the tomatoes into small cubes.
- Finely slice the garlic.
- Deseed and chop the red pepper into 1cm/½in cubes.
- Deseed and finely chop the fresh chillies (if using).
- Finely chop the fresh herbs (if using).

2. Add 1 teaspoon of the olive oil to a small frying pan on a medium heat. Add the onion and garlic and sauté for 3 minutes.

3. Add the tomatoes, red pepper and chillies, cayenne or dried chilli/hot pepper flakes and cook for another 2 minutes until soft.

4. Now add the tamari/soy sauce, sweetener, black pepper and salt and stir well.

5. Taste and adjust the seasonings, if needed. Mix in the herbs (if using) and the remaining olive oil, then serve.

SERVES: 4 | TIME: 45-60 MINUTES

BBQ OYSTER MUSHROOMS

EQUIPMENT

Sharp knife, deep pan, wooden spoon, large frying pan, ovenproof dish, tongs or a fork, hand-held/immersion blender or regular blender

INGREDIENTS

16 large oyster mushrooms, wiped clean

Olive or rapeseed/canola oil, for frying

For the BBQ Sauce (you can make this in advance to store in an airtight container/jar in the refrigerator up to 3 months)

1 small onion

½ thumb-size piece root ginger

2 cloves garlic

¼ red Scotch bonnet chilli or ¼ teaspoon cayenne pepper (optional)

2–3 sprigs of fresh thyme or ½ teaspoon dried thyme

1 bay leaf

5–7 allspice/pimento berries, slightly crushed or ½ teaspoon ground allspice

½ teaspoon freshly grated nutmeg or ¼ teaspoon ground nutmeg

1 cinnamon stick or ¼ teaspoon ground cinnamon

4 teaspoons smoked paprika

1 teaspoon cayenne pepper

1 teaspoon dried oregano

400g/14oz passata

2 tablespoons apple cider vinegar

60ml/2fl oz/¼ cup fresh pineapple juice (optional)

4 tablespoons date syrup

2 tablespoons black treacle/molasses (optional)

2 tablespoons tamari

1. Let's prepare the veg.
- Cut each mushroom into three.
- Dice the onion.
- Finely slice the ginger and garlic.
- Remove the seeds and finely slice the Scotch bonnet (if using).

2. For the BBQ sauce, heat a teaspoon of oil in a deep pan, then add the onion, ginger, garlic, Scotch bonnet, thyme, bay leaf, allspice/pimento, nutmeg and cinnamon and cook for a few minutes until the onion has softened.

3. Add all the remaining BBQ sauce ingredients into the pan, stir well and place on a medium heat. Bring gently to the boil, then reduce the heat and simmer for about 20–30 minutes until it has thickened and reduced in volume.

4. Preheat the oven to 180°C/350°F/gas 4.

5. Put a large frying pan on a medium heat and add 1 teaspoon of oil. When hot (after a minute), add the mushrooms (do not overcrowd as you want them to brown without losing lots of liquid) and fry until golden brown on both sides. This should take about 5 minutes.

6. Tip the mushrooms into a baking dish. Next use 2 forks, one to hold each mushroom in place, the other to pull the mushroom apart to shred it. You will get better at this with practice.

7. Once the BBQ sauce is ready, let it cool for 2 minutes, then use tongs or a fork to remove the thyme twigs, bay leaf and cinnamon stick. Blend the sauce until smooth using a hand-held/immersion blender or in a regular blender.

8. Cover the mushrooms with the BBQ sauce, then bake for around 10–15 minutes until golden brown in colour.

SERVES: 4 | TIME: 15 MINUTES

BAKED PLANTAIN

TIPS & TRICKS
Plantain For Newbies p 378

EQUIPMENT

Sharp knife, baking sheet, pastry/silicone brush, spatula/fish slice

INGREDIENTS

1 firm plantain
Neutral oil suitable for baking (such as vegetable oil) or coconut oil

1. Preheat the oven to 180°C/350°F/gas 4.

2. Peel the plantain by cutting off both ends, then gently run the knife down the side to remove the rest of the skin but be careful not to cut too deep as you don't want to cut into the flesh.

3. Slice the plantain on the diagonal, medium thickness (under 1cm/½in), so that they're more oval shaped than round.

4. Lightly grease a baking sheet with oil so that the plantain slices do not stick.

5. Brush both sides of the plantain lightly with oil, then place on the baking sheet and pop in the oven.

6. Bake for 10 minutes until golden brown, then flip over and continue to cook for another 5–10 minutes until golden brown on both sides. Remove from the oven and serve as a side.

SERVES: 4 | TIME: 5 MINUTES

SIMPLE PEAR (AVOCADO) SALAD

EQUIPMENT

Sharp knife, serving bowl

INGREDIENTS

2 medium or 4 small ripe avocados
Small handful of fresh coriander/cilantro or parsley
2 limes
Black pepper

1. Peel, pit and chop the avocados into small cubes and chop the fresh herbs.

2. Next squeeze the juice from the limes over the avocado.

3. Add the chopped herbs and a pinch of black pepper to taste and stir gently to mix.

4. Taste and adjust the seasoning if needed, then serve.

SERVES: 4 | TIME TO MAKE EVERYTHING: 1½ HOURS

SHARON'S VERSION OF TRINI CURRY, BODHI AND BUSS UP SHOTS

"I'm Jamaican heritage with Trini family via my niece – so these recipes are not 100% traditional but adapted for my plant-based lifestyle. Trinidad and Tobago, like other Caribbean islands, are a melting pot of cultures; from the indigenous Arawak South American settlers, to enslaved Africans, indentured Indians, Chinese and a variety of other European peoples. This diversity is reflected throughout the dishes the island has to offer. I love Channa Aloo – it's the ultimate representation of the gorgeous Indian-Afro-Caribbean fusion that is Trinidadian cuisine. It's full of spices and protein. It freezes well so it's good for batch cooking. You can serve the dishes in two separate bowls or together on a plate and rip the roti with your fingers and dip it into the dishes. I recommend eating with your hands.

MAKES: 4 SMALL BUSS UP SHOTS TIME: 40 MINUTES

BUSS UP SHOTS

EQUIPMENT

Large bowl, fine sieve/fine-mesh strainer, long wooden spoon, clean dish towel, frying pan, rolling pin, 2 wooden spatulas

INGREDIENTS

- 250g/scant 2 cups plain/all-purpose flour, plus extra for dusting
- 1½ teaspoons baking powder
- ½ teaspoon sea salt
- 175ml/6fl oz/¾ cup room temperature water (you may need a little more or less)
- 2 tablespoons soft coconut oil or neutral oil (or you could use vegan ghee or butter)
- 2–3 tablespoons neutral oil, such as olive oil or rapeseed/canola oil (use this in step 11 to go on top of roti when cooking)

TIP ***Prep all your veg and ingredients for the curry and the bodhi so you can make these quickly while the dough is resting.***

1. Using a fine sieve/fine-mesh strainer, sift the flour, baking powder and salt into a large bowl.

2. Gradually add the water and use clean hands to combine the dry and wet ingredients to make a soft dough. Do not knead the dough like you're making bread – just bring it together into a soft ball.

3. Cover with a clean dish towel and let it rest for 15 minutes. If the dough is very soft it may only need 5–10 minutes of resting time. While the dough is resting you can start making your curry and bodhi – don't worry if the dough rests a bit longer than 15 minutes. But if it rests longer than 30 minutes it might become too sticky to work with. They'll be another resting period, so you can keep making the other dishes then too.

4. Divide the dough into four equal pieces. Press each piece of dough into a large flat circle using your fingers or with a rolling pin on a floured flat surface. Go around the edge of the circle with your fingers to press it into shape. >>

5. Using your fingers (or the bottom of a spoon), rub the surface of the dough with the coconut or neutral oil. The larger the circle the flakier the roti will be.

6. Sprinkle the roti with a little flour, then cut a line down the dough from the middle of the top edge (12 o'clock) to the middle of the dough.

7. Now roll the dough clockwise into a cone. Push the tip of the cone downwards back into the dough. Let it rest for 20 minutes under a dish towel. Repeat to make the rest.

8. When ready to cook the roti, heat your frying pan on a medium heat until hot. Working with one ball of dough at a time (keep the remaining dough covered to stop it drying out), using just enough flour to prevent the dough sticking on the work surface, flatten the dough into a small flat circle about 10cm/4in wide, adding a dust of flour to prevent the rolling pin from sticking.

9. Now use a rolling pin to roll the dough out into a circle. Rotate and roll the dough until it becomes a thin, even round (as large as your pan), making sure that the edges are not too thick. If you can't make it round, don't worry, it tastes just as good whatever shape.

10. Lightly flour your hands, pick up the dough, placing it on the palm of your hand and then lay it on the pan by quickly flipping your hand over the pan – splat – it's a quick movement.

11. Drizzle or brush about ¼ teaspoon of the oil over the surface of the roti. Flip. Drizzle or brush another ¼ teaspoon of oil over the other side. Flip again. Cook until the roti has puffed up and has golden brown spots on both sides, this should take about 15–30 seconds per side.

12. When the roti is fully cooked, use a pair of wooden spatulas to beat the roti gently in the pan – to buss it up – pushing the edges toward the middle until the layers separate. Alternatively, place the roti into a clean, dry dish towel and crunch it together (like you're playing an accordion) until it looks 'bussed up'! It sounds like loads of work but it happens very quickly.

13. Store the buss up shot wrapped tightly in a clean, dry dish towel. Repeat rolling out and cooking the remaining dough, stacking and wrapping the finished roti in the dish towel. Once they are all cooked, let them rest in the dish towel until ready to serve. The more you make these, the quicker you get at it.

SERVES: 4 | TIME: 20 MINUTES

BODHI (GREEN BEANS)

EQUIPMENT

Sharp knife, pestle and mortar, large, heavy saucepan, wooden spoon

INGREDIENTS

350g/12oz long green beans

3 ripe tomatoes or 2 tablespoons tomato purée/paste

1 teaspoon cumin/ jeera seeds

30g/1oz fresh coriander/ cilantro

1 tablespoon olive oil or other neutral oil

2 teaspoons ground coriander

Pinch of cayenne pepper/ chilli powder

1 teaspoon amchoor (mango powder) or juice of ½ lime

¼ teaspoon ground turmeric

5 tablespoons water (may need a little more)

Pinch of sea salt

¼ teaspoon black pepper

1. Let's get the vegetables ready.

- Trim the ends off the green beans and cut into 5cm/2in pieces.
- Dice the tomatoes (if using).
- Crush the cumin seeds with a pestle and mortar.
- Roughly chop the fresh coriander/cilantro.

2. Add the oil to a heavy pan on a medium heat. Once the oil is hot, add the crushed cumin seeds and leave to splutter and brown for 30 seconds.

3. Now add the tomatoes (if using) and cook for 3–5 minutes until soft and broken down.

4. Next, add the green beans, ground coriander, cayenne pepper/ chilli powder, amchoor (if using) and turmeric and mix well to combine. If you didn't use fresh tomatoes, add the tomato purée/ paste now and mix again.

5. Now add the water, mix well, then cook on a medium heat with the lid on for about 10 minutes until the beans are tender.

6. If you didn't use the amchoor, add the lime juice, mix, then season with the salt and black pepper. Add the fresh coriander/ cilantro and mix in just before serving.

SERVES: 4 | TIME: 30 MINUTES

CHANNA ALOO CURRY

EQUIPMENT

Colander, sharp knife, small bowl, heavy pot/ saucepan, wooden spoon

INGREDIENTS

120g/4¼oz/¾ cup dried chickpeas/garbanzo beans or 1 x 400g/14oz can chickpeas/ garbanzo beans

1–2 onions

2 cloves garlic

⅕ red Scotch bonnet chilli (see Scotch Bonnet for Newbies on p 379) (optional)

3 medium potatoes

1 tablespoon fresh coriander/cilantro, or 1 teaspoon dried fenugreek leaves

1 tablespoon curry powder (preferably a Caribbean one)

5 tablespoons water, plus an (optional) 1 teaspoon

1 tablespoon rapeseed/ canola or extra virgin olive oil

1 teaspoon black pepper

½ teaspoon sea salt

200ml/7fl oz/scant 1 cup water (you may need a little more), or use the reserved cooking water if you cooked the chickpeas from scratch (see method)

1 teaspoon ground cumin/jeera

1. If cooking chickpeas/garbanzo beans from dry, remove any stones and wash with several changes of water. Then cover the chickpeas/ garbanzo beans with cold water in a bowl and leave to soak overnight.

2. Next morning, drain the chickpeas, place in a saucepan and cover with fresh water. Bring to the boil on a high heat. After it comes to a vigorous boil, reduce the heat to medium. Continue cooking for 40–50 minutes, adding more water if needed. Strain and reserve any liquid.

3. Now let's prepare the ingredients.
- Drain and rinse the chickpeas if using canned and catch the aquafaba to use in another recipe.
- Dice the onion(s).
- Finely slice the garlic.
- Finely slice the Scotch bonnet and remove the seeds.
- Cut the potatoes into large bite-size pieces.
- Chop the coriander/cilantro (if using).

4. Put the curry powder into a small bowl and mix with 2 tablespoons of the water to make a paste.

5. Pour the oil into a large, heavy pot/saucepan and heat on a medium heat for a minute. Add the curry powder paste into the oil and cook for 2–3 minutes. Add in an extra teaspoon of water if the curry is already looking very thick.

6. As it cooks down, add the onion(s), garlic, Scotch bonnet (if using) and coriander or fenugreek, stir, then add the remaining 3 tablespoons of water and cook for 2–3 minutes. Add more water if the sauce is getting too thick. Now add the potatoes and stir to coat with the curry and onion mixture, followed by the chickpeas, black pepper, salt and the 200ml/7fl oz/scant 1 cup of water. You can use any reserved cooking water you kept in step 2.

7. Stir and bring to the boil, then reduce the heat to medium. Cover with a lid and simmer for 20–25 minutes until the potatoes are tender.

8. If the potatoes are cooked and the sauce is still thin, use your spoon to mash some of the potatoes and chickpeas in the pot. Stir in the cumin and turn the heat off. Serve with your bodhi and roti.

SERVES: 4 GENEROUSLY | TIME TO MAKE EVERYTHING: 2 HOURS

MICHAEL'S TRINIDADIAN CARNIVAL FOOD – CORN SOUP, PHOLOURI, TRINI CHOW AND TRIO OF SAUCES

"I grew up in Trinidad and never missed carnival, which we celebrate over two days from early morning with Canboula, *which means burnt sugar cane and is a symbol of rebellion where people dress up and satirize colonial characters from slavery times. There are lots of elements to this meal, so invite a friend over and cook together.*

Pholourie is a delicious deep-fried, street food snack that is a must to eat over carnival time. The Corn Soup is a classic Trini dish and tastes amazing the day after you cooked it as the flavours have had time to infuse. All Trini chefs have their own recipe for green seasoning or what we call locally Chadon Beni sauce. Chadon Beni is a green herb that grows in Trinidad, also called culantro, but it's not to be confused with cilantro (fresh coriander) as that's a different plant. If you're lucky you can buy it from specialist Caribbean retailers, but for this recipe I've replaced it with fresh coriander/cilantro, which is what I've used since I moved to the UK.

Trini Chow is a spicy, fruity salad and is a staple of Trini cuisine. I like mine spicy so I use a whole Scotch bonnet, but you may want to start with a small amount. The Mango Sauce I've shared is a sweet, spicy sauce – it's a classic example of the Indian-African culinary fusion of Trinidadian cuisine. You can use it with doubles, Buss Up Shots (p 97) or to dip the Pholourie into. Finally, Tamarind Sauce has a complex flavour profile that's both sweet and sour. You can buy tamarind in blocks with its big seeds still in it – this is the real deal – but tamarind paste is fine and is more readily available."

STEPS FOR MAKING THE WHOLE MEAL

1. Soak your yellow split peas overnight in cold water or boil them for 1 hour.

2. Make your Pholouri batter and leave to rest for 1–2 hours so it doubles in size.

3. While the batter is rising, make your Corn Soup.

4. While the Corn Soup is simmering, make your batch of Chadon Beni (Green Seasoning) and then your Mango Sauce.

5. While your Mango Sauce is cooking, make your Chow and Tamarind Sauce.

6. Serve together with soca music blasting for the ultimate Trinidad and Tobago carnival street food feast. >>

SERVES: 4 | TIME: 25 MINUTES, PLUS 1–2 HOURS RESTING

PHOLOURIE

EQUIPMENT

Sharp knife, large bowl, wooden spoon, high-sided saucepan, 2 metal tablespoons, metal slotted spoon, plate lined with paper towels

INGREDIENTS

- ¼–1 red Scotch bonnet chilli (see Scotch Bonnet for Newbies on p 379)
- 1 teaspoon fresh coriander/cilantro or ground coriander
- 240g/8½oz/1¾ cups plain/all-purpose flour
- 60g/2¼oz/scant ½ cup chickpea/gram flour
- 1½ teaspoons baking powder
- 2 teaspoons sea salt
- 2 teaspoons ground turmeric
- 2 teaspoons fast-action/instant active dried yeast
- ¼ teaspoon ground cumin/jeera
- 350–450ml/12–16fl oz/1½–1¾ cups warm water
- About 700ml/24fl oz/3 cups vegetable oil, for deep-frying

1. Finely slice the Scotch bonnet and finely chop the fresh coriander/cilantro (if using).

2. Combine all the dry ingredients – that's everything except the water and oil – in a large bowl and mix gently. Add the Scotch bonnet and fresh or ground coriander. When handling the Scotch bonnet, be sure to wear food hygiene gloves or wash your hands thoroughly afterwards.

3. To make sure the batter is not too runny, add the warm water a little at time and mix the ingredients together until you get a batter consistency similar to a very thick pancake mix. Use a wooden spoon to begin with, then revert to using your hands.

4. Leave the mixture to rest in a warm place, covered with a clean dish towel, for 1–2 hours. It will rise and double in size. If making the other elements of this meal, do this while the batter is rising.

5. Now your batter has rested, add your vegetable oil to a high-sided saucepan and bring to a high temperature. This should take a minute or two. To check your oil is ready, drop a speck of dough into the oil. If it immediately turns golden and rises, your oil is hot enough. Take this dough out using your metal slotted spoon.

6. Use two spoons, one to scoop up the batter, the other to neaten, gently transfer a portion of batter into the saucepan so as not to splash the oil. This method gets you a nice even shape. The traditional method involves scooping up a portion of mix with your hands and using your fists like a piping bag to squeeze it out of the bottom of your fist. This requires practise and is messy. Have a go!

7. Add 3–4 to the hot oil and turn them over if needed to ensure they cook evenly. Each pholourie should take 4–5 minutes to cook – you're aiming for a golden brown colour.

8. Remove with a metal slotted spoon (for the oil to drain) onto a plate lined with paper towels to absorb the excess oil.

9. Pholourie is best eaten fresh within minutes of deep-frying, so gather around and tuck in. Once cooked, they can be left to cool, then warmed up (in the oven or air fryer) and eaten later – but they're not as good.

     use gluten-free vegetable stock cubes.

SERVES: 4 | TIME: 1–12 HOURS SOAKING; 1 HOUR 15 MINUTES ACTIVE COOKING

CORN SOUP

EQUIPMENT

Strong sharp knife, large saucepan

INGREDIENTS

1 large carrot
2 potatoes (optional)
2 corn on the cobs
1 large onion
4 cloves garlic
25g/1oz celery (optional)
2.5cm/1in piece root ginger
Bunch of fresh coriander/cilantro
¼–1 red Scotch bonnet chilli (see Scotch Bonnet for Newbies on p 379)
315g/11oz/1¾ cups dried yellow split peas
1 tablespoon olive oil
475ml/17fl oz/2 cups water
3 low-sodium vegetable stock cubes
¼ teaspoon sea salt
½ teaspoon black pepper
800ml/28fl oz/scant 3½ cups coconut milk

1. Let's get the ingredients ready.
- Thinly slice your carrot into discs.
- Cube your potatoes (if using).
- Remove the outer leaves and the silks from your corn cobs, then chop into 2.5–5cm/1–2in pieces.
- Dice your onion and celery.
- Finely slice your garlic. Finely slice your ginger.
- Roughly cut your coriander/cilantro into ribbons.
- Finely slice your Scotch bonnet. Remove the seeds for low heat levels, keep in if you like it hot.
- Rinse your split peas in cold water and drain.

2. In a frying pan on a medium heat, sauté all the chopped/sliced items in the olive oil. After 4–5 minutes, add the split peas and water, cover and cook for 20 minutes.

3. Now add the crumbled up stock cubes, the salt, black pepper and coconut milk. Stir well, then cover and leave to simmer on a medium heat for 30–40 minutes. I usually add a tablespoon of sugar, but as MIH is concerned about community health I omit this step in my classes for them.

While the soup is cooking, you can make your chow and sauces.

SERVES: 4 | TIME: 5 MINUTES

CHADON BENI SAUCE (GREEN SEASONING)

EQUIPMENT

Sharp knife, blender

INGREDIENTS

- 30g/1oz fresh coriander/cilantro
- 30g/1oz fresh parsley
- 235ml/9fl oz/1 cup water (you may need a little more)
- 2–3 cloves garlic
- Small thumb-size piece root ginger (optional)
- ¼–1 red Scotch bonnet chilli (see Scotch Bonnet for Newbies on p 379) (seeds removed for milder heat, kept for stronger)
- ½ lime, without the skin
- Pinch of sea salt

1. Roughly chop the fresh herbs.

2. Add all the ingredients to a blender and blend till smooth! You may need to drizzle in an extra teaspoon or two of water to help the blending.

3. Set aside as you're going to use this in the Trini Chow and Tamarind Sauce. This makes 1 quantity of green seasoning.

SERVES: 4 | TIME: 10 MINUTES

TRINI CHOW

EQUIPMENT

Sharp knife, large bowl with lid, wooden spoon

INGREDIENTS

- 1 pineapple or 2 cucumbers
- 2 unripe/firm mangoes
- ¼–1 red Scotch bonnet chilli (see Scotch Bonnet for Newbies on p 379)
- ½ quantity of Chadon Beni Sauce (Green Seasoning) (see above)
- Pinch of sea salt
- Pinch of black pepper

1. Remove the skin from the pineapple or cucumbers, depending on which you're using, and chop into chunks. (Use the pineapple skin to make Tepache, see p 356.)

2. Peel and pit the mangoes and chop into 5 x 1cm/2 x ½in lengths. This doesn't need to be precise.

3. Finely slice the Scotch bonnet. You're going to be eating this raw so only use what you can enjoy from a heat point of view.

4. Add all the ingredients to a bowl with a lid and shake vigorously. If you don't have a bowl with a lid just mix well. Taste and enjoy.

EQUIPMENT

Small frying pan, sharp strong knife/cleaver, saucepan with lid, stick blender, bowl

INGREDIENTS

- 2 teaspoons cumin/jeera seeds
- 1–2 cloves garlic
- 2 raw firm green mangoes
- ¼–1 red Scotch bonnet chilli (see Scotch Bonnet for Newbies on p 379)
- About 950ml/32fl oz/4 cups water (you may need a little more)
- 120g/4¼oz/⅔ cup soft dark brown sugar or sweetener of choice (such as maple, date or rice syrup)
- 2 teaspoons amchar masala, or use 1 teaspoon garam masala and 1 teaspoon ground cumin/jeera
- ¼ teaspoon ground turmeric
- ½ teaspoon sea salt
- 1 teaspoon ground culantro/bandhania/coriander (optional)

SERVES: 4 | TIME: 45–60 MINUTES

MANGO SAUCE

1. Toast the cumin seeds in a dry frying pan on a medium heat for 2 minutes. Meanwhile, finely slice your garlic. Set both aside.

2. Chop through each mango down the middle making sure to halve the pit/seed. Chop it again into a few more pieces, keeping the pit/seed as part of the pieces.

3. Finely slice your Scotch bonnet. I keep the seeds for a hotter sauce or discard them.

4. Add all the ingredients to a saucepan and cook on a high heat with the lid on for 45 minutes–1 hour, or until the mango is properly cooked down – it should feel soft when you prick it with a fork.

5. As the sauce is cooking, you can add more water if needed – the consistency you're aiming for is looser than ketchup but not runny like water. You can use a stick blender to blend and thicken to a loose sauce, leaving some chunks.

6. Serve hot, warm or cold with the mango pit/seed still in the sauce – just don't swallow the bits of pit/seed when eating.

EQUIPMENT

Sharp knife, blender

INGREDIENTS

- Small bunch of fresh coriander/cilantro (about 30g/1oz)
- 1 x 100g/3½oz tube of tamarind paste
- 3–5 cloves garlic (to taste preference)
- ½ quantity of Chadon Beni Sauce (Green Seasoning) (see p 105)
- 50g/1¾oz/¼ cup soft dark brown sugar, or for a lower sugar option use 2 tablespoons date or maple syrup
- 2 teaspoons sea salt

SERVES: 4 | TIME: 5 MINUTES

TAMARIND SAUCE

1. Roughly chop the coriander/cilantro.
2. Add all the ingredients to a blender and blend until smooth!
3. Serve with the Pholourie (p 102).

SERVES: 4 | TIME: 1 HOUR 20 MINUTES, PLUS 1-24 HOURS MARINATING TIME

OLLIE'S PHISH AND CHIP SUPPER

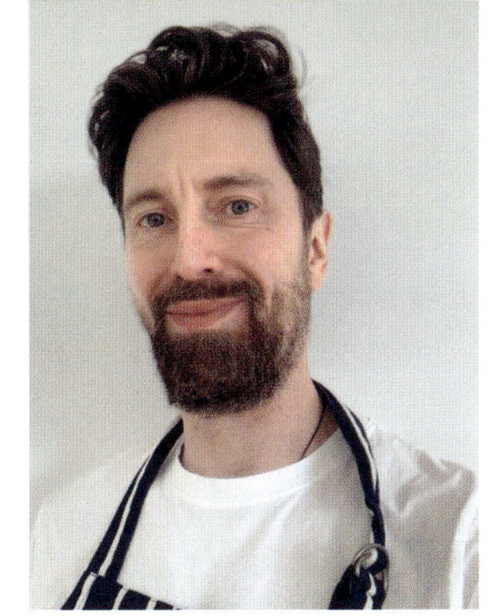

"Before I became vegan I grew up loving fish and chips, so there was a lot of nostalgia and pressure to create a good vegan version. Here is the result. When I eat the Phish, I dip every forkful into Tartar Sauce, so I've provided the recipe for it too. It's utterly delicious. The Pea Purée recipe is a lighter, fresher take on traditional mushy peas. In the UK, the mushy peas served in fish and chip shops are marrowfat peas. They have a high starch content and are larger than regular peas – and they have a very different taste and texture. Finally, homemade chips are healthier than chip-shop chips because they're cooked in less oil. They'll never taste quite as good as chip-shop chips – but they're still delicious."

TO MAKE THE WHOLE MEAL:

1. Marinate the banana blossom or tofu phish for at least an hour but ideally overnight.
2. Make the tartar sauce.
3. Make the homemade chips. While the chips are roasting in the oven, make your phish batter.
4. After turning the chips over, make the pea purée and then start to fry your phish.
5. Finish frying your phish and serve hot along with the chips, phish and tartar sauce.

EQUIPMENT

Sharp knife, bowl, storage containers with lids

INGREDIENTS

For The Marinade

- 2–3 shiitake mushrooms (if using dried, hydrate them first in some boiling water)
- 1 clove garlic
- 250ml/9fl oz/1 cup hot (tap) water
- 1–2 x 4–5cm/1½–2in pieces of dried kelp/kombu
- 2 tablespoons tamari or dark soy sauce
- 1 tablespoon maple syrup
- 2 tablespoons apple cider vinegar or brine from pickles
- Sea salt

For The Phish

- 1½–2 x 395g/14oz blocks of firm tofu or 2 x 400g/14oz cans banana blossom

GF use gluten-free soy sauce or swap for tamari.

SERVES: 4 | TIME: 6 MINUTES, PLUS 1-24 HOURS MARINATING

PHISH MARINADE

1. Finely slice the shiitake mushrooms and crush the garlic.
2. Mix all the marinade ingredients together in a bowl.
3. If using tofu, cut the tofu into 8 x 1.5cm/3¼ x ⅝in wide strips (keep it the length of the block), then pop in a bowl or container. If using banana blossom, drain the banana blossom, pull it apart with your fingers, place in a bowl and pat dry with paper towels or a clean dish towel.
4. Pour the marinade over the tofu or banana blossom, cover and leave for a few hours or ideally overnight in the refrigerator.
5. Drain before using.

Use the leftover marinade and mushrooms to make another dish such as a broth or dipping sauce. To batter and cook the fish, see the next page.

EQUIPMENT

Bowl, wooden spoon, sharp knife, high-sided saucepan, metal slotted spoon, plate lined with paper towels, tongs

INGREDIENTS

- 270g/9¾oz/2 cups plain/all-purpose flour (or preferably 135g/4¾oz/1 cup each plain/all-purpose and rice flour)
- 1 teaspoon baking powder
- 1 teaspoon ground turmeric
- Pinch of sea salt
- 375ml/13fl oz/1½ cups sparkling water
- 2 nori sheets
- Squeeze of lemon juice
- 500ml–1 litre/17–35fl oz/2–4¼ cups cooking oil (such as groundnut/peanut or rapeseed/canola oil), for deep-frying, or 1 teaspoon vegetable or olive oil, for air-frying
- 1 x quantity pre-marinaded tofu or banana blossom (see above)

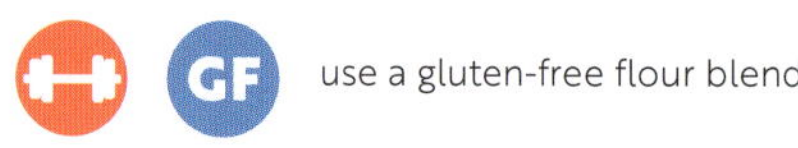

SERVES: 4 | TIME: 25 MINUTES

PHISH

1. TO DEEP-FRY: Mix all the dry ingredients together in a bowl using a wooden spoon. Gradually add the water and mix together to form a thickish batter, like a custard. Put aside.

2. Remove the tofu or banana blossom from the marinade, then cut the nori sheets to fit the tofu or banana blossom pieces and stick a piece of nori to both sides of each piece of tofu/banana blossom with a little lemon juice.

3. Heat the oil in a high-sided saucepan on a medium-high heat until hot. Check it is hot enough by dropping a small piece of batter – it should immediately crisp and float to the top.

4. Dip the tofu or banana blossom pieces into the batter until fully coated, then gently lower a couple into the hot oil (you'll need to fry them in batches).

5. Fry each batch for around 1–1½ minutes ensuring they're fried on all sides. If using less oil you'll need to turn over. Transfer with a metal slotted spoon to a plate lined with paper towels to remove excess oil.

6. Serve with your chips, pea purée and tartar sauce. For the full works, you could make some of Asa's Fermented Ketchup too (see page 341).

1. TO AIR-FRY: If you'd like to air-fry your phish, make a slightly thicker batter by upping the flour quantity by 50g/1¾oz/generous ⅓ cup.

2. Add 1 teaspoon of olive or vegetable oil to the air fryer, then add the battered vegan phish. Do not stack the vegan phish pieces on top of each other – cook them in a couple of batches if necessary (adding another teaspoon of oil to the second batch, if you like).

3. Air-fry at 180°C/350°F for 10 minutes until golden brown. The batter will drip off into the basket which is a little messy. For ease, serve the phish with batter on one side. For all round batter, re-dip the bottom of the piece in the batter and air fry again for 10 minutes with the freshly dipped side facing up.

Air-fried batter doesn't have the same crispiness of a deep-fried version, but it's still tasty and much healthier.

TIPS &
TRICKS
Shopping For
Shiitake Mushrooms
and Seaweed
p 380

SERVES: 4 | TIME: 5 MINUTES

TARTAR SAUCE

EQUIPMENT

Medium-size bowl, Microplane/grater

INGREDIENTS

200g/7oz (drained) pickled gherkins
2 tablespoons fresh dill
200g/7oz vegan mayonnaise
Juice of 1 lemon
1–2 tablespoons (drained) small capers (optional)
¼ teaspoon black pepper

1. Cut your pickled gherkins into small cubes and finely chop your fresh dill.

2. Add the mayonnaise to a medium-size bowl and stir in the lemon juice.

3. Add the gherkins, dill, capers and black pepper and stir together. Cover and store in the refrigerator, then enjoy with your vegan phish and chips.

SERVES: 4 | TIME: 10 MINUTES

SIMPLE PEA PURÉE

EQUIPMENT

Saucepan, blender, fine sieve/fine mesh strainer (optional)

INGREDIENTS

500g/1lb 2oz/4 cups frozen peas
2 tablespoons olive oil
Pinch of dried lavender or a few leaves of fresh mint (optional)
A squeeze of lemon juice
Sea salt

1. Bring a pan of salted water to the boil, add the peas and blanch them for 3 minutes.

2. Drain, then add the peas to a blender with the olive oil and the lavender or mint (if using) and blitz. Add more oil or water if needed. Blend for 2–3 minutes until smooth and thick.

3. If you want a silky finish use a fine sieve/fine-mesh strainer and push the purée through it. This will take some time and it's just as delicious without doing this step.

4. Season with a pinch of salt and add a squeeze of lemon juice.

Serve warm with your phish and chips. It will discolour over time so make it shortly before eating.

TIP *Chips also work brilliantly cooked in an air fryer on the Max Crisp setting for 18 minutes, tossing/turning them every four minutes. Most air fryers would not fit all these chips in one go so you'd need to cook them in two batches, hence the oven is more convenient.*

EQUIPMENT

1–2 baking sheets, peeler, sharp knife, saucepan, colander, pastry brush, baking parchment

INGREDIENTS

- 5–6 large Maris Piper potatoes (but any white potatoes are fine)
- Olive oil, for brushing
- Generous pinch of sea salt
- Generous pinch of B12-enriched nutritional yeast (optional)

SERVES: 4 | TIME: 50 MINUTES

HOMEMADE CHIPS

1. Preheat the oven to 180°C/350°F/gas 4. Line 1–2 baking sheets with baking parchment.

2. Peel and slice the potatoes into chips about 1cm/½in wide.

3. Pop your chips into a pan and cover with cold water. Put the pan on a high heat and bring to a rolling boil (you'll see bubbles). Leave to cook for 2 minutes, then drain in a colander.

4. Tip the chips onto the lined baking sheet(s) and arrange so they're not on top of each other, using 2 baking sheets if needed.

5. Brush the chips with olive oil and then sprinkle with the salt and nutritional yeast.

6. Pop in your pre-heated oven for 15 minutes. Bring them out and turn the chips over and pop back in the oven for another 10-15 minutes or until they've turn golden brown but aren't burning.

7. Remove from the oven and tip into a paper-lined basket or onto some paper for an authentic chippy experience.

NN **IF I'M NOT EATING FISH, WHERE DO I GET OMEGA-3 FATS?**

Fish contain omega-3 fats, but fish get them from algae. So why not go straight to the source? You can't buy algae at the grocers but you take it as a supplement – as an EPA and DHA algae-derived oil. We recommend the capsules as the oil has a strong taste. For people who can't swallow capsules add the oil to a flavoursome drink. ALA Omegas (a different type to the EPA and DHA that's in algae) can be found in tofu, chia seeds, ground linseed/flax, hemp, pumpkin and sunflower seeds and walnuts. The body converts ALA omegas into EPA and DHA omegas. More research needs to be done into whether an EPA and DHA supplement is necessary, but it is recommended for pregnant and lactating women following a plant-based diet.

SERVES: 4 | TIME: 2 HOURS FOR EVERYTHING

STEVE'S ALL-OUT SUNDAY LUNCH

"Who doesn't love a Sunday roast? The plant-based version is often more flavoursome as more care is given to elevating the trimmings. Instead of the classic nut loaf, I've created a seed loaf, which is a more affordable source of protein and it's packed full of umami flavours. The process is similar to an upside-down pineapple cake. I hear MIH's founder Sarah's family has it every year made in a circular cake pan for Christmas dinner – so it must be good. Root vegetables have a lot of natural sweetness. Roasting them brings the sweetness out and increases the richness of the vegetable. Get them nicely browned as that is where the flavour's at. I like a side of tasty greens whenever eating a roast, both because they're good for you, and they taste really good. Tangy mustard and pungent garlic are the perfect combination for whichever greens you use. You can apply the same technique of blanching then dressing to any greens. These recipes are budget-conscious, accessible and a bit healthier than what a restaurant would serve, but with no compromise on flavour."

  (without the miso paste)  use gluten-free stuffing mix, gluten-free vegetable bouillon powder and swap the yeast extract for tamari sauce.

SERVES: 4 | TIME: 1 HOUR

PARSNIP AND CRANBERRY SEED LOAF

EQUIPMENT

2 saucepans with lids (wash between uses), sharp knife, 1 x 900g/2lb loaf pan or 1 x 27cm/10¾in diameter springform cake pan, 2 non-stick frying pans (preferably non-stick), 2 mixing bowls, tongs, 2 wooden spoons

INGREDIENTS (next page)

1. Put the lentils in a saucepan, cover with the water and season with the pinch of salt. Bring to the boil, then reduce the heat and simmer the lentils for 20 minutes until tender. Strain and leave to cool.

2. Meanwhile, prepare the veg and seeds.
- Finely dice the onions and garlic.
- Slice the parsnips into long thin strips – you should get about 6 thin strips per parsnip.
- Roughly chop the sunflower seeds, leave some whole and have some in pieces.

3. Preheat the oven to 190°C/375°F/gas 5. Line the loaf pan or springform cake pan with baking parchment.

4. Sauté the onions in the rapeseed/canola oil in a frying pan on a medium heat for about 5 minutes until soft and golden, then add the garlic and sauté for a further minute. Set aside. **>>**

INGREDIENTS

120g/4¼oz/⅔ cup dried Puy lentils
1 litre/35fl oz/4¼ cups water
Pinch of sea salt, plus extra for the parsnip water
2 onions
2–4 cloves garlic
2 parsnips
160g/5¾oz/scant 1¼ cups sunflower seeds
1–2 teaspoons rapeseed/canola oil, plus extra for greasing
40g/1½oz sage and onion stuffing mix
40g/1½oz brown rice miso paste (optional)
20g/¾oz yeast extract
1 teaspoon vegetable bouillon powder
2 tablespoons potato flour (or other thickener like cornflour/cornstarch or tapioca)
100g/3½oz cranberry sauce

5. Add the parsnip strips to a pan of salted boiling water and cook for 4 minutes until tender. Drain and set aside.

6. Toast the sunflower seeds in a dry frying pan on a medium heat until golden to bring out their nutty flavours. Set aside.

7. In a large bowl, mix all the nut roast ingredients together – so that's everything except the cranberry sauce and parboiled parsnips.

8. Put the cranberry sauce at the bottom of the prepared loaf/cake pan and spread it out over the baking parchment 0.5cm/¼in thick.

9. Layer the parsnip slices in the bottom of the loaf/cake pan on top of the cranberry sauce. Make it look pretty – as although it's the bottom now, it's going to be the top of your loaf.

10. Add the seed and lentil mixture to the top of the parsnips and press it down. Bake for 25 minutes until firm and darker in colour.

11. Now for the magic bit. Take it out of the oven, leave to stand for 2 minutes, then flip it upside down and let the loaf slide out. Gently peel off the baking parchment if it is stuck on. Doesn't it look pretty?!

SERVES: 4 | TIME: 50-55 MINUTES

CRISPY FLUFFY ROAST POTATOES

"As we're making a healthier version of roast potatoes we're going to go lighter on the cooking oil than with usual roasties, but we'll still use enough oil so they go nice and crispy."

EQUIPMENT

Peeler, saucepan, colander, roasting pan, tongs

INGREDIENTS

1kg/2lb 4oz potatoes (use a fluffy rather than a waxy variety, like Maris Piper)
1 tablespoon sea salt, plus an extra pinch
2 litres/70fl oz/8½ cups water
100ml/3½fl oz/scant ½ cup vegetable oil
Pinch of black pepper

1. Preheat the oven to 220°C/425°F/gas 7.

2. Peel the potatoes and cut them into similar bite-size pieces. Place them in a pan, add the tablespoon of salt and cover with the water. The salt will penetrate to the middle of the potatoes during this boiling phase, giving you a tastier potato.

3. Bring the water to the boil on a high heat, then reduce to a medium heat and gently simmer for around 8 minutes. You're looking to just cook the potatoes through to the middle, but not to overcook them. You want them to hold their shape for the shaking and roasting stages.

4. Once the potatoes are cooked, strain in a colander. Now give the colander a good shake so that you fluff up the sides of the potatoes,

this will give you a good coating for getting crispy during roasting – so don't be shy. Alternatively, you can rough up the edges with a fork.

5. Place the cooking oil into a roasting pan and heat up in the oven for 5 minutes. You want the oil to be really hot so that when you pop your potatoes in, they will fry in the oil, creating a crispy layer on the outside of the potatoes, rather than boiling in the oil and the potatoes soaking up the oil like a sponge. Shake the potatoes around in the oil to get them well coated, and then put them back into the oven to roast for an initial 30 minutes.

6. After 30 minutes, take the potatoes out of the oven and carefully turn them over with a pair of tongs. Pop them back in the oven to roast for a further 30 minutes.

use gluten-free vegetable stock and gluten-free Dijon mustard.

SERVES: 4 | TIME: 30 MINUTES

MISO GRAVY

"Let's face it, store-bought gravy just doesn't cut it. We can do better. This plant-based gravy combines umami-rich miso paste with sweet cranberry sauce and other flavourings to make a delicious sauce to smother your roast dinner with."

EQUIPMENT

Sharp knife, saucepan, hand-held/immersion blender

INGREDIENTS

1 onion
1 clove garlic
2 tablespoons olive oil
600ml/20fl oz/2½ cups vegetable stock
2 tablespoons brown rice miso paste
1 tablespoon Dijon mustard
2½ tablespoons cranberry sauce (or raspberry jam)
½ tablespoon balsamic vinegar (or other vinegar, but not malt)
Pinch of sea salt
Pinch of black pepper

1. Roughly chop the onion and the garlic. Mix the crushed garlic, mustard, vinegar and olive oil together in a small bowl.

2. In a saucepan, sauté the onion and garlic in the olive oil on a medium heat with a lid on for 10 minutes until soft.

3. Add all the other ingredients to the pan, then boil for 20 minutes until reduced by a third.

4. Using a hand-held/immersion blender, blend the ingredients together until smooth. Pour over your roasties or wherever you prefer to have your gravy. Happy Sunday!

   use a gluten-free Dijon mustard as occasionally malt vinegar isn't gluten-free.

SERVES: 4 | TIME: 10 MINUTES

GARLIC AND MUSTARD GREENS

EQUIPMENT

Sharp knife, small bowl, saucepan, colander

INGREDIENTS

16 stems of purple-sprouting broccoli or slim stalks of broccoli
2 cloves garlic
2 teaspoons Dijon mustard
2 teaspoons apple cider vinegar
2 teaspoons extra virgin olive oil
Sea salt

1. Prepare the broccoli and garlic.
- Cut the broccoli stalks in half lengthways if you have large pieces.
- Finely chop and crush the garlic. This will release all the pungency from inside.

2. Mix the crushed garlic, mustard, vinegar and olive oil together in a small bowl. This will be the dressing for your greens.

3. Heat up a pan of lightly salted boiling water. Blanch the broccoli for 2 minutes.

4. Drain the broccoli into a colander and shake off the excess water before dressing with your garlic mustard mixture.

SERVES: 4 | TIME: 35 MINUTES

ROAST CARROTS

EQUIPMENT

Sharp knife, small roasting pan

INGREDIENTS

4 carrots
1 tablespoon extra virgin olive oil
2 star anise (optional)
Finely grated zest of ½ orange (optional)
1 tablespoon orange juice (optional)
1 tablespoon maple syrup (optional)

1. Preheat the oven to 220°C/425°F/gas 7.

2. Cut off the tops and bottoms of the carrots and discard. Cut each carrot into two long pieces by cutting lengthways through the middle of the carrot. If you have very large carrots, quarter them.

3. Mix the carrots with the olive oil and star anise (if using) and pop them into a small roasting pan. Roast for 30 minutes.

4. After 25 minutes, take them out and dress the carrots in the orange zest, orange juice and maple syrup (if using) and roast for a further 5 minutes.

SERVES: 4 | TIME: 1 HOUR

JAH SPIRIT'S (RIP) ITAL STEW

Jah Spirit was a much-loved community class teacher and dear friend to MIH founder Sarah. He passed away in 2018. This is how he described his ital stew: *"I've been making Ital stew long time. It's a big one-pot dish good for feeding a lotta' people at a gathering, dance or at carnival where I've served it from mi' stall every year. It'll keep your belly full and it's nice and flavoursome. It freezes good so cook up a big batch and have it on days you nah hav' time to cook."*

EQUIPMENT

Sharp knife, Jamaican Dutch pot or large saucepan with lid, heatproof jug/pitcher

IINGREDIENTS (next page)

1. Let's start by preparing our vegetables.
- Cut the skin off the pumpkin, discard the seeds and cut into 2cm/¾in cubes.
- Cut the onions into large 2cm/¾in dice.
- Peel and cut the plantains into slanted 2cm/¾in pieces.
- Peel and cut the sweet potato and yam (if using) into 2cm/¾in chunky pieces.
- Finely slice the kale or spinach.
- Cut the limes in half.
- Finely slice the ginger and garlic.
- Finely slice the Scotch bonnet – removing or keeping the seeds as per your heat preference.

2. Heat the coconut oil in a large saucepan on a medium heat. Add the diced onions and fry for 3 minutes until soft and golden.

3. Add both ground spices, the thyme, garlic and ginger to the pan, stir and cook for 1 minute.

4. Add the coconut milk along with the plantains, pumpkin, sweet potato and yam (if using).

5. Open the cans of butter/lima beans, drain, rinse and add to the stew. Add the Scotch bonnet.

6. Measure the boiling water into a jug/pitcher with the crumbled stock cubes or bouillon powder. Once it's dissolved, add to the stew. Gently stir a couple of times.

7. Cover with a lid and gently simmer on a medium heat for 15–20 minutes until the roots and tubers are soft all the way through. Test this by pricking them with a fork. >>

REMEMBERING JAH SPIRIT
See what a special man Jah Spirit was by reading his obituary online in the *Hackney Gazette*.

INGREDIENTS

200g/7oz pumpkin

2 onions

2 ripe plantains (see p 378 for shopping tips)

200g/7oz sweet potato

200g/7oz poona yam (optional)

100g/3½oz kale or spinach (in Jamaica, we'd use fresh callaloo)

2 limes

2 thumb-size pieces root ginger

3 cloves garlic

¼–1 red Scotch bonnet chilli (optional) (see Scotch Bonnet for Newbies on p 379)

½ tablespoon coconut oil

2 tablespoons Caribbean curry powder

1 tablespoon ground allspice/pimento

2 tablespoons dried thyme

2 x 400ml/14fl oz cans coconut milk

1½–2 x 400g/14oz cans butter/lima beans

300ml/10½fl oz/1¼ cups boiling water

2 vegetable stock cubes or 1 tablespoon vegetable bouillon powder

Sea salt and black pepper

Cooked grain of choice (basmati or short-grain brown rice) to serve alongside

8. While the Ital stew is cooking, you can cook your grain of choice if eating with a grain. We recommend short-grain brown rice, basmati rice or quinoa for a lighter grain (for cooking instructions, see p 57).

9. Once the harder veg are soft, you can add the chopped kale or spinach and squeeze the juice of the limes into the Ital stew.

10. Season with salt and pepper and serve in a bowl along with your grain of choice.

Jah Spirit, Caroline and Ogu sharing recipes in a class for Hackney Museum.

LET'S TALK ABOUT... WHAT IS ITAL FOOD?

With Chef Ekowa Paul

You know what they say, Ital is vital. It's food that's vital for your mental, physical and spiritual wellbeing. It's a way of eating developed by Rastafarians in Jamaican around the 1930s that gives life and nah deal with death. It doesn't use any meat, fish or animal products so, yes, Ital food is vegan. It's usually also low to no salt, but that can change chef to chef, and is centred around wholefoods and fresh produce, stays away from anything excessively processed from the capitalist food system, and ideally uses organic food if it's available. It's food grown, produced and cooked in harmony with nature. In the kitchen as an Ital chef you try to avoid plastic and aluminium cooking utensils, and some Rastas eat from a calabash bowl and carry this around with them. Some Ital chefs follow the late, great Haitian health visionary Dr Sebi's diet recommendations of eating a mainly alkaline diet. I'm influenced by this but I don't only cook like that. This way of eating is part of livity, the Rasta way of living life to the fullest.

   use gluten-free soy sauce or swap for tamari.

SERVES: 4 | TIME: 45 MINUTES

DR SUNNI'S CAULIFLOWER MANCHURIAN

"This is a favourite restaurant dish in India, its popularity demonstrating the growing interest in fusion food there. It's great as a first course but it's usually served as a main course alongside hakka noodles or fried rice. This recipe is less oily and greasy than many versions you get in restaurants, but it's just as flavoursome and satisfying. Enjoy."

EQUIPMENT

Sharp knife, saucepan, baking sheet, wok or shallow frying pan

INGREDIENTS (next page)

1. Let's prep the ingredients for the sauce.
- Deseed and dice the red pepper and dice the celery.
- Finely slice the spring onions/scallions, keeping the white and green parts separate.
- Finely slice the ginger.
- Finely chop the garlic.
- Finely chop the green chillies.

2. Chop or break the cauliflower or broccoli into medium- or small-sized florets, but do not discard the stem or leaves – use them in a ferment or to make a veg stock.

3. Cook the florets in a pan of boiling water for 5 minutes, then drain and keep aside.

4. Preheat the oven to 200°C/400°F/gas 6. Line a baking sheet with baking parchment.

5. While the cauliflower or broccoli is cooking, make the batter. In a bowl, mix together the flour, cornflour/cornstarch, soy sauce or tamari, black pepper, chilli powder and salt. Add the water and whisk to make a smooth batter without any lumps.

6. Dip each floret in the batter and place on the lined baking sheet in a single layer. Bake for 20 minutes until crispy.

7. For the sauce, in a wok or shallow pan, heat the olive oil until hot, then sauté the ginger, garlic and green chillies on a medium heat until the ginger and garlic look more translucent, about 5 minutes.

8. Add the red pepper, celery and spring onion white parts. >>

INGREDIENTS

1 medium cauliflower or 1 medium head of broccoli

For The Batter

130g/4¾oz/1 cup plain/all-purpose flour, rice flour or chickpea/gram flour

4 tablespoons cornflour/cornstarch

1 teaspoon dark soy sauce or tamari

¼ teaspoon black pepper

½ teaspoon chilli powder

Pinch of sea salt

240ml/8½fl oz/1 cup water

For The Sauce

1 red pepper (green or yellow work well too)

2 celery stalks

Bunch of spring onions/scallions

4cm/1½in piece root ginger

3–4 cloves garlic

2 fresh green chillies

2 tablespoons olive oil

1 tablespoon dark soy sauce or tamari

1 tablespoon tomato purée/paste

½ teaspoon black pepper

Pinch of sea salt

1 teaspoon rice vinegar (or white wine vinegar or apple cider vinegar)

Your choice of cooked grain (such as basmati rice, short-grain brown rice or noodles), to serve

Increase the heat to high and stir-fry till the pepper is almost fully cooked, about 3 minutes.

9. Add the soy sauce or tamari, tomato purée/paste, vinegar, black pepper and salt. Give it a good stir.

10. Add the baked cauliflower or broccoli florets, then mix well to ensure that the sauce coats the cauliflower/broccoli well.

11. Lastly, add the rice vinegar, stir well and then mix in the spring onion greens. These don't need to cook.

12. Serve with your choice of grain – basmati rice, short-grain brown rice or noodles (see Cooking Staples on p 55).

Nutrition Nugget... The Gut Microbiome With Dr Sunni Patel p 371

**DR SUNNI'S TOP TIPS
FOR MAINTAINING A HEALTHY GUT MICROBIOME**

1. Ensure you eat a varied diet rich in whole plant foods of differing colours.

2. Add fermented foods to your diet such as sauerkraut, kimchi, fermented nut and seed cheeses and drinks such as homemade kombucha (see p 358) and kefir.

3. Eat foods rich in fructans (asparagus, onions, garlic, barley, wheat) and short-chain fatty acids (wholegrains, fruits, vegetables and legumes).

4. Remain active to help increase levels of endorphins, serotonin and dopamine.

5. Do what you can to ensure you're getting enough sleep as this helps with your melatonin levels, overall body clock and gut health balance. We understand how frustrating this advice can be for people with young children, doing shift work or who have health conditions such as a hormonal imbalance and are experiencing insomnia due to perimenopause and menopause, sleep apnoea, overactive thyroid and other conditions known to disrupt sleep. Don't worry about it too much; humans can survive on very little sleep, just get rest as and when you can.

use a gluten-free stock cube (if using) for the stew peas and use gluten-free flour to make the spinners.

SERVES: 4 GENEROUSLY | TIME: 1 HOUR, 20 MINUTES, PLUS OVERNIGHT SOAKING AND 40 MINUTES COOKING IF USING DRIED PEAS – USING DRIED KIDNEY BEANS IS THE TRADITIONAL METHOD, BUT YOU CAN REMOVE THIS STEP BY USING CANNED

MELISSA'S STEW PEAS AND SPINNERS

"This is one of my go-to comfort dishes, as it transports me back to the Caribbean with its warm, nourishing flavours. I'm a big advocate for having enough fibre in the diet and kidney beans are a favourite of mine; it's one of the many reasons I love to teach this dish. People are aways pleasantly surprised with how something as simple and overlooked as kidney beans can make such a delicious dish."

EQUIPMENT

Large, deep saucepan, sharp knife, large cast iron Dutch pot (traditional vessel) or large stew pot/ saucepan, small ramekin, wooden spoon, metal slotted spoon, medium mixing bowl

INGREDIENTS (next page)

START AT STEP 3 IF USING CANNED KIDNEY BEANS.

1. Take the kidney beans that have been soaking overnight and discard the water. Rinse the beans, then add to a large deep saucepan and cover with fresh water.

2. Bring to the boil and boil for 40 minutes, adding more water as needed, until the beans are pierceable with a fork. Do not cook them until easily mashable as they will cook more in the stew. Drain the beans and reserve the cooking water to use in step 4.

3. Now let's prepare the vegetables.
- Chop the onion into medium chunks.
- Finely slice the garlic and celery (into discs not sticks).
- Finely slice the Scotch bonnet and remove the seeds unless you enjoy very hot food.
- Deseed and finely dice the red pepper and finely dice the carrot.
- If using whole allspice/pimento berries, grind them in a pestle and mortar.
- Finely chop the spring onion/scallion (if using) – this is for the garnish.

4. Reserve 400ml/14fl oz/1⅔ cups of the water the beans were cooked in as this will develop the stew's flavour, or make up 400ml/14fl oz/1⅔ cups of vegetable stock from the stock cube. Set aside.

5. Heat a heavy duty, cast iron pot (or a high-sided pot/pan) on a medium-high heat and add the olive oil. **>>**

INGREDIENTS

For The Stew Peas

- 350g/12oz/generous 2 cups dried kidney beans (soaked overnight) or 2 x 400g/14oz cans kidney beans
- 1 large yellow onion
- 6 large cloves garlic
- 1 large celery stalk
- ½–1 red Scotch bonnet chilli (see Scotch Bonnet for Newbies on p 379)
- 1 large red pepper
- 1 large carrot
- 4–5 allspice/pimento berries or 2 teaspoons ground allspice
- 1 spring onion/scallion (optional)
- About 400ml/14fl oz/1⅔ cups reserved kidney bean water OR 1 vegetable stock cube
- 1 tablespoon olive oil
- 4–5 sprigs of fresh thyme, plus 1–2 extra (optional) sprigs to garnish
- 1 tablespoon black pepper
- 1 tablespoon dried mixed herbs
- ½ tablespoon sea salt, or to taste
- 400ml/14fl oz/1⅔ cups coconut milk
- 1 tablespoon cornflour/cornstarch
- 360g/12½oz/2 cups uncooked brown basmati rice, quinoa or grain of choice (see Cooking Staples on p 55)

For The Spinners

- 180g/6¼oz/1⅓ cups plain/all-purpose flour, plus extra for dusting
- 2 teaspoons sea salt
- 100ml/3½fl oz/scant ½ cup water

6. Distribute the oil around the pot and add in the onion, leaving it to fry until slightly translucent. Add the garlic and sauté for a further minute, stirring occasionally.

7. Add the celery, Scotch bonnet, red pepper, carrot and thyme sprigs and give it a quick stir. Leave to cook for 3–4 minutes. Now add in the allspice, black pepper, dried herbs and salt and stir.

8. Add the cooked kidney beans to the pot and mix thoroughly. Leave to sauté for a minute or two.

9. On a low-medium heat, add and mix in the coconut milk and the reserved water from the cooked kidney beans or the vegetable stock (if using canned beans).

10. To a small ramekin, add the cornflour/cornstarch and a few tablespoons of liquid from the stew and mix into a thick paste. Stir it back into the stew to thicken it.

11. Leave to simmer gently on a low heat for 15–20 minutes. The dish will naturally thicken due to the starchiness of the beans, the coconut milk and, eventually, with the addition of the spinners.

12. To prepare the spinners, add the flour and salt to a medium mixing bowl. Add the water and lightly work the mixture with your hands to make a dough.

13. Tip onto a lightly floured surface and knead (see How to Knead on p 374) for a few minutes until the dough is slightly firm.

14. Shape the dough into a log and tear off small pieces. Roll each piece first into a ball and then spin it back and forth to form sausages, each about 6–8cm/2½–3¼in in length. I like larger spinners, so I make mine 10cm/4in in length, but the traditional way is smaller.

15. Add the spinners to the stew and ensure they're covered with the stew liquid. Cover with a lid and simmer for 20–25 minutes so the stew thickens and the spinners become firm.

16. In the meantime, cook your accompanying grain. I recommend brown basmati rice or quinoa (see Cooking Staples on p 55).

17. Remove the thyme stalks, then serve the stew with your grain of choice and enjoy. Ensure each portion has at least 4 spinners (if made the traditional size). Garnish with the spring onion (if using) or a sprig or two of thyme on top.

LET'S TALK ABOUT... DIVERSITY & HEALTH EQUITY

With Melissa Saint Hill, co-founder of the Diverse Nutrition Association

When I started out in clinical nutrition, I worked mainly with type 2 diabetes patients and those with prediabetes. Often, they were being told by healthcare professionals to cut out traditional staples from their diet, which led to dissatisfaction, decreased adherence and eventual dropouts from dietary interventions that they were enrolled onto. I found it upsetting to see people so frustrated and confused when they'd be told that they could not include foods they were used to. There wasn't a standardized body with culturally relevant information, so I decided that I'd do something about it.

The Diverse Nutrition Association provides culturally tailored educational eating resources, works with communities for health education and advocacy, and teaches healthcare practitioners about cultural sensitivity. People need to be aware of how healthy nutrition works for them based on what they know from their culture. That goes for the layperson and probably even more importantly the healthcare practitioner. We need to have practitioners who are knowledgeable about how to work with people from an ever-growing diverse population. This is how we achieve health equity. The lack of representation in the nutrition/dietetics space is problematic because, naturally, not everyone practising in the field is going to understand various cultures, or be comfortable asking certain questions, or be skilled to look for cues that may be part of someone else's cultural norms. There are various barriers that may be present, and if not identified or mitigated, someone could be walking away from a service or intervention that could save their life. In a healthcare setting, people care if you understand them and where they're coming from. When the right level of interest is displayed and the correct questions asked in the correct way, the conversation will open up, and key information is shared. The result is someone receiving the advice they need to help them.

Participants from Micro-Rainbow, an amazing charity that provides safe homes for LGBTQIA plus asylum seekers, with their delicious bakes.

     use a gluten-free Dijon mustard.

SERVES: 4 | TIME: 25 MINUTES

SARETA'S OCEAN CAKES

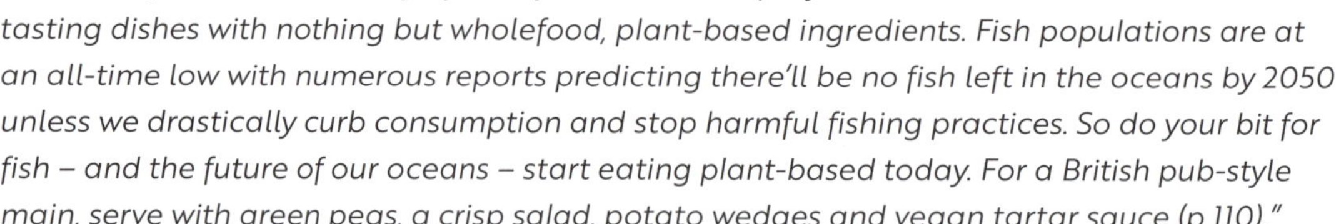

"I made these for a tasting session with the Fuller's pubs team when we were trialling dishes for a fundraising item for their menu. They were blown away by how you can create fishy-tasting dishes with nothing but wholefood, plant-based ingredients. Fish populations are at an all-time low with numerous reports predicting there'll be no fish left in the oceans by 2050 unless we drastically curb consumption and stop harmful fishing practices. So do your bit for fish – and the future of our oceans – start eating plant-based today. For a British pub-style main, serve with green peas, a crisp salad, potato wedges and vegan tartar sauce (p 110)."

EQUIPMENT

Sharp knife, medium-size bowl, masher, non-stick frying pan, flipper

INGREDIENTS (next page)

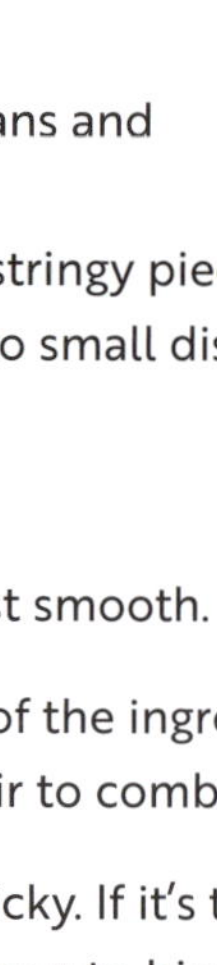

1. Let's prep the ingredients.
- Drain and rinse the chickpeas/garbanzo beans and artichoke hearts.
- Finely dice the artichoke hearts into small, stringy pieces.
- Cut the spring onion/scallion and celery into small discs.
- Finely chop the dill.
- Quarter the capers.

2. In a bowl, mash the chickpeas until almost smooth.

3. Add the artichoke pieces and all the rest of the ingredients – except the vegetable oil – to the bowl and stir to combine.

4. The mixture should be smooth but not sticky. If it's too sticky, add an extra ½ teaspoon of chickpea/gram flour to bind it. You can taste it at this stage – it should be slightly salty and smoky with a vinegar taste.

5. Divide the mixture into 8 small or 4 large balls (your preference) and flatten into cake-shaped discs. They won't expand when cooking so make them the size you want your final phish cakes to be. I like mine about 10–12cm/4–4½in across.

6. Heat the vegetable oil in a non-stick pan on a medium heat. When it's hot, add 2–3 cakes at a time, depending on the size of your pan. Cook for approximately 5 minutes until browned, then flip over and repeat on the other side. >>

INGREDIENTS

1 x 400g/14oz can chickpeas/garbanzo beans

1 x 400g/14oz can artichoke hearts in brine or water (both work)

1 spring onion/scallion

½ celery stalk (approximately 30g/1oz)

Handful of fresh dill

8 (drained) capers

2 teaspoons nori sprinkles (optional)

2 tablespoons caper brine

2 tablespoons Dijon mustard

2 tablespoons vegan mayonnaise

3 tablespoons chickpea/gram flour

1 teaspoon smoked paprika

¼ teaspoon cayenne pepper

¼ teaspoon black pepper

¼ teaspoon sea salt

1–2 tablespoons vegetable oil

To Serve

Watercress salad

OR

Fresh dill

Vegan Tartar Sauce (see p 110)

Simple Pea Purée (see p 110)

Homemade Chips (see p 111)

Lemon wedges

Nutrition Nugget... Plant-Based Omega Oils p 111

7. Alternatively, add ½ teaspoon of oil to an air fryer with the cakes and air-fry at 190°C/375°F for approximately 12 minutes, flipping over halfway through until browned.

Serve with a watercress salad, or for a larger meal with a sprig of fresh dill, vegan tartar sauce, pea purée, some chunky chips and lemon wedges.

LET'S TALK ABOUT... THE JOY OF FISH *by Sarah Bentley*

Fish get a crappy deal when it comes to human empathy. Until recently scientists weren't convinced they felt pain or distress (they certainly do), hence the close to non-existent welfare standards when it comes to fishing and fish farming. Fish are incredibly unique, diverse and intelligent creatures that are our direct ancestors. Yes, humans evolved from fish. Studies have found they have musical preferences, friendship groups and complex courtship rituals. Japanese puffer fish build stunning sand mosaics to attract a mate and recently a fish was discovered in Vietnam where the males have their phallus positioned on their head – that's right, there are dickheads in the fish world too.

But our fish friends and indeed everything that lives in the ocean are in serious trouble with a complete collapse of ocean life predicted to happen by 2048 unless drastic interventions are made. How did it get to this? In the last 50 years industrial fishing, particularly super trawlers, have wiped out 90% of the world's largest fish. Apex predators such as sharks and many types of whales – creatures at the top of the ocean food chain vital for sustaining a healthy eco-system – are being killed in such vast quantities they cannot birth offspring quick enough to sustain population levels. Fishing kills 30,000 sharks every hour. Try to visualize that. Yes you might not be eating shark, but most fish eating contributes to the death of them. People fret about plastic straws polluting the ocean, but few people want to talk about the fact 70% of large macro plastics polluting the sea comes from fishing tackle. And perhaps just as disturbing as the bottom trawlers that indiscriminately scrape up everything on the sea bed are the line fishing boats that cast enough line to wrap around the earth 500 times – per day! This also means coastal indigenous communities who survive off fishing using tiny, non-polluting canoes and other low impact vessels are struggling to survive. It's a disaster all around. We know this might be hard to hear, but if you love fish and the abundance of aquatic life the ocean holds, the best thing you can do is stop eating them. And if this isn't motivation enough, consider the high levels of contamination in oceans these days – micro plastics, mercury, industrial pollutants – that all become particularly concentrated in larger fish, and much less so in algae.

SERVES: 4 | TIME FOR THE WHOLE MEAL: 1 HOUR, 15 MINUTES

SARETA'S HAGGIS, NEEPS 'N' TATTIES

"Growing up I enjoyed the times around Burns Night when my dad would get a veggie haggis from the shops and we'd eat something a bit different to our usual fare. When I started to flex my cooking skills in adulthood, making one from scratch was high on my agenda. Haggis is a delicious nutty, peppery dish perfect for a winter's night. The traditional recipe contains the liver, heart and lungs of a sheep minced and mixed with beef or mutton suet. Eugh. Even for non-vegans, a lot of people are squeamish about the ingredients. This plant-based version is delicious and is teamed with neeps (creamed swede/rutabaga – which the Scots call turnips) and tatties (mashed potatoes). It also makes for a great Christmas dinner option. Leftovers can be kept and made into various new dishes e.g. stirred through pasta, a topping for pizza, made into samosas or sausage rolls!"

TO MAKE THE WHOLE MEAL

1. Chop your veg for the neeps and tatties and leave in cold water.
2. Make the haggis according to the haggis method on the next page.
3. While the haggis is in the oven, boil the vegetables – starting with the swede as it takes 5 minutes longer than the potatoes. See methods for neeps and tatties recipes on the next page.
4. While the vegetables are boiling and the haggis is in the oven, you can make the cream sauce as per the recipe on the next page. Once the cream sauce is made, turn off the heat but keep covered to stay warm, and make the neeps and tatties according to the recipe.
5. By now your haggis should be done! It's all come together brilliantly, well done. >>

    use gluten-free vegetable stock, gluten-free oats and swap the soy sauce for tamari or use gluten-free soy sauce.

SERVES: 6-8 | TIME: 1 HOUR, 10 MINUTES

HAGGIS

EQUIPMENT

Deep ovenproof dish, large saucepan, sharp knife, masher, food processor

INGREDIENTS

- Vegetable oil, for greasing
- 150g/5½oz/generous ¾ cup dried split red lentils
- 500ml/17fl oz/2 cups vegetable stock
- 200g/7oz carrots
- 2 portobello mushrooms or 150g/5½oz chestnut/cremini mushrooms
- 1 x 200g/7oz can kidney beans
- 125g/4½oz/scant 1 cup mixed seeds (50/50 sunflower and pumpkin works well)
- 150g/5½oz/1½ cups rolled oats
- 1 tablespoon dark soy sauce
- 2 teaspoons dried sage
- 1 teaspoon ground nutmeg or mace
- 1 teaspoon ground cinnamon or ground allspice/pimento
- 1 tablespoon black pepper (or more if you like it spicy!)
- ½ teaspoon sea salt

TIPS & TRICKS

Just Freeze It p 375

1. Preheat the oven to 180°C/350°F/gas 4. Grease a deep ovenproof dish and set aside.

2. Rinse the lentils. Heat the stock in a large pan and add the lentils. Bring to the boil, then cover and simmer for 15–20 minutes until the lentils are translucent but not mushy.

3. While the lentils cook, let's prepare the other ingredients.
- Coarsely grate the carrots.
- Finely dice the mushrooms.
- Drain and rinse the kidney beans, then mash in a bowl.
- Finely chop or blitz the seeds in a food processor until they're in small chunks but not completely ground.

4. Once the lentils are cooked, stir through the oats – you might need to add a little water at this point so there is enough liquid to soak up the oats. Stir and cook for 2–3 minutes.

5. Stir through the carrots, mushrooms, kidney beans, soy sauce, sage, both ground spices, black pepper and salt. Don't add the seeds yet.

6. Simmer for 5–10 minutes until it thickens to a porridge-like consistency. Add a little more water during this stage if it's too dry, thick or sticking to the pan.

7. Stir through the seeds. Taste and adjust the seasoning if necessary. It should have a salty, peppery and almost nutty flavour from the oats and seeds. If in doubt, add more pepper. The flavours subside as the haggis cooks. The final consistency should be thick, almost like a coarse dough.

8. To finish it off, cook it in the oven. Spoon the haggis mixture into the prepared ovenproof dish and bake for 25–30 minutes until the top is crispy. While it's in the oven, you can start to boil your veg for the neeps and tatties.

9. Remove from the oven and leave it to cool for a few minutes before serving.

Serve it in mounds using a large spoon or ice cream scoop, doing the same with the neeps and tatties, or mould it into a round layer topped with neeps and tatties.

use a gluten-free wholegrain mustard.

SERVES: 4 | TIME: 25 MINUTES

TATTIES

EQUIPMENT

Large saucepan, peeler, sharp knife, colander, masher or ricer

INGREDIENTS

- 600g/1lb 5oz potatoes (I recommend Maris Piper)
- 50g/1¾oz cavolo nero or kale (optional)
- 75–100ml/2½–3½fl oz/⅓–scant ½ cup plant-based milk
- 4 tablespoons vegan butter or olive oil
- 1 tablespoon wholegrain mustard
- Pinch of sea salt
- Pinch of black pepper

1. Bring a pan of water to the boil. Peel and dice the potatoes. Remove the thick stems and finely chop the cavolo nero/kale (if using).

2. Add the potatoes to the boiling water and simmer on a medium heat for about 15 minutes until very soft. Drain but retain the water.

3. Return the potatoes to the pan and add in 1–2 tablespoons of the potato water. This helps to give them an even creamier finish!

4. Stir through the plant-based milk, vegan butter or olive oil and the mustard and season with the salt and black pepper, then mash until smooth. Use a potato ricer if you have one for super smooth tatties.

5. If using cavolo nero/kale, stir it through. Taste and adjust the seasoning. Add more potato water or milk for a creamier consistency.

SERVES: 4 | TIME: 25 MINUTES

NEEPS

EQUIPMENT

Saucepan, peeler, sharp knife, colander, masher or ricer or blender

INGREDIENTS

- 1 large swede/rutabaga (roughly 800g/1lb 12oz)
- 4 tablespoons vegan butter
- Pinch of sea salt
- Pinch of black pepper

1. Bring a pan of water to the boil. Peel and dice the swede/rutabaga.

2. Add the swede to the pan and simmer for about 15–20 minutes.

3. Drain and return to the pan. Stir through the butter and season with the salt and black pepper.

4. Mash with a masher or in a blender.

GF use a gluten-free wholegrain mustard.

SERVES: 4 | TIME: 5 MINUTES

CREAMY SAUCE

EQUIPMENT

Small saucepan, wooden spoon

INGREDIENTS

- 150ml/5fl oz/⅔ cup plant-based double/heavy cream
- ¼ teaspoon wholegrain mustard
- ¼ teaspoon black pepper
- ⅛ teaspoon sea salt

1. Bring the cream to a simmer in a small pan.

2. Add the rest of the ingredients and stir through until combined.

3. Taste and adjust the seasoning if required. Oidhche Bhlas Burns!

   GF use gluten-free certified poppadoms.

SERVES: 4 GENEROUSLY | TIME: 1 HOUR

DR NITU & ROHINI'S EDAMAME & LENTIL KHICHADI

"Lentils are nutritional powerhouses, packed with protein, fibre and iron. According to the Environmental Working Group, they are the top 'climate-friendly protein'. This is a staple in South Asian kitchens, often given to you if you have a tummy bug or cold. It's rich in all nine essential amino acids and saves on washing up as a one-pot dish. It also freezes well. If you have a pressure cooker, it only takes ten minutes to prepare."

EQUIPMENT

Large bowl, sharp knife, medium-sized saucepan with lid, small frying pan

INGREDIENTS

- 210g/7½oz/scant 1¼ cups uncooked brown rice of choice (or half and half rice and quinoa)
- 450g/1lb/2½ cups dried split yellow lentils (toor dal)
- 2 carrots
- 125g/4½oz green beans
- 2.2–2.8 litres/77–96fl oz/9½–12 cups water
- 2 teaspoons ground turmeric
- 80g/3oz/⅔ cup frozen peas
- 75g/2¾oz/⅔ cup frozen edamame beans (green soybeans)
- 1–2 teaspoons sea salt
- 1 teaspoon olive oil (optional)
- 2 teaspoons cumin/ jeera seeds
- 1 teaspoon asafoetida/ hing (optional) (see p 276 for more information)
- 2–4 dried red chillies
- 1–2 tablespoons water (optional)

To Serve

- Corn or lentil papads/ poppadums
- Soy yogurt
- Mango pickle

1. Soak the brown rice and yellow lentils together in room temperature water for 3–4 hours. Ensure they are covered by at least 5cm/2in of water while soaking. Rinse thoroughly before using.

2. Now prepare your veg.
- Dice the carrots and green beans.

3. Add the rice and lentils to a saucepan, add 2.2 litres/77fl oz/9½ cups of the measured water and bring to the boil on a high heat.

4. Once boiling, add half the turmeric, then turn down the heat, part-cover the pan with the lid and simmer for 30 minutes.

5. Add in the carrots, green beans, peas and edamame beans and stir thoroughly. Lentils absorb a huge amount of water so ensure the mixture is quite liquid, adding remaining water, if needed.

6. Part-cover with the lid and simmer on a medium heat for 30 minutes or a bit longer. The mixture should be soft and almost mushy when fully cooked. Stir in the salt to taste.

7. Finally, let's make the tadka – the seasoning for the khichadi. Heat the olive oil (if using) in a small frying pan on a medium-high heat. Once hot, add in the cumin seeds, the remaining turmeric and the asafoetida/hing, then break the red chillies into the pan.

8. Turn the heat down to low, taking care not to burn the spices, and stir for a minute until fragrant. Add the tablespoon or two of water if the mixture is sticking.

9. Add the tadka to the khichadi mixture and stir thoroughly, then turn off the heat and leave to rest for 5 minutes with the lid on.

Amino Acids and the Food Combining Myth p 368

SERVES: 4 | TIME: 20 MINUTES, PLUS 10-15 MINUTES RISING

ANNA'S FRYING PAN YOGURT FLATBREADS

Renowned chef Anna Jones is one of our celebrity supporters who has delivered amazing fundraising cookery classes for us. She is a Hackney local and author of acclaimed cookbooks. She says: *"These are pleasingly simple and work brilliantly on a BBQ."*

EQUIPMENT

Food processor (optional) or bowl, frying pan or griddle/grill pan

INGREDIENTS

200g/7oz/1½ cups plain/all-purpose flour, plus extra for dusting (I use spelt)
1 teaspoon baking powder
200g/7oz/scant 1 cup vegan yogurt or 150ml/5fl oz/⅔ cup warm water

1. Put all the flatbread ingredients into the bowl of your food processor and pulse until the mixture forms a ball. If you don't have a food processor, use a bowl and fork to begin with, then your hands. It will take 3–4 minutes longer, that's all. Vegan yogurt varies in thickness, so add it gradually until you get the desired consistency of a flatbread dough which needs to be not too sticky, nor too dry.

2. Tip the dough out onto a clean work surface dusted with flour. Knead for a minute or so to bring it all together (see How to Knead on p 374).

3. Put the dough into a flour-dusted bowl and cover with a plate. Put to one side to rise a little for 10–15 minutes covered with a dish towel. Don't expect it to rise like normal dough, but it may puff up a tiny bit.

4. Dust a clean work surface and rolling pin with flour, then divide the dough into four equal pieces.

5. Using your hands, pat and flatten out the dough, then use the :rolling pin to roll each piece into a disc roughly 20cm/8in in diameter and 2–3mm/ ⅛ in thick.

6. Warm a frying pan or griddle/grill pan that's a bit larger than your flatbreads on a medium-high heat.

7. Once your pan is nicely hot, cook each flatbread (one at a time) for 1–2 minutes on each side, until nicely puffed up, turning with tongs. Keep the cooked flatbreads warm in a clean dish towel and serve them warm.

SERVES: 4 | TIME: 55 MINUTES

ANNA'S QUICK COURGETTE AND RED ONION FLATBREADS

"This is a cheat's way to a white pizza with courgettes/zucchini. If you'd like to add more green, pile it with peppery salad leaves/greens in the summer or shaved asparagus in spring when it's hot out of the oven. In the cooler months, you could use new potatoes instead of the courgettes.."

EQUIPMENT

Sharp knife, mandolin (if you have one), frying pan, baking sheet, zester or Microplane, oven

INGREDIENTS

- 2 red onions
- 2 large or 4 small courgettes/zucchini, a mix of colours works nicely
- 40g/1½oz vegan parmesan-style cheese, or 2 tablespoons nutritional yeast
- ½ tablespoon olive oil
- 4 flatbreads (see previous page or use store-bought)
- 8 tablespoons vegan oat crème fraîche
- Grated zest of ½ lemon (do not pre-zest)
- A few sprigs of fresh thyme, oregano or marjoram (leaves picked)
- Pinch of sea salt
- Pinch of black pepper

1. Preheat the oven to 200°C/400°F/gas 6.

2. Finely slice your red onions and courgettes/zucchini – if you have a mandolin, slice the courgettes on that. You want to slice them wafer thin and lengthways. Finely grate your cheese (if using).

3. Put a frying pan on a medium heat, add the olive oil and the sliced onions and cook for about 10 minutes until soft and sweet.

4. Lay the flatbreads on a baking sheet. If you've made them from scratch, wait for them to cool first before continuing.

5. Spread the crème fraîche over the flatbreads and then top with the onions, courgettes, the grated cheese or nutritional yeast, lemon zest, herb leaves and the salt and black pepper.

6. Bake for 8–10 minutes until everything has melted together and the flatbreads have slightly changed colour. Eat straight out of the oven while still warm.

TIP ***If you wanted to add some protein to this flatbread, sprinkle with a handful of crushed chickpeas/garbanzo beans before popping it in the oven.***

use gluten-free oats and gluten-free soy sauce or swap for tamari.

SERVES: 4 (2 GOOD-SIZE SAUSAGES EACH) | TIME: 35 MINUTES

JORDAN'S CHICKPEA AND SOY SAUSAGES

"I developed this vegan gluten-free sausage recipe for a cooking demo at a vegan festival aiming to provide a quick, easy, healthy alternative to traditional meat sausages. I love sausages so I wanted to recreate that familiar taste but without the animal cruelty. My taste testers all loved them – and my fellow chefs appreciated the flavour and their relatively straightforward preparation. I hope you do too. Double, triple or quadruple the recipe to make a big batch for your freezer."

EQUIPMENT

Large bowl, food processor, colander, spatula, wooden spoon, ice-cream scoop or tablespoon, frying pan

INGREDIENTS

50g/1¾oz dried soy chunks (also known as TSP chunks)
Boiling water, to cover
120g/4¼oz/scant 1 cup (drained weight) canned (or cooked) chickpeas/garbanzo beans (½ x 400g/14oz can)
60g/2¼oz/⅔ cup rolled oats
4 tablespoons cornflour/cornstarch (also called maizena)
2 tablespoons tomato purée/paste
3 tablespoons B12-enriched nutritional yeast
1 tablespoon tamari or dark soy sauce
2 teaspoons sea salt
2 teaspoons garlic granules
2 teaspoons dried oregano
¼ teaspoon dried thyme
¼ teaspoon dried rosemary
½ teaspoon black pepper
1–2 teaspoons olive oil

1. Place the soy chunks in a bowl and fully submerge with boiling water. Leave to rehydrate and plump up for at least 10–15 minutes.

2. In a food processor, combine all the ingredients – except the soy chunks and olive oil.

3. Tip the chunks into a colander to drain and press down on them using a spoon or bowl to squeeze as much water out as possible. I use my hands but it's easy to burn yourself as the water in the soya chunks is still hot. Add them to the food processor.

4. Process the mixture until it forms a smooth dough, like playdough. If necessary, use a spatula to scrape down the sides and bring everything to the middle of the processor. Add a little water, a teaspoon at a time, if needed, to achieve the right consistency, which should be like a thick paste.

5. Once the mixture is smooth, use an ice-cream scoop or tablespoon to portion the dough onto a wooden chopping board into 8 portions.

6. With slightly moist hands, roll each portion into a sausage shape. Use the palm of your hands and apply gentle pressure, rolling back and forth until you achieve the desired size – about 8–9cm/3¼–3½in long.

7. Leave the sausages to rest on a plate for 5 minutes in the refrigerator. They will firm up a little and become less sticky.

8. Heat a frying pan on a medium-high heat and add the olive oil. Place the sausages in the pan about 3–4 at a time, depending on the size of your pan – but no more, as you need space to move them around to fry. Put a lid on the pan.

 Once you've made this recipe a few times, experiment with different herbs and seasonings to craft your own custom vegan sausages. You could also shape the mix into burger patties or meatballs. Experiment and have fun.

What does the NHS recommend as the maximum amount of meat anyone should eat a day? Find out on p 370

9. Cook for 6–8 minutes, turning every couple of minutes or so, until the sausages are golden brown on all sides. When you take the lid off, watch out for the oil spitting.

10. While you fry the next batch of sausages, keep the ones you've just cooked warm in a low oven or just cover with a dish towel or bowl to keep warm. Voilà.

Serve as a healthy hot dog in a spelt flour flatbread with fresh toppings (see Asa's Fermented Ketchup on p 341 and potato wedges on p 111), or on top of mashed potatoes and gravy. I recommend tripling the recipe and making a big batch for the freezer.

TIP *To freeze the cooked sausages, ensure they are fully cooled, then wrap well in baking parchment and freeze for up to 1 month (they'll keep for longer than that but 1 month is best for optimal quality). To cook/reheat from frozen, heat 2 teaspoons of olive oil in a frying pan on a medium heat, then fry the sausages for 14–16 minutes, turning regularly, until hot all the way through.*

LET'S TALK ABOUT... TOXIC KITCHEN CULTURE

With Jordan Bourzig

I went to chef school in France when I was a teenager to learn classic gastronomy then went straight to work in restaurants. In many ways it was an incredible learning experience, but in many kitchens – not all, of course – it was quite toxic. To cope with the stress I numbed myself and became robotic. During high intensity services you can't think, you just have to act and respond constructively to your superiors' critiques, which can be pretty harsh. I worked in a Michelin-starred restaurant and that was a whole next level of stress and tension. I learned so much – it was amazing – but mostly I learned I didn't want to be a Michelin-starred chef. In that environment people lose themselves, they're on edge and very aggressive. They don't get enough breaks and they're not supported with their mental health. In France it was quite a macho culture and I saw chefs bullying female chefs and sabotaging their dishes. It was crazy.

I hear similar stories of kitchens in the UK and the US, with chefs working crazy hours, for days on end with no break. Some places have bad reputations for the way they treat their staff. I think there's a new generation of chefs emerging who don't want to replicate the trauma of their peers, are less ego-driven and are trying to make kitchens a safe and enjoyable place to work. When I started working in the MIH community meal service kitchen, I loved the energy and atmosphere. I'd never worked in a kitchen with so many lead female chefs and it was such a good energy and caring culture. We all came together to share our stories, our cuisines and ideas. Volunteers helped out for weeks or sometimes for just one shift, but they always came with the best energy. We were all cooking with a purpose for our community. That's a beautiful feeling. This level of human connection in a kitchen was a completely new experience for me. When people we had provided meals for said we had helped their family get through a rough time, it was very emotional and hugely rewarding. I was giving but I was also receiving, it was such a boost for my mental health and wellbeing. It was magical, and that feeling is what I'm about now as a chef.

 use gluten-free mustard and gluten-free vegetable stock.

SERVES: 4 | TIME: 1 HOUR, 20 MINUTES

JORDAN'S TOMATE FARCIE

"This is a comforting dish for me as it carries memories as rich as the flavours. My mum used to make it when I was a child. She's Portuguese but we lived in France and she loved this dish. It was popularized by several French chefs and writers such as Alexandre-Balthazar-Laurent Grimod de La Reynière (long name, yes!) in 1803 in his book Almanach Des Gourmands. *My mum made big batches, so when I came home from school as a teenager and she wasn't in, I'd warm up a portion from the freezer. My grandad grew massive tomatoes that Mum used for this meal. I've updated the family recipe by veganizing it and swapping white rice for protein rich quinoa. I love the lentil mixture as you can use it to make burgers or other dishes that require a plant protein."*

EQUIPMENT

Saucepan, sharp knife, frying pan, wooden spoon, bowls, deep ovenproof dish

INGREDIENTS (next page)

1. For the lentil stuffing, rinse and drain the lentils, then cook in a pan of boiling water for 15–20 minutes until tender. Drain and set aside.

2. While the lentils are cooking, prep the vegetables.
- Dice the onion.
- Finely chop the mushrooms into very small cubes.
- Thinly slice the garlic.
- Chop the parsley.

3. Sauté the onion in the oil in a frying pan on a high heat for 1 minute.

4. Add the mushrooms and garlic to the frying pan with the cumin and salt and cook for 5 minutes until the mushrooms reduce in size and go soft.

5. Add the miso paste and tomato purée/paste, stir and then take it off the heat.

6. Mix the mushroom mixture with the cooked lentils in a bowl.

7. Add the oats, nutritional yeast, mustard, black pepper and parsley to the lentils and mushrooms. Using clean hands or a wooden spoon, mix it together until combined. Taste, adjust the seasoning if needed, and set aside ready to stuff the tomatoes.

8. Preheat the oven to 180°C/350°F/gas 4.

9. For the tomato farcie, rinse the quinoa and put to the side.>>

Mr Organic
ITALIAN ORGANIC
EXTRA VIRGIN OLIVE OIL
COLD PRESSED
PERFECT FOR DRIZZLING, DIPPING, DRESSINGS AND ADDING FLAVOUR TO ANY DISH
500ml

INGREDIENTS

For The Lentil Stuffing

- 100g/3½oz/generous ½ cup dried Puy lentils
- 1 yellow or white onion
- 10–12 mushrooms
- 2 cloves garlic
- Medium bunch of fresh parsley (about 40g/1½oz)
- 2 tablespoons olive or rapeseed/canola oil, plus 2 teaspoons for frying
- 1 teaspoon ground cumin/jeera
- Pinch of sea salt
- 1 teaspoon brown rice miso paste
- 1 tablespoon tomato purée/paste
- 40g/1½oz/scant ½ cup rolled oats
- 1 tablespoon B12-enriched nutritional yeast
- 1 tablespoon yellow mustard
- Pinch of black pepper

For The Tomato Farcie

- 250g/9oz/1½ cups quinoa
- 4 large beefsteak tomatoes
- Pinch of sea salt
- 180ml/6fl oz/¾ cup vegetable stock
- 1 tablespoon dried herbes de Provence or dried mixed herbs
- A few fresh parsley or basil leaves or sprigs of thyme, to finish (optional)

10. Now let's prep the tomatoes. Chop the top quarter off a tomato and set it carefully aside to use later as a little hat. Now slice off a thin layer of the bottom of the tomato so it can stand more easily.

11. With a small knife, cut inside the middle of the tomato in a circular motion. Using a spoon, scoop out all the middle flesh, chop it and set it aside to use later. Repeat with the other tomatoes.

12. Now stuff the tomatoes with the lentil and mushroom mixture. Fill them to just above the top to create a little dome of filling poking out the top.

13. Place the quinoa in a deep ovenproof dish, add the salt, cover with the vegetable stock and the reserved tomato flesh and sprinkle over the dried herbs.

14. Place the tomatoes on top of the stock and quinoa – for now without the tops – and bake for 25 minutes, then bake for an additional 20 minutes with the hats on.

15. When ready, they should look soft enough to cut easily with a knife. Taste the quinoa to make sure it is cooked through (every oven behaves a little differently), but be careful not to burn yourself.

To serve, for each portion use a light-coloured plate to contrast with the red of the tomatoes. Make a small mound of quinoa (if you have one, use a ring mould to shape the quinoa) and then place a tomato on top. On top of each tomato either scatter with chopped fresh herbs or top with a sprig of herbs. Beautiful.

Chef Jordan and Sukhin leading a cooking demo at Vegan Life Live.

  use gluten-free soy sauce or swap for tamari.

MAKES: 4 SUSHI SANDWICHES; EACH FILLING MAKES ENOUGH FOR 4 SANDWICHES | TIME: 35-40 MINUTES (IF MAKING 1 FILLING); 1 HOUR (IF MAKING 2 FILLINGS)

SARA'S SCRAMBLED SEAWEED TOFU AND PULLED JACKFRUIT ONIGIRAZU

"Onigirazu or "sushi sandwich" is Japanese rice plus any fillings, wrapped up in a sheet of nori seaweed like an edible bundle/package. You don't need to be a pro to get it right and you can get enough filling in there for a substantial meal. I make 2 onigirazu per person. If you don't have nori sheets, you can make a rice bowl and top your rice with the fillings. If you're short of time, just make one filling."

EQUIPMENT

1 medium saucepan with lid, sharp knife, 2 frying pans, fine sieve/fine-mesh strainer, wooden spoon, spatula, small bowl

4 dried nori sheets (each filling makes enough for 4 sandwiches)

INGREDIENTS (next page)

JAPANESE RICE

1. Before cooking the rice, rinse and drain it 3 times in cold water. This makes the best sticky sushi rice. Add the dry rice and water to the pot you will cook it in, then rub the rice in the water to remove as much cloudy starch as possible. Drain and repeat twice more.

2. Drain off the rinsing water and add the measured water for cooking.

3. Cover and bring to the boil, then simmer for 15 minutes.

4. Remove from the heat without opening the lid and leave to rest for 5 minutes. Let it cool before using. You can use it warm or at room temperature – refrigerated rice won't stick together well.

SCRAMBLED SEAWEED TOFU FILLING

1. Finely chop the leek or spring onions/scallions, then sauté in 1–2 teaspoons of the oil in a frying pan on a medium heat until it softens.

2. Push to one side, then add the remaining oil to the pan. Drain the tofu, then add it to the pan and gently press down on the tofu to break it up.

3. Sprinkle the tofu with the turmeric, salt, sugar, garlic powder and wakame seaweed. Leave the tofu untouched for about 5 minutes, then stir gently to mix with the leek/spring onion.

4. Cover with a lid so the seaweed will expand from the moisture and cook gently for 5–10 minutes.

5. Serve hot or cold. It keeps in an airtight container in the refrigerator for up to 24 hours. >>

TAMARI

INGREDIENTS

For The Japanese Rice

300g/10½oz/scant 1¾ cups uncooked sushi rice

360ml/12fl oz/1⅓ cups water

For The Scrambled Seaweed Tofu Filling

½ small leek or 2 spring onions/scallions

2–4 teaspoons toasted sesame oil or any neutral oil

1 x 300g/10½oz block silken tofu (any tofu will work but silken works best)

¼ teaspoon ground turmeric

½ teaspoon black Indian salt (kala namak) or any sea salt

Pinch of sugar (I use coconut palm, but any sugar will work)

Pinch of garlic powder

1 teaspoon dry 'instant' wakame seaweed (optional)

For The Savoury Pulled Jackfruit Filling

1 x 400g/14oz can jackfruit

3–4 tablespoons odourless coconut oil

1–2 teaspoons toasted sesame oil (optional)

For The Jackfruit Filling Sauce

1–2 tablespoons tamari (or any Japanese soy sauce)

1 teaspoon brown rice miso paste

1 teaspoon toasted sesame oil

1 teaspoon coconut palm sugar or soft dark brown sugar

1 teaspoon gochugaru (Korean chilli powder), or ½ teaspoon each paprika and mild chilli powder

½ teaspoon garlic powder

SAVOURY PULLED JACKFRUIT FILLING AND SAUCE

1. Drain the jackfruit and break into smaller chunks.

2. Heat the coconut oil and sesame oil (if using) in a frying pan, then add the jackfruit. You can use different oil but coconut oil gives a "meat-like" mouthfeel to the jackfruit.

3. Fry on a medium-high heat, stirring occasionally, until reduced to half its original volume – this will take 20–25 minutes. Add another teaspoon of coconut oil if it looks dry – it should look slightly glossy.

4. Stir the sauce ingredients for the jackfruit filling together in a bowl. When the jackfruit is done, remove from the heat, add the sauce and mix until glossy.

5. Serve hot or cold. This keeps in an airtight container in the refrigerator for a few days.

TO ASSEMBLE

1. Now assemble the sandwiches by wrapping the rice and fillings into the nori, like a small bundle/package, 1 nori sheet per sandwich. To make 8 sandwiches, double the quantity of nori sheets and rice and make both fillings.

2. Place a nori sheet on a work surface in a diamond position – one corner pointing toward you

3. Use 150–200g/5½oz–7oz of cooked rice per onigirazu. The rice can be warm but not hot. Place half of the rice portion in the middle of the nori, using wet fingers (stops the rice from sticking), and make a square shape 1.5–2cm/⅝–¾in thick and 8cm/3¼in wide. It seems counter-intuitive but don't line the edge of the rice up with the nori sheet, instead rotate it along one of the rice's corners to point to the middle of each sheet edge. (There are plenty of tutorials online!)

4. Top the rice with some tofu or jackfruit filling, levelling it out to an even thickness. Then add another layer of rice. Once you've made a few of these you will work out how thick you can make the layers.

5. Now to wrap! Imagine sealing a package. Fold the nori sheet from the right and left edges into the middle and stick them together. You may need to moisten the parts of the nori sheet you're sealing together.

6. Do the same with the top and bottom corners – pulling them together to meet in the middle to make a tightly-wrapped nori square.

7. Using a very sharp knife, cut it in half and serve. These are best served freshly made.

use gluten-free soy sauce or swap for tamari, and gluten-free gochujang.

SERVES: 4 | TIME: 1 HOUR

REBECCA'S BIBIMBAP BOWL

"Bibim *means to mix and* bap *means rice. This dish was born out of laziness to take all the banchan, side dishes, and eat them all at once, to get rid of all the small bowls and plates. I ate this dish when I was little without calling it bibimbap. When my mom didn't feel like cooking, she'd chuck all the banchan into a big bowl with sesame oil and gochujang and mix it. It was such a nice meal because the family would gather around one big bowl and eat in close proximity, so I always thought it was fun. It's a lot of work to prepare the veg separately – so you can skip all the blanching and sautéing by steaming everything together in a steamer basket. This vegan bibimbap recipe is vibrant and customizable, allowing you to enjoy the rich flavours and textures of the natural vegetables.*"

EQUIPMENT

Saucepan, sharp knife, large stainless steel steamer, frying pan, wooden spoon, small bowl, 4 ramekins

INGREDIENTS

400g/14oz/2¼ cups uncooked sushi rice

3 carrots

4 courgettes/zucchini

12 shiitake, oyster or button mushrooms

800g/1lb 12oz/2 cups spinach

400g/14oz/2 cups bean sprouts

500g/1lb 2oz/2 cups medium-firm tofu

Pinch of sea salt

1 tablespoon neutral oil, such as rapeseed/canola or avocado oil

2 tablespoons dark soy sauce

Pinch of black pepper

For The Sauce

2–3 cloves garlic

5 tablespoons vegan gochujang

4 teaspoons rice or apple cider vinegar

6 tablespoons sesame oil

150–200ml/5–7fl oz/⅔ cup–scant 1 cup water

To Serve And Garnish

300g/10½oz vegan kimchi (75g/2¾oz per portion, but I'm Korean, so I usually double this)

4 teaspoons sesame oil

Sesame seeds

1. Put the rice on to cook (see Cooking Staples on p 56).

2. Now we're going to prepare the vegetables.
- Cut the carrots and courgettes/zucchini into matchsticks.
- Finely slice the mushrooms.
- Shred the spinach (if using whole/large leaves).
- Finely dice the garlic for the sauce and set aside.

3. Using a large stainless steel steamer basket, add the carrots and steam them for 5 minutes.

4. Now add all the remaining vegetables – the courgettes, mushrooms, spinach and bean sprouts and steam together for another 5 minutes. Set a timer so you don't forget to turn them off after 5 minutes.

5. While the veg is steaming, work on your tofu. Press the water out of it and cut into 1.5cm/⅝in cubes or thin 1.5cm/⅝in-thick slices. Your preference. Sprinkle the salt over the tofu cubes/slices.

6. Sauté the tofu in a frying pan with the oil on a medium heat until golden brown on both sides, about 5 minutes. Pour the soy sauce over the tofu, add the black pepper and fry for an additional 3 minutes. Set aside.

7. Time to make the sauce. In a small bowl, combine all the sauce ingredients and stir until well mixed, adding enough water to your preferred thickness.

8. Pour into 4 small ramekins so everyone has their own portion of sauce.

HOW TO ASSEMBLE THE BIBIMBAP

1. Place a serving of cooked rice into each person's bowl.

2. If presenting for a dinner party or you want to do it restaurant-style, arrange the prepared vegetables (carrots, courgettes, mushrooms, spinach, bean sprouts and kimchi) neatly around the edges of the rice and add the tofu in the middle. Most Koreans don't arrange it when cooking at home.

3. Drizzle with the sesame oil and sprinkle with sesame seeds to garnish.

4. Serve with the gochujang sauce on the side.

TO EAT THE BIBIMBAP

1. Add the desired amount of gochujang sauce to the bowl.

2. Mix everything together thoroughly. Hence people not arranging it when cooking at home. Enjoy your delicious, colourful and nutritious vegan bibimbap!

  use gluten-free miso paste and gluten-free soy sauce or swap for tamari.

SERVES: 4 (MAKES 12 SUMMER ROLLS) | TIME: 30 MINUTES

SONALI'S RAINBOW SUMMER ROLLS

"Over the years I've experimented with numerous variations of these Summer Rolls. One version stands out, which I've prepared for a few private clients. Their enthusiastic feedback confirmed what I had hoped – the miso adds a subtle depth of umami, while the aromatic Thai basil infuses the rolls with a fresh, vibrant flavour that elevates them to another level."

EQUIPMENT

Sharp knife, saucepan, colander, small bowl, medium bowl, large, shallow dish, damp dish towel, serving platter

INGREDIENTS **(next page)**

1. First let's prepare the ingredients.
- Cut the carrots and cucumber into thin matchsticks. Deseed the red peppers and cut into thin matchsticks.
- Pick the leaves off the mint and Thai basil stems. Discard the stems.
- Roughly chop the peanuts or bash them in a pestle and mortar.

2. Cook the rice vermicelli noodles according to the package instructions. While the rice noodles are cooking, thinly slice your ginger for the dressing and the red chillies for the peanut dipping sauce. Set aside.

3. Once the noodles are cooked, drain and rinse under cold water to stop the cooking process. Set aside.

4. In a small bowl, combine all the dressing ingredients. Mix well and set aside to allow the flavours to infuse.

5. In a separate bowl, mix the peanut butter, soy sauce and caster sugar for the dipping sauce. Add the sliced chillies to the sauce and stir until smooth. If the sauce is too thick, you can thin it with 1 teaspoon of warm water at a time, until it reaches your desired consistency.

6. Fill a large, shallow dish the size of your rice paper sheets with warm water. Dip one sheet into the water for 10–15 seconds, or until it becomes pliable. Or, mist each rice paper with a water spray bottle.

7. Carefully lay the softened rice paper on a clean, damp dish towel or chopping board.

8. In the middle of the rice paper, place a small handful of rice vermicelli noodles and a few slices of carrot, cucumber and red pepper. Add a few mint and Thai basil leaves and a sprinkle of chopped peanuts. Arrange the filling in the length you want your final summer roll to be.

INGREDIENTS

For The Rice Paper Rolls
- 4 large carrots
- 1 cucumber
- 2 red peppers
- Medium bunch of fresh mint
- Small handful of fresh Thai basil
- 160g/5¾oz/scant 1¼ cups roasted, salted peanuts
- 300g/10½oz dried rice vermicelli noodles
- 12 rice paper sheets

For The Dressing
- Large thumb-size piece root ginger
- 4 teaspoons white miso paste
- 4 teaspoons dark soy sauce
- Juice of 1 lime
- 2 teaspoons shichimi togarashi or Japanese 7 spice

For The Peanut Dipping Sauce
- 2 fresh red chillies
- 300g/10½oz/1⅓ cups smooth peanut butter
- 4 tablespoons dark soy sauce
- 2–4 tablespoons caster sugar (optional)

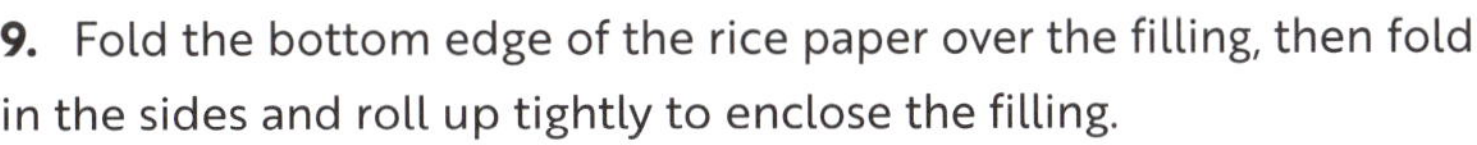

9. Fold the bottom edge of the rice paper over the filling, then fold in the sides and roll up tightly to enclose the filling.

10. Repeat with the remaining rice paper sheets and fillings.

11. To serve, arrange the rice paper rolls on a serving platter. Serve with the peanut dipping sauce on the side and drizzle the prepared dressing over the rolls or serve on the side for additional flavour.

Enjoy your fresh and healthy plant-based rice paper rolls with the tangy peanut dipping sauce.

SERVES: 4 (8-10 DUMPLINGS EACH AS A MAIN)
TIME: 1½ HOURS (IF MAKING THE SKINS FROM SCRATCH), 30 MINUTES IF USING READY-MADE SKINS

FLO'S HAPPY CHEF'S GYOZA

"If you haven't made gyoza before, please try. It's easier than you think. When I introduce them to a class, participants leave happy and satisfied with what they've made. I give everyone the same amount of flour and water and somehow everyone's dough comes out differently and needs to be adjusted. After we've prepped the veg, we sit around the table and a peaceful focus descends as everyone masters the pleating technique. There are lots of different ways to fold dumplings. Whatever method you choose, remember they most likely won't be perfect the first time, but you'll be surprised at how quickly you pick it up. They can be eaten as a main course, side or a first course. If eating for a main course, you may want to add stir-fried veggies or a ramen broth. Experiment and have fun."

EQUIPMENT

2 large bowls, measuring jug/pitcher, spatula, dough scraper (if you have one), sharp knife, damp dish towel to cover dough, rolling pin, 8cm/3¼in diameter cookie cutter, whisk, small bowl, large frying pan with a tight-fitting lid

INGREDIENTS (next page)

1. If using ready-made wrappers, go to step 8 to make the filling.

2. If not, let's make gyoza wrappers! Sift your flour into a large bowl.

3. Boil the water and decant into a measuring jug/pitcher. Add the salt to the water and stir until it dissolves.

4. Add the hot water to the flour, a little at a time, stirring with a spatula as you go. Keep stirring until all the flour and water are combined to form a dough. You may need to add more water, a teaspoon at a time – but go easy. For the last stage, use your hand to form the dough. If it feels a little sticky, add more flour, a teaspoon at a time. Practise makes perfect here.

5. Dust a generous pinch of flour over a clean, flat work surface, transfer the dough onto it and knead for 10 minutes (see How to Knead on p 374). You might find it helpful to set a timer as it's easy to lose track of time. The texture of the dough should be smooth.

6. Using a dough scraper, cut the dough in half. If you don't have one, break it apart with your hands.

7. Shape each half into a long sausage, about 3–4cm/1¼–1½in or just under in thickness. Wrap in cling film/plastic wrap (sorry, yes, for this it's important) and let it sit at room temperature for 30 minutes. While the dough is sitting, start your filling. **>>**

Clearspring
ORGANIC
SHICHIMI
TOGARASHI
七味

INGREDIENTS

32–40 ready-made fresh gyoza wrappers

OR

For the homemade gyoza wrappers

240g/8½oz/1¾ cups plain/all-purpose flour, plus extra for dusting

120–150ml/4–5fl oz/½–⅔ cup water

½ teaspoon sea salt

For The Filling

100g/3½oz/¾ cup frozen peas

400g/14oz mixed mushrooms

20g/¾oz fresh chives

2 cloves garlic

Thumb-size piece root ginger

1 tablespoon dark soy sauce

1½ teaspoons sesame oil

1 teaspoon shichimi togarashi or Japanese 7 spice (optional)

¼ teaspoon white pepper

Pinch of sea salt

Cornflour/cornstarch, for dusting

Sesame or vegetable oil, for frying

200ml/7fl oz/scant 1 cup water

For The Dipping Sauce

2 tablespoons dark soy sauce

1 tablespoon rice vinegar

To Serve And Garnish

Chilli oil (optional) (if you've not used shichimi togarashi but like heat, you will want to add this)

1 tablespoon toasted sesame seeds

NOW LET'S PREPARE THE FILLING

8. - Defrost your frozen peas.
- Finely chop the mushrooms, chives and garlic and grate the ginger.

9. Add the prepped ingredients to a bowl, then add all the remaining ingredients – except the cornflour/cornstarch, oil for frying and water – and mix well. We are not going to pre-cook the gyoza filling – it will cook when you boil, steam or fry your whole gyoza. Set the filling aside. **If using pre-made gyoza wrappers, go to the next page to learn how to assemble the gyoza.**

10. If the dough has rested for 30 minutes (if not, use this time to clean down), unwrap the dough now.

11. Sprinkle a clean, flat work surface with flour (or cornflour if you plan to freeze the gyoza – see Tip below), take each dough sausage and cut them into about 2cm/¾in-wide pieces (about 20 pieces per dough sausage as you'll make about 40 gyoza in total). Cover the dough with a damp dish towel to keep it moist – this is important so don't skip this step.

12. Now to shape the dough pieces into wrappers. Pick a single portion of dough up and roll into a ball. Place it onto your floured surface and press down with the palm of your hand into a flat circle.

13. Using a rolling pin, roll out the dough on one side, rotate 90 degrees, roll again, rotate 90 degrees, roll again, until you've completed a full circle and rolled out a thin, flat circle.

14. If you'd like perfectly round wrappers (I like them like this), use a 8cm/3¼in diameter round cookie cutter and cut out as many wrappers as you can from what you've rolled out. Stack in a pile with a little cornflour sprinkled on top of each to prevent sticking. Keep the stack under a damp paper towel to stay moist.

15. Scrunch any leftover dough into a ball and repeat steps 12–15 until you've used up all the dough.

TIPS & TRICKS

What Is Shichimi Togarashi or Japanese 7 Spice? p 379

TIP *The One Directional Pleating Method*

1. Place a teaspoonful of filling in the middle of your gyoza wrapper.

2. Slightly dampen your fingers.

3. Bring the wrapper ends together nearest your hand.

4. You're going to keep one half of the wrapper skin smooth and unpleated, and the other side you're going to do multiple pleats in one direction to create a curved, half-moon shape.

5. To do the pleats, fold the wrapper back on itself 0.5cm/¼in and gently press.

6. Repeat this process along the whole of one side and seal at the end by pinching the wrapper together.

7. As a final step, you might wish to run your fingers along the top ridge of the gyoza pinching it together.

NOW LET'S ASSEMBLE THE GYOZA

1. Dust a plate or tray with a thin layer of cornflour. Work with one wrapper at a time and cover the other wrappers with a damp dish towel to prevent them from drying out.

2. Hold a wrapper in the palm of your hand and use your finger to moisten around the edge with water.

3. Place a teaspoonful of filling in the middle, then fold and pleat the edges together (see Tips left). Place each one, bottom-down, on the plate/tray you've prepared with the cornflour.

4. Repeat until you've used all the wrappers and filling. Cover with a damp dish towel.

5. Make the dipping sauce by whisking the soy sauce and vinegar together in a small bowl.

6. Pour a thin layer of sesame or vegetable oil into a large frying pan (with a lid) and place it on a medium heat, let it warm up a little, then place the gyozas in, bottom-down. I work around the edge of the pan so they're all hugging each other facing the same direction in a circle, and then I place two or three in the middle. But that's me!

7. They will start to brown quickly on the bottom. If the heat is uneven and some are browning more than others, move the dumplings around. This takes about 5 minutes.

8. When the colour is golden brown on the bottom, CAREFULLY pour in the water – it will make a ferocious noise as it hits the pan. Cover the pan immediately with a lid, then turn the heat down a bit.

9. After 5 minutes, see if the water has evaporated. If not place the lid back on until it has. Once the water has evaporated, if you like them really crispy on the bottom, leave on the heat for a few minutes.

10. When ready, turn them onto a plate and serve with the dipping sauce and chilli oil (either drizzled over or for dipping) and garnish with a sprinkling of sesame seeds. Well done!

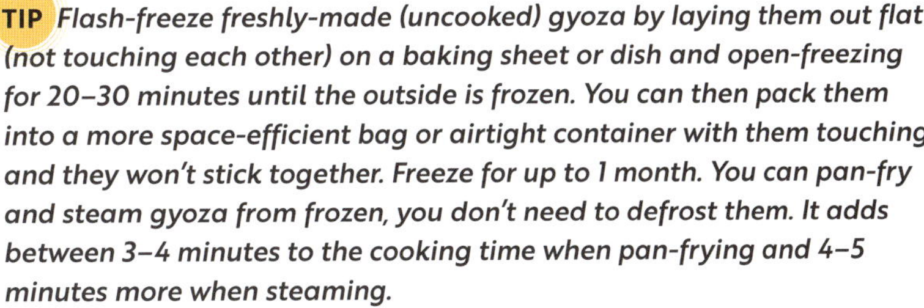

TIP *Flash-freeze freshly-made (uncooked) gyoza by laying them out flat (not touching each other) on a baking sheet or dish and open-freezing for 20–30 minutes until the outside is frozen. You can then pack them into a more space-efficient bag or airtight container with them touching and they won't stick together. Freeze for up to 1 month. You can pan-fry and steam gyoza from frozen, you don't need to defrost them. It adds between 3–4 minutes to the cooking time when pan-frying and 4–5 minutes more when steaming.*

use gluten-free vegetable stock.

SERVES: 4 (WITH LEFTOVERS) | TIME: 45 MINUTES

FLO'S AFGHAN-STYLE BEAN CURRY

"I love the simplicity and speed of this recipe, a good crowd-pleaser and a great one to batch-cook for the freezer. How something this simple can be so moreish and tasty always astounds me. I've cooked thousands of portions of this dish. It means a lot to me that it's what we served at MIH's former finance officer Amber's wake. It was simple, nourishing and comforting at a time when we were all very shocked and sad. I hope she would have liked it."

EQUIPMENT

Colander, large saucepan or stew pot, hand-held/immersion blender, sharp knife

INGREDIENTS

2 x 400g/14oz cans kidney beans
2 tablespoons rapeseed/canola oil
1 tablespoon ground coriander
2 teaspoons ground cumin/jeera
1 teaspoon dried mint
2 x 400g/14oz cans plum tomatoes
2 red onions
4 cloves garlic
300ml/10½fl oz/1¼ cups vegetable stock
Pinch of sea salt
Pinch of black pepper

To Serve And Garnish

Your choice of grain (such as basmati rice, short-grain brown rice or noodles). I usually do basmati rice with ½ teaspoon of turmeric powder to give it a lovely yellow colour.
Small bunch of fresh coriander/cilantro
1 red onion

1. Drain and rinse your cans of kidney beans and set aside.

2. Add 1 tablespoon of the rapeseed/canola oil to a large saucepan or stew pot and warm it up on a medium heat for 1 minute.

3. When it's hot, add the ground coriander and cumin. When they smell fragrant, add the dried mint and the canned tomatoes.

4. Mash the tomatoes down with a fork. Cook for 5 minutes.

5. Meanwhile, finely dice your red onions and thinly slice your garlic.

6. Use a hand-held/immersion blender to blend the tomatoes and spices into a smooth sauce. Empty the sauce into a bowl and set aside, then rinse your pan/pot out ready for the next step.

7. Add the remaining oil to the pan/pot and warm up on a medium-low heat for 1 minute. Add the onions and cook for 10 minutes, stirring occasionally, until softened and starting to turn golden.

8. Next add the garlic and continue to cook for 5 minutes, stirring often so it doesn't burn.

9. Once the onions are nice and caramelized, add the vegetable stock, spiced tomato sauce, kidney beans, salt and black pepper.

10. Simmer, uncovered, on a low heat for about 15 minutes. Adjust the seasonings to taste. Pop your grain of choice on to cook now while the dish is simmering (see Cooking Staples on p 55).

11. Now prepare your garnish – chop your fresh coriander/cilantro and dice your red onion. Garnish the curry with the coriander and chopped onion and serve with your cooked grain of choice. It looks really beautiful served with yellow basmati rice cooked with ground turmeric, a pinch of black pepper and a few saffron threads if you have it.

TIPS & TRICKS
Chopped Versus Plum Canned Tomatoes
p 379

LET'S TALK ABOUT... COMMUNITY CARE

With Flo Francis

Community care in the context of food means many things to me. One part of what we do at MIH is the gathering of people, and giving people time to connect, which is so much easier over food. At the same time as connecting, we're nourishing. We all like to be fed in different ways. Whether that's through conversation or connection or memory. When I cook with community members, I try to connect with each person. I try to love them all in that space and time and make each individual person feel seen and like they all matter – because we do all matter. For the people I don't see but I cook meals for in the wider community – I cook for you like I cook for myself, never any less. I cook you the best meal I've got, with the best ingredients we can afford with the best standard of nourishment and the best flavours. After all, we all deserve a good meal.

London's always been a hard place to cover all your basic costs, but since I moved here in 2000 the difference is astronomical. Although the media never talks about it anymore the cost-of-living crisis is ongoing and prices are still going up. With astronomical rents and mortgages to pay to live in this city, many people are compromising on what they eat, or not eating at all. And that's wrong. It saddens me that so many people don't have access to enough nutritious food. It does something energetically to you. If you're already down, it double downs you. You exist on a lower frequency. It might seem like providing a free meal isn't a lot but in many ways it is. It's a stepping-stone to work from. One thing that's taken care of so you can focus on improving other areas of your life. There are so many people who know how to cook and what good food is, but they don't have the funds or they're living in hostels with poor facilities so can't provide their family good food. This infuriates me and I'm so glad to be able to provide meals for families in this situation. We drop meals at a nearby school twice a week and for those families that pick them up that's one fewer thing to think about, to find money for, and with what you save you can put more money on your Oyster Card (London travelcard) or take the kids out or whatever.

That's what's so great about distributing and utilizing surplus food; it benefits us all and together we're saving food that would otherwise be wasted. Nobody should be going without, there's enough for us all to share. And that's what I love about Made In Hackney. It's not us and them – them over there that need help and us over here giving it. No. It's us. It's we. It's community.

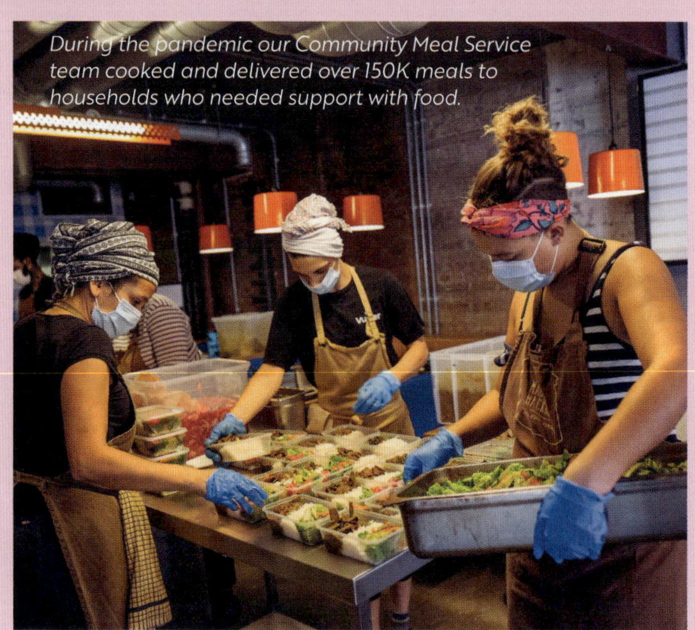

During the pandemic our Community Meal Service team cooked and delivered over 150K meals to households who needed support with food.

IN CONVERSATION WITH...

Community Kitchens in Peru

A conversation with MIH's Global Plant Kitchen mentees Alison Hamje and Jorge Arango of Ollas Comunes Veganas, about the world's largest nationwide network of community kitchens.

When did Peru's thriving network of community kitchens begin?

Alison: They existed long before the Spanish colonizers arrived in the 16th century. Communal living was the way of life back then. Even to this day, in communities in the highlands, which is where the Incan Empire thrived, throughout the Andes, the land is owned communally and needs are met communally. The community kitchens we have today emerged in the 1980s during the violent clashes between the Shining Path and the Army, which caused rural people to move into the cities in droves. It was a true emergency. People didn't have anything. They'd left their whole way of life behind. So the women got together to cook in order to feed everyone. Immersed in this story is the story of women's rights and activism in Peru. It was a huge victory when the kitchens became formally recognized for their work and received support from the government. It meant the work and rights of women were starting to be recognized.

How does the network of kitchens work today?

Alison: There are two types of kitchens in Peru, which for an English translation we're calling community kitchens and communal kitchens. The community kitchens are more formal in terms of venue, equipment, funding, frequency of operation and staff training. And the communal kitchens, which are the one's we've been supporting, are more spontaneous and pop up in response to emergencies. They're often run by women who are not trained, supported or funded in any way. They know their community has a need, so they set up a kitchen and cook. In the Quechua and Aymara indigenous languages there are words that refer to the different types of community-orientated cooperation projects and workdays. It's part of Incan culture. It's really something to see. The community spirit is so strong and heart-warming. Jorge has volunteered in these kitchens much longer than I have – in four or five different districts of Lima since 2020 when the pandemic hit and these kitchens were vital.

In what way does the government support the kitchens today?

Jorge: The government supports them with funding and supplies during times of crisis, most recently during the COVID-19 pandemic. Many people in Lima and across Peru relied on community and communal kitchens for their food. The government sent supplies – beans, rice, spaghetti and other ingredients traditional to Peruvian meals. They also provided equipment and gas cylinders for cooking. And some basic training in food hygiene, first aid, how to manage budgets and how to report on all the help they've received.

Alison: It's important for people in the UK and Global North to visualise these kitchens as something very rustic. An open, outdoor space with no walls, no running water, tables or furniture. Just three rocks with some sticks underneath and a pot on top. That's the most extreme example, but it's common. And then there are kitchens located in a large room or hall with some gas stoves, a big pile of supplies and one basic tap for cooking and washing. It's basic even in the better equipped kitchens.

How many community and communal kitchens are there in Peru?
Jorge: No one really knows because the kitchens come and go. They pop up when they're needed, then close again. The government website says there are over 13,000 community kitchens, but these are the more established ones, so if you include the communal ones, the figure would be higher.

Is everyone a volunteer or are some people paid to work in the kitchens?
Alison: No one is paid. It's voluntary. You get free meals and take donations home if there is a surplus.

How often do the kitchens open and how much are meals?
Alison: Monday to Fridays – on school days. One of the main objectives of the kitchens is to ensure the children go to school with some food. That is the main focus of food security in Peru. So usually the kitchens provide breakfast and lunch. Culturally, lunch is the main meal of the day.

Jorge: In times of emergency, food is often free. But generally, the kitchen charges two to four soles, about 50 US cents, to cover costs. If you have no money, most kitchens will serve you anyway. Usually there's one lead volunteer person there every day supported by different volunteers. Roles are rotated to share the responsibility. There's sometimes a few seats and tables but not always. When the food is ready a bell is rung or some kind of noise is heard through the community, or a text message is sent out. Soon everyone starts showing up with their "tuppers" – bowls and containers. Everyone has to bring dishware for the people they're taking food for. It's not a communal dining experience, people chat while in the queue, then take the food home.

Do most people in Peru support the kitchens? Are they associated with right or left politics?
Jorge: Most people support the kitchens, yes. During election times politicians use the kitchens for publicity and to improve their image by donating rice and potatoes. They take advantage as opposed to really wanting to help the community.

You mentioned it's mainly women cooking in the kitchens. Is this still the case?
Jorge: In Peru the majority of people working in jobs are men while women work at home. So when emergencies happen women are most able to activate the kitchens. I'm a Scout leader so I'm used to working at social events that help people. Vegan activism is usually focused on campaigning, pamphleting on the street – but working in the kitchens is very different. We spread the message of the many benefits of vegan food while helping people.

The larger kitchens prepare 200 to 400 meals daily. But most of the kitchens we work with serve 100 meals.

The same reason I started MIH. How easy is Peruvian cuisine to make plant-based?
Jorge: Peruvian gastronomy is a fusion of different traditions with influences from China – called chifa cuisine – Japan, Italy and the Middle East. Dishes in Peru are usually rice and potatoes, vegetables and beans, with chicken or pork. We swap the meat for soy chunks, soy beans or seitan. We use a lot of beans – at least ten different types. Some of the women cooking think of it as a game, adding the right amount of spices and seasoning so nobody notices it's not meat. When we first started using the dehydrated soy, the people we were cooking with thought it was dog food because they'd never seen it before and complained. But once we cooked with it they were won over. Ceviche is a very popular dish made from fish. The soy version works very well. And vegan burgers – people love the burgers.

Tell us about the work of Ollas Comunes Veganas in the kitchens.
Jorge: We work with about 25 to 30 kitchens in Lima and one in the north of the country. Some operate independently and receive donations of soy from us. In other kitchens we're more involved and offer training on how to prepare the meals and cook with soy. Sometimes we bring in a vegan nutritionist to do a class. The women are

busy with children and family so making training part of the meal prep time works best. The larger kitchens prepare 200 to 400 meals daily. But most of the kitchens we work with serve 100 meals.

A key motivation is to improve the nutritional value of food for those most in need.

What practical motivation is there for people to adopt vegan products in Peru?
Alison: Imagine you're living way up the side of a mountain. And the only way out is to climb 150 steps down a ladder with no railings to the market. And then you need to carry all your shopping back up again. A 15kg (33lb) sack of dehydrated soy that needs no refrigeration is very practical. It's a very liveable, cost effective and practical way to cook and prepare your food.

Jorge: A key motivation is to improve the nutritional value of food for those most in need. Many people in Peru get by on coffee and bread for a meal. This is not okay for children. They need better nutrition. And likewise, people who are ill or disabled or have had accidents and can't work, they need support to eat well. It's part of a vegan philosophy to help those in need. Vegan food is the best type of food to provide this support and nourishment.

Is plant-based eating part of Peruvian culinary culture?
Alison: To an extent yes, although a lot of meat is also eaten. Peru is a bread basket with a vast variety of grains, beans and varieties of produce. In the new year we have something called The Seven Grains Ritual where we wish friends and family abundance in the new year by giving them a cone or jar containing quinoa, lentils, barley, rice, cañihua, split peas, corn, white and black beans and one traditional huayruro seed for good luck. It matters what order you put them in and each has a different meaning. But essentially it's all you need to bring you abundance in the new year. So yes, it's in the culture.

    GF use gluten-free soy sauce or tamari.

SERVES: 4 | TIME: 25 MINUTES

MARK'S SWEET AND SOUR FRIDGE FORAGE STIR FRY

"Fridge forage is when we're making the most out of the ingredients we already have instead of wasting them to buy new ones for a specific recipe. It's better for the environment and our pockets. This fridge forage stir fry is versatile and the sauce is a healthier and simpler spin on the popular takeout dish. The flavour totally pops in a way that means you'll make it again and again. I loved teaching for MIH – the conversations I had with participants put energy and love into my week and are now treasured memories."

EQUIPMENT

Sharp knife, bowl, wok or frying pan, saucepan, wooden spoon

INGREDIENTS

1 onion

185g/6½oz mixed fridge-foraged raw vegetables (mushrooms, pepper, green beans – whatever you have)

1 x 400g/14oz can pineapple chunks in fruit juice (optional)

1 tablespoon oil (coconut, sesame, vegetable – whatever you have)

180g/6¼oz/1 cup uncooked basmati rice or 240g/8½oz dried noodles of choice

1 x 400g/14oz can chopped tomatoes

1 x 400g/14oz can butter/lima or cannellini beans

¼ teaspoon dried chilli/hot pepper flakes (optional)

For The Sauce

2 tablespoons vinegar (rice vinegar would be great but use whatever vinegar you have; avoid malt vinegar if gluten-free)

2 tablespoons date syrup

2 tablespoons dark soy sauce

1. First let's prep the veg and pineapple.
- Thinly slice your onion.
- Slice the fridge-foraged vegetables into ribbons, matchsticks or small chunks (your preference).
- Drain the can of pineapple (if using) and set the chunks aside (you can drink the juice).

2. Now make the sauce by stirring all the sauce ingredients together in a bowl. Set aside.

3. In a wok or large frying pan, heat the oil on a high heat. Add the onion and cook, stirring often, for about 3 minutes until it starts to lose moisture and change colour.

4. Add the fridge-foraged vegetables and stir-fry for another 3 minutes. If you like your veg very crunchy, stir-fry for less time.

5. While your veg is stir-frying, boil a pan of water to cook either your basmati rice or noodles. See Cooking Staples on p 55.

6. Add the tomatoes and pineapple (if using) and stir-fry for 5 minutes.

7. Drain and rinse the beans, add to the pan with the chilli/hot pepper flakes and stir.

8. Add the sauce to the wok or frying pan and stir until the mixture has thickened slightly. This should take around 2 minutes.

9. Taste and adjust the sweet/sour balance to your liking with additional date syrup, vinegar and/or soy sauce.

Serve in bowls with either the basmati rice or noodles.

LET'S TALK ABOUT... THE FOOD WASTE PROBLEM *by Sarah Bentley*

Food waste is a global issue. And surprisingly, according to the UN Environment Programme's Food Waste Index, it's not just a "rich nation" issue, but an "all nations" one – albeit the reasons for it often differ. In 2022 (more up to date figures are yet to be crunched), the world wasted 1.05 billion tonnes of food a year – that's one-fifth of all available food. This is in addition to the 13% of the world's food being lost in the supply chain. But despite this huge figure the majority of food waste occurs in households – 631 million tonnes versus the 290 million in the food service sector and 131 million in the retail sector. These staggering losses happen against a backdrop of rising global hunger. Right now over 783 million plus people are hungry and a third of humanity faces food insecurity. And yet the food lost in households every day could provide 1 billion meals – which is more than enough to feed everyone. A painful irony. Despite this irony, it's important to note food waste isn't the root cause of hunger. War, poverty, imperialism, climate change, inequality, rampant unchecked capitalism and food being weaponized to starve people to death – are the causes of hunger. So saving food doesn't tackle any of these issues, but that doesn't mean it still isn't a great thing to do to reduce the carbon emissions of our food supply. I'll leave you with one more startling fact: food waste and loss generates 8–10% of global greenhouse gas emissions – nearly five times the total emissions of the aviation sector. Wild.

OUR TOP FIVE FOOD WASTE INTERVENTIONS

1 REDISTRIBUTION

In 2016, France ruled it was illegal for retailers to dispose of food surplus and that they needed to find charities supporting people experiencing food insecurity to donate it to. Alas, other countries have not followed suit, but across the world businesses and charities have formed partnerships and created innovative projects such as community shops, refrigerators, pantries, food co-ops, community kitchens, community feasts and pay-what-you-feel cafés that all utilize food surplus.

2 INDUSTRY UTILIZATION

We love the growing market of products that utilize food that would otherwise be wasted. From smoothies and crisps made from wonky fruit and veg, ale made from stale bread and sweeteners made from byproducts of tequila – this is a powerful way to reduce waste at an industry level.

3 ROOT TO TIP COOKING

Given that the bulk of food waste occurs in the home, this is surprisingly one of the most important interventions. Our Hannah Walker has some great tips on p 373 that revolve around fermenting, preserving, dehydrating, blending and freezing ingredients to utilize as many parts of fresh produce as possible – including bits most commonly discarded such as peels and stalks.

4 INNOVATION

New machinery and processes either on farms or in factories to reduce waste, particularly for big businesses that grow or process a lot of food, can save vast amounts of food. For example, controlled atmosphere storage regulates the air composition in storage facilities to reduce post-harvest losses.

5 LOCALIZED COMMUNITY SOLUTIONS

We love localized community-driven solutions such as gleaning – the practice of people being invited onto farmland to harvest unwanted crops – and green energy-powered refrigeration and freezing systems shared by communities who are otherwise off-grid.

use gluten-free vegetable stock cube, gluten-free lasagne sheets and gluten-free flour blend.

SERVES: 4 GENEROUSLY | TIME: 1 HOUR 20 MINUTES

MARK'S LASAGNE

"I like this recipe as it takes a little bit of skill to make but is simple enough to still be quite relaxing. It's a delicious, homely meal you can enjoy over good conversation or a podcast. It tastes even better the next day as the flavours have had time to develop. When I've made it in community classes it's always gone down well and people suggested twists such as adding chilli or dark chocolate to the tomato sauce. It's not the Italian approach, but why not. Experiment and enjoy."

EQUIPMENT

Sharp knife, large non-stick saucepan, medium non-stick saucepan, wooden spoon, metal whisk, 40 x 30cm/16 x 12in ovenproof lasagne dish, oven

INGREDIENTS (next page)

1. Let's prepare our ingredients.
- Wash the red lentils and drain.
- Finely slice the onion, garlic and mushrooms (if using).
- Cut the aubergine/eggplant and courgette/zucchini into small cubes – about 1cm/½in. Deseed the red pepper and cut into small cubes as well.
- If using kale, remove any tough stalks and shred the leaves.

2. Heat the olive oil (for the vegetable mixture) in a large, non-stick saucepan on a medium heat and fry the onion for 3–4 minutes, or until softened and lightly browned.

3. Add the aubergine/eggplant, courgette/zucchini, red pepper and mushrooms (if using) and fry for 12 minutes, stirring regularly until soft.

4. Add the garlic and cook for a few seconds more, then stir in the lentils, canned tomatoes, tomato purée/paste (if using), the dried oregano and crumbled stock cube.

5. Refill one of the tomato cans with water and pour into the pan. Stir well, bring to a simmer and cook for 15 minutes on a medium heat, stirring regularly.

6. Add the baby spinach or shredded kale to the pan, a handful at a time, and cook for 1–2 minutes more – a bit longer for kale.

7. Meanwhile, preheat the oven to 180°C/350°F/gas 4.

8. While the vegetables are simmering (before the spinach/kale is added), let's make the white sauce.

9. Heat the olive oil in a medium saucepan. When it is hot, add the flour and cook for 1 minute, stirring. Gradually stir in the milk, **>>**

ITALIAN ORGANIC
TOMATO
PUREE

INGREDIENTS

100g/3½oz/generous ½ cup dried red split lentils
1 large onion
2 cloves garlic
75g/2¾oz button mushrooms (optional)
1 small aubergine/eggplant
1 courgette/zucchini
1 red pepper
150g/5½oz baby spinach leaves or kale
4 tablespoons olive oil
2 x 400g/14oz cans chopped tomatoes
2–4 tablespoons purée/paste (optional)
2 teaspoons dried oregano
1 low-salt vegetable stock cube
9–10 dried egg-free lasagne sheets

For The White Sauce
3 tablespoons olive oil
100g/3½oz/¾ cup plain/all-purpose flour
800ml/28fl oz/scant 3½ cups oat milk
3 tablespoons B12-enriched nutritional yeast
1 bay leaf
¼ teaspoon ground nutmeg
Pinch of sea salt
Pinch of black pepper

then add the nutritional yeast, bay leaf, nutmeg, salt and pepper.

10. Turn up the heat slightly to bring the sauce to a simmer, whisking constantly with a metal whisk on a medium heat for 4–5 minutes, or until smooth and thickened.

11. To assemble your lasagne, spread a third of the vegetable mixture over the base of a 40 x 30cm/16 x 12in ovenproof lasagne dish and cover with a single layer of lasagne sheets. Top with another third of the vegetable mixture (don't worry if it doesn't cover evenly) and a second layer of lasagne.

12. Remove the bay leaf from the white sauce, then pour just under half of it gently on top of the lasagne sheets, then top with the remaining vegetable mixture.

13. Finish with a final layer of lasagne and the rest of the white sauce.

14. Bake for 35–40 minutes, or until the pasta has softened and the topping is browned and bubbling.

15. Remove from the oven and leave to stand for 5 minutes before cutting to allow the filling to settle. Enjoy.

TIP WHY WASH GRAINS & LENTILS?

Grains and lentils are small crops and can contain pieces of grit and debris, so are best washed before using. Rinsing also releases surface level starch – which is why the water goes cloudy. Although not essential, rinsing surface level starch off means they are less likely to stick together when cooking.

LET'S TALK ABOUT... LANGUAGE MATTERS *by Sarah Bentley*

When utilizing food surplus in community support services such as community shops, fridges, pantries, cooking classes and food banks (if you're still using that term, we don't) – semantics matters. Being offered "waste" doesn't conjure up dignity, quality or care. But being offered food surplus and by utilizing it you are "saving food" and "doing your bit for the environment", it's the same thing, just more appealingly described. When describing wastage within the food industry, calling it what it is – waste – is fine. But when you're offering it out as a key source of nourishment for your community, you need to exercise stringent quality control and reduce stigma of eating surplus by not referring to it as waste.

SERVES: 4 GENEROUSLY | TIME: 40 MINUTES, PLUS 1–2 HOURS YEAST ACTIVATION TIME; 1 HOUR PROVING TIME

FI'S PIZZA NIGHT SPECIAL

"This is a versatile, straightforward dough recipe that can be used as a base for numerous dishes. Making pizza from scratch may seem like a faff but once you've discovered how easy, cheap and delicious it is, you won't look back. And when making pizza at home, you can use whatever toppings you have in – get experimental and go beyond what you see in restaurants and takeouts. I've made this recipe with so many families and young people over the years and it's always a big hit."

EQUIPMENT

Small bowl, large bowl, medium-sized bowl, clean dish towel, sharp knife, food processor or pestle and mortar, saucepan with lid, two baking sheets, rolling pin

INGREDIENTS

For The Pizza Base

- 7g/⅛oz/dried active yeast granules
- 320ml/11fl oz/scant 1½ cups warm water
- 1 teaspoon date syrup
- 500g/1lb 2oz/3½ cups strong wholemeal/whole-wheat or spelt flour, plus extra for dusting
- 1 teaspoon sea salt
- 2 tablespoons extra virgin olive oil, plus extra for greasing

(Continued next page)

MAKE THE PIZZA BASE DOUGH

1. First make the dough for the pizza base. In a small bowl, mix together the yeast, a teaspoon or two of the warm water and the date syrup, then leave in a warm place – this wakes the yeast up and it's great if you can do this step a couple of hours, or at least 1 hour, before you want to make your pizza.

2. Once the yeast mixture is ready, in a separate larger bowl, sift the flour and salt together, then add the olive oil and yeast mixture.

3. Now the fun part. Mix with your fingertips in a clockwise motion, then pour in a third of the remaining warm water, continuing to mix with your fingertips – the mixture should start to look like breadcrumbs.

4. Keep mixing with your fingertips and pour in half of the remaining water – the mixture now looks like shredded fabric – then pour in the remaining water, keep mixing and the mixture should start to look like a sticky dough.

5. Shape the dough into a ball and leave in the oiled bowl, covered with a clean dish towel, in a warm place to prove for 1 hour. When the dough has roughly doubled in size, it's ready. Depending on the temperature of the room, this could be less or more than an hour. Now start prepping your toppings. >>

For The Toppings

2 peppers (different colours – red, yellow, green or orange)

50g/1¾oz mushrooms or pitted black olives (for umami taste)

1 red onion

50g/1¾oz (drained weight) canned sweetcorn or canned pineapple chunks (for sweet taste) (optional)

8 sun-dried tomatoes (optional)

1 teaspoon dried oregano or mixed herbs

Handful of rocket/arugula leaves

For The Tomato Sauce

1 red onion

Handful of fresh basil leaves

2 cloves garlic

½ tablespoon olive oil

1 x 400g/14oz can chopped tomatoes

2–4 tablespoons tomato purée/paste (optional)

For the Cashew Cheese Crumbs

100g/3½oz/scant 1 cup raw cashews

2 tablespoons B12-enriched nutritional yeast

1 teaspoon sea salt

½ teaspoon garlic powder

MAKE THE TOPPINGS, TOMATO SAUCE AND CASHEW CHEESE CRUMBS

1. First let's prepare the ingredients.

- Deseed and slice the peppers. Slice the mushrooms or olives.
- Chop 1 red onion and slice the other. Keep them separate.
- Chop the pineapple (if using) and the sun-dried tomatoes into smaller pieces.
- Thinly slice your basil and slice your garlic into little squares or use a garlic crusher. If you find garlic repeats on you, see Tips & Tricks on p 374 about crushing versus slicing.
- Blitz all the cashew cheese ingredients in a food processor or break down and combine in a pestle and mortar. This is a dry mixture. Set aside.

2. For the tomato sauce, add your olive oil to a saucepan and heat on a medium heat until hot, then add the chopped red onion and garlic and cook gently to infuse the oil with its flavour, about 3 minutes.

3. Now add the chopped tomatoes and tomato purée/paste and let it simmer for 20 minutes. Start with the lid on to infuse the flavours, then after about 10 minutes remove the lid to allow the liquid to cook off and thicken. Simmer until the sauce has reduced and become thicker.

4. Take the sauce off the heat, add the basil leaves and set aside.

5. You can use the sliced red onion (for the toppings) raw and add to the top of the pizza before going in the oven, or lightly fry it or do a quick caramelization. Adding it raw to cook in the oven is the healthier option but caramelized is a classic pizza topping (see Tip).

TIP ***Caramelizing onions can take up to 45 minutes, but you can do a quick version by adding the sliced red onion to a pan with ½ tablespoon of olive oil, fry on a high heat for 5 minutes, then add a teaspoon of vinegar (apple cider, balsamic or malt works) and ¼ teaspoon of soft brown sugar or date syrup (or whatever sweetener you have) and fry for 10 minutes.***

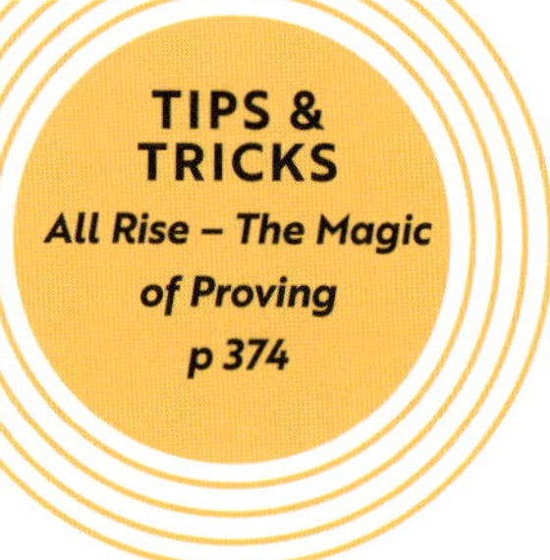

TO ASSEMBLE AND COOK THE PIZZAS

1. Preheat the oven to 200°C/400°F/gas 6 and line 2 baking sheets with baking parchment.

2. Divide the dough into four equal-size balls.

3. Scatter flour on a flat surface or large wooden chopping board and rub your rolling pin with flour – this is to stop the dough sticking. Take one of the balls of dough and roll out to your desired pizza base thickness, about 0.5–1cm/¼–½in, and transfer to a lined baking sheet. Do this for a second ball of dough as well.

4. Smear the tops of the first two pizzas with a thin layer of the tomato sauce and evenly spread the raw toppings of your choice across the pizza, then top with some of the cashew cheese crumbs.

5. Bake in the oven for 20 minutes on a low shelf (or bake one on the low shelf and the other on the middle shelf) until golden and crispy. If baking the two pizzas on separate shelves, take the highest one out when ready, move the bottom one up and bake for another 2 minutes or so to fully cook. Serve hot.

6. Repeat this process for the other two pizzas.

More On Garlic p 369

LET'S TALK ABOUT… TAKING THE PRESSURE OFF FAMILY MEAL TIMES *With Fi McCallister*

One of the things I love most about cooking with families and young people is that when you cook together communally it really takes the pressure off. Conversation flows freely and organically. People open up and share about their home cooking, cultural foods and food experience. I've had numerous families come to sessions with children with really challenging selective eating that have told me the classes substantially increased the range of foods their children will try and eat, which has been a huge relief. I think the transformation happens as the young people are invested in the creative process of cooking. They're handling the ingredients themselves and they have agency to adapt things and customize dishes to their preference. The pressure is also off the carers as they're not leading the class and they didn't buy the ingredients so the whole thing is more relaxing and enjoyable – and that opens up the possibility to try new things and for behaviours associated with control or stress to adapt. I always ask the young people to try things but reassure them they won't be forced to finish their portion or to eat something they don't like. I just ask them to give it a go. We spend time talking about what we like and don't like and why, and developing a vocabulary around it. The beauty of plant-based ingredients is that it's very safe for children to handle both when raw and cooked, so they can really get familiar with the ingredients. Seeing the young people get more confident with cooking as the weeks pass is really satisfying, and it's particularly sweet when they say now they've been part of the process they'll try to help more with the washing up at home.

use gluten-free vegetable stock cubes.

SERVES: 4 | TIME: 1½ HOURS

MAURO'S PUMPKIN, GINGER & LEMON RISOTTO

"Risotto is a dish I grew up seeing my mum cook at home, especially if you come from the north of the country like me where it is seen as the perfect Sunday afternoon dish. During the autumn when pumpkins are in season, and the weather starts to cool, rice and pumpkin make an amazing pairing. The twist of adding ginger I learnt from a Brazilian chef called Malu' on one of my many cookery experiences. Roasting the pumpkin in the oven, then adding the hazelnuts for a crunchy bite give it an extra special touch."

EQUIPMENT

Sharp knife, frying pan, baking sheet, large non-stick saucepan with lid, blender or masher, sieve/ fine-mesh strainer, medium non-stick saucepan, wooden spoon

INGREDIENTS (next page)

1. Preheat the oven to 180°C/350°F/gas 4.

2. Cut your pumpkin or butternut squash into large, rough (4cm/1½in) chunks, then cut off the skin and deseed. If you cannot cut a pumpkin or squash, pop it in the oven whole and bake for 1 hour.

3. After baking, you can easily remove the skin with a sharp knife, deseed, then cut it into chunks. Pan-fry the chunks in a frying pan on a medium heat with 1 tablespoon of the olive oil, all the herbs, the garlic and a pinch of salt and pepper, for 10 minutes to ensure the flavours infuse.

4. If you have cut the raw pumpkin/squash, pop your chunks on a baking sheet, drizzle over 1 tablespoon of the olive oil, then add the herbs and garlic. Sprinkle over a pinch of salt and pepper. Bake for 30 minutes until tender.

5. Now let's prep the ingredients for the vegetable broth (if using).
- Roughly chop all the veggies into 2.5cm/1in chunks.
- Or, if you're not making your own, add the crumbled stock cubes to the boiling water and stir. Go to step 6.

6. Add all the veggies to a large saucepan or pot with a lid, cover with the cold water and add the garlic, bay leaf, salt and black pepper.

7. Bring to the boil, then turn down to a low-medium heat, cover with a lid and simmer for 1 hour.

INGREDIENTS

1 medium pumpkin or butternut squash (about 500g/1lb 2oz)

2½ tablespoons extra virgin olive oil

Small bunch of fresh sage (20g/¾oz)

Small bunch of fresh rosemary (20g/¾oz)

Small bunch of fresh thyme (20g/¾oz)

2 bay leaves

2 cloves garlic

2 vegetable stock cubes (optional)

1.2 litres/40fl oz/5 cups boiling water (optional)

50g/1¾oz root ginger

Juice of ½ lemon

10–12 whole (skin-on) hazelnuts

500g/1lb 2oz/scant 2¾ cups risotto, arborio or carnaroli rice

3 tablespoons B12-enriched nutritional yeast

Sea salt and black pepper

For The Homemade Vegetable Broth (if making)

1 onion

1 carrot

1 celery stalk

1.2 litres/40fl oz/5 cups water

1 clove garlic

1 bay leaf

Pinch of sea salt

Pinch of black pepper

8. Now let's get the rest of the risotto ingredients ready.
- Grate the ginger.
- Roll the lemon (to release the juice) and squeeze the juice from one half into a small bowl.
- Roughly chop the hazelnuts (if using) and set aside.

9. When the broth (if using) is ready, strain out the vegetables and set aside (you won't need these now for the risotto but you could keep them to make a soup). Keep the liquid in the pot (or the stock-cube made stock) on a medium heat as it needs to be simmering when we use it for the risotto.

10. Take the pumpkin/squash out of the oven, remove the herbs and garlic (again, you won't need these now, but you could add them to a soup). Add the pumpkin/squash to a blender and blend into a purée.

11. Let's prepare the risotto. Add the rice to a sieve/fine-mesh strainer and wash under cold running water for 30 seconds. To save water, you can add to a bowl, stir vigorously, drain the water and repeat.

12. Put a medium, non-stick saucepan or pot on a low-medium heat. Add the rice and toast until it becomes translucent. Use a wooden spoon to stir it. This should take 1 minute

13. Turn up the veggie broth/stock so it's gently bubbling, then start to gradually add it to the pan/pot, a ladleful or so at a time until the rice is covered. Keep stirring. Once the rice has absorbed this broth/stock, gradually add the rest in stages, stirring until each ladleful is absorbed.

14. After 9 minutes (roughly half the risotto cooking time), add the pumpkin purée and mix together, then continue to add the rest of the broth/stock as before until absorbed.

15. When the risotto is cooked (usually after 18 minutes, but check on the packaging as it varies depending on the brand), turn the heat off and stir in the ginger, the lemon juice, the rest of the olive oil and the nutritional yeast. If needed, add a pinch more salt and pepper.

Serve the risotto with the hazelnuts sprinkled on top. Enjoy.

use gluten-free vegetable stock and gluten-free flat breads.

SERVES: 4 GENEROUSLY | TIME: 1 HOUR

YASMIN'S SQUASH, LENTIL AND APRICOT ONE-POT STEW

Yasmin Khan is an award-winning cookbook author, broadcaster – and former MIH project manager. She says: *"Not quite a soup or a stew but something in between, this nourishing meal is inspired by the Moroccan soup harira but with added squash and dried apricots in sweet spices. Serve on its own or with flatbreads or toast. My husband was vegan when we met, which inspired me to veganize a lot of classic recipes. MIH changed the way I ate and cooked; I learned so much and for that I'll always be grateful."*

EQUIPMENT

Sharp knife, 1 large non-stick saucepan with lid, wooden spoon, pestle and mortar

INGREDIENTS (next page)

1. First let's prepare the ingredients.
- Finely dice the onions and celery.
- Mince the garlic.
- Peel, deseed and dice the butternut squash into small chunks.
- Halve the dried apricots.
- Rinse and drain the chickpeas/garbanzo beans and set aside.
- Rinse and drain the red lentils and set aside.
- Finely chop the fresh coriander/cilantro (for the finish/garnish).

2. Heat the vegetable oil in a large pot on a medium heat. Add the onions and sauté until softened, stirring occasionally, for about 15 minutes.

3. Add the celery, garlic and all the spices apart from the saffron. Fry for 2 minutes.

4. Boil the 720ml/24fl oz/3 cups of water in a kettle. Add the lentils and this boiling water to the pan. Cover and cook until softened, about 12 minutes.

5. Grind the saffron strands (if using) with the sugar in a pestle and mortar. Add the 2 tablespoons of just-boiled water and leave to steep.

6. When the lentils are soft, add the squash, saffron, chickpeas/garbanzo beans, apricots, vegetable stock, tomatoes, rice, ¾ teaspoon of salt and ½ teaspoon of black pepper to the pan. Stir to combine.

7. Cover and simmer on a medium-low heat, stirring occasionally, until the squash is completely cooked and beginning to melt into the stew. This will take 25–30 minutes. >>

INGREDIENTS

2 onions
2 celery stalks
4 cloves garlic
350g/12oz butternut squash
10 dried apricots
1 x 400g/14oz can chickpeas/garbanzo beans
170g/6oz/1 cup dried split red lentils
3 tablespoons vegetable oil
1½ teaspoons ground cumin/jeera
1½ teaspoons ground coriander
1 teaspoon smoked sweet paprika
½ teaspoon ground cinnamon
½ teaspoon ground ginger
720ml/24fl oz/3 cups water (plus 120ml/4fl oz/½ cup extra if needed later)
¼ teaspoon saffron strands (optional)
Pinch of sugar
2 tablespoons of just-boiled water
500ml/17floz/2 cups vegetable stock (made from 1 stock cube)
1 x 400g/14oz can chopped tomatoes
45g/1½oz/¼ cup white basmati rice
Sea salt and black pepper

To Finish And Garnish

Large handful of fresh coriander/cilantro leaves (optional)
3 tablespoons extra virgin olive oil, plus extra for the flatbreads/toast
Juice of ½ lemon
Dried chilli/hot pepper flakes

Flatbreads or toasted sourdough, to serve

Add the extra 120ml/4fl oz/½ cup (boiling) water if the stew is dry. While the stew is cooking, you can clean down and set the table.

8. In the last 5 minutes of cooking, add most of the chopped coriander/cilantro and the olive oil to finish.

9. Taste and season as needed with the lemon juice and more salt and black pepper. Serve garnished with the remaining coriander/cilantro and some chilli/hot pepper flakes.

10. Serve with flatbreads or toasted sourdough, drizzled with extra virgin olive oil. The flavours improve after the stew has rested overnight (in the refrigerator, then reheat to serve) and it also freezes well so is ideal for batch cooking.

TIP ***Freeze the stew in an airtight container for up to 3 months. Defrost, then reheat gently until piping hot to serve.***

TIPS & TRICKS
Getting to Know Saffron p 375

"The classes have inspired me to eat better, healthier, and how to do so for less money."

SERVES: 4 GENEROUSLY | TIME: 1 HOUR LEISURELY COOKING

SAMI'S MUSAQA'A

"Musaqa'a (also spelled Musaqqā'a) is a traditional dish that is popular in several Middle Eastern and Mediterranean countries, particularly in Palestine, Egypt, Lebanon, Syria and Turkey. The dish is often cooked in a pan or oven-baked, made with layers of aubergines, tomatoes and, depending on the regional variation, other vegetables. My mum, who passed away when I was six, used to make the dish in the summer and serve it at room temperature, perfect for hot days. I like to think of my book Falastin *and all my cooking as love letters to my mum."*

EQUIPMENT

2 large baking sheets, sharp knife, large bowl, wooden spoon, large frying pan

INGREDIENTS (next page)

1. Preheat the oven to 220°C/425°F/gas 7 and line two large baking sheets with baking parchment.

2. Chop the aubergines/eggplants into 3cm/1¼in cubes and place them in a large bowl. Add 75ml/2½fl oz/⅓ cup of the olive oil, 1 teaspoon of salt and 4 grinds of black pepper.

3. Mix together, then tip out and spread onto the lined baking sheets.

4. Place one baking sheet on the middle shelf and the other on the high shelf in the oven and roast for 30 minutes, swapping the baking sheets around halfway through, until the aubergines/eggplants have softened and lightly browned. Remove from the oven and set aside.

5. While the aubergines are roasting, prepare the other vegetables and chickpeas/garbanzo beans.
- Dice the onion and crush the garlic.
- Roughly chop the tomatoes. Deseed and roughly chop the green peppers.
- Roughly chop the coriander/cilantro.
- Drain and rinse the chickpeas/garbanzo beans.

6. Now let's make the sauce. Add the remaining olive oil to a large frying pan and place on a medium-high heat. Add the onion and cook for about 5 minutes until softened.

7. Add the garlic, chilli/hot pepper flakes, cumin, cinnamon and tomato purée/paste, stir and cook for another minute.

8. Add the chopped tomatoes, green peppers, chickpeas, canned tomatoes, water, 1¼ teaspoons of salt and a good grind of black >>

INGREDIENTS

5 medium aubergines/ eggplants
100ml/3½fl oz/scant ½ cup olive oil, plus extra to serve
1 onion
5 cloves garlic
2 plum tomatoes
2 green peppers
10g/¼oz fresh coriander/ cilantro (average size of a package in supermarkets)
1 x 400g/14oz can chickpeas/ garbanzo beans
1 teaspoon dried chilli/ hot pepper flakes
1¼ teaspoons ground cumin/jeera
½ teaspoon ground cinnamon
2 teaspoon tomato purée/paste
1 x 400g/14oz can chopped tomatoes
200ml/7fl oz/scant 1 cup water
Sea salt and black pepper

pepper. Reduce the heat to medium and cook for 20 minutes with no lid.

9. Stir in the roasted aubergine and three-quarters of the coriander/ cilantro and cook for 5 more minutes, still keeping the lid off.

10. When ready to serve, top with the remaining coriander, drizzle over a teaspoon of olive oil and serve either warm or at room temperature.

Serve the dish with pickles, olives and lots of bread for mopping up all the lovely juices. Alternatively, musaqa'a can be served with cooked rice, couscous or other grains.

Sami Tamimi visiting our community meal service.

use gluten-free breads or pittas.

SERVES: 4 | TIME: 1 HOUR, PLUS 2–3 HOURS (OR OVERNIGHT) RESTING TIME

ROSHNI'S HERBED CHICKPEA KUKU SABZI

"This is my version of the Iranian herbed omelette that I developed for my supper club 8 Plates. It's high in protein, gluten-free and very adaptable. I shared this recipe in a Plant Prospects workshop, I've used it for community cooking classes and made it for my Iranian friends at my other work, which was slightly nerve-racking, but thankfully they loved it. It's a great example of shared food histories being used to build community bonds. If you can't find barberries, you can use dried sour cherries or cranberries."

EQUIPMENT

Whisk, large bowl, 20cm/8in round or square cake pan, baking sheet, blender/food processor (optional), sharp knife, spatula, sieve/fine-mesh strainer, small bowl

INGREDIENTS (next page)

1. For the batter, in a large bowl, whisk together the chickpea/gram flour, salt, water and olive oil, then cover and leave to rest for 2–3 hours at room temperature or overnight in the refrigerator. Leaving batter mixtures to rest allows the flour to absorb the water fully, usually giving a lighter, more enjoyable result.

2. Preheat the oven to 180°C/350°F/gas 4. Line a 20cm/8in round or square cake pan with baking parchment and grease with olive oil.

3. Roughly chop the walnuts and hazelnuts, add to a baking sheet and roast for 5 minutes. Keep the oven on after removing the nuts as you'll need it again soon. Set the nuts aside.

4. Let's prep the veg and herbs.
- Finely chop the spring onions/scallions and spinach.
- Finely chop the coriander/cilantro and chives.
- Alternatively, you can blend the spring onions, spinach and herbs together in a blender to make a green paste. For future recipes, you can experiment using dill, wild garlic, mint and other greens.
- I keep the barberries/cherries/cranberries whole, but you can cut them into smaller pieces if you like.

5. Now add all the remaining batter ingredients to the rested batter and stir together to combine.

6. Pour the mixture into the prepared cake pan. Bake for 45–50 minutes at 180°C.

INGREDIENTS

For The Batter

- 90g/3¼oz/⅔ cup chickpea/gram flour
- 1 teaspoon sea salt
- 240ml/8½fl oz/1 cup water
- 1 tablespoon olive oil, plus extra for greasing
- 40g/1½oz/⅓ cup mixed roasted walnuts and whole (skin-on) hazelnuts (to save budget, use just walnuts)
- 3 spring onions/scallions
- 30g/1oz spinach
- 100g/3½oz fresh coriander/cilantro
- 20g/¾oz fresh chives
- 1 tablespoon barberries or dried sour cherries or dried cranberries
- 1 tablespoon lemon juice

For The Cucumber-Yogurt Dressing, To Serve (optional)

- ½ cucumber
- 1 clove garlic
- 4 tablespoons plain vegan yogurt

To Serve

- Pitta bread
- 4 teaspoons pickles (such as pickled mixed veg)

7. While it's baking, you can make your cucumber-yogurt dressing. Cut the cucumber into 1.5cm/⅝in cubes and finely slice the garlic.

8. Add the yogurt to a small mixing bowl. Add the cucumber and garlic to the yogurt, stir and then set aside.

9. The sabzi is baked when the top looks set – it will have cracked slightly and the edges will be slightly browned. Don't test with a cocktail stick/toothpick – this is misleading as the dish will set more when cooling. Remove from the oven and leave to cool in the tin for 20–30 minutes.

10. Once cooled, carefully remove the sabzi from the tin and cut into 8 slices (2 slices per portion). Serve warm or cold with pitta bread, the pickles and the cucumber-yogurt dressing (if using).

TIP ***The sabzi keeps in an airtight container in the refrigerator for up to 3 days and it also freezes well (cut into slices first) for up to 1 month (defrost before eating). If you want to serve it hot, you can fry the slices in 1–2 teaspoons of olive oil on a medium heat until crisp on each side.***

Sami Tamimi and team after his Ultimate Falafel fundraising class for us at Leiths Cookery School.

RAHA'S KHORESHT GHEYMEH & SALAD SHIRAZI

"Khoresht Gheymeh (also spelt Gheime) is a beloved Persian dish that dates back to the Safavid dynasty in the 16th century. It traditionally features lamb or beef – which we will replace with mushrooms – cooked with split peas, onions, tomatoes and spices to make a really flavourful stew. Over time, Khoresht Gheymeh has evolved with regional variations, but its essence as a comforting and nourishing dish has remained. Today, it holds a cherished place in Persian cuisine, served in my family home, restaurants and enjoyed by people around the world. Salad shirazi is a refreshing Persian salad. It is a delicious and traditional accompaniment to most Persian stews."

SERVES: 4 | TIME: 1½ HOURS; PLUS OVERNIGHT SOAKING

KHORESHT GHEYMEH

EQUIPMENT

Large bowl, medium-sized bowl, cup, sharp knife, stew pot or large saucepan with lid, frying pan, wooden spoon

INGREDIENTS (next page)

1. Rinse the split peas, then place in a bowl, cover with cold water and leave to soak overnight. The next day, drain and rinse again.

2. Let's prepare the vegetables.
- Peel your potatoes, then cut them into thin sticks and submerge in a bowl of cold water for 15–20 minutes to remove the starch.
- Dice your onion and finely chop your mushrooms.
- If using saffron, crumble the strands into a cup, add the ice cube and let the it melt while you're cooking. We're going to add it to the cooked rice at the end.

3. Heat the vegetable oil in a stew pot or high-sided pan on a medium heat. Add the chopped onion and a pinch of the salt and cook until golden, about 6–10 minutes.

4. Add the turmeric and stir, then add the mushrooms and cook until they're soft, about 5 minutes.

5. Next add the soaked yellow split peas and the tomato purée/paste and sauté for about 2–3 minutes.

6. Pierce the dried limes with a fork, or squeeze the juice from the fresh limes, then add to the pot.

7. Now pour in enough of the measured water to cover the yellow split peas and the dried limes (if using). Add the remaining pinch of salt, the black pepper and cinnamon. **>>**

INGREDIENTS

- 215g/7½oz/scant 1¼ cups dried yellow split peas
- 1 medium russet or other floury potato
- 1 large onion
- 500g/1lb 2oz chestnut/cremini mushrooms
- Pinch of saffron strands (optional)
- 1 ice cube (optional)
- 3–4 tablespoons vegetable oil
- 2 pinches of sea salt
- 1 teaspoon ground turmeric
- 3 tablespoons tomato purée/paste
- 4 dried limes or 2 fresh limes
- 600ml/20fl oz/2½ cups water
- Pinch of black pepper
- ½ teaspoon ground cinnamon
- 180g/6¼oz/1 cup uncooked basmati rice
- 4–5 tablespoons rapeseed/canola oil

8. Bring to the boil and boil for 5 minutes, then lower the heat. Cover the pot with a lid and leave the stew to simmer for 1–1½ hours to really let the flavours settle. This will allow the split peas to soften and give time for the flavours to develop. Set a timer in case you forget it! Once ready, if you find that the consistency is too watery, turn up the heat for 5–10 minutes to reduce it.

9. When the stew is coming to the end of its cooking time, cook the basmati rice (see Cooking Staples on p 55).

10. Remove the potatoes from the water and pat dry.

11. Heat the rapeseed/canola oil in a non-stick frying pan on a medium heat until hot. Add the potato sticks and shallow-fry until they're crispy and golden – this should take around 4–6 minutes.

12. If there is excess oil, remove the potato sticks from the pan and pat dry with paper towels to absorb the oil. Add the potato sticks to the top of the stew immediately before serving.

13. Serve with the steamed basmati rice. If you're adding saffron, mix half of the cooked rice with the prepared saffron until fully combined and yellow. Add the yellow rice over your white rice and enjoy!

SERVES: 4 | TIME: 10 MINUTES

SALAD SHIRAZI

EQUIPMENT

Sharp knife, bowl, lemon squeezer/juicer

INGREDIENTS

- 3 salad tomatoes
- 1 cucumber
- 1 onion (red or yellow)
- Bunch of fresh parsley
- Bunch of fresh mint
- 1 tablespoon dried mint
- 2 limes
- 3 tablespoons olive oil
- Pinch of sea salt
- Pinch of black pepper

1. First prepare the ingredients.
- Finely chop the tomatoes and cucumber.
- Finely chop the onion.
- Finely chop the parsley and mint.

2. In a bowl mix the chopped ingredients together with the mint.

3. Squeeze the juice of the limes into the bowl.

4. Add the olive oil, salt and pepper and then finish by stirring it all together to combine. Serve.

SIX KEY INGREDIENTS FOR PERSIAN COOKING

1 TURMERIC *(or 'Zardchoobe) – indispensable in Persian cuisine for its vibrant colour, earthy flavour and anti-inflammatory benefits, enriching everything from stews and rice dishes to kebabs and soups.*

2 SAFFRON *– cherished in Persian cooking for its aroma, deep golden hue and delicate flavour, elevating rice dishes, desserts and stews to another level. It is the most expensive spice in the world and is known as red gold.*

3 ROSE WATER *– a treasured ingredient that adds a subtle floral essence to sweets, beverages and savoury dishes.*

4 SUMAC *– another staple in Persian cuisine, prized for its tangy, lemony flavour that brightens and balances kebabs, rice dishes and salads.*

5 POMEGRANATES *– the national fruit of Iran, pomegranates are integral to Persian cuisine, celebrated for their sweet-tart flavour and jewel-like seeds that enhance salads and desserts, and stews using pomegranate molasses.*

6 PISTACHIOS *– Iran's prized export, these nuts are cherished for their rich, nutty flavour and crunchy texture, adding depth to sweets, rice dishes and other savoury recipes.*

SERVES: 4 | TIME: 40–45 MINUTES

NENA'S EGUSI SOUP WITH UNRIPE PLANTAIN FUFU

"Egusi soup is a stew-like soup made with ground melon (egusi) seeds and is very popular in West Africa, with considerable local variation, both regionally and across countries. This is the Igbo variation, Igbo being my ethnic tribe in Nigeria. Africans call what Europeans know as stew, soup. We love to have it with lots of chunky bits in it that we call 'obstacles' in pidgin English. If the soup is thin with hardly any veg or meat, people complain and say it's too scanty. So make sure you make a nice thick soup with plenty of obstacles that no one could call scanty. It freezes well, so double up the quantities and make a batch for future meals."

EQUIPMENT

Sharp knife, large saucepan/stew pot

INGREDIENTS

- 1 onion
- ½ red Scotch bonnet chilli (see Scotch Bonnet for Newbies on p 379)
- 90g/3¼oz spinach
- 15g/½oz fresh uziza leaves (optional) (see p 380), or use extra spinach or 1 teaspoon dried uziza seeds
- 300g/10½oz whole egusi seeds, or 120g/4¼oz ground egusi
- 450g/1lb mushrooms
- 180ml/6fl oz/¾ cup red palm oil
- 1½ teaspoons iru (fermented locust beans – p 182) or dark soy sauce
- 500ml/17fl oz/2 cups water, plus (optional) extra 250ml/9fl oz/1 cup if the soup is too thick
- 3 tablespoons vegetable bouillon powder or 2 vegetable stock cubes (ideally low-salt)
- 70g/2½oz dried soy chunks (also known as TSP chunks)
- ½ teaspoon sea salt

1. Let's prepare the ingredients.
- Cut the onion into thin slices.
- Thinly slice the Scotch bonnet, including the seeds if you like heat (without the seeds if you want less heat).
- Slice the spinach and fresh uziza (if using) into ribbons.
- If using whole egusi seeds, blend into a flour.
- Quarter the mushrooms.

2. Pour the red palm oil into a large saucepan or stew pot and heat on a medium heat for 1 minute.

3. Add the sliced onion and iru or soy sauce and stir-fry for a minute, or until golden. Add the ground egusi and mix well, then stir-fry for 5 minutes.

4. Add the 1 litre/35fl oz/4¼ cups of water, the Scotch bonnet and bouillon powder or crumbled stock cubes, cover with the lid and cook on a medium heat for 20 minutes. Stir at intervals to stop the soup from burning or sticking to the bottom of the pan/pot. The soup/stew is done when the oil has separated from the mix.

5. Now add the mushrooms, soy chunks and salt and cook for a further 5 minutes. Add the extra water if the soup is too thick to enjoy and heat through. The soup/stew should be thick not watery.

6. Finally, add the spinach and uziza leaves or seeds. Cover the pan/pot and leave to simmer for 1 minute. Enjoy!

The soup freezes well in an airtight container for up to 1 month. Defrost, then reheat gently until piping hot to serve.

LET'S TALK ABOUT... OFFENDING THE ANCESTORS

With Duchess Nena

When I first started sharing my recipes online, I would get a lot of outrage saying I was offending the ancestors with my vegan dishes, that I would burn, and all sorts of wahala (pidgin English for trouble). In fact, our ancestors were eating way more plant-based foods than what is regarded as traditional West African food now, and in fact the heavy meat consumption we see today, especially amongst wealthier parts of society, is a status symbol and is heavily influenced by colonization. When I try to order meals with no meat in a restaurant, they often try to reassure me that the meat is cheap as they presume it's a budget thing, rather than an ethical, lifestyle thing. Let me take it back. Nigerians were not originally heavy meat eaters. A lot of meat eaten nowadays in Nigeria comes from Niger where there is a lot of cattle rearing. Nigerians were traditionally plant-farmers. We didn't do a lot of animal husbandry. We had chickens and goats roaming about, which were used for eggs and milk and were only very rarely killed to mark special occasions. Hunters would catch wild game but this takes a lot of effort and the hunt was often not successful. So eating meat was a rarity and a treat. Coastal and river communities caught fish and smoked it to preserve it for many days. The way we eat meat today in such large quantities is a new thing. Even when I was growing up, we only ate a small amount of meat and it certainly would not be every meal. The sorts of diseases we're seeing in Nigeria today – high cholesterol, cardiovascular disease – there are no native names for them, as they weren't prevalent. So to conclude – my food is actually much closer to our ancestral food than today's prevailing diet.

SIX WEST AFRICAN SPICES TO GET TO KNOW WITH DUCHESS NENA

There are many spices used in West African cooking, but here are my favourites. You can buy them online or, if you're lucky enough to live near specialist West African stores or markets, get them there. Unlike with fresh produce where there's a lot of crossover, in London and cities like New York you won't find these spices in Afro-Caribbean stores; you need a specialist West African cuisine vendor. Names vary from country to country, which will affect whether the vendor understands what you're asking for. Google translate is your friend. Enjoy the culinary adventure!

1 **GRAINS OF SELIM PODS,** *also called Uda, are typically used for soups and have a strong black peppery taste. The pods are used whole or lightly crushed.*

2 **IRU** *is fermented locust beans. They have a pungent smell and are used as a food flavouring instead of stock cubes. They give an umami flavour to dishes and you only need a small amount.*

3 **AIDAN FRUIT,** *also known as Prekese, is also used in soups and stews. It has a complex taste that's predominantly sweet but with bitter, tangy notes.*

4 **ALLIGATOR PEPPERS** *have a mild pepper taste and add a beautiful aroma to soups and stews.*

5 **SCENT LEAVES,** *also called Efirin, are just what their name says. They add a strong minty aroma to dishes.*

6 **UZIZA SEEDS,** *also called West African Pepper, is an African spice with a pungent peppery flavour and unique aroma, often used in African dishes.*

SERVES: 4 | TIME: 20 MINUTES

NENA'S UNRIPE PLANTAIN FUFU

"Fresh fufu is a West African staple. You may have seen the instant version you can buy in shops in boxes, but these products can have a lot of other unnecessary ingredients added so we're going to make it fresh the traditional way. Go online and watch some videos of West African chefs stirring fufu to see how intensely and vigorously you stir it to get a good consistency. Spoiler alert – you give it your full effort!"

EQUIPMENT

Sharp knife, blender, saucepan, rolling pin (optional)

INGREDIENTS

1–2 teaspoons vegetable oil
3 green/unripe plantains* (green in colour – it would not work if the plantains are ripe)
240ml/8½fl oz/1 cup water

****Make sure they are green plantains and not green bananas. See p 378 for tips on shopping for plantains and spotting the difference between plantains and bananas.***

1. To prevent your hands getting covered in the sticky residue on an unripe plantain's skin, rub your hands with the vegetable oil before handling them.

2. Peel and cut the plantains into small pieces. Add the plantain pieces to a blender with the water and blend until smooth, like a purée.

3. Pour the mixture into a clean saucepan and cook on a medium heat for 15 minutes, constantly stirring to avoid sticking or burning, until a dough consistency is formed.

4. You can present your fufu in a round dumpling shape created by scooping out a portion (a quarter of the mix) from the pan, adding to a small bowl and rolling from side to side so it forms a ball. Or if you're feeling fancy, you can roll it (like a Swiss roll) using baking parchment (see below). I present mine like this.

TIP HOW TO ROLL FUFU

1. Pull out a sheet of baking parchment from its roll roughly 40cm/16in long and fold it in half.
2. Take a portion of fufu (a quarter of the mixture as you want to make 4 servings) and place it onto the baking parchment, then roll out into a 12 x 18cm/4½ x 7in rectangle (roughly), about 0.5cm/¼in thick. I would never measure it – only eye ball it.
3. Lift up the bottom end of the baking parchment (the shortest sides are top and bottom), encourage the fufu to curl over onto itself and then steadily keep lifting the parchment up as you roll the fufu up.
4. You're now serving food bouji-Lagos-restaurant style – well done!

DUCHESS NENA'S PARTY JOLLOF & KELEWELE

"Jollof rice is a celebratory dish enjoyed by many West African people. It is a spicy one-pot rice dish with a rich tomato base originating from the Wolof tribe found in Senegal, Gambia and Mauritania. There is much chat about which nation's jollof is better, which is called in a tongue-in-cheek way the jollof wars. I could say Nigeria's is best, but I'm too diplomatic for that. Each nation brings their own spin, delicious in their own way. Party jollof is jollof elevated. It's a dish we take to parties and we add in extra veggies and recreate the smoky flavour of cooking it over an open fire by putting it in the oven at the end. To get in the mood, put some afro-beats on. I like 'Jollof On The Jet' by Dj Cuppy ft Rema. Serve my Party Jollof with Kelewele: Plantain is the ultimate comfort food. Sweet and satisfying, it brings smiles to faces and comfort to tummies. It is used across West Africa. You can serve plantain fried or roasted, or season it like in this popular Ghanaian dish. At parties, there are big platters full of kelewele and it's always very popular."

use gluten-free vegetable stock cubes.

SERVES: 4 | TIME: 45–60 MINUTES

PARTY JOLLOF

EQUIPMENT

Blender/food processor, frying pan, sharp knife, wooden spoon, sieve/fine-mesh strainer, saucepan/pot with lid, ovenproof dish, parchment paper

INGREDIENTS (next page)

1. Let's prepare the ingredients.
- Halve and deseed the red pepper.
- Halve the brown onion. Slice one half and leave the other half whole.
- Finely dice the red onion.
- Finely chop the chives to serve (if using).

2. To a blender/food processor, add the canned tomatoes, red pepper, brown onion half, Scotch bonnet, garlic and ginger. Blend together until smooth.

3. Heat the oil in a frying pan on a medium heat. Add the chopped red onion and stir-fry for 1 minute until the onion starts to glisten and shrink in size. Then add the tomato purée/paste and cook for a further minute.

4. Add the mixture from the blender to the pan, along with the bay leaves, curry powder, dried thyme and rosemary, the crumbled stock cubes and the salt and cook on a medium heat for 10–12 minutes until the liquid reduces a little and looks thicker. Stir occasionally to avoid burning. This stew will be the base for the jollof. **>>**

INGREDIENTS

1 red pepper
1 large brown onion
1 large red onion
2 x 400g/14oz cans plum or chopped tomatoes
½–1 red Scotch bonnet chillies (depending on your heat tolerance)
2 cloves garlic
½ thumb-size piece root ginger
60ml/2fl oz/¼ cup cooking oil, preferably avocado for its health benefits, but any vegetable oil is fine
200g/7oz tomato purée/paste
2 bay leaves
1 teaspoon curry powder
½ teaspoon dried thyme
½ teaspoon dried rosemary
2 vegetable stock cubes
Pinch of sea salt
420g/15oz/2⅓ cups uncooked Golden Sella basmati rice or easy-cook long-grain rice
140g/5oz frozen mixed vegetables

To Serve (optional)
2 stalks of fresh chives
4 fresh basil leaves

5. Meanwhile, wash the rice in a sieve/fine-mesh strainer under cold running water for 10–15 seconds until the water runs clear, then add to a separate pot, cover with fresh water, bring to the boil and par-boil for 5 minutes.

6. Drain and rinse the rice. This removes the starch and prevents it from turning to pottage. Add to the stew and gently mix.

7. Cover the pot with baking parchment and push down so it's just above the rice, then put a lid on. Cook on a low heat for 30 minutes. Halfway through, stir the rice once as the sauce will stay at the bottom of the pot. This will ensure the rice cooks evenly.

8. Meanwhile, preheat the oven to 200°C/400°F/gas 6.

9. Once the rice is done, add the sliced brown onion and the frozen mixed vegetables and stir through.

10. To get the 'party' flavour, transfer the jollof into an ovenproof dish and bake for 10 minutes. This will slightly burn and dry out the rice on the top to give it a smoky taste like it's been cooked over an open fire. Don't cover the dish; this effect is desired and intentional.

If you want to be fancy, you can serve with some chopped chives scattered on top and a few fresh basil leaves. This is UK Nigerian diaspora vibes – you wouldn't serve with basil in Nigeria.

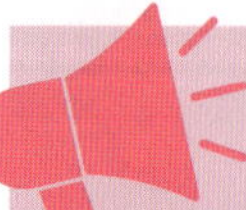

LET'S TALK ABOUT… PALM OIL

With Duchess Nena

Veganism and sustainable food in general in the West can be very white-washed and there's a lack of education around palm oil. When I first went vegan I kept hearing about the displacement of orangutans and how palm oil was causing the Brazilian and south Asian rainforest to be cut down. This is true but not the full picture. Across West Africa there are many sustainable farms growing palms for palm oil. There are also a lot of palms growing in the wild. There has been no animal displacement. Palm trees are native to West Africa. And when we say palm oil, people think about palm kernel oil, which is a saturated fat like coconut oil from the kernel inside, but it is different from the cold pressed palm oil made from the flesh, which is what I sell in my online shop. Palm oil actually has many beneficial health properties. You don't want to heat it to high temperatures, but as a drizzle on top of food to enhance flavour, it's good. All this confusion often leads me to teach people about palm oil. But sometimes I feel it should not be on me to educate people. If you're going to be against something, go beyond the headlines and do your research.

SERVES: 4 | TIME: 30 MINUTES

KELEWELE

EQUIPMENT

Sharp knife, food processor (or hand-held/immersion blender with a processor attachment), medium-size bowl, wooden spoon

INGREDIENTS

2 ripe plantains (with predominantly black skins)
120ml/4fl oz/½ cup water
½ thumb-size piece root ginger
1 clove garlic
½ onion
¼–½ red Scotch bonnet chilli (with seeds for extra heat, without for a milder taste) (see Scotch Bonnet for Newbies on p 378), or 1 teaspoon smoked paprika
1 grains of selim pod (optional) (see p 182)
½ teaspoon black pepper
Pinch of sea salt

TIPS & TRICKS
Scotch Bonnet For Newbies
p 379

1. Peel and cut the plantains into roughly 2cm/¾in cubes

2. To a blender or food processor, add all the ingredients – except the plantain – and blend into a paste.

3. Tip the paste into a bowl and add the cubes of plantain. Stir to cover the plantain in the delicious paste.

4. Now you have three options.
- To oven-cook, preheat the oven to 180°C/350°F/gas 4 and line a baking sheet with baking parchment. Tip the plantain cubes onto the lined baking sheet and spread out so they have space, then bake for 20 minutes until golden-red and crispy on some edges.
- Alternatively, air-fry the plantain cubes at 180°C for 12 minutes (remembering to take out and shake every 3 minutes) until golden-red and crispy.
- Or fry in 1–2 teaspoons of rapeseed/canola or olive oil in a frying pan on a medium heat until golden-red and a little crispy. I like to oven-bake as I can do something else while it's in the oven and it uses less oil than pan-frying.

TIPS & TRICKS
Plantain For Newbies
p 378

     use gluten-free vegetable stock cubes.

SERVES: 4 | TIME: 1 HOUR 15 MINUTES (BUT THIS INCLUDES TIME TO DO ALL THE WASHING UP AND SET THE TABLE BECAUSE THERE'S QUITE A LOT OF TIME WHEN THE STEW IS COOKING)

BETTY'S GROUNDNUT, CHICKPEA, CARROT & SPINACH STEW

"This dish is inspired by my Sierra Leonean culinary heritage of Granat (Groundnut) soup that my beautiful late mother would lovingly cook for me, my sisters and father. It truly speaks comfort for the soul. Even when I became an independent adult, I'd periodically call my mother in the family home in Liverpool and talk about what life in that there big London was throwing at me. If it was getting too much I'd plan a quick weekend escape to get back home and rest. 'Should I make granat soup?' was all she had to say for me to know I was truly coming home. My meal of return. My comfort."

EQUIPMENT

Sharp knife, blender/food processor or large pestle and mortar, medium pot or saucepan with lid, wooden spoon

INGREDIENTS (next page)

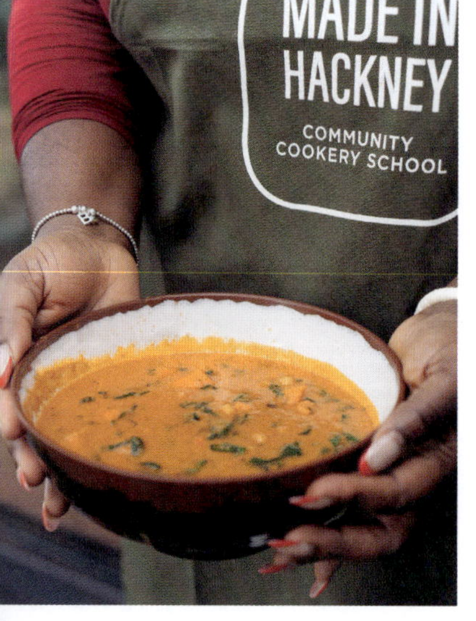

1. Let's prepare the veg.
- Quarter the onion.
- Chop the Scotch bonnet chilli in half, deseed and quarter.
- Deseed and slice the red pepper.
- Chop the carrots into 2.5cm/1in chunks.

2. Place the onion, Scotch bonnet, red pepper, garlic, ginger, canned or fresh tomatoes and tomato purée/paste in a blender or food processor and blend to a medium-smooth consistency. If you don't have a blender/food processor, use a large pestle and mortar to achieve a medium-smooth consistency.

3. In a medium pot, combine the 200ml/7fl oz/scant 1 cup of water and the crumbled stock cubes and heat until the cubes have completely dissolved.

4. Slowly pour the tomato mixture into the pot of stock and simmer on a low heat for 2–3 minutes, then cover and simmer for 10 minutes, or until the stew base is cooked. At this point, the stew should be slightly darker in colour.

5. Stir thoroughly, then add the chopped carrots, cover and cook for 10 minutes.

6. Add the cinnamon, black pepper and peanut butter and stir until

INGREDIENTS

1 onion

½ red Scotch bonnet chilli (see Scotch Bonnet for Newbies on p 379)

1 red pepper

2 carrots

2 cloves garlic

Thumb-size piece root ginger

1 x 400g/14oz can chopped tomatoes or 3 fresh tomatoes

1 tablespoon tomato purée/paste

200ml/7fl oz/scant 1 cup water (you may need an extra tablespoon)

2 vegetable stock cubes

½–1 teaspoon ground cinnamon

1 teaspoon black pepper

3 tablespoons peanut butter (crunchy or smooth)

1½ x 400g/14oz cans chickpeas/ garbanzo beans

150g/5½oz baby spinach (2 heaped handfuls)

Pinch of sea salt

To Serve

Steamed rice of choice or couscous (see Cooking Staples on p 55)

Fresh green salad

combined. Cover and simmer for an additional 10–15 minutes. The oil from the peanut butter will naturally begin to rise to the top and the stew will become thicker. If the sauce is getting too thick, add a tablespoon more water.

7. Drain and rinse the chickpeas/garbanzo beans (don't forget to catch the juice – aquafaba – to use in another recipe), then add them and the spinach to the pot, and cook on a low-medium heat until the chickpeas and carrots are tender – this will take about 10 minutes.

8. Stir occasionally to ensure the dish does not burn or stick. Don't worry if it looks like there is a lot of spinach to start with, the steam from the stew will wilt the spinach reducing it substantially in size.

9. Add the pinch of salt, stir and then turn off the heat.

Serve with steamed rice or couscous and a fresh green salad to bring a cooling balance.

LET'S TALK ABOUT... REPRESENTATION IN VEGANISM *With Betty Vandy*

When veganism first started entering the mainstream a few years back it was white-washed, and Black and brown people that had been there all along were side lined. Plant-based foods and veganism are not a white movement and never have been. It's why myself and fellow vegan chefs Esme Carr and Michaella Palmer decided to host a pioneering event in Peckham – UK Vegans Of Colour – to showcase the talent in our community. There was a huge amount of innovation coming from Black and brown vegan businesses and then larger brands with financial backers would come along, take their ideas and run with them. We were being marginalized and very few people championed us except Sean from FatGayVegan who now works for Made In Hackney. He financially backed the event along with the founder of RG Vegan. So it was a white gay man and a Black man who supported us to make it happen. We got a huge amount of support but also a lot of incredulousness – how dare these Black women do this? Who do they think they are? Other people made it their business not to be involved. But in the end a huge number of businesses came through from across the UK. We had over 60 stalls, talks and workshops and thousands of people passed through over the two days. It was amazing, and many of the businesses had never had that kind of platform before. People were not holding space for us, so we had to hold space for ourselves. If you don't hold space for each other, you can't flourish. Events and community like this are so important for underrepresented people. For those running vegan businesses in less diverse places, if you are feeling alone, there are places to find your tribe.

WOIN'S KEI MISER WOT & TIKEL GOMEN

"These Ethiopian dishes are delicious, straightforward and affordable to make. I recommend eating them with Injera, which is fermented Ethiopian bread. You can buy these from specialist retailers or online. If you can't access these breads, then a naan bread, tortillas, flatbreads or any other bread that is nice to dip into tasty dishes will work. Miser Wot is a spiced red lentil stew. I love to make it as it's simple, requiring no specialist equipment or spices but is still really delicious. In Ethiopian cuisine we give the flavours time to infuse, so don't rush the various cooking steps or you won't achieve the right depth of flavours. Tikel Gomen is a vegan dish that Ethiopian Christian orthodox followers often eat during lent. You can make this same recipe but replace the cabbage with spring/collard greens, spinach or kale. Finally, I have provided recipes for two spice mixes. Mekelesha is known as the 'finishing spice blend' in Ethiopian cuisine. It is added to the dish toward the end of cooking time so that the heat does not destroy the spices' aromatics. It is made up of seven hand-roasted spices. In Ethiopia, we leave the spices out to dry in the sun for three days, but in cooler climates you'll need to roast them in a pan. Like the Berbere Spice (see p 194), it won't taste the same as something purchased in Ethiopia, but it's a good replacement. Indian long pepper can be found in South-East Asian and East African stores."

TO MAKE BOTH DISHES FOR A MEAL

1. Prepare the ingredients in step 1 of both recipes.
2. Start with the Kei Miser Wot. At step 4 where the dish cooks for 20–30 minutes, start making the Tikel Gomen. Set a timer so you don't burn your lentils and remember to stir regularly.

SERVES: 4 TIME: 1 HOUR 10 MINUTES

MISER WOT

EQUIPMENT

Sharp knife, garlic crusher (optional), medium-sized saucepan, wooden spoon

INGREDIENTS (next page)

1. First let's prepare the ingredients.
- Finely dice the onions.
- Finely slice or crush the garlic.
- Finely slice or grate the ginger.
- Wash the lentils in a bowl of cold water until the water becomes clear. >>

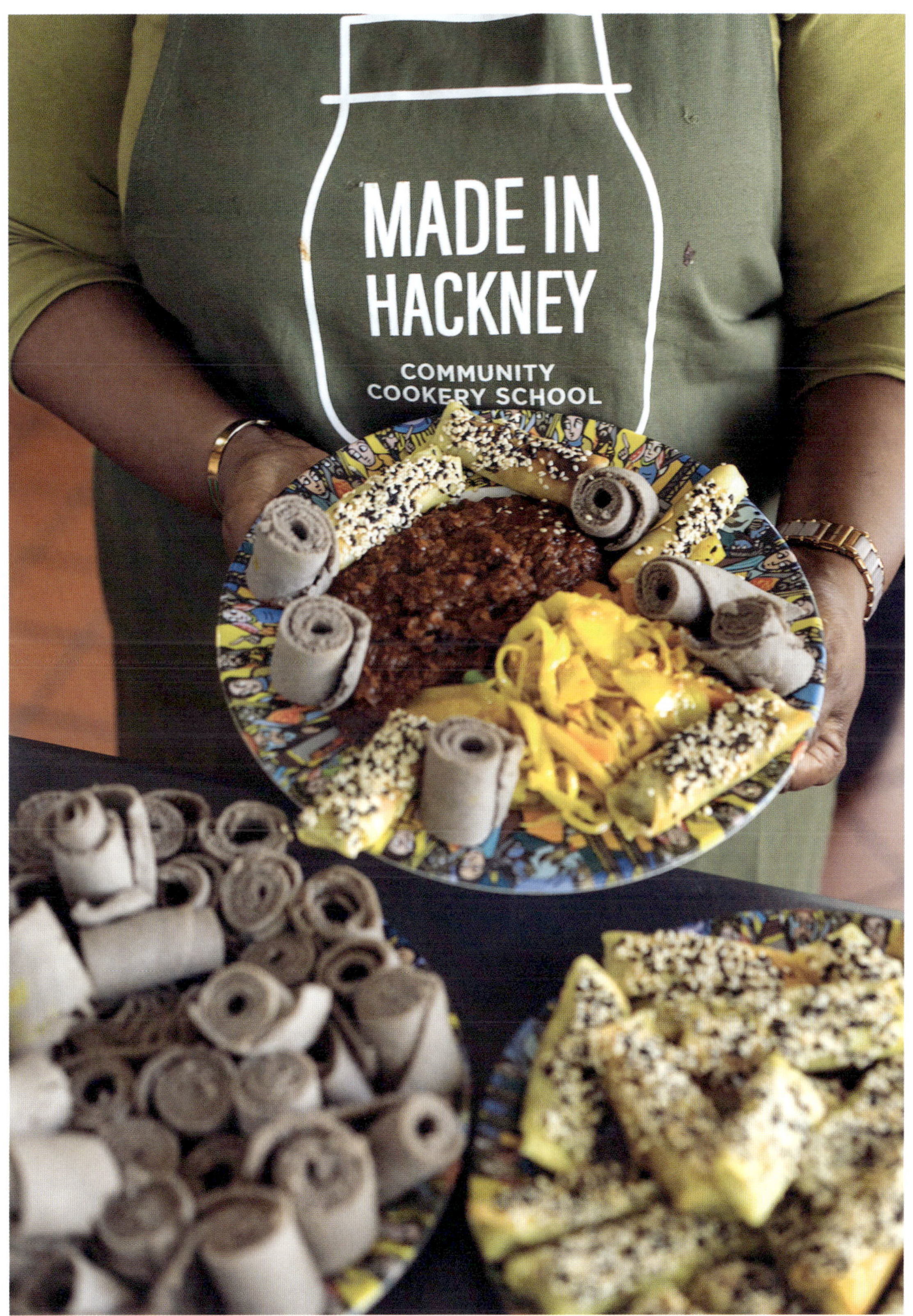
MADE IN
HACKNEY
COMMUNITY
COOKERY SCHOOL

INGREDIENTS

- 2 onions
- 2–4 cloves garlic
- 2.5cm/1in piece root ginger
- 200g/7oz/generous 1 cup dried split red lentils
- 5 tablespoons olive oil
- 200g/7oz tomato purée/paste
- 3 tablespoons Berbere Spice (see DIY recipe on p 194) or chilli powder
- About 800ml/28fl oz/scant 3½ cups boiling water
- Pinch of sea salt
- Pinch of black pepper
- 1 tablespoon Mekelesha (see DIY recipe on p 193)
- Injera (fermented Ethiopian bread) or other flatbreads, to serve

2. In a medium saucepan, dry-fry the onions on a medium heat. Stir regularly until the water released from the onions has evaporated, this will take between 5–8 minutes.

3. Add the olive oil and continue cooking the onions on a medium heat for a further 10 minutes, then add the garlic and ginger and cook for another 5 minutes. The onion should now be caramelized.

4. Now add the tomato purée/paste and Berbere spice or chilli powder and cook on a medium heat for 20–30 minutes, stirring regularly to avoid anything sticking. The colour should change to a deep, dark red. If you don't want to stand by it the whole time stirring, you will need to turn it down to a low heat.

5. Add the lentils to the pan, stir and cook for 5 minutes, then add 700ml/24fl oz/3 cups of the boiling water and put the lid on.

6. Simmer on a medium heat until the lentils are cooked and have started to disintegrate and become smoother in texture. You may need to add the remaining boiling water. This will take around 10–15 minutes – some lentils are harder than others so you'll need to judge by eye.

7. Add the salt, black pepper and Mekelesha (or replacement spices if making your own – see next page to make your own blends), stir through and cook for another 10 minutes.

8. Remove from the heat and serve on top of the injera (so you're using the injera like a serving plate) along with the Tikel Gomen. Break pieces of the injera off with your hands and use it to scoop the other dishes into your mouth (see Eating With Our Hands on p 372).

SERVES: 4 | 55 MINUTES LEISURELY COOKING

TIKEL GOMEN

EQUIPMENT

Sharp knife, garlic crusher (optional), medium-sized saucepan, wooden spoon

INGREDIENTS (next page)

1. First let's prepare the ingredients.
- Finely slice the onion.
- Crush or finely slice the garlic.
- Cut the tomatoes (if using) into quarters.
- Finely slice the cabbage.
- Cut the carrots into matchsticks.
- Peel and cut the potatoes into matchsticks.
- Cut the green chillies into matchsticks (deseed if you prefer less heat).

INGREDIENTS

1 large onion
2–4 cloves garlic
2 tomatoes (optional)
200g/7oz white cabbage (or any type of cabbage or any spring/collard greens such as chard or kale)
2 carrots
2 potatoes
2 fresh green chillies
5 tablespoons olive oil
½ teaspoon ground turmeric
Pinch of sea salt
Pinch of white pepper

2. Add the olive oil to a medium saucepan and heat on a medium heat for 1 minute. Add the onion and garlic and cook for 5 minutes, stirring regularly.

3. Add the tomatoes (if using) and turmeric and cook for a further 10 minutes. Stir in the carrots and cook for another 10 minutes. Stir occasionally throughout to prevent sticking.

4. Add the potatoes and cook for a further 5–10 minutes. Stir in the cabbage and cook for another 10 minutes.

5. Finally, add the green chillies, salt and white pepper, stir and then remove from the heat. That's right, the chillies are almost raw.

6. Remove from the heat and serve on top of the injera along with the Kei Miser Wot.

WOIN'S SPICE BLENDS

MAKES: ABOUT 140–150G/5–5½OZ SPICE MIX | TIME: 5 MINUTES

MEKELESHA

EQUIPMENT

Frying pan, wooden spoon, spice grinder/coffee grinder/blender or pestle and mortar, airtight jar

INGREDIENTS

2 tablespoons green cardamom pods
2 tablespoons black peppercorns
2 x 5cm/2in cinnamon sticks, broken into pieces
1 tablespoon cumin/jeera seeds
1 tablespoon whole cloves
2 teaspoons ground nutmeg
4 pieces of timiz (Indian long pepper) (optional but recommended)

1. Lightly toast all the spices in a dry frying pan on a medium heat for 3–4 minutes until they release their aroma. Leave to cool.

2. Add all the toasted spices to a spice grinder, clean coffee grinder or blender and blend together into a ground mixture. You can use a pestle and mortar to do this, but it will take a while to grind everything down.

3. Transfer the ground spice mixture into a clean airtight jar, seal and label. Store in a cool, dark cupboard for up to 3 months.

MAKES: ABOUT 140–150G/5–5½OZ SPICE MIX | TIME: 5 MINUTES

BERBERE SPICE

Most of the berbere spice blends you can buy in the Global North are not authentic as the spices are prepared differently and the blends don't contain the local herbs – the rue, besobila and Ethiopian rosemary, which are dried and prepared in a specific way. In Ethiopia, the preparation is a long process that begins by washing the whole cayenne peppers and all the spices, then drying them in the sun. Next you wash all the herbs, mix all the ingredients together with a big mortar, dry them in the sun again and when completely dry, blend the mix again in a big machine. Most households in Ethiopia prepare a year's supply in one go and make a large quantity, 20kg/44lb or more. I only buy Berbere Spice in the Global North when we've run out of supplies from Ethiopia, but it never tastes as good. If you've never had the authentic Ethiopian blend, those you can find in the Global North are ok, but just know the real thing tastes far superior. Ajwain spice can be find in South-East Asian and East African stores.

EQUIPMENT

Frying pan, wooden spoon, spice grinder/coffee grinder/blender or pestle and mortar, airtight jar

INGREDIENTS

- ½ teaspoon fenugreek seeds
- 1 teaspoon coriander seeds
- 1 teaspoon green cardamom seeds (6–8 pods, crushed, and seeds removed)
- ½ teaspoon cumin/ jeera seeds
- 1 teaspoon black peppercorns
- ½ teaspoon whole cloves
- 1 teaspoon ground cinnamon
- ¼ teaspoon ajwain seeds
- ¼ teaspoon nigella seeds
- 135g/4¾oz chilli powder

1. Lightly toast all the spices – except the chilli powder – in a dry frying pan on a medium heat for 2–3 minutes until they release their aroma and become slightly darker. Leave to cool.

2. Add all the toasted spices to a spice grinder, clean coffee grinder or blender and blend together into a ground mixture. Add the chilli powder and blend again. You can use a pestle and mortar to do this, but it will take a while to grind down.

3. Transfer the ground spice mixture into a clean airtight jar, seal and label. Store in a cool, dark cupboard for up to 3 months. Use to season your Ethiopian dishes or any dish of your creation.

NOTE:

This recipe is so we can make this spice blend with what's available. It's not the same as the one in Ethiopia, but it's as close as we can get it.

GF use gluten-free wraps.

SERVES: 4 | TIME: 20 MINUTES

SARA'S WILD GARLIC PESTO PINWHEELS

"I love to cook with fresh ingredients of the season. Wild garlic is in season February to April (in the UK and areas with a similar climate in the US) and is utterly delicious. You can replace the wild garlic with another green such as nettles, spinach or basil."

EQUIPMENT

Several bowls, sharp knife, saucepan, wooden spoons, masher, colander, grater, peeler, food processor or blender, lemon juicer

INGREDIENTS

For The Wild Garlic Pesto

- 100g/3½oz/1½ cups pumpkin seeds
- Juice of 2 lemons
- 60g/2¼oz wild garlic (ramsons), or use nettles, spinach or basil
- 20g/¾oz fresh parsley (optional)
- 1 clove garlic (optional – add if not using wild garlic)
- 4 tablespoons B12-enriched nutritional yeast
- ½ teaspoon sea salt
- ½–1½ tablespoons water

For The Pinwheels

- 200g/7oz mushrooms
- 20 cherry tomatoes
- 12 sun-dried tomatoes (optional)
- 2 x 400g/14oz cans white/cannellini beans or butter/lima beans
- 1 tablespoon olive oil
- 1 batch of Wild Garlic Pesto (see above)
- 4 large wraps (regular, wholegrain or gluten-free wraps)
- 20g/¾oz baby spinach

1. First let's prep the ingredients for the pinwheels.
- Slice your mushrooms.
- Dice your cherry tomatoes and chop your sun-dried tomatoes.
- Drain and rinse the canned beans.

2. Sauté your mushrooms in the olive oil in a saucepan on a medium heat for 5–8 minutes until they change colour and go soft.

3. While the mushrooms are cooking, make the pesto.

4. Add all the ingredients for the pesto to a food processor or blender and blend to a smooth consistency. Depending on how powerful your food processor is will affect how much water you need to add. Start with ½ tablespoon and add more if necessary.

5. In a bowl, mash together the white beans and the wild garlic pesto.

6. Now spread the mashed mixture over each wrap.

7. Next, layer your filling ingredients in rows on each wrap. Start with a row of baby spinach, then a row of mushrooms and then the cherry tomatoes and sun-dried tomatoes (if using). Starting from one end, roll up each wrap tightly like a sushi roll.

8. Refrigerate for at least an hour before slicing into bite-size pieces. If you're short on time, or hungry, enjoy your wraps straight away without slicing into pinwheels.

TIP ***You can swap ramsons/wild garlic for another wild allium called three cornered leek. Like ramsons, three cornered leeks have a strong onion-garlic flavour. They are sometimes easier to forage for in urban areas than ramsons.***

NISHMA'S BHARAZI, SUKUMA WIKI AND UGALI

"Bharazi is a delicious East African dish of pigeon peas, or carlin peas, simmered in coconut milk. It's a fusion dish influenced by the Gujarati diaspora who introduced the use of ginger, cumin/jeera and other spices to the local dishes. Many Gujaratis migrated to Kenya in the 1930s as there was a bad drought in Gujarat, plus the British were always seeking labourers to work in the docks in Mombasa. Because of migration and the trading routes, there is a huge amount of culinary fusion between Burmese, Portuguese, Indian, East African and Caribbean cuisines. Serve your Bharazi with Sukuma Wiki, which means collard greens in Swahili. It is a crop known for enhancing food security in East Africa as it can stay in the fields for a long time and is quite disease-resistant. You can swap it for cavolo nero or curly kale, but try to find collard greens.
Pair these with Ugali, a cornmeal which is eaten across East Africa with your hands. It doesn't have a strong flavour but you dip it into dishes to mop up all the flavours. Wheat isn't really grown in this part of the world – it's millet, barley and polenta/cornmeal, hence this being the staple carbohydrate. In Kenya meals are often served on a large sharing plate. The ugali is positioned in the middle so everyone has access to it with the beans, greens and other dishes around it. It's a lovely and enjoyable way to eat."

SERVES: 4 | TIME: 25 MINUTES

EQUIPMENT

Sharp knife, fine grater/ Microplane, colander, small saucepan

INGREDIENTS (next page)

BHARAZI

1. Let's prep the ingredients.
- Finely dice the onions to similar size pieces as the carlin peas.
- Finely chop the chillies (deseed if you prefer less heat).
- Peel, core and finely dice the cooking/baking apple.
- Finely grate the ginger.
- Pour the cans of carlin peas into a colander to drain the water, and then rinse them with fresh water.

2. In a small pan, warm the oil on a medium heat and then add the diced onions. Cook for about 5 minutes until they become translucent. If the onions are sticking to the pan, add 1–2 teaspoons of water rather than more oil. **>>**

INGREDIENTS

2 large white onions

3–5 fresh green chillies (depending on desired heat)

¼ cooking/baking apple

20g/¾oz root ginger

2 x 400g/14oz cans carlin peas*

2 tablespoons vegetable, sunflower or rapeseed/canola oil

2 x 400ml/14fl oz cans coconut milk (thick and pure version, rather than that used for teas/coffee/cereal)

1 teaspoon sea salt

1–4 tablespoons water (optional)

8 sprigs of fresh coriander/cilantro, to garnish (optional)

**You can buy canned or dried carlin peas. If you buy the dried ones, you will need to soak them for 24 hours in cold water and then cook them (see Tip). Canned gungo peas, also available in supermarkets, can be used instead of carlin peas.*

3. Add the canned (or cooked soaked) carlin peas, the coconut milk, grated ginger, salt and chopped chillies to the mixture and cook for 2 minutes.

4. Now add the diced cooking apple. Leave to cook on a low simmering heat for about 10 minutes, allowing the flavours to infuse.

5. Add more water if the sauce is becoming too thick.

6. Taste the curry to check you are happy with the flavours. Serve in a bowl and garnish with the coriander/cilantro sprigs.

TIP *If using dried carlin peas, weigh out 200g/7oz and place them in a bowl. Cover with 600ml/20fl oz/2½ cups of cold water and leave to soak overnight. The next day, drain the peas, then add them to a pressure cooker, along with 1 litre/35fl oz/4¼ cups of fresh water and cook at pressure for 20 minutes, then release the steam, drain and discard the cooking water. Your carlin peas are now cooked and ready to use. If you don't own a pressure cooker, I recommend using canned carlin peas as a more cost-effective option.*

SERVES: 4 | TIME: 20 MINUTES

SUKUMA WIKI

EQUIPMENT

Sharp knife, fine grater/Microplane, heavy frying pan with lid, wooden spoon

INGREDIENTS (next page)

1. Remove the hard stalks/veins from the collard greens or kale and shred the leaves. Slice the cherry tomatoes in half.

2. Finely dice the onions. Finely grate the garlic.

3. Warm the oil in a heavy frying pan on a medium heat. Add the diced onions and cook for 5 minutes until they soften.

4. Add the collard greens or kale and cook until it softens. This will take about 5–8 minutes, depending on the greens/kale.

INGREDIENTS

- 300g/10½oz collard greens or curly kale
- 20–30 cherry tomatoes
- 2 large white onions
- 6 cloves garlic
- 2 tablespoons rapeseed/canola or olive oil
- ½ teaspoon sea salt
- ½ teaspoon ground turmeric
- 100ml/3½fl oz/scant ½ cup water

5. Now stir in the cherry tomatoes and garlic. Add the salt and turmeric, stir and leave to cook for 1–2 minutes.

6. Stir in the water, then cover the pan to speed up the cooking process and cook for 5 minutes.

7. Lower the heat and continue to cook until the collard greens/kale, tomatoes and garlic have merged together and everything is soft – this should take another 6–10 minutes. After it's become soft, leave on a low heat to stay warm until ready to serve. While this is cooking, you can start making your ugali.

SERVES: 4 | TIME: 15 MINUTES

UGALI

EQUIPMENT

Fine grater/Microplane, saucepan, rolling pin

INGREDIENTS

- 10g/¼oz root ginger
- 600ml/20fl oz/2½ cups boiling water
- 200g/7oz/1⅓ cups fine polenta/cornmeal
- ½ teaspoon sea salt
- 2 teaspoons rapeseed/canola or sunflower oil (to grease the rolling pin)
- ½–1 teaspoon dried chilli/hot pepper flakes

1. Finely grate the ginger.

2. Add the measured boiling water from the kettle to a saucepan on a medium heat. Stir in the grated ginger, the polenta/cornmeal and salt.

3. Rub the oil over one end of a rolling pin and use that end to vigorously stir the polenta/cornmeal to prevent any lumps. You're aiming for the grains to be soft but the mixture to be quite dense.

4. After 5 minutes of stirring, add the chilli/hot pepper flakes. Continue stirring using the rolling pin until the polenta/cornmeal has absorbed all the water, becomes a little stiff and has come together like a soft dough. It is now ready.

5. Serve the ugali while it is hot. You can use a greased bowl or ramekin to shape the ugali and tip it onto your serving plate, or just scoop it out. Serve on the same plate alongside the other two dishes.

To eat, break off some ugali with your fingers and dip it into the Bharazi and Sukuma Wiki to soak up their juices. Delicious.

GF use gluten-free soy sauce or tamari.

SERVES: 4 | TIME: 1 HOUR

BRUNA'S FEIJOADA

"Feijoada is Brazil's go-to Saturday lunch when loved ones gather for a hearty feast accompanied by samba tunes and caipirinhas flowing all afternoon. My plant-based version offers a lighter take that's packed with nutrition and flavour. Beans are the star, loaded with fibre for gut health and protein. They're not just good for filling you up – they're a powerhouse of nutrients like iron, magnesium, potassium, folate and zinc. Plus, they've got resistant starch to keep your gut happy. The Feijoada is served with Simple Brown Rice, Stir-fried Greens and Quick Pickled Onions."

EQUIPMENT

Sharp knife, large saucepan or stew pot, wooden spoon

INGREDIENTS

- 1 large potato (or you can use 1 sweet potato or ¼ butternut squash or 1 patty pan squash)
- 2 carrots
- 150g/5½oz mushrooms
- 1 large onion
- 2–3 cloves garlic
- 1 fresh red chilli
- 200g/7oz vegan sausages or smoked firm tofu (optional)
- 1½ tablespoons olive oil
- 1½ teaspoons ground cumin/jeera
- 1½ tablespoons tomato purée/paste
- 2 bay leaves
- 1 teaspoon smoked paprika
- 1½ x 400g/14oz cans black beans or 250g/9oz/1½ cups dried black beans (see Tip)
- 1½ tablespoons dark soy sauce (gluten free)
- 2 tablespoons water (optional)
- Pinch of sea salt

1. First let's prepare the ingredients.
- Chop the potato, carrots and mushrooms into chunky 2cm/¾in cubes (do the same for the sweet potato or peeled and deseeded squash, if using instead of the potato).
- Dice the onion and garlic.
- Slice the chilli in half lengthways. If you prefer mild heat, remove the seeds, then chop into small chunks. If you like high heat, keep the chilli whole with the seeds and chop into small chunks.
- If using vegan sausages or smoked tofu, chop the sausages or cube the tofu.

2. Using a stew pot, big saucepan or casserole dish, heat the olive oil on a medium heat, then add the diced onion. Cook for about 5 minutes or until starting to turn golden.

3. Add the chopped mushrooms to the pot and cook for another 5 minutes, or until the mushrooms look like they've absorbed the cooking oil, adding a teaspoon of water if necessary to prevent sticking to the pan. Keep stirring.

4. Stir in the garlic and continue to cook on a medium heat for another 5–7 minutes.

5. Now add the rest of the vegetables, the chilli, cumin, tomato purée/paste, bay leaves and smoked paprika and stir to combine.

6. Now add the canned (or cooked soaked) black beans, including the liquid from the cans, to the pot and the soy sauce. If you'd prefer to not use the liquid from the cans (or are using cooked soaked beans), add the 2 tablespoons of water. Stir and season with the pinch of salt. >>

7. If you are using vegan sausages or smoked tofu, add them now.

8. Turn the heat down and let it simmer for at least 25 minutes but preferably longer, ideally 40 minutes. The sauce should be nice and thick. Serve the Feijoada with Simple Brown Rice, Stir-fried Greens and Quick Pickled Onions (see below) and enjoy.

TIP ***If using dried black beans, place them in a bowl, cover with plenty of cold water and leave to soak overnight. The next day, drain the beans, then add them to a pan, cover with fresh water, add a bay leaf, bring to the boil and cook for about 50 – 60 minutes until tender. Drain the beans and discard the cooking water. Your black beans are now cooked and ready to use.***

SERVES: 4 | TIME: 50 MINUTES

SIMPLE BROWN RICE

"Traditionally, feijoada is served with white rice, but for our version, we will be serving it with simple brown rice for its superior nutrient and fibre content."

EQUIPMENT

Sieve/fine-mesh strainer, large pot/saucepan with lid

INGREDIENTS

- 315g/11oz/1¾ cups uncooked brown rice (short, medium or long grain)
- 2.1 litres/72fl oz/9 cups water
- Pinch of sea salt

1. Rinse the rice in a sieve/fine-mesh strainer under cold running water for 30 seconds until the water runs clear.

2. Bring the water to a rolling boil in a large pot/saucepan – you'll see bubbles.

3. Add the rinsed rice to the boiling water, cover and cook for 30 minutes, maintaining a steady boil. Turn down the heat if needed to prevent the water from boiling over.

4. Drain any remaining cooking water from the rice and return it to the pot. Cover the pot and let the rice rest, off the heat, for 10 minutes. This resting period is the secret to lovely, not too soft, not too hard rice. Fluff the rice with a fork, add the pinch of salt and serve.

SERVING SUGGESTION: ***Peel 1 orange and slice into rounds. Serve 1–2 orange slices with each helping of Feijoada.***

Brown Rice Vs White Rice p 371

SERVES: 4 | TIME: 10 MINUTES

STIR-FRIED GREENS

"Over time, Brazilians developed a traditional way of serving Feijoada, and nowadays it always comes with a side of garlic stir-fried kale. Kale is a nutritious food rich in antioxidants, vitamin C, vitamin K and beta-carotene."

EQUIPMENT

Sharp knife, frying pan, wooden spoon

INGREDIENTS

150g/5½oz kale (any type), chard or spinach
1 clove garlic
½ tablespoon olive oil
Pinch of sea salt

1. Let's prepare the vegetables.
- Cut or rip the kale leaves away from the stalks and cut into thin ribbons. You can roll the kale leaves up into a tight bunch and then finely slice them – this technique is called chiffonade.
- Finely dice the garlic.

2. Add the olive oil to a frying pan on a medium heat. Add the garlic and lightly fry until it turns brown, about 3 minutes.

3. Stir in the kale and either cook for 1 minute or turn off the heat immediately. You want crunchy almost raw kale. Sprinkle the pinch of salt over it. That's it!

SERVES: 4 | TIME: 10 MINUTES, PLUS 20 MINUTES INFUSING

QUICK PICKLED ONIONS

"This condiment is perfect to add acidity and helps to bring all the flavours in Feijoada together. It's not essential, but for me it's worth the extra step. You can make it while the Feijoada is cooking."

EQUIPMENT

Sharp knife, bowl

INGREDIENTS

1 large onion
1 small red chilli
1½ tablespoons white vinegar
Pinch of sea salt
Pinch of black pepper
1½ tablespoons olive oil

1. Dice the onion and red chilli (deseed if you prefer less heat).

2. Transfer the onion to a bowl, add the vinegar, salt and black pepper and stir.

3. Add the chilli, then the olive oil and stir. Set aside for 20 minutes to allow the flavours to infuse.

Up Your Iron p 369

SERVES: 4 | TIME: 35 MINUTES

BRUNA'S ULTIMATE EGG-FREE OMELETTE

"Aquafaba, the liquid from cooked chickpeas/garbanzo beans, when whipped works wonders in mimicking the airy quality of eggs. I created many variations of this recipe and I'm really happy with how light and airy this omelette turns out. It's a plant-based version of a classic breakfast that is tasty and comforting. The more you work with aquafaba you get to know its ways – so don't be put off if your first go isn't perfect. Save the chickpeas/garbanzo beans to use in another meal rather than adding to the filling or it could be an overload for your digestion. This batter also makes a wonderful savoury waffle mix."

EQUIPMENT

Sharp knife, skillet or frying pan, large bowl, wooden spoons, sieve/fine-mesh strainer, 2 large bowls, electric hand whisk/beater or food processor with a whisk attachment, small (22cm/8½in) non-stick frying pan with lid

INGREDIENTS (next page)

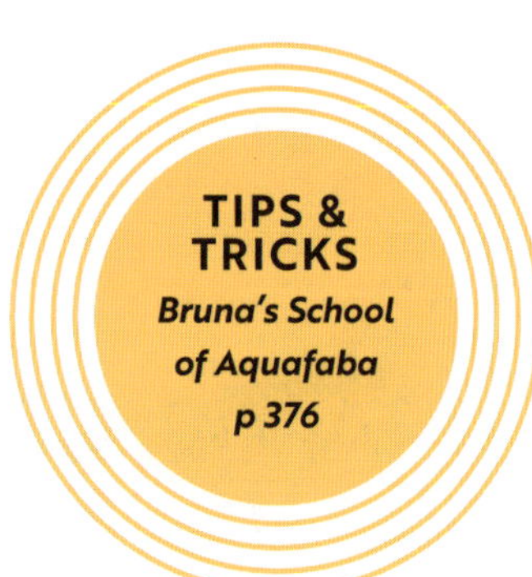

1. First prepare the filling ingredients.
- Halve the cherry tomatoes.
- Slice the mushrooms.
- Finely slice the garlic.

2. To make the filling, heat up a skillet or frying pan on a medium heat for 1 minute. Add the olive oil, garlic and mushrooms and cook for 4–5 minutes until the mushrooms are soft and have changed colour.

3. Now stir in the herbs, season with salt and pepper and cook for another 2–3 minutes.

4. Turn off the heat and add the tomatoes. Mix well and set aside. This will be used as the filling for the omelettes.

5. For the omelettes, in a large bowl and using a wooden spoon, combine the chickpea/gram flour, nutritional yeast, turmeric, garlic powder, smoked paprika (if using) and salt.

6. Once everything is mixed, pass the mixture through a sieve/fine-mesh strainer to remove any lumps. Set aside.

7. Now let's prepare the whipped aquafaba. In a separate large bowl, using an electric hand whisk/beater or a food processor with a whisk attachment, whip the aquafaba with the cream of tartar for 9–13 minutes until stiff peaks form. Yes, that's a long time, but it's how you get amazing whipped aquafaba. You know it's stiff enough when you can scoop some up with a spoon and when you try to shake it off the spoon it stays on.

MIH cheese queens Ellie and Bruna at one of our Vegan Cheese fundraising parties where they did demo's and sold their delicious cheeses.

INGREDIENTS

For The Omelettes

220g/8oz/1⅔ cups chickpea/gram flour

3 tablespoons B12-enriched nutritional yeast

¾ teaspoon ground turmeric

1 teaspoon garlic powder

¾ teaspoon smoked paprika (optional)

½–1 teaspoon black salt or regular sea salt

470ml/16fl oz/scant 2 cups aquafaba (the liquid from inside 2 x 400g/14oz cans chickpeas/garbanzo beans), chilled

¼ teaspoon cream of tartar (found in baking aisle)

Rapeseed/canola

For The Filling

150g/5½oz cherry tomatoes

70g/2½oz button mushrooms

1 clove garlic

½ tablespoon olive oil

½ tablespoon dried oregano or dried mixed Italian herbs

Sea salt and black pepper

Fresh green salad, to serve

8. Gently fold the sifted dry ingredient mixture into the whipped aquafaba, being careful not to deflate the mixture too much. Gently mix until the batter is well combined.

9. Now preheat the oven to 110°C/225°F/gas ¼ (as you'll use it to keep the omelettes warm in between frying).

10. Heat a small (22cm/8½in) non-stick frying pan on a medium heat. Add about ½ teaspoon of rapeseed/canola oil to the pan, then tilt the pan to spread it over the surface. Scoop up about 240ml/8½fl oz/1 cup of the batter, then pour it into the pan so it covers the surface. If your frying pan is a little larger, you will need a bit more batter to cover the base. Spread out the batter evenly (you should have enough batter and filling to prepare 4 omelettes). Cook until the top of the omelette forms bubbles and the edges just begin to set.

11. Place a quarter of the filling onto one half of the omelette. Carefully fold the other half over the filling using a spatula.

12. Cover the pan with a lid and cook for an additional 1–2 minutes, or until the inside of the omelette is fully set and not raw.

13. Pop the omelette on a plate in the oven to keep warm while you make the other omelettes in the same way, or ideally, serve them fresh out of the pan. The longer they sit and cool, the firmer they become.

Serve with a fresh green salad.

use a gluten-free flour blend and gluten-free stock.

SERVES: 4 | TIME: 1 HOUR, 10 MINUTES

ANDI'S RED LENTIL & PLANTAIN DHAL WITH PARSNIP FRITTERS

TV presenter, author, podcast host and now national treasure, Andi Oliver is one our celebrity ambassadors. She says: *"I loved making this dish with the MIH chefs at the Community Meal Service. They gave me a knife, a gastro and we just got on with it. My kind of kitchen. Seeing the work and love the team pour into the meals was amazing – and it was humbling going out delivering to community members. No one should be going hungry in London. It's an outrage. When times are hard, this is the kind of meal that brings comfort and joy. At least I hope that's what it brought to everyone we delivered it to."*

EQUIPMENT

Sharp knife, grater, medium-size bowl, sieve/ fine-mesh strainer, frying pan, 2 medium saucepans, metal slotted spoon, plate with paper towels or baking parchment or an old clean dish towel on it

INGREDIENTS (next page)

1. Let's prep the ingredients for the fritters.
- Grate the parsnips.
- Finely slice the white onion, garlic and parsley. Pick the leaves off the thyme.

2. In a bowl, combine all the fritter ingredients – except the oil for deep-frying – then cover and refrigerate for 15–20 minutes.

3. Now let's prep the ingredients for the dhal.
- Thinly slice your onion and garlic.
- Finely chop your chillies (deseed if you prefer less heat).
- Grate the ginger.
- Roughly chop the spring onion/scallion and fresh coriander/cilantro.
- Peel and slice your plantain on the diagonal.
- Rinse your red lentils in a sieve/fine-mesh strainer under cold running water.

4. Sauté your onion, garlic and chillies in 2 teaspoons of the olive or rapeseed/canola oil in a frying pan on a medium heat. Once soft and translucent (after about 8–10 minutes), add all the spices, the ginger and a teaspoon more oil and continue to fry for a few more minutes.

5. Next add your red lentils and give them a good stir so that they are covered with the spices.

6. Add 700ml/24fl oz/3 cups of the vegetable stock (yes, hold back 100ml/3½fl oz/scant ½ cup), take the heat down and simmer gently for 20–25 minutes, stirring occasionally. If it looks like it's getting too thick during this time, add the tablespoon of water. >>

INGREDIENTS

For The Parsnip Fritters

320g/11¼oz parsnips (any mix of hard root vegetables – carrots, beetroots/beets, etc)

1 small white onion

4 cloves garlic

8g/¼oz fresh flat-leaf parsley

1 sprig of thyme

70g/2½oz/½ cup self-raising/self-rising flour

1 teaspoon ground turmeric

1 teaspoon cumin/jeera seeds

1 teaspoon dried chilli/hot pepper flakes

Big pinch of sea salt

Pinch of black pepper

500ml/17fl oz/2 cups neutral oil (vegetable, rapeseed/canola or sunflower oil),

For The Dhal

1 onion

4 cloves garlic

1–2 fresh red or green Bird's Eye chillies

20g/¾oz root ginger

1 spring onion/scallion

Small handful of fresh coriander/cilantro

1 plantain

140g/5oz/¾ cup dried split red lentils

2 tablespoons olive or rapeseed/canola oil

1 teaspoon cumin/jeera seeds

1 teaspoon ground coriander

1 teaspoon ground turmeric

1 teaspoon Caribbean curry powder

2 star anise

800ml/28fl oz/scant 3½ cups vegetable stock

1 tablespoon water (optional)

Pinch of sea salt

To Serve

Cooked grain of choice (see Cooking Staples on p 55)

Simple green salad

Stir-fried greens

7. Once the lentils are tender, give it a stir, add the remaining vegetable stock and the salt and turn off the heat to let the flavours develop.

8. While the dhal is cooking, pop your accompanying grain on to cook, and start deep-frying your fritters – not something that's common in a health-conscious MIH class but sometimes it's necessary!

9. Heat your neutral oil in a deep, heavy saucepan (or deep-fat fryer, if you have one) to around 170°C/340°F. To test if the oil is hot enough, pop in a pinch of the fritter mix – be careful not to splash yourself with the hot oil. If it rises and goes golden quickly, it's ready to fry.

10. Gently slide 1 tablespoon of the fritter mix at a time into the hot oil and cook each one until golden. Depending on the size of your pan, I recommend cooking 2 or 3 at a time. It's helpful to keep them a modest size (no bigger than two golf balls combined), otherwise you'll find they cook on the outside and remain raw in the middle! Don't worry about them being perfectly shaped, nice straggly edges is fine.

11. Get a plate or bowl lined with paper towels ready to one side of your pan (or fryer), remove the cooked fritters with a metal slotted spoon and pop them on the paper towels to absorb any excess oil. Keep them warm in a low oven, while you deep-fry the remaining fritters in the same way.

12. Now let's fry the plantain. Add the remaining olive or rapeseed oil to a frying pan and ensure it coats the whole pan by turning it from side to side. Now fry your plantain pieces on a medium heat (you can fill the pan but you need some space between the pieces to move them around so they don't stick) until golden on both sides. You'll need to turn them over after about 2–3 minutes of frying to do both sides.

13. When it's time to serve, take half of the chopped coriander/cilantro and the spring onion/scallions and stir gently through the dhal. Next lay the fried plantain on top of the dhal and sprinkle over the last of the chopped coriander to garnish. Serve the fritters piled high alongside.

Serve with something fresh like a simple green salad, stir-fried greens and your choice of cooked grain.

LET'S TALK ABOUT....
THE DEMONIZATION OF SINGLE INGREDIENTS *With Sarah Bentley*

Some plant-based ingredients are regarded as problematic, written off as bad for this or that reason, usually with a sensational clickbait headline. These demonizations tend to come from quite a Westernized angle – and it is usually the colonized, capitalist system of food production that is the issue, rather than the ingredient itself.

As you've learned with Nena (p 378), palm oil has received a lot of negative press as the mass farming of palms has destroyed the homes of orangutans and great swathes of rainforest in the Amazon and parts of south Asia. But palm oil made from palms grown in small holdings in West Africa is a completely different story. Yet many people have developed the opinion that all palm oil equals bad, with no nuance or wider understanding.

The rise in the consumption of quinoa was reported as causing hunger amongst Bolivian communities who could no longer afford to eat the staple grain they've been growing for hundreds of years as it was so in demand from the global market. This is true, but it's not the full picture. The value of the crop (about three times what it was prior to its boom in popularity) means farmers were generating more wealth because of it, but for local folk who weren't farmers their staple grain was suddenly far too expensive. Is this an issue? Yes, absolutely. But would stopping eating quinoa solve it? No. Addressing the colonized, capitalist system of food production and unjust manner with which farmers and farming communities are treated, not to mention the issue of food commodity traders, would be a more productive way to tackle global inequities in the food system. (See p 211 for How to be a Good Global Food Citizen.) And besides, quinoa can be sourced from all over the world, including colder European climates, and is even grown in the UK by a company called Hodmedod.

Almond milk was reported to be extremely environmentally unsustainable due to the industrial almond farms in California consuming water at an alarming rate and causing droughts. Does this mean all almonds and almond milks are cancelled? Almonds are grown in many parts of the world other than California, so we'll leave you to consider that one. My personal bugbear with almond milk is the tiny number of almonds most store-bought milks contain versus water. If you have a high speed blender and a nut milk bag – make your own. And if you think plant-milks are a Millennial invention – you'd be wrong. Coconut milk has been used across Asia for centuries and almond milk was used in medieval cuisine across Europe.

Other ingredients surrounded by controversy include avocados (their popularity has triggered the avocado wars in Mexico with rival mafias competing to control the trade), soy (virgin rainforest cut down to grow soy – but largely this is for animal feed and not for the consumption of vegans and veggies) and coconuts (reports of chained up monkeys being used to harvest them). All these issues are valid and do happen – but does it mean we have to cancel a whole ingredient? We don't think so.

So to sum up – let's all be mindful not to label an ingredient good or bad just because we've read a compelling story about it. Instead, do wider research and look at the sourcing options carefully. Talk to people from communities that use this ingredient in their cultural cuisine and get a deeper, more nuanced understanding.

 use gluten-free soy sauce or swap for tamari.

SERVES: 4 | TIME: 45 MINUTES

EDDIE'S CHORIQUESO

"Mexican chorizo is an intensely spiced sausage crumble that's typically made with pork, vinegar and a variety of herbs, spices and chillies. It's often combined with eggs for breakfast or served as an appetizer on top of a bowl of stretchy cheese dip. Hence, the name of this dish, Choriqueso – 'Chori' for chorizo (or sausage) and 'queso' for cheese. For a healthier twist on this northern Mexico starter, we take those traditional seasonings and combine them with protein-packed chickpeas to top our cashew-based cheese dip. You're going to love it."

EQUIPMENT

Sharp knife, large bowl, food processor (optional), large frying pan, wooden spoon, high-speed blender, small saucepan

INGREDIENTS (next page)

1. First make the chickpea chorizo. Let's prepare the ingredients.
- Finely dice the onion and sun-dried tomatoes.
- Drain the chickpeas/garbanzo beans – catch the liquid, the aquafaba, to use in another recipe.
- Soak the cashews (for the cheese dip) in hot water for 20 minutes.

2. Pulse the chickpeas to a crumble in a food processor. You want them to be broken up and look like taco meat, not a paste. If you don't have a food processor, use a fork to bash them up.

3. In a large frying pan, heat the sesame oil on a medium-high heat. Add the onion and sauté for 4–5 minutes, or until translucent.

4. Stir in the garlic, then add all the dry ingredients and sun-dried tomatoes and mix well.

5. Add the tomato purée/paste, the crumbled chickpeas, the soy sauce and vinegar and toss until well combined and the chickpeas are evenly coated in the seasoning.

6. Sauté the "chorizo" mix on a medium-high heat for 5–7 minutes, stirring occasionally. Keep warm on a low heat.

7. To make the cheese dip, first drain and rinse the soaked cashews.

8. Toss all the ingredients in a high-speed blender and blend til smooth.

9. Pour the mixture into a small saucepan and cook on a medium-high heat for about 5–7 minutes, stirring constantly, until the "cheese" is nice and stretchy.

10. Pour the cheese dip into a serving bowl and top with chickpea "chorizo". Enjoy.

INGREDIENTS

For The Chickpea Chorizo

½ onion

20g/¾oz (drained weight) sun-dried tomatoes in oil

4 cloves garlic

1 x 400g/14oz can chickpeas/ garbanzo beans

1½ tablespoons sesame oil

½ teaspoon ground cumin/jeera

¼ teaspoon dried thyme

½ teaspoon dried oregano

¼ teaspoon black pepper

¼ teaspoon ground cinnamon

⅛ teaspoon ground cloves

1 teaspoon ground coriander

½ teaspoon smoked paprika

¼–½ teaspoon chipotle powder

1 tablespoon tomato purée/paste

1 teaspoon dark soy sauce

2 teaspoons red wine vinegar

For The Cheese Dip

70g/2½oz/⅔ cup raw cashews

240ml/8½fl oz/1 cup water

½ tablespoon B12-enriched nutritional yeast

1 teaspoon lemon juice

½ teaspoon sea salt

½ teaspoon garlic powder

½ teaspoon mustard powder

3 tablespoons tapioca starch

¼ teaspoon black pepper

HOW TO BE A GLOBAL FOOD CITIZEN *With Sarah Bentley*

SUPPORT LOCAL FOOD SYSTEMS

Support your local farmers' market, local veg box scheme, shop at independent stores and cafés and buy from local artisan producers.

REDUCE YOUR WASTE

Follow our tips for reducing your food waste on p 373.

GO VEGAN, OR AT LEAST EAT MORE VEGAN MEALS

Try eating vegan two or three days a week and increase from there.

BUY ORGANIC – IF YOUR BUDGET ALLOWS

Join an organic food buying cooperative, sign up to a community-run veg box scheme or look for organic budget lines in supermarkets.

SUPPORT THE GLOBAL PEASANT FARMERS MOVEMENT

Smallholders and peasant farmers produce 30–34% of the global food supply on just 24% of gross agricultural land. They protect biodiversity and save local seeds. Support movements such as La Via Campesina.

DEMAND CHANGE

Get involved and demand action from governments, local councils, retailers, institutions and large food and farming corporations.

LEARN TO COOK, AND DO IT

Cook from scratch using wholefood plant-based ingredients.

PARTICIPATE IN FOOD ACCESS/SOLIDARITY PROJECTS

According to Action Against Hunger, more than 733 million people regularly go hungry. Find out about projects in your area tackling hunger and either volunteer, make a donation or amplify their work.

GET INFORMED

There are many powerful and destructive forces at play in our global food system. Learn about them – watch documentaries, read books.

RACIAL JUSTICE IS FOOD JUSTICE

From land access to health inequalities, these issues disproportionately affect black and brown communities in the Global North and lower income communities in the Global South. Follow and read works by Karen Washington, Deidre Woods and Sareta Puri's article for **Sustain** ***"Why Racial Justice Has to be at the Heart of Food Justice".***

GROW YOUR OWN, BY ANY MEANS NECESSARY

You don't need a garden; a balcony or window ledge will do. Growing is about sparking a connection to your food and our incredible ecosystem.

use gluten-free vegetable stock and gluten-free soy sauce or swap for tamari.

SERVES: 4 | TIME: 1 HOUR, 15 MINUTES

NIKI'S LENTIL & SWEET POTATO COTTAGE PIE

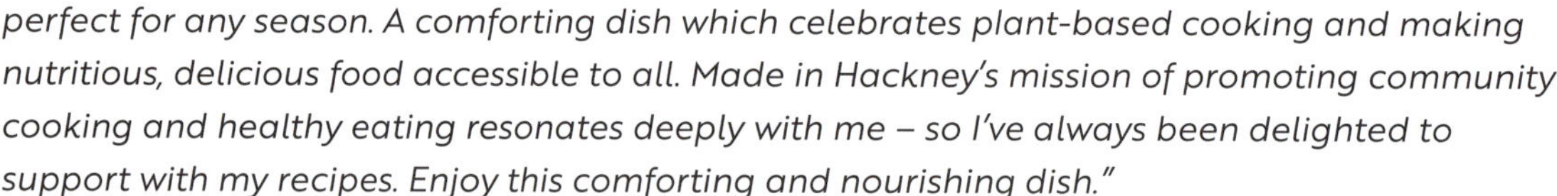

"My Lentil and Sweet Potato Cottage Pie blends hearty lentils with vibrant veggies and a creamy sweet potato topping, perfect for any season. A comforting dish which celebrates plant-based cooking and making nutritious, delicious food accessible to all. Made in Hackney's mission of promoting community cooking and healthy eating resonates deeply with me – so I've always been delighted to support with my recipes. Enjoy this comforting and nourishing dish."

EQUIPMENT

Sharp knife, sieve/fine-mesh strainer, 2 large saucepans with lids, wooden spoon, peeler, colander, masher, large ovenproof dish (approx. 30 x 20cm/12 x 8in)

INGREDIENTS (next page)

1. For the filling, let's prepare the ingredients first.
- Dice the onion, carrots and celery.
- Deseed and dice the red pepper.
- Finely slice the garlic.
- Rinse the lentils in a sieve/fine-mesh strainer under cold water.

2. Heat the olive oil in a large saucepan on a medium heat. Add the onion, carrots, celery, red pepper and garlic and sauté for about 10 minutes until the vegetables are softened.

3. Add the lentils, sun-dried tomato paste, chopped tomatoes, vegetable stock, dried oregano and smoked paprika to the pan.

4. Stir well to combine, then turn the heat up to high and bring to the boil. Once boiling, reduce the heat to low-medium, cover with a lid and simmer for about 30–35 minutes, or until the lentils are tender and the mixture has thickened.

5. Stir in the Worcester sauce, tahini, soy sauce, balsamic vinegar and frozen peas. Season with a pinch of salt and pepper to taste. Set aside.

6. While the filling is simmering, make the topping. Peel and chop your sweet potatoes into small cubes, about 1.5cm/⅝in across. Place the chopped sweet potatoes in a large pot and cover with water.

7. Cover the pan and bring to the boil on a high heat, then reduce the heat and simmer for about 15–20 minutes, or until the sweet potatoes are tender. You can test them with a fork.

8. Drain the sweet potatoes and return them to the pot. >>

INGREDIENTS

For The Filling
1 large red onion
2 carrots
2 celery stalks
1 red pepper
4 cloves garlic
200g/7oz/scant 1¼ cups dried green or brown lentils
2 tablespoons olive oil
3 tablespoons sun-dried tomato paste
1 x 400g/14oz can chopped tomatoes
1 litre/35fl oz/4¼ cups vegetable stock
1 teaspoon dried oregano
1 teaspoon smoked paprika
2 tablespoons vegan Worcester sauce
2 tablespoons smooth tahini
2 tablespoons dark soy sauce
1 tablespoon balsamic vinegar
200g/7oz/1⅓ cups frozen peas
Sea salt and black pepper

For The Sweet Potato Topping
750g/1lb 10oz sweet potatoes
3 tablespoons olive oil or vegan butter
3 tablespoons B12-enriched nutritional yeast

Stir-fried greens or side salad, to serve

9. Add the olive oil or vegan butter and nutritional yeast. Mash until smooth and creamy.

10. Season the mashed sweet potatoes with salt and pepper to taste.

11. Preheat the oven to 200°C/400°F/gas 6. Now assemble the cottage pie.

12. Spread the lentil and vegetable filling evenly in a large ovenproof dish. Spoon the mashed sweet potatoes over the top of the filling, spreading out evenly.

13. Bake for about 20–25 minutes, or until the topping is golden brown and the filling is bubbling around the edges.

Enjoy with stir-fried greens or a salad on the side.

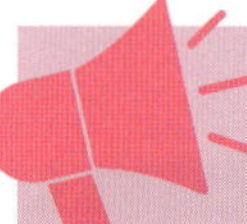

LET'S TALK ABOUT... FOOD SOCIAL ENTERPRISES *With Steve Wilson*

Food is our primary connection to the soil and each other. But the food industry can feel like a disaster – the way people are treated in kitchens, the waste, the lack of sustainability that is driven by caring for profit above all else. If you're constantly striving to drive down prices then something has to be lost; that's usually community, social values, nutrition – all things we need to include in the price of food. But more people are thinking about the bigger picture and resisting food that does more harm than good. People are hungry for change. That means there's room for improvement, disruption, new ideas. My social enterprises sought to inspire people to eat better or cook fresh ingredients from scratch, which leads to healthier, more sustainable food. Producing food ethically, in a way that looks after the earth and pays people a fair wage, does cost more, but it's mutually beneficial. There needs to be more investment in food enterprises working like this. Most of my projects have been about bringing people together around food, so on the one hand you could say it isn't political, but on the other you could say it's highly political, breaking down barriers, doing things differently, not accepting business as usual. Food social entrepreneurship and access is a big challenge – and something I sought to address with People's Kitchen and You Make Kit. If you're creating something that can only be afforded by certain people, is it doing enough? It's challenging creating a business that considers these things but can still wash its own face financially. The best thing about working in food social enterprises has been the people I've met along the way. The experiences we've shared. And of course the incredible food. If you're thinking of setting up a food social enterprise go for it. There's plenty of opportunity. Surround yourself with good people, make it fun, and never underestimate where a good dose of grit and determination will get you.

    use a gluten-free chipotle paste (in case it has malt vinegar in it) and corn not wheat tortillas.

SERVES: 4 | TIME: 15 MINUTES

KARLA'S CREAMY CHIPOTLE MUSHROOM TACOS

"In my family, my dad was the biggest mushroom fan. He used to cook them in different ways, but this is probably my favourite recipe. I love the fact that it's easy and quick to make. The chipotle chilli adds so much flavour to them and it can be spicier if you add more. The cream just makes the whole dish comforting and delicious. A perfect dish for a crowd or just as a mid-week meal."

EQUIPMENT

Sharp knife, 2 large frying pans, wooden spoon

INGREDIENTS

1 small onion
500g/1lb 2oz chestnut/cremini mushrooms
50g/1¾oz fresh coriander/cilantro
3 tablespoons vegetable oil
½ teaspoon sea salt
3 tablespoons store-bought chipotle paste
5 tablespoons plant-based double/heavy cream or vegan crème fraîche

To Serve
25g/1oz fresh coriander/cilantro
12 corn tortillas

Note: These mushrooms can be served with a salad, rice and fried beans on the side for a more generous meal. Make sure to buy good corn tortillas from a good sypplier like Cool Chile or Mextrade

1. First let's prepare the ingredients.
- Thinly slice the onion.
- Thinly slice the mushrooms.
- Chop the coriander/cilantro (for the mushrooms and to serve).

2. In a large frying pan, heat the vegetable oil on a medium heat.

3. Add the onion and fry for 3 minutes, then add the mushrooms and season with the salt.

4. Fry until the mushrooms reduce in size, making sure to mix from time to time, so they cook evenly – this will take around 5 minutes or a bit more.

5. Add the chipotle paste and stir well, so all the mushrooms are evenly coated with it.

6. To finish the dish, stir in the plant-based cream or crème fraîche and the chopped coriander. Cook for a further 2 minutes and then remove from the heat.

7. Meanwhile, heat the corn tortillas in a dry frying pan, according to the package directions.

8. To serve, place the mushrooms on a platter with the tortillas alongside, so you and your guests can make your own tacos. Scatter over the chopped coriander to finish.

TIPS & TRICKS
What's Chipotle Paste?
p 376

IN CONVERSATION WITH...

Exploring Decolonizing the Food System

A conversation with food writer, poet and academic Anna Sulan Masing

What does to decolonize the food system mean?
Anna: In its simplest form, it's to look away from Western systems, structures and approaches to food and drink. To examine power dynamics and structures and understand that we live in a world that has been for a long time, and it can be argued still is, subjected to capitalist structures created by European and white settler states. So if we're decolonizing our food systems, we're looking at the power dynamics between the Global North, white settler states and European powers, and the Global South, and interrogating those systems to see what the dynamics are.

What kind of dynamics might we be looking at?
The Global South has fed and continues to feed the Global North. So that's a power structure that puts the Global South potentially in a vulnerable place to be exploited. It's a power dynamic that needs to be examined and interrogated, more than just thinking about the legacy of colonialism. It's not just spaces that are south of the equator or were colonized, or were referred to previously as "the developing world", because you can get Global South spaces in Global North locations.

How does this show up in everyday aspects of British food culture?
One way to look at it is through narratives. If we think about chefs on popular media, it's understanding what's considered good or of value is not something that has to be rooted in European traditions. It's understanding that non-European, global majority cuisines, techniques and flavour profiles have complex systems of deep and ancient knowledge, of innovation. It's knowing that food and culinary histories anchored in European histories are often seen as more important or of more value. And when global majority culinary foods are seen as having value, it's often only when it's been touched by a white hand, say a white chef cooking Thai food on TV, and suddenly everyone thinks Thai food is great. It's shifting that understanding to allow for people whose heritage is anchored in those cuisines to be given the same value as white chefs.

So an example might be how in the UK French cuisine is exalted for its deep culinary lexicon, but unless someone's from the diaspora, or is intentionally seeking it out, people might not have considered the equally deep culinary culture of, say, Ghana.

And that's because we live in a European culture. So these kinds of European histories are more accessible. French chefs were here for hundreds of years; there's geographic and cultural proximity. Georges-Auguste Escoffier created the kitchen brigade system at the Savoy Hotel in the 19th century with the strict chain of kitchen command that is still used in kitchens today. So of course we're influenced by it. But it's understanding that just because you don't know something, doesn't mean it doesn't exist or doesn't have value. And if you value something it doesn't mean something else is not valued. We can hold multiple understandings at once. To decolonize our thinking is to reject that there is one way to do things, as opposed to multiple ways.

What about the international products we find in supermarkets? Are these part of decolonizing the food system? Or the opposite?
This brings in ideas about cultural appropriation and exoticization. Brands jump on trends without understanding the deep history or story behind these foods. It's not that hard to do it well, and yet so often it's done badly. And it's not necessarily that

the food tastes bad, but the narrative doesn't acknowledge the history or is treating it like a trend. Let's take for example the "Chinese Wrap" I bought the other day for lunch and was laughing at. It used ingredients that weren't Chinese. Taste wise, it was good, it was almost there. But it's so homogenizing. It lacks that extra bit of thought to do it well. These products need developing with people from those cultures, and I don't know how often they are. It's better when an individual person or region is attached to it to anchor it so you can get a story that's a bit more nuanced.

So how could those products be done better?
If we stay with the "Chinese Wrap", I think they were trying to create a wrap reminiscent of a British Chinese takeaway dish, which if you were doing the storytelling better you could say: a wrap that's developed from or brings together Cantonese flavours with a British diaspora food experience. That's too long, but the copy writers could do a better job, right? Things don't always have to be so reductive. A Chinese Wrap with nothing in it that is Chinese. And what do you mean by Chinese? It's so homogenizing. But saying "inspired by" is a lazy short cut too. You can't just be like: "This is inspired by Vietnamese coffee". And then it's not even Vietnamese coffee. Be specific.

What about products such as Levi Roots' "Reggae Reggae" sauce?
Levi Roots is great. It's a positive example, as it's his interpretation of his cultural heritage. That's the crux of it. You're not saying: "This is Jamaican hot sauce", because everyone has a different recipe and story about Jamaican hot sauce. And this is what happens when someone is really integral to a product's development. We get to see more Black and brown faces and understand they are people who create products of excellence. Instead of constantly seeing white faces in the world. So that's important. I don't think representation is the answer to all this. But it is helpful and gives more nuanced storytelling.

What else is important to understanding decolonizing the food system?
The understanding of authenticity in relation to the Western way of thinking, which is more about nostalgia than authenticity. When Western tourists or Westerners who have lived in another country for years talk about authenticity, it's through a lens of whiteness. They might be eating from hawker stalls in Singapore declaring it's an authentic experience. But I don't think white people can ever talk about something being authentic or not if it's outside their culture. Because the experience they had is just a snapshot that isn't anchored in histories. Whereas I think to other predominantly global majority cultures that sit outside of the Western structural system, that idea of authenticity is based on individual history, and the idea of authenticity is always changing and is about dynamism, innovation, growth and personal history. It's about looking back and saying my great-grandmother did this, my grandmother did that, and my mother did this – but this is my way. It's an authentic story through multiple generations. So what I'm creating is innovative and new, whereas the Western idea of authenticity through a white lens is about static tradition.

So these are two very different understandings of authenticity.
It's two entirely different conversations. The idea of authenticity grounded in a Western cultural way of thinking is different to the concept of authenticity in global majority spaces. And it's quite damaging. I would say that a lot of people here, who are of the diaspora, also see this understanding of authenticity that is really about a snapshot in time. They're not interrogating their nostalgia and the idea of authenticity; they're placing it within a value system that is possibly a much more capitalist system. So people here might be talking about how authentic a type of Singaporean noodle is, without realising right now in Singapore young chefs are doing crazy interesting stuff that is nothing like the Singapore noodles you're eating in London. And they would say they're doing authentic cooking, which they are, because they're Singaporean chefs, in Singapore, cooking Singaporean noodles, you know what I mean?

If people want to be part of decolonizing the food system, what can they do?
I'm a reader and writer, so I say decolonize your bookshelf, your cookbooks. It could be really fun. Like, get a map and put pins in all the different places your cookbooks come from. Or if you can't buy many cookbooks, look up recipes online. And this will open up how different cultures

have complex ideas of how to build flavour. Another fun thing is look up different cultures' favourite quick and easy foods. That takes you on a whole other journey of discovery.

What about decolonizing veganism?

In the Western world there needs to be serious conversations about decolonizing veganism. Which is what MIH does a lot of, showcasing global cuisines and chefs that are plant-based or vegan. For so long veganism in the media was portrayed as this white, rich, female, wellness-centred thing. It's like, what? They didn't invent this.

What about sourcing and ingredients like quinoa – where does this come into the discussion?

This is based on marketing and capitalism. One product gets promoted like it's going to solve all your issues and suddenly it's the hot food that everyone wants – even though it's been around for thousands of years. These trends can mess up systems and cause prices to spike. A decolonizing approach to sourcing is to have multiple different grains in your pantry and look into where and how these grains are grown. It's difficult, but worth doing. It's understanding you have to source from multiple places and spaces. We live in a global food system and have done so for thousands of years. We need to go back to relying more on local, seasonal products and then carefully source the other international items.

Let's talk about mock meats. They've long been part of Chinese cuisine, but faux meats are often presented like a new innovation.

They've been part of Chinese cuisine for thousands of years and are a part of millions of people's food culture. The tech bros want us to think that they've solved the environmental crisis, particularly the environmental issues around meat, but it's so much more complex than that. But many of these companies are still acting within a very capitalist structure that's got nothing to do with a vibrant, regenerative food system. It's a technology that has its place, but it has completely different labour structures to the rest of the food system, which is important to recognize.

Should we be thinking about where we spend our money?

I know this is hard to do, especially if you have a big family to feed, but if you can avoid shopping in the big supermarkets, which have too much power and influence on our food system and take up too much space in our communities, that's a good thing to do. Spend money with smaller, independent retailers. Shop at markets and farmers' markets if you have one nearby.

So decolonizing our food system doesn't mean eating lots of global food?

Not necessarily. We don't need to force ourselves to eat differently. Food is a biological and cultural right. You shouldn't force yourself to eat foods from other cultures, unless you're curious. You should eat foods you find delicious and comforting. So if you don't feel comfortable going into an Asian supermarket then don't; it's not for you. It's for the Asian community. Not every space is for everybody. And that's ok. Part of decolonizing is not thinking you're entitled to every space. Or making the employees work harder so you understand the space and the products. You're not entitled to that extra labour. If you're comfortable exploring it for yourself, go for it. But if not, go somewhere else where you are comfortable. Decolonizing is about interrogating and understanding the power structures within our food system, and how we play a part.

Anything else that you'd like to share about decolonizing the food system?

Decolonization is a constant and moving process that in 10, 50, 100 years is going to look different to now. It's a constantly moving conversation, which is why I like to root it in this idea of power and space. It's a way of interrogating it that makes sense to me. And it's important people see it as constant internal, personal work. And just because you're of the diaspora it doesn't mean you don't need to do the work too, because if you've grown up in Western spaces, you've absorbed colonial structures. Decolonization is a difficult thing for everybody to go through, talk about, negotiate, think and rethink.

SIDE SHOW

Welcome to the side show where we celebrate and share recipes traditionally regarded as side dishes, first courses, snacks and accompaniments.

We've got everything here from delicious salads created by TV doctors to treasured family recipes for a pan-fried Gujarati snack, a celebratory Czech potato salad and a fermented soybean Japanese dish that's a nutrition powerhouse.

We'll also show you some zero waste cooking tricks, including turning citrus peels into deep flavour enhancers and banana skins into delicious pulled pork imitating taco fillings. Yes, we said banana skins!

So fire up your hob/stovetop, blender or oven and let's get going.

SERVES 4 | TIME: 20 MINUTES

SARAH'S CHICKPEA THUNA

"When I have people over for a gathering or one of our Skank & Grill parties (sweet tunes and a vegan BBQ), this is one of the dishes I whip up for the buffet. Most people at first glance think it's tuna and do a double take. Hosting and feeding beautiful souls is a great privilege and a practice I learned from my mum. Her epic party tables always groaned with food and I think of her whenever I make a big spread for lots of people."

EQUIPMENT

Sharp knife, colander, large bowl, masher or food processer, small bowl, oven

INGREDIENTS

1 x 400g/14oz can chickpeas/garbanzo beans
1 x 200g/7oz can sweetcorn
30g/1oz fresh dill
30g/1oz fresh chives (optional)
125g/4½oz (drained) capers
Finely grated zest and juice of 1 lemon
1 tablespoon extra virgin olive oil
2–3 tablespoons vegan mayo
½ teaspoon mustard powder (optional)
2 tablespoons brine/vinegar from the jar of capers or from a jar of gherkins
Pinch of sea salt
Pinch of black pepper

1. Let's prep the ingredients.
- Drain and rinse the chickpeas/garbanzo beans and sweetcorn, but ensure to catch the juice from the chickpeas – the aquafaba – to use in another recipe.
- Finely chop the dill and chives if using.

2. Add the chickpeas/garbanzo beans to a bowl and mash with a potato masher, fork or your hands. The finished result shouldn't be mush but crumbled chickpeas. If making a large batch for a party, use a food processor to crumble them.

3. Add the sweetcorn, dill, chives, capers and lemon zest and mix.

4. In a small bowl, mix together the olive oil, vegan mayo, mustard powder (if using), lemon juice and caper/gherkin brine/vinegar.

5. Stir the sauce through the chickpea mix. Add the salt and black pepper and stir again. Serve as is or as a topping for a jacket potato or sandwich filler.

use gluten-free soy sauce or swap for tamari.

SERVES 4 | TIME: 25 MINUTES

SARAH'S SOY CHUNKS

"My household loves soy chunks or textured soy protein as they're less catchily called. Little chewy pieces of yum. We throw them on top of tomato pasta, inside a wrap or burrito or have them on the side in a bowl. I first tried textured soy protein many years ago in Kingston, Jamaica at an Ital food takeout run by chef Ras Pablo. He made a different budget meal every day for the equivalent of £2/$2.60 and kept many hungry bellies full when money was short. Chunks are a cost-effective, easy-to-store source of plant protein and a happy reminder of my former days as a reggae-dancehall music journalist."

EQUIPMENT

Large heatproof bowl, colander, frying pan, wooden spoon

INGREDIENTS

100g/3½oz dried soy chunks (also known as TSP chunks)
Boiling water, to cover
1 tablespoon rapeseed/canola oil
1–2 tablespoons dark soy sauce
75g/2¾oz tomato purée/paste

1. Add the soy chunks to a large heatproof bowl and cover with boiling water. The water should be 2cm/¾in above the chunks. Leave to hydrate for 10–15 minutes.

2. Once the chunks have hydrated and grown in size, tip them into a colander resting in the sink.

3. Squeeze the water out of the chunks with your hands. You might want to wear rubber gloves as the water will be hot.

4. Add ½ tablespoon of the oil to a frying pan on a medium heat. Tilt the pan to spread the oil all over it.

5. When the oil is hot, after about 1 minute, add the chunks and cook on a medium-high heat for 5 minutes. Stir often.

6. Add the remaining oil, stir, then cook for another 5 minutes.

7. When the chunks have changed colour all over, tip them into a bowl and coat them all over with the soy sauce, then tip them back into the pan. If you pour the sauce into the pan instead, it will burn on the pan surface.

8. Turn the heat down to medium and cook for 3 minutes.

9. Add the tomato purée/paste to the pan and stir to evenly coat the chunks. Cook for another 3–5 minutes. Enjoy.

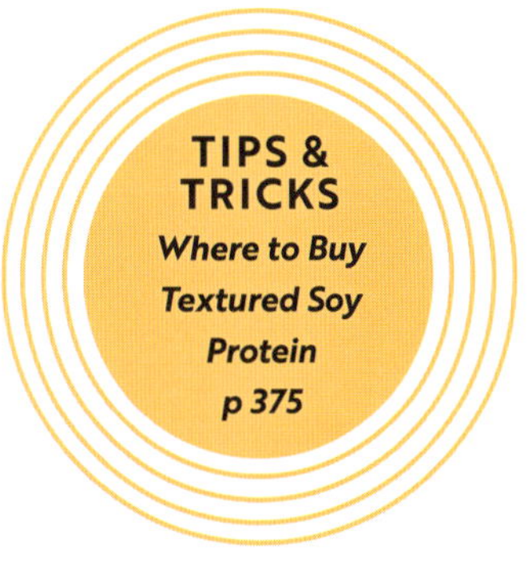

TIPS & TRICKS

Where to Buy Textured Soy Protein p 375

GF swap the yeast extract for a teaspoon of tamari.

SERVES 4 | TIME: 1 HOUR, PLUS 4-8 HOURS SOAKING

SARAH'S CHEESY KALE CRISPS

"These crisps are one of the few ways I can get my son to eat kale and seeds. The trick is to make them super cheesy and umami rich. For a cheaper sauce you can omit the cashew nuts and use more sunflower seeds. We use a dehydrator to make raw kale crisps – but not many people have a dehydrator, so this recipe uses an oven. Our former Community Programmes Manager Veryan, who tested this recipe, described them as "The (ethical) Rolls Royce of kale crisps". Eat them as a snack or scatter them on top of soups and stews for a tasty crunch."

EQUIPMENT

3 bowls, sieve/fine-mesh strainer, high-speed blender, large bowl, 2–3 baking sheets lined with baking parchment, wooden spoon

INGREDIENTS

200g/7oz/scant 1¾ cups raw cashew nuts
2 tablespoons sunflower seeds
1 tablespoon pumpkin seeds
50ml/1¾fl oz/scant ¼ cup water (you may need a little extra)
3 tablespoons B12-enriched nutritional yeast
1 teaspoon yeast extract
1 teaspoon brown rice miso paste (optional)
1 tablespoon tomato purée/paste
2 teaspoons apple cider vinegar
Pinch of black pepper
400g/14oz curly kale
1 teaspoon olive oil
Sea salt

1. Soak the cashew nuts and seeds in cold water in separate bowls for 4–8 hours. Or if you are short of time, soak in separate bowls of boiling water for 30 minutes instead.

2. Preheat the oven to 120°C/250°F/gas ½.

3. Drain and rinse the nuts and seeds in a sieve/fine-mesh strainer, add to a high-speed blender with all the other ingredients – except the kale and olive oil – adding a pinch of salt too.

4. Blend into a smooth paste. If you need to loosen it a little, add more water, 1 teaspoon at a time. You want a creamy paste, not runny.

5. Tear the kale leaves away from the stalks and rip the leaves into 2–4cm/¾–1½in pieces. Rinse the kale to clean it then dry it with a dish towel so it crisps up nicely in the oven.

6. Compost the stalks or pop in a ziplock bag to use later in a veg broth or a ferment.

7. Add the kale to a large bowl. Add the olive oil and a pinch of salt and massage the kale with your hands for 3 minutes so it becomes soft as if it has been cooked.

8. Pour the sauce over the kale and mix together, ensuring all the leaves are evenly coated with no big dollops of sauce.

9. Spread the kale out on the lined baking sheets, ensuring they don't overlap.

10. Bake on the middle and bottom shelves of your oven for up to 40–50 minutes. Check them after 25 minutes as kale burns easily and every oven behaves differently. The ones on the middle shelf will be done first. Once they are, you might need to move up the lower

TIPS & TRICKS
Sourcing Cashew Nuts
p 375

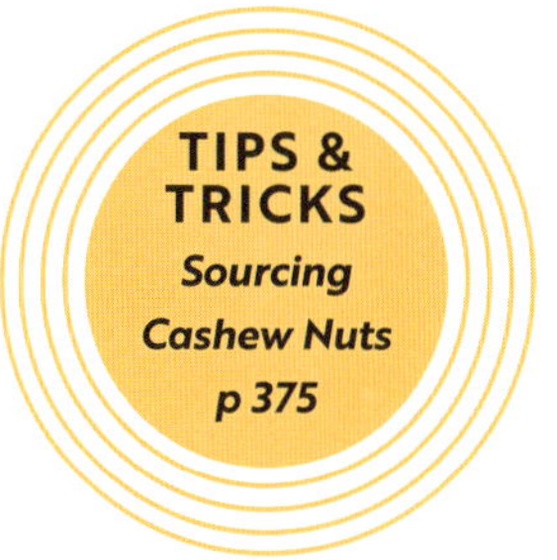

baking tray and bake for 5–10 more minutes. The kale pieces should be crispy and the sauce dried. If some crisps still have patches of wet sauce on, pop just these pieces back in the oven for 5–10 minutes.

11. Ensure the crisps cool completely on the baking trays before storing them in an airtight container at room temperature. They keep for up to a week but you may need to crisp them up again in the oven (same temperature as before) for 3–5 minutes before serving, as they will soften over time.

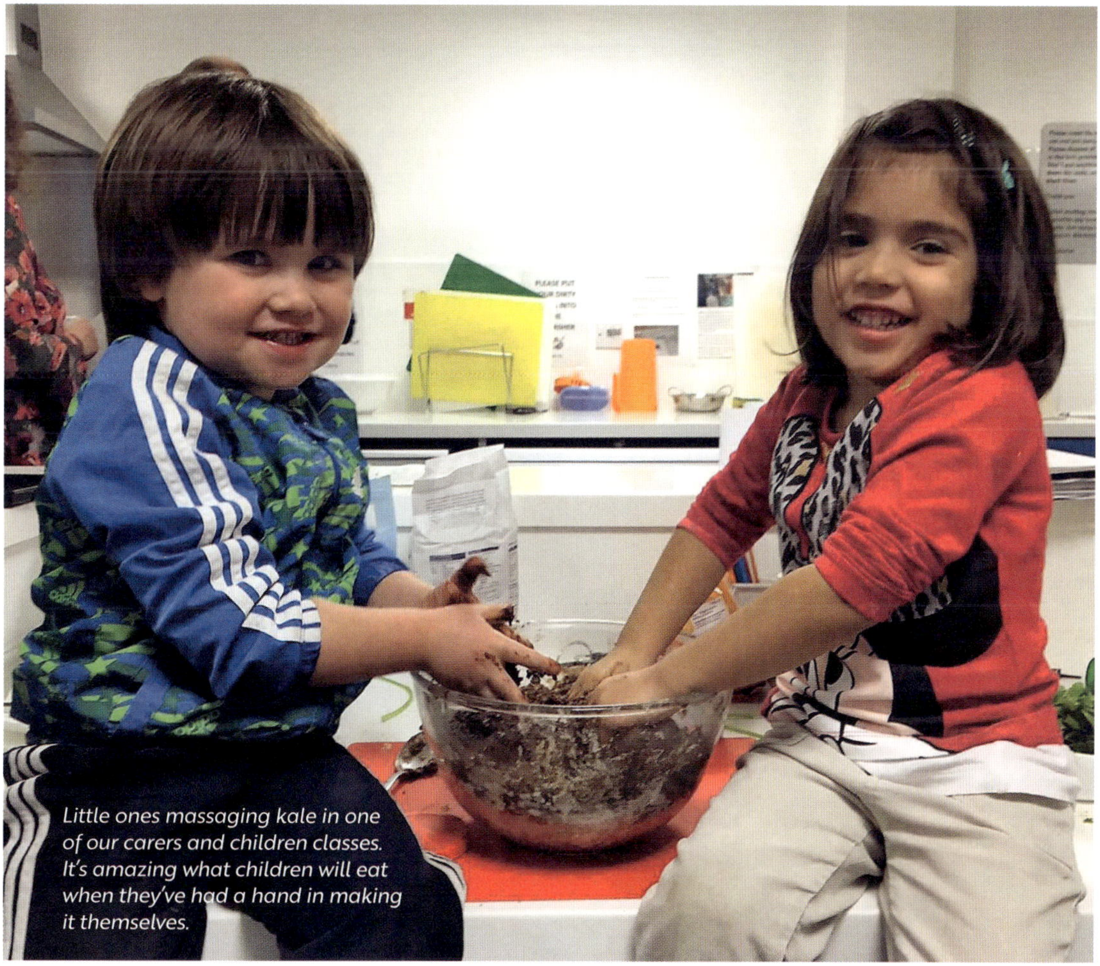

Little ones massaging kale in one of our carers and children classes. It's amazing what children will eat when they've had a hand in making it themselves.

MAKES 6 PATTIES | TIME: 45-60 MINUTES

EKOWA AND ZAHIRA'S BEEF-STYLE PENG PATTY

"At Peng Patties we want to bring about a world where regardless of where a young person is from or what their background is, they are nurtured to develop the skills and confidence to fulfil their potential and make their dreams come true. In the early stages of the project, we lost a young man to youth violence, which was utterly devastating. It was his idea to name the group Peng Patties, so the name is very special to us. This is a beef-style patty modelled on ones you'd find in a patty shop but without the flaky pastry and with a healthier, Ital filling."

EQUIPMENT

Saucepan, sharp knife, peeler, frying pan, wooden spoon, small saucepan, measuring jug/pitcher, hand-held/immersion blender, baking sheet, large bowl, rolling pin, pastry brush

INGREDIENTS (next page)

1. Rinse the lentils for the filling, then put them on to cook in a pan. Cover them in water so it sits about 1cm/½in above the lentils, bring to the boil, then turn the heat down and simmer for 20 minutes until soft.

2. Meanwhile, let's prepare the vegetables.
- Peel, deseed and cut the butternut squash into 2cm/¾in cubes.
- Dice the onion.
- Deseed and dice the red pepper.
- Finely slice the garlic and ginger.

3. Add the rapeseed/canola oil to a frying pan and heat on a medium heat until hot.

4. Add the onion, garlic and ginger to the pan and cook for 3–4 minutes, stirring occasionally.

5. Add the butternut squash and cook for a further 5 minutes. Add extra oil if the veg are sticking too much.

6. Add the red pepper and all the ground spices and cook for 10 minutes, stirring occasionally.

7. In a separate small pan, add the mixed frozen veg, cover with water and bring to the boil. Cook for 5 minutes until they have cooked but aren't soft and mushy. Strain and set aside.

8. Once the lentils are ready, strain, then add to the frying pan and stir. Combine the boiling water and stock cubes in a measuring jug. >>

The young Peng Patties chefs in session honing their cooking and entrepreneurial skills.

INGREDIENTS

For The Patty Crust

- 360g/12¾oz/3 cups plain/all-purpose or white spelt flour, plus extra for dusting
- 2 teaspoons sea salt
- 2 teaspoons ground turmeric
- 4 tablespoons grapeseed or rapeseed/canola oil
- 240ml/8fl oz/1 cup plant-based milk, plus 1 tablespoon (for brushing on top at end)

For The Filling

- 100g/3½oz/½ cup dried brown/green lentils
- 200g/7oz butternut squash
- ¼ white or red onion
- ¼ red pepper
- 1 clove garlic
- ½ thumb-size piece root ginger
- 1 teaspoon rapeseed/canola oil (you may need an extra teaspoon or two)
- ½ teaspoon Caribbean curry powder
- ¼ teaspoon ground cloves
- ¼ teaspoon ground turmeric
- ¼ teaspoon smoked paprika
- ¼ teaspoon cayenne pepper
- ¼ teaspoon ground allspice/pimento
- 75g/2¾oz/½ cup frozen mixed vegetables
- 235ml/8fl oz/1 cup boiling water
- 1 vegetable stock cube

9. Now slowly add your vegetable stock to the frying pan so the level is just above the lentil mixture, then simmer on a medium heat for 10 minutes until the stock has reduced substantially. Turn off the heat.

10. Use a hand-held/immersion blender to blend the mixture into a thick purée. When you add it to the patties you don't want it to leak, so it shouldn't be watery. Add the cooked frozen veg and stir.

11. Preheat the oven to 180°C/350°F/gas 4. Line a baking sheet with baking parchment.

12. Let's make the pastry. Mix all the dry ingredients in a large bowl.

13. Add the wet ingredients and mix until you get a dough. It's nice to use your hands to bring it together. Use a hand-held/immersion blender to blend the mixture into a thick purée. When you add it to the patties you don't want it to leak, so it shouldn't be watery. Add the cooked frozen veg and stir through.

14. Scatter flour over a clean, flat surface. Place the dough on the floured surface and roll out with a rolling pin to 0.5cm/¼in thickness. Brush your rolling pin with flour to stop it sticking to the dough.

15. Place a soup or cereal bowl (about 14 – 16cm/5½ - 6in in diameter) onto the dough and cut around it to make a circle shape. Repeat this process until you have four circles of dough.

16. To one semi-circular side of each circle, add 3 tablespoons of the patty filling, ensuring to leave a 0.5cm/¼in border free around the edges so it doesn't ooze out.

17. Fold the empty side of the pastry circle over the top of the filling side and press down to seal. Use fork prongs to pattern the edge. In Peng Patty sessions, the young people use a fork to prick their initials into the top of the patty. Add a line of three pricks or whatever pattern you like.

18. Brush the remaining 1 tablespoon of plant-based milk over the top of each patty, then place on the lined baking sheet.

19. Bake on the middle shelf for 22–25 minutes. The pastry will turn a little darker. Eat the patties hot or warm as is, or with a dip.

SERVES: 4 | TIME: 25-30 MINUTES

EKOWA'S ITAL QUINOA

"This is a nice, tasty dish, but you can get it out the door quick to feed the children dem. I started eating more quinoa as I'm interested in the work of the late, great Dr Sebi, a Honduran herbalist, healer and nutrition adviser who promoted alkaline diets that are easy to follow. The idea is after you've eaten like that for a while, you're more in-tune with your body and know what it needs. I find quinoa lighter and easier to digest than rice."

EQUIPMENT

Sieve/fine-mesh strainer, saucepan, wooden spoon, sharp knife, frying pan

INGREDIENTS

For The Quinoa
- 200g/7oz/scant 1¼ cups quinoa
- 1 tablespoon coconut or olive oil
- 350ml/12fl oz/1½ cups water
- Pinch of sea salt
- 1 white onion
- 1 red onion
- 2 spring onions/scallions
- ½ each colour pepper – red, green and yellow
- 3 large mushrooms or 6 closed cup mushrooms
- 6 cherry tomatoes
- 3 thumb-size pieces root ginger
- 1 clove garlic
- ¼–1 red Scotch bonnet chilli (see Scotch Bonnet for Newbies on p 379)
- 1 tablespoon olive oil
- 1 teaspoon dried thyme
- 1 teaspoon dried oregano
- 1 tablespoon onion powder
- 1 teaspoon garlic powder
- 1 teaspoon all-purpose seasoning (see p 376)
- Pinch of sea salt
- Pinch of black pepper

1. Rinse the quinoa in a sieve/fine-mesh strainer under cold running water to clean it, then drain.

2. Place a saucepan on a medium heat, add the quinoa to the dry pan and cook for 2–3 minutes to toast it, then add the oil and cook for 3–5 minutes. When the quinoa starts to pop, add the water, salt and stir!

3. Cover, reduce the heat to very low and leave for 15 minutes. It's gently steaming at this point. Now you can prep the veg but remember to set a timer so you can turn the heat off.

4. Let's prep your veg.
- Finely slice both onions and the spring onions/scallions.
- Deseed and finely slice the peppers. Finely slice the mushrooms.
- Finely slice or quarter the cherry tomatoes.
- Finely slice the ginger, garlic and Scotch bonnet (deseed for less heat).

5. Heat the olive oil in a frying pan until hot, add the white onion and cook on a medium heat for 3 minutes until it's changed colour.

6. Add the garlic and tomatoes and cook for another 3 minutes until they've slightly cooked down.

7. Add the ginger, mushrooms, red onion, spring onions/scallions and Scotch bonnet and cook for another 3 minutes.

8. Now add the peppers and cook for a further 2 minutes. You want them crunchy and fresh still so there's no need to cook them for long.

9. Add the quinoa, herbs and all the remaining ingredients and stir!

10. Put on a low heat, cover and cook for 4–6 minutes to warm up. Serve as a tasty side or as a simple lunch or dinner.

  GF use gluten-free soy sauce or swap for tamari.

SERVES: 4 | TIME: 20 MINUTES

SARETA'S JACKFRUIT TOPPING

"You see jackfruit on a lot of chain restaurant menus and often it's cooked really badly so can put people off using it. This recipe is really simple and always goes down well. It's chewy and spicy, and a great topper for salads, tacos and sandwiches. Although used as a kind of replacement for pulled pork, it's not as high in protein but does have good amounts of fibre, vitamin C, potassium and also has B6 and folic acid."

EQUIPMENT

Baking sheet, sieve/fine-mesh strainer, large bowl

INGREDIENTS

- 1 x 400g/14oz can young green jackfruit
- 1 teaspoon ground cumin/jeera
- 1 teaspoon smoked paprika
- 1 teaspoon garlic powder
- ½ teaspoon black pepper
- ½ teaspoon cayenne pepper or chilli powder
- 2 tablespoons dark soy sauce (or tamari for gluten-free)
- 2 tablespoons olive oil

1. Preheat the oven to 180°C/350°F/gas 4. Line a baking sheet with baking parchment.

2. Drain and rinse the jackfruit in a sieve/fine-mesh strainer.

3. Using clean hands, pull the jackfruit apart into strands. Cut the core bits into 1–2cm/½–¾in cubes.

4. Mix all the remaining ingredients – except the soy sauce and olive oil – in a bowl, then add the jackfruit and stir to ensure it is nicely coated in the spice mixture. Add the soy sauce and stir it in or rub it in with your fingers.

5. Drizzle the olive oil over the lined baking sheet, spread the seasoned jackfruit out on top and then stir to coat in the oil.

6. Bake for 15 minutes until crispy.

Serve hot or warm in a sandwich, on top of tacos or on top of a salad.

Two Hackney locals enjoying the food and good vibes at one of our Community Feasts in partnership with Clapton Commons.

SERVES: 4 | TIME: 20 MINUTES

SARETA'S BEETROOT AND CABBAGE THORAN

"This recipe is super-quick and really tasty. I like it from an Ayurvedic point of view because it doesn't have onion or garlic, which can all be quite heavy on the digestion. Feel free to use whatever vegetables are in season – usually only one or two veg at a time."

EQUIPMENT

Peeler, grater, sharp knife, frying pan, wooden spoon

INGREDIENTS

375g/13oz raw beetroots/beets

190g/6¾oz Savoy cabbage

1½ fresh green finger chillies

3 tablespoons vegan ghee or coconut oil (you may need 2–3 teaspoons extra, or water)

2½ teaspoons brown mustard seeds

6 fresh curry leaves or 6–8 dried

¾ teaspoons ground turmeric

1½ teaspoon ground cumin/jeera

60–75g/2¼–2¾oz/scant 1 cup–1 cup unsweetened desiccated/dried shredded coconut

½ teaspoon sea salt

1. Let's prepare the veg.
- Peel and grate the beetroots/beets.
- Finely slice the cabbage.
- Finely slice the green chillies (deseed if you prefer less heat).

2. Heat the 3 tablespoons of vegan ghee or coconut oil in a frying pan on a medium heat for 1 minute.

3. Add the mustard seeds and curry leaves and cook until the seeds start to pop, about 2–3 minutes.

4. Add the green chillies, turmeric and cumin and stir. Then almost immediately add the beetroot and cabbage and stir until coated in the spices.

5. Cook on a medium heat for 8–10 minutes until the beetroot and cabbage are soft. If needed, you can add 2–3 teaspoons of extra ghee/oil or water if it dries up but the natural waters from the vegetables should be enough.

6. Once the vegetables are softened, stir through 60g/2¼oz/scant 1 cup of the coconut and season with the salt.

7. Cook for another 1–2 minutes. Taste and, if desired, add the remaining coconut. Stir through, then take off the heat and serve.

The Deal With Coconut Oil p 369

IN CONVERSATION WITH...

Exploring Body Inclusivity and Fatphobia

A conversation with sustainable, ethical fashion and size inclusion activist Aja Barbar

Body shape and size exclusion is endemic in the food, health and wellbeing space. How do you see this intersecting with your work in the fashion sphere?

Aja: Size inclusivity is an intersectional issue. Food is connected to fashion. Fashion is connected to feminism. Everything is connected. Whenever I say something about the fashion industry, there's always someone that says, you know, that applies to food as well.

You use the term fatphobic in your work while other people say size inclusivity. Why do you prefer fatphobic?

I use the phrase fatphobic as it's a good umbrella phrase for the way in which the world is weird about people with bigger bodies, where there's a fear of the bigger body. It ranges depending on which country and culture you're in, but at the end of the day, we live in a world where people who are fat are on the fringes of society. A society where it's perfectly acceptable for someone to say, "Oh, I'm not going to make that size in clothing", even if they have the ability to do it. Or, "I'm not going to employ someone with a larger body to promote my smoothie company or my supplement line." Or "I'm not going to make the seats comfortable on my bus, train or plane for people with this size body." Or "I'm not going to employ that yoga teacher because their body type doesn't fit our brand image." And it goes totally unchallenged.

And what's the broader impact of this?

Fatphobia has a detrimental impact on the human race in so many ways, and it gets in all our heads whether we want it to or not. It's as prevalent in the health and wellbeing space as the fashion space, and it intersects with medical racism and medical exclusion. How if a person who is bigger goes to the doctor for any ailment – any ailment – there's a good chance the doctor will start talking about their weight. That's what it means to live in a fatphobic society. To be like: "Help, I think I broke my arm." And to have someone be like, "Have you tried losing weight?" We could also talk about the ways in which people view themselves, about disordered eating, about diet culture. Diet culture is insidious, the way it makes people view themselves and what it causes them to do in order to seek acceptance that they shouldn't need to seek just to be human. And it's so entrenched that if you don't stop to intentionally think about it, you'll never really think about it, because it's so normalized in our society.

And when it is spoken about or opposed, it can trigger quite an aggressive, visceral reaction, particularly on social media.

Absolutely. There's this section of social media of supposed

Size inclusivity is an intersectional issue. Food is connected to fashion. Fashion is connected to feminism. Everything is connected.

health professionals who lambast anyone in a larger body who's unapologetically living their life for promoting obesity, just by daring to exist. It's really weird and toxic but largely goes unchallenged. And the reason these health professionals can get away with saying this kind of stuff without fear of repercussion is because we live in a fatphobic society where that sort of behaviour is fully acceptable. And it's stuff we don't even realize is pernicious. Like, when you're watching a comedy show and the fat person is the butt of every joke or portrayed as unintelligent. The larger body person is never the lead role, the boss role. It's these things in our society that are so accepted and not questioned that makes it so insidious.

You've mentioned on your socials a few times there's no payment for doing this work.

Unlike other forms of activism there's no payment or career prospects for promoting size inclusivity. The payment is brands start to make larger sizes, and you know you've been part of the conversation to make that happen. No one's paying you to do this work. No one values it enough to put funding into it.

You mentioned medical racism. How does fatphobia intersect with racism generally?

We live in a white supremacist society where there are very rigid rules to exist. Any deviation from these rigid rules you get criticized or much worse – abused, marginalized, incarcerated, excluded. So if you have a queer identity, a non-white identity or a plus size identity, just existing, just living, is much harder for you when it shouldn't be. As a society we need to start unpicking some of this but we're not getting there, or anywhere close to there, yet. And that's why I think everything intersects and that to start solving some of these issues, we need to see how they all interlink.

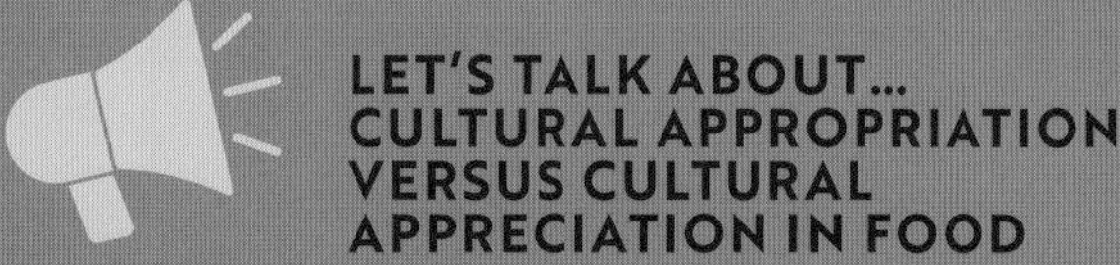

LET'S TALK ABOUT... CULTURAL APPROPRIATION VERSUS CULTURAL APPRECIATION IN FOOD

With Sarah Bentley and Sareta Puri

As a white woman in a white-centric colonizer culture, it took me a while (and I am still learning) to grasp cultural appropriation versus appreciation. As someone who loves exploring other cuisines and went vegan thanks to the nourishing powers of Ital Rastafarian food, I made some slip-ups along the way. The process of learning and unlearning, being challenged and stretched is one of the great joys of being alive today. It's not always easy on the ego, but the collective gains far outweigh the discomfort. So let's hear what Sareta Puri has to say:

"Cultural appropriation is where something is taken from another culture – food, music, a spiritual practice – and used without paying respect, homage or referencing its origins. It's problematic when it's done in a non-transparent way, the essence of something is being diluted and when someone is making money without giving back to the founding culture. No one should be profiting inappropriately off the culture, heritage and stories of other people.

When it comes to food the difference between appropriation and appreciation is quite nuanced and depends on the situation. It usually comes down to someone creating food but taking away the heritage and meaning behind it, which is what makes it so powerful in the first place. That's not to say you have to be Indian to cook or teach Indian food, but it's really about grounding yourself in the knowledge, heritage and landscape of it and recognizing why you're doing it and being honest about that. There might be plenty of people in the diaspora that don't have strong links to their heritage's food culture, and someone not of that heritage with really strong links to it who's doing a really good job of showing its authentic origins and stories. It's not one size fits all.

You see cultural appropriation a lot in food when businesses try to be very catch-all – lumping all East Asian cuisines together for example. Or when TV chefs bring out dubious products based on a national dish that has nothing to do with their own culture or heritage, and often even the original dish. Bastardization of a dish and a lack of acknowledgment of its roots are probably the most common problematic behaviours with regards to cultural appropriation in food. But it's a big topic, and everyone will have different views on what's appropriating or appreciating.

GF

SERVES: 4 | TIME: 25-30 MINUTES

SARETA'S MASALA POTATOES

"These potatoes are delicious, and class participants always want seconds, so I know they're good. My mum passed away when I was little so Dad took me and my sister to work a lot with him, so I grew up watching him cook these in restaurants in Scotland. They're more an Anglo-Indian dish than a traditional Indian one, but they're really tasty."

EQUIPMENT

Sharp knife, saucepan, colander, frying pan, wooden spoon

INGREDIENTS

600g/1lb 5oz potatoes
2 sprigs of fresh coriander/cilantro (optional)
3 tablespoons vegetable oil, plus (optional) 1 teaspoon
1½ teaspoons cumin/jeera seeds
¾ teaspoon brown mustard seeds
Pinch of asafoetida/hing (optional)
1½ teaspoons ground cumin/jeera
¾ teaspoon ground coriander
¾ teaspoon ground turmeric
½ teaspoon garlic powder (optional)
½ teaspoon chilli powder or dried chilli/hot pepper flakes (optional)
Sea salt
Coriander chutney, to serve (optional)

1. Cut the potatoes into roughly 2.5cm/1in cubes. Finely chop the fresh coriander/cilantro (if using) for the garnish and set aside.

2. Bring a saucepan of salted water to the boil. Add the potatoes and cook for 10 minutes until par-boiled. You want them soft enough to bite but not crumbly. Drain the water and set aside.

3. While the potatoes are boiling, heat the vegetable oil in a frying pan on a medium heat. When the oil is hot, add the cumin seeds and toast until lightly brown, about 2 minutes.

4. Add the mustard seeds and asafoetida/hing. When the mustard seeds start to pop, add the ground cumin, ground coriander, turmeric, garlic powder and chilli powder or flakes (if using) and cook on a medium-low heat for 1 minute, then turn the heat off.

5. Add the potatoes to the spice mix and then add a pinch of salt. Stir to ensure the potatoes are well coated. If they stick to the pan, add another teaspoon of oil.

6. Cook on a medium heat for 8–10 minutes, stirring occasionally, until the potatoes are soft, lightly browned and crisp.

7. Garnish with the chopped coriander (if using) or serve with coriander chutney on the side.

SERVES: 4 | TIME: 10 MINUTES

XIMENA'S BEETROOT AND WALNUT DIP

"I love this recipe as it reminds me of the first lesson I taught for MIH in 2012 with a wonderful group of Irish women from a charity called Mind Yourself, which supported the Irish community in London with health and wellbeing services. I was nervous how they'd take to the all-vegan menu but was pleasantly surprised when everything was eaten up and appreciated. This dip is amazing due to the sweet, earthiness from the beetroots, tanginess from the lemon, smokiness of the walnuts and creaminess of the tahini. It's a taste explosion and filling too."

EQUIPMENT

Sharp knife, food processor or blender, frying pan

INGREDIENTS

500g/1lb 2oz cooked beetroots/beets
Small handful of fresh coriander/cilantro
100g/3½oz/1 cup walnuts
3 tablespoons tahini
3 tablespoons olive oil
1–2 cloves garlic
2 teaspoons ground cumin/jeera
Juice of 1 lemon
Pinch of sea salt

1. Let's prep the ingredients.
- Chop the beetroots/beets into rough chunks.
- Chop the coriander/cilantro (for the garnish) and set aside.

2. Place the beetroot/beets in a food processor and whizz until smooth.

3. Dry-fry the walnuts in a frying pan on a medium heat, stirring occasionally, until they have slightly changed colour and are aromatic. This should take about 3 minutes.

4. Add the walnuts and all the rest of the ingredients – except the coriander/cilantro – to the food processor and whizz until they form a rough paste. Taste and add a squeeze more lemon, a pinch more salt and/or an extra teaspoon of olive oil if you think it needs it.

5. Decant the dip into a bowl and sprinkle with the chopped coriander to serve.

Ximena teaching a herb growing and cookery class in a children's centre with carers and under 3s.

MAKES: APPROX. 200G/7OZ JAR | TIME: 20 MINUTES, PLUS 4 HOURS, 15 MINUTES FOR RESTING AND PREPPING

AMANDEEP'S PUNJABI CONDIMENTS

"Nothing says autumn like an apple achar. It's seasonal, low cost and bursting with sweet and spicy flavours. I used cooking/baking apples but any sour and tart apple will work. I remember as a child, my mum would make achar in batches whenever we had an abundance of apples and then gift jars of it to relatives and friends. Achar adds a tangy flavour to any meal. It's an excellent accompaniment to a paratha or simple rice and dhal."

EQUIPMENT

Sharp knife, large bowl, large frying pan, sterilized 200g/7oz glass jam jar (see p 383)

INGREDIENTS

- 1 large cooking/ baking apple
- 1 teaspoon sea salt
- 4 tablespoons rapeseed/ canola or vegetable oil
- 2 heaped teaspoons achar masala (see p 239 to make your own)
- 1 teaspoon ground turmeric
- ¼ teaspoon black pepper

TO MAKE THE APPLE ACHAR

1. Core and cut the apple into approx. 3cm/1¼in cubes.

2. Put the apple cubes in a bowl, add the salt and mix well. Cover and set aside for 4 hours.

3. After 4 hours, drain off any juices that may have been released from the apple.

4. Heat the oil in a large frying pan on a high heat for 2 minutes.

5. Add the achar masala, turmeric and black pepper and stir continuously for about 30 seconds, making sure the masala and turmeric do not burn.

6. Add the apple cubes to the pan and mix well, making sure all the cubes are coated with the masala mix. Cook for 4 minutes on a high heat until the apple cubes are slightly soft.

7. Take off the heat and leave the mixture to cool completely.

8. Once cool, add to your sterilized jar, seal and label. The achar can be eaten straight away or kept in the refrigerator for about 2 weeks.

SERVES: 4 GENEROUSLY | TIME: 10 MINUTES

AMANDEEP'S RAITA

"Raita is a yogurt-based condiment traditionally eaten with curries to reduce the heat. Raita recipes can vary. Vegetables and fruits added to the yogurt can be cooked or raw to add different textures. Fresh herbs are always used, like coriander or mint, and the dry spices vary from garam masala to mustard seeds, which give the raita its rich flavour. This is a family recipe."

EQUIPMENT

Small frying pan, wooden spoon, pestle and mortar, sharp knife, grater, sieve/ fine-mesh strainer, bowl

INGREDIENTS

½ teaspoon cumin/ jeera seeds
Small handful of fresh coriander/cilantro
¼ small red onion
¼ cucumber
½ tomato
250g/9oz plant-based Greek-style yogurt
½–1 tablespoon plant-based milk (optional)
Pinch of sea salt
Pinch of black pepper

1. Heat a small dry frying pan on a high heat for 1 minute, then add the cumin/jeera seeds and dry-roast for about 1 minute. They will release an aroma and start to turn dark. Stir to prevent burning.

2. Remove from the pan and crush them lightly in a pestle and mortar.

3. Prepare the other ingredients.
- Roughly chop the coriander/cilantro.
- Finely slice the onion.
- Grate the cucumber.
- Finely chop the tomato.

4. Now let's get the water out of the prepped cucumber and tomato by squeezing them with your hands or pushing down with a sieve/ fine-mesh strainer until most of their water content is out.

5. Add the yogurt to a bowl. If it is a very thick style of yogurt, loosen it up with enough of the plant-based milk.

6. Add the chopped coriander/cilantro, all the prepped veg, the roasted cumin seeds, the salt and black pepper to the yogurt and give it a good mix. Eat straight away or chill before serving (it will keep for up to 2 days in the refrigerator), and enjoy with any dhal or curry dish.

MAKES: 75G/2¾OZ | TIME: 5 MINUTES

AMANDEEP'S HOME BLENDED ACHAR MASALA

"My mum doesn't trust the quality of blended spices, so I grew up watching her make her own at home. This blend is easy to make and you can adjust to your own and your household's taste preferences. It works brilliantly with apples but you can also use it to pickle other fruits and vegetables. Experiment and have fun."

EQUIPMENT

High-speed blender or spice grinder, clean jar

INGREDIENTS

4 tablespoons cumin/ jeera seeds
4 tablespoons fennel seeds
4 tablespoons nigella seeds
3 tablespoons fenugreek seeds
3 tablespoons black mustard seeds
1 teaspoon sea salt

1. Add all the spice seeds and the salt to a high-speed blender or spice grinder and blend into a powder.

2. Pour into a clean jar and seal. This achar masala powder will keep in a cool, dry place for up to a year.

LET'S TALK ABOUT... ANGLICIZED INDIAN FOOD

With Roshni Shah

Anglicized Indian food means Indian food adapted for the British market. Good examples of this are Balti and Chicken Tikka Masala, which is one of the UK's favourite meals. It's not traditional Indian food but it has its own place in the culinary lexicon. It's slightly different to bastardizations of Indian dishes such as kedgeree. The original kedgeree (khichdi) is a spiced vegetarian rice and lentil mix, but thanks to our dear friends the colonizers (eye roll) it started to be made with fish and eggs. There is a difference between food that has come over as a result of immigration, food culture as a result of empire and colonization, food that has been adopted or adapted by people living in the UK, and fusion and hybrid food the diaspora creates. My family are Gujarati heritage but from Kenya, so we eat a lot of African-Indian food using cassava, green bananas and sweetcorn. I've grown up in the UK so I like ketchup as a condiment with muthia. When I was growing up if my mum ran out of time to cook she sometimes added masala to baked beans. India and its diaspora are so huge with a vast number of regional cuisines. The famous curry houses on Brick Lane in East London that many people think of as Indian are largely Bangladeshi-owned and the cuisine is very different to Gujarati. There are so many food cultures within one country a lot of non-Gujarati Indians would have never tried muthia. Even within my own family my mum's sister has only ever made it with cooked rice, never with poha. That's why I wanted to share my recipe on p 269. It's simple, delicious but hard to come across unless your family makes it.

    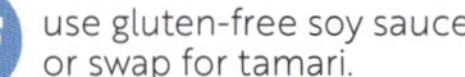

GF use gluten-free soy sauce or swap for tamari.

SERVES: 4 | TIME: 30 MINUTES

HANNAH'S BANANA PEEL CARNITAS & CARROT TOP CHIMICHURRI

"Banana peels are one of the most underappreciated ingredients most people have but don't realize they can eat! Banana skins make up as much as 40 per cent of the weight of a banana, and most people throw away (or hopefully compost) this super nutrient-rich part. They're a great source of fibre, protein, calcium, iron, vitamins A and C, potassium and essential fatty acids. And importantly, when prepared appropriately, they're delicious! Loaded with warming spices and bright citrus, once cooked, you'd have no idea that it was banana peel you were eating!"

EQUIPMENT

Bowl, sharp knife, frying pan with lid, wooden spoon

INGREDIENTS (next page)

1. First things first is to peel your bananas and set aside the fruit to use in another recipe or eat later (you can refrigerate or freeze the fruit to use in a smoothie or nice cream).

2. Now wash your banana skins. If using organic – which we highly recommend as we'll be eating the skins – give them a light scrub and rinse. If using non-organic, soak the skins in a bowl of cold water and vinegar – 1 part white vinegar to 4 parts water – and leave for 20 minutes.

3. Rinse the skins, then cut both ends off and pop them in the compost.

4. Use a spoon to scrape out the remains of the fleshy white part of the fruit and set aside or eat.

5. Use two forks to shred the banana skins into strips. Use one to hold the skin in place and the other to shred it. To create shorter strands after pulling them, cut them in half or even into thirds.

6. In a bowl, mix the banana peel strips with the seasonings – cumin, smoked paprika, oregano, onion and garlic powders and salt and pepper. Set aside.

7. Now finely slice the onion, garlic and red chilli (seeds removed for less heat).

8. Heat the olive oil in a frying pan on a medium heat until hot, then add the onion, garlic and red chilli. Sauté for 5–6 minutes, or until the onion is soft. **>>**

INGREDIENTS

- 5–6 (ideally organic) banana skins
- White vinegar, for soaking (only if using non-organic banana skins)
- 2 teaspoons ground cumin/jeera
- 1 teaspoon smoked paprika
- 1 teaspoon dried oregano
- ½ teaspoon onion powder
- ½ teaspoon garlic powder
- ¼ teaspoon sea salt
- ¼ teaspoon black pepper
- 1 small onion
- 2–3 cloves garlic
- 1 fresh red chilli
- 1 tablespoon olive oil
- 1 tablespoon dark soy sauce (or use tamari if gluten-free)
- 3–4 tablespoons freshly squeezed orange juice (from 1 orange)**
- Juice of 1 lime**
- Small handful of fresh coriander/cilantro leaves, to garnish (optional)

9. Next, add the seasoned banana peel strips to the pan and stir to combine.

10. Finally, add the soy sauce and orange and lime juices. Save the peels of the orange and lime to zest, preserve (see p 246), use as a tea, or to candy them for a dessert.

11. Increase the heat to medium-high and bring to a simmer, then reduce to a low heat and cover. Cook like this with the lid on for 25–30 minutes until the banana peel strips are softly stewed.

12. Remove from the heat, taste and adjust the seasoning if needed. Add more salt/soy sauce or lime juice to taste and garnish with the coriander/cilantro leaves.

Enjoy as a side dish, on top of a salad or in a taco. Although it's imitating a pulled meat, it doesn't have any protein, so adding to black beans or tofu would be great.

Founder Sarah, volunteer Tina, chef Hannah, ambassador Dr Rupy and Oatly nutritionist Kate working at a children's bowel health day at The Royal London Hospital

SERVES: 4 | TIME: 10 MINUTES

HANNAH'S CARROT TOP CHIMICHURRI

"Chimichurri is a flavour-packed condiment that originated in Argentina and Uruguay. You can use most green leafy vegetables, herbs or those old wilting salad leaves in the back of your refrigerator. It makes a vibrant green, zesty addition to any meal. As well as a dressing, it can be stirred through beans or lentils, used as a dip or as a marinade. Carrot greens contain a whopping six times more vitamin C than the root, as well as being a good source of calcium and other phytonutrients. They have a slightly bitter flavour that contributes to their ability to aid digestion, so they're best paired with other herbs or spices."

EQUIPMENT

Sharp knife, food processor, small bowl, whisk

INGREDIENTS

1–2 cloves garlic
1 fresh red chilli
1 shallot or ½ onion
2 tablespoons chopped preserved lemons (see Hannah's recipe on p 246), plus 2 tablespoons preserving brine, OR 2 tablespoons lemon juice, finely grated zest of 1 lemon and ½ teaspoon sea salt
40g/1½oz/1 cup carrot top greens (or beetroot/beet greens, spinach or leftover salad leaves/greens, etc.)
30g/1oz/½ cup fresh herbs (parsley, coriander/cilantro, mint, chives or a mixture)
1 teaspoon dried oregano
½ teaspoon ground paprika
½ teaspoon ground cumin/jeera
½ teaspoon sea salt
2 tablespoons red wine vinegar
2 tablespoons olive oil
Pinch of sea salt
Pinch of black pepper

1. Finely slice the garlic, red chilli (deseeded if you prefer less heat) and shallot/onion.

2. Put all the ingredients – except the olive oil, salt and black pepper – in a food processor and pulse briefly until finely chopped but not completely blended.

3. Transfer into a small bowl and whisk in the olive oil.

4. Stir in the salt and black pepper, then serve drizzled over tacos or oven-roasted veggies, or like here on top of the banana peel carnitas.

MAKES: 800ML–1 LITRE/28–35FL OZ/3½–4¼ CUPS | TIME: 1½ HOURS (GOOD TO DO WITH A FRIEND TO REDUCE TIME)

HANNAH'S HEDGEROW BBQ SAUCE

"I got into wild food on holiday. I went on a coastal walk with a forager who introduced me to the culinary possibilities of wild plants. Pineapple weed blew my mind as it really does smell like pineapple. I was hooked. I attended courses, self-studied and became a foraging leader. What I love about wild food is it opens up a new flavour cabinet. It connects you to the seasons and forces you to slow down and pay attention to what's around you. There's plenty of wild food in urban areas – sometimes more than the countryside because of agriculture. There's nothing in this sauce that can be easily confused with anything poisonous, but do use a foraging book or trusted plant ID app to make sure. These wild foods are available in the UK late August to September/October. In the US, they're available at different times depending on where you live. This recipe is fun to make in large batches with a group of friends as a social activity."

EQUIPMENT

Sharp knife, grater, large saucepan with lid, food processor, sieve/fine-mesh strainer (better than a muslin cloth/cheesecloth), masher, sterilized glass bottles or jars with metal lid for storage

INGREDIENTS **(next page)**

1. First let's prepare our ingredients.
- Finely slice the red onion.
- Chop the dates into small pieces.
- Grate the apples and carrot.
- Grate the ginger.

2. Add all the hedgerow berries – except the rosehips – to a large saucepan with the measured water and the vinegar and simmer on a medium heat for 25–30 minutes until they start to disintegrate. Put the lid partially on so it doesn't bubble over and maintains the heat.

3. Meanwhile, blend the rosehips in a food processor to a rough texture (not a purée) and add to a separate saucepan with enough water to fully cover. Bring to the boil and simmer on a medium heat for 25–30 minutes.

4. Once the hedgerow berries start to disintegrate, remove from the heat and mash in the pan with a masher. Pass the mixture through a sieve/fine-mesh strainer and collect as much pulp as you can.

5. Repeat this process of mashing and straining with the simmered rosehips to remove the fine hairs and seeds within the hips.

6. Repeat this process one or two times more by adding another 100–200ml/3½–7fl oz/scant ½–scant 1 cup of water each time to the remaining fruit solids (skin and seeds of both the hedgerow berries and rosehips), boiling for another 5 minutes and then straining again

INGREDIENTS

½ red onion
100g/3½oz dates
3 cooking/baking or eating/dessert apples
1 carrot
Thumb-size piece root ginger
500g/1lb 2oz/4 cups mixed hedgerow fruits (I used a mix of elderberries, hawthorn berries, rowan berries and rosehips)
300ml/10½fl oz/1¼ cups water, plus extra as needed (see method)
150ml/5fl oz/⅔ cup red wine/apple cider/ white vinegar (red wine vinegar tastes nicest)
1 tablespoon black treacle/molasses
1 star anise
1 cinnamon stick
2 teaspoons smoked paprika
2 teaspoons black mustard seeds
1 teaspoon cumin/jeera
1 teaspoon ground cinnamon
¼ teaspoon ground allspice/pimento
1 teaspoon sea salt

TIPS & TRICKS

Foraging Tips p 381

to get as much pulp as possible. A bit of a faff but we want to get as much of that superfood goodness out of these wild fruits as we can!

7. Once you've got as much sieved pulp as possible, mix the hedgerow berry and rosehip pulps in a large saucepan on a low-medium heat and then add all the remaining ingredients.

8. Cook, uncovered, on a medium heat for 15 minutes, stirring occasionally, until the liquid starts thickening.

9. Remove the star anise and cinnamon stick, then spoon the mixture into a blender and process until a smooth consistency. Alternatively, you can use a hand-held/immersion blender or even leave it chunky!

10. Decant into hot sterilized glass bottles or jars (see How To Sterilize Jars on p 383), seal and label. Enjoy! Don't forget to take this condiment out with you to friends' houses, picnics and dinners – something as cool as hedgerow BBQ sauce has got to be shared! And you worked hard to make it!

It keeps for a month or so unopened in the refrigerator. Once opened, enjoy within 1–2 weeks.

Hannah foraging ramsons aka wild garlic in the woods near her home in Totnes.

MAKES: 1 JAR; SERVES: 4+ | TIME: 15 MINUTES, PLUS 3–4 WEEKS STANDING TIME

HANNAH'S PRESERVED LEMONS

"Preserved lemons are a lovely condiment for adding a depth of lemony flavour to dishes. They're traditionally used in Middle Eastern and North African cooking. You pickle or ferment the lemons in a brine of salt and lemon juice to preserve them. It's a great way of using the whole lemon, but you can also make it just from the lemon rinds, after using lemon juice in other recipes. In this recipe, I've added herbs and spices to the brine to give a Moroccan flavour, but experiment with alternative additions such as a fresh sprig of rosemary. You can use the same method to preserve limes and orange peel or do a combination of all of them! Once you've done this, you'll never throw citrus peel away again!"

EQUIPMENT

Sharp knife, sterilized jar approx. 10cm/4in diameter and 18cm/7in tall (approx. 350–500ml/ 12–17fl oz/1⅓–2 cups)

INGREDIENTS

- 4–6 lemons (depending on size of lemons and jar) – organic and unwaxed if possible
- 3–4 tablespoons sea salt (or other non-iodized salt that doesn't contain anti-caking agents often found in table salt)
- 2–3 bay leaves
- 1 cinnamon stick
- 4–6 cracked green cardamom pods
- 4 star anise
- 4 whole cloves
- ½ teaspoon coriander seeds
- ½ teaspoon black peppercorns
- Extra lemon juice, to cover

1. Wash the lemons, slice the tops and ends off (these can be added to your compost bin) and then cut into quarters. Try to remove the seeds but don't worry too much about getting them all out. If using waxed, non-organic lemons, see p 53 for how to pre-soak them.

2. Cover the base of the sterilized jar with a layer of the salt and pack the lemons in, adding more layers of the salt as you go. It seems like a lot of salt, but don't worry, it's part of the preserving method and can be rinsed off before eating.

3. As you layer the lemons, squeeze them down to release their juice, adding in the herbs and spices as you pack your jar.

4. Once your jar is filled, pour over extra lemon juice (or cold filtered water if you run out of juice) so the lemons are completely submerged. Tightly seal the jar.

5. Leave to sit at room temperature for 3–4 weeks. Shake every couple of days to redistribute the liquid.

6. Once ready, refrigerate. The jar of preserved lemons will keep in the refrigerator for up to 1 year (ensure they remain submerged in the brine liquid once opened).

7. To use the lemons in your cooking, use a clean spoon or tongs to remove them from the jar. Rinse off the salt before using, or leave on for flavour but don't add any more salt to the dish. They're great finely sliced or blended as part of dressings, sauces and stews. Enjoy!

Citrus Skins p 369

Super

use gluten-free spring roll wrappers made from rice or coconut.

SERVES: 4; MAKES 24 SPRING ROLLS (6 SPRING ROLLS EACH) | TIME: 1 HOUR, PLUS TIME MAKING YOUR OWN GARLIC PURÉE

WOIN'S LENTIL SPRING ROLLS

"This is a delicious spring roll recipe I created fusing my Ethiopian heritage with East Asian cuisine. In Ethiopia, we make brown lentil samosas but this recipe is simpler to roll. In our cuisine we cook things over many hours, letting all the flavours infuse, so don't rush during the frying. My three girls love this recipe as a snack and I make it for events and share with the local community at different gatherings. These are best eaten hot out of the pan but they are still delicious eaten cold. I hope you enjoy them."

EQUIPMENT

Medium-sized saucepan, sharp knife, large frying pan, wooden spoon, mixing bowl, 2 medium frying pans

INGREDIENTS (next page)

1. Wash the lentils thoroughly, then add to a pan of water, bring to the boil and cook on a medium heat for 20–25 minutes. Drain and set aside.

2. While the lentils are cooking, let's prepare the ingredients.
- Finely dice the onions.
- Finely slice the leeks.
- Deseed and finely slice the peppers.
- Finely slice the chillies (deseed if you prefer less heat).

3. Take a large frying pan and heat on a medium heat. Add the olive oil. Once the oil is warm, add the onions and leeks and cook for 10 minutes until golden, stirring now and again.

4. While these are cooking, make the garlic purée/paste (see p 374), if not using store-bought.

5. Add the garlic purée to the onions/leeks and cook on a low-medium heat for a further 20 minutes, stirring occasionally. While this is cooking, set the table and prep any dipping sauces (if using).

6. Add the peppers and cook for a further 2–3 minutes.

7. Add the green chillies, salt and black pepper and cook for a further 2–3 minutes.

8. Add the cooked lentils, stir to combine and then set aside until cool enough to handle.

9. Add the water to a bowl – you will use this to dip your fingers in to stick the pastry.

INGREDIENTS

- 500g/1lb 2oz/scant 3 cups dried brown lentils
- 1kg/2lb 4oz red onions
- 2 leeks
- 2–3 mixed red and yellow peppers
- 10–12 fresh green chillies
- 1 tablespoon olive oil
- 1 tablespoon garlic purée/paste (for homemade see p 374)
- Pinch of sea salt
- Pinch of black pepper
- 50ml/1¾fl oz/scant ¼ cup water
- 24 spring roll pastry wrappers
- 200ml/7fl oz/scant 1 cup neutral oil like vegetable or rapeseed/canola oil
- 80g/3oz/generous ½ cup sesame seeds
- 2 tablespoons vegan mayo or 1 tablespoon olive oil (either is fine)

10. Take a spring roll wrapper and lay it on a clean, flat surface. Add 1–2 tablespoons of the lentil mix to the far left edge of the paper (leave a 3cm/1¼in margin) and spread it from top to bottom in a column.

11. Now roll the spring roll wrapper into a cigar shape about 10cm/4in long and 2cm/¾in diameter. Rub the ends with a small amount of water, then fold them over to stick them together. Repeat for the rest of the spring roll wrappers/lentil mixture.

12. Heat the neutral oil in a frying pan on a medium heat. Once the oil is hot, add the spring rolls – about 4–5 in the pan at one time – and lightly fry until golden on each side, about 8–10 minutes per batch.

13. Meanwhile, toast the sesame seeds in a separate dry frying pan on a low heat for 1–2 minutes until golden, then decant onto a dry plate.

14. Smear a small amount of vegan mayo or olive oil across the length of each cooked spring roll and scatter the sesame seeds on top so they stick.

Serve as is or with a fresh salad or a dipping condiment such as vegan mayo mixed with Ethiopian chilli powder. They're delicious just as they are.

TIPS & TRICKS

DIY Garlic Purée/Paste p 374

    use a gluten-free Dijon mustard without malt vinegar in it.

SERVES: 4 GENEROUSLY | TIME: 25 MINUTES

DR RUPY'S AVOCADO KALE PROTEIN PACKED SALAD

Culinary health legend Dr Rupy started his brand The Doctor's Kitchen after experiencing a debilitating heart condition as a junior doctor. He volunteered with us to learn about the challenges people faced around healthy eating and remains a charity ambassador for us to this day. He says: *"I love including additional nutritious ingredients along with punchy flavours to salads. Adding to the fibre, healthy fats and protein of the salad, pumpkin seeds bring zinc, a vital mineral."*

EQUIPMENT

Large bowl, blender or food processor, sharp knife

INGREDIENTS

400g/14oz kale
2 ripe avocados
2 x 400g/14oz cans haricot/navy beans
Juice of 2 lemons
6 tablespoons extra virgin olive oil
2 teaspoons Dijon mustard
2 teaspoons garlic powder or granules
1 teaspoon maple syrup
2 tablespoons B12-enriched nutritional yeast
8 tablespoons pumpkin seeds
1–2 tablespoons water (optional)
Generous pinch of sea salt
Generous pinch of black pepper
2 tablespoons hulled/shelled hemp seeds (optional)

1. Let's prep the ingredients.
- Wash the kale. Remove the leaves from the stalks (save the stalks and use in a ferment or veg broth) and tear the leaves into bite-size pieces.
- Peel and pit the avocados and cut into bite-size pieces.
- Drain the haricot/navy beans and rinse well. You could save the liquid to use as aquafaba in another recipe.

2. Add the kale to a large bowl, squeeze the juice of 1 lemon over it and add 1 tablespoon of the olive oil.

3. Using clean hands, rub the lemon juice and oil into the kale – this is called massaging. The kale will become softer, get darker in colour and reduce in volume, giving the impression that it's been cooked while maintaining all the nutrients of raw kale. If you've never done this before, 2–4 minutes of massaging should be long enough, but it depends on how hard you're massaging.

4. Now we're going to make the pesto. Remove half the kale from the bowl and add to a blender or food processor with the remaining olive oil and lemon juice, the mustard, garlic powder/granules, maple syrup, nutritional yeast and half of the pumpkin seeds and blend until smooth.

5. If you need to add more water as you blend to loosen the mixture, do so 1 teaspoon of water at a time. Add the salt and black pepper.

6. Now add the haricot beans and pesto into the bowl with the remaining kale and mix to combine.

7. Serve the salad topped with the avocado, the remaining pumpkin seeds and the hemp seeds (if using). Enjoy on its own as a light meal or serve with some crusty bread and soup for something more satiating.

 use white wine vinegar not malt vinegar.

SERVES: 4 | TIME: 40 MINUTES, PLUS OVERNIGHT TO DRAIN AND FIRM UP

ELLIE'S RICOTTA CHEESE

Ellie is the founder of one of the UK's biggest independent vegan cheese companies Kinda Co. *"I think Sarah believed in Kinda Co before I even did – she was such a cheerleader for the brand in its early days and I loved my early classes for MIH, which were called, 'Life Beyond Cheese', as the line I often heard and still do here is, 'I couldn't live without cheese.' Unlike many vegan cheeses, which are cultured, this one is cooked, curdled, then left overnight to drain and firm up. It has minimal ingredients and is really delicious and versatile. Let's make plant-based ricotta cheese!"*

EQUIPMENT

Saucepan, wooden spoon or whisk, bowl, sieve/fine-mesh strainer lined with muslin cloth/cheesecloth, cheese basket (optional), 15cm/6in piece of string

INGREDIENTS

- 1 litre/35fl oz/4¼ cups soy milk (use a brand with no added sweetener or oil)
- 2–4 tablespoons white wine vinegar or malt vinegar
- ¾ teaspoon fine sea salt or 1 heaped teaspoon flaky sea salt

1. Pour the soy milk into a saucepan and put on a medium-high heat without a lid, so you can see when the milk is ready. Stir occasionally to make sure the milk doesn't burn on the bottom.

2. Bring the temperature up until the milk is steaming and almost boiling. If you see the milk starting to gently bubble, then it's ready.

3. Take the milk off the heat and gently stir 2 tablespoons of vinegar into the milk for 30 seconds until the vinegar is fully mixed into the milk. You should see clumps of milk coming together – these are curds. Leave untouched for 5 minutes so the curds can fully form. If curds don't appear, add another 1–2 tablespoons of vinegar, stir gently through and leave for 5 minutes.

4. Now get a bowl ready and a sieve/fine-mesh strainer lined with muslin cloth/cheesecloth. Take the mixture and pour it into the cloth-lined sieve set over the bowl.

5. Leave to stand for 5 minutes so the watery "whey" can drain from the curds. If you like, you can lift up the sides of the cloth and give it a gentle squeeze to remove more of the liquid.

6. Sprinkle the salt over the curds and stir to evenly distribute.

7. Now to shape your ricotta.
Option 1: With a cheese basket. Spoon the ricotta curds into the basket, nudging them into place with the back of a spoon. Put in the refrigerator on an upturned bowl over a container to catch the drips.
Option 2: With a muslin cloth/cheese cloth. Bring together the corners of the cloth and gather the ricotta into a ball, then tie with a string. Pop the cheese in the cloth into a sieve over a bowl and put in the refrigerator.

8. Leave the ricotta in the refrigerator overnight to continue draining and to firm up.

Serve the ricotta in a rollatini, or with grilled vegetables layered in a lasagne, or piped into cannelloni.

SERVES: 4 | TIME: 10–15 MINUTES, PLUS MINIMUM OF 15 MINUTES SOAKING TIME FOR CASHEWS

FRAN'S NO-MAYO COLESLAW

"Sometimes you just can't beat a simple coleslaw. This with a jacket potato has become one of my quick go-to dinners. I love it because it's a healthy twist on a classic comfort food. When we made it in class the attendees looked skeptical – I think it was the cashew nuts – but it wasn't long before they were won over. One student was so thrilled after trying it, she broke into a spontaneous joyful dance. So enjoy this recipe but beware, may cause uncontrollable boogying and other enthusiastic outcomes. Serve the slaw with a jacket potato or a selection of other salads."

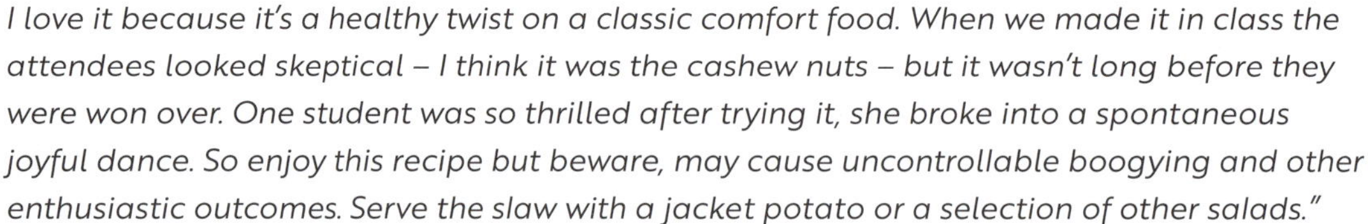

EQUIPMENT

Large bowl, grater, sharp knife, food processor/blender

INGREDIENTS

70g/2½oz/scant ⅔ cup raw cashew nuts
2 carrots
½ green cabbage
2 spring onions/scallions
½ clove garlic
Grated zest and juice of 1 lemon
About 2 tablespoons water
Sea salt and black pepper

TIP ***Add some finely sliced or chopped red onion and radishes to the slaw, if you like. This slaw is best eaten fresh on the day you make it.***

1. Put the cashew nuts in a bowl, cover with cold water and leave to soak for a minimum of 15 minutes (4–8 hours is best). Or if you are short of time, soak the cashews in a bowl of boiling water for 30 minutes instead. Drain and rinse before using.

2. Now let's prep the veg.
- Grate the carrots.
- Thick slice the cabbage.
- Thinly slice the spring onions/scallions.

3. Chuck the cashew nuts, garlic, lemon zest and juice and a pinch of salt and pepper into a food processor or hand-held/immersion blender with a bowl attachment. Blend to a smooth paste.

4. Taste and adjust the seasoning as needed with additional salt, pepper and extra lemon. It should be pretty punchy because it's going to be diluted when it's added to the other ingredients.

5. Thin down the dressing with enough water until it's closer to the consistency of a vinaigrette.

6. Put the carrot, cabbage and spring onions/scallions in a bowl, add the dressing and mix together.

SERVES: 4 | TIME: 5 MINUTES

RACHEL'S DANDELION BUTTER

Rachel has worked in the kitchens of Heston Blumenthal and Peter Gordon, was Head of Fantastic Food at Abel & Cole and is the author of seven cookbooks. She says: *"This is a brilliant way of making the most of late spring's golden swathes of dandelions and it's an uncanny alternative to butter. I love this recipe as it reminds me of all the wonderful classes I used to teach at Made in Hackney. Make sure to only use the dandelion petals and not any of the green bits as, although edible, they are very bitter. In the UK and many parts of the US, dandelions flower from May to October but are most prolific from May to June."*

EQUIPMENT

Blender or food processor, spatula, airtight container

INGREDIENTS

4 tablespoons dandelion petals or 1 teaspoon ground turmeric
4 tablespoons coconut oil
2 teaspoons lemon juice
Pinch of sea salt

1. Add the dandelion petals or turmeric to a blender or food processor with the coconut oil, lemon juice and salt (you don't need to melt the coconut oil first). Blend together.

2. When you have a smooth consistency, scrape it out with a spatula into a container and store either in the refrigerator or at room temperature.

3. It will keep in an airtight container in the refrigerator for up to 6 weeks or at room temperature for up to 1 week. It's delicious on toast or crumpets, on top of baked potatoes, or dotted/drizzled over steamed vegetables.

Ken Greenway our foraging teacher leading an edible wild plants walk in Tower Hamlets Cemetery Park.

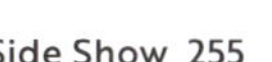

   use a gluten-free flour blend.

SERVES: 4 (3 CAKES EACH) | TIME: 1 HOUR

LINDA'S BRAMBORÁKY (CZECH POTATO CAKES), SUNFLOWER SEED DIP AND CABBAGE SALAD

"I'm a Czech food lover and health enthusiast dedicated to supporting people to have the happy, healthy lifestyle they deserve. Czech food is traditionally very meat- and dairy-heavy with a lot of salt and oil, so I adapt recipes to make them better for people and the planet. These potato cakes are a Czech street food dish served with sauerkraut and sour cream, or in a restaurant you might order it as a first course or side. I have created a dip from sunflower seeds to replace the sour cream. In this recipe, we use dried marjoram but in the Czech Republic, we use fresh. It grows everywhere and is a staple of our cuisine. The traditional size of these cakes is dinner-plate size, but I adapted them to be palm-sized as they're easier to flip. Our food is very heavy – we do a lot of frying – so the cabbage salad is like a palate cleanser. And it's not always a vegetable salad; sometimes it's a fruit salad. When I stay in small villages in rural Czechia, as a wholefoods plant-based eater, I'm a complete oddity. If I go out to eat in a restaurant I might get some tomatoes and cabbage, that's it. Prague is completely different. There are many amazing plant-based restaurants and the scene is growing all the time. The Sunflower Seed Dip is a replacement to sour cream, which is very popular in Czechia and is served with the potato cakes. It's nutritious and works for people with nut allergies. You can replace the sunflower seeds with the same quantity of raw cashew nuts but this makes it more expensive."

EQUIPMENT

Grater, large bowl, colander, garlic crusher, frying pan with lid, ladle, flipper, ovenproof dish

INGREDIENTS

- 500g/1lb 2oz potatoes
- Pinch of sea salt or black salt (kala namak)
- 5 cloves garlic
- 3 teaspoons dried marjoram or 30g/1oz fresh
- About 5 tablespoons plain/all-purpose flour
- 1 tablespoon olive oil, plus extra if needed

TIP ***If making all elements of this recipe, start by putting the sunflower seeds for the creamy dip in to soak in cold water for 1 hour and then get started with the other dishes.***

1. Wash, peel and grate the potatoes with a coarse grater and lay them in a large colander placed over a bowl.

2. Sprinkle the salt over the potatoes (black salt gives an egg flavour) and leave to stand for 20 minutes to let the water drain out. Discard this water.

3. Mince the garlic in a crusher and add to a large bowl along with the grated potatoes and marjoram. If using fresh marjoram, roughly chop it before adding. **>>**

4. Sprinkle the flour onto the potatoes to cover them so the flour absorbs any remaining water in the potatoes and forms a thick mass. Depending on the water content of the potatoes, the amount of flour needed will vary. If you use too much, the cakes will be hard and tough.

5. Heat the olive oil in a frying pan on a medium–high heat for 1 minute. Take a ladle's worth of mixture, press it together in your hands, then add it to the pan and press down into a palm sized disc. You should be able to fit 3 or 4 potato cakes in the pan. Aim for a thin 0.5cm/¼in thickness; if they're too thick, they won't get crispy.

6. Cover with a lid, then after 3 minutes, turn the potato cakes over and fry for 2–3 minutes on the other side until they're golden brown and crispy. Every pan behaves differently but if you need to add a little more oil between batches (I usually don't) add 1 teaspoon for every new batch.

7. Add the cakes to an ovenproof dish and keep warm in a low oven (110°C/225°F/gas ¼) while you cook the rest of the cakes, adding more oil if needed. If you don't have an oven or want to save energy costs just cover with a tea towel.

Serve hot with sauerkraut (see p 342), Cabbage Salad (see below) and Creamy Sunflower Seed Dip (see right).

use apple cider vinegar instead of malt vinegar

SERVES: 4 | TIME: 10 MINUTES

CABBAGE SALAD

EQUIPMENT

Grater, sharp knife, large bowl

INGREDIENTS (next page)

1. Let's prep the ingredients.
- Coarsely grate or finely slice/shred the cabbage.
- Coarsely grate the onion.
- Chop the dill.

2. Add the cabbage, onion and dill to a large bowl.

3. Add all remaining ingredients to the bowl and massage for 3-5 minutes to release the juices until the cabbage becomes soft. The longer you massage your cabbage, the more water it will release.

SERVES: 4 (WITH LEFTOVERS FOR ANOTHER DAY) | TIME: 10 MINUTES, PLUS 1 HOUR SOAKING

CREAMY SUNFLOWER SEED DIP

EQUIPMENT

Large bowl, grater, sharp knife, high-speed blender

INGREDIENTS

- 75g/2¾oz/½ cup sunflower seeds
- About 250ml/9fl oz/1 cup cold water, to cover
- 1 cucumber
- 20g/¾oz fresh dill
- 20g/¾oz fresh mint leaves
- 1–2 cloves garlic
- 1 tablespoon coconut oil (melted or unmelted)
- 1–2 tablespoons lemon juice
- 1 teaspoon sea salt
- 100ml/3½fl oz/scant ½ cup water

1. Soak the sunflower seeds in enough cold water to cover for at least 1 hour (and up to 8 hours). Drain and rinse well before using.

2. Let's prep the other ingredients.
- Grate the cucumber.
- Finely chop the dill and mint.
- Finely chop or crush the garlic.

3. Drain the soaked sunflower seeds and add them to a high-speed blender along with the coconut oil, lemon juice, salt and water and blend until smooth.

4. Mix everything together in a bowl and serve with the potato cakes and cabbage salad. Yum.

INGREDIENTS

- 1 small green cabbage (about 400g/14oz)
- ½ onion
- 40g/1½oz fresh dill
- 50ml/1¾fl oz/scant ¼ cup water (optional, if you massage for longer the cabbage will release enough water)
- 1 tablespoon malt vinegar (I use apple cider vinegar but this isn't traditional)
- ¼ tablespoon sea salt, plus an (optional) extra pinch

4. The traditional recipe would add 2–3 tablespoons of white sugar at this point. But I omit this.

5. Taste and add a pinch more salt if needed, then serve.

This salad is best made and eaten fresh for maximum crunch, but it will keep in an airtight container in the refrigerator for up to 24 hours.

SERVES: 4 | TIME: 25 MINUTES, PLUS 4 HOURS–OVERNIGHT COOLING, PLUS 1–24 HOURS STANDING BEFORE EATING (THE FLAVOURS IMPROVE THE LONGER YOU LEAVE IT)

LINDA'S BRAMBOROVÝ SALÁT (POTATO SALAD)

"This is our traditional potato salad, which we enjoy at celebrations. Every family tweaks the recipe. As you visit different people's homes over the holidays, you taste their potato salad. You compliment it, but hold fast that your family's recipe is best. This one is my grandma's, which I have veganized. When you make it you always make a large amount, like 5kg/11lb. It's eaten over a week and the flavours get better everyday. Do I think my family's recipe is the best? Of course."

EQUIPMENT

Large saucepan with lid, peeler, small saucepan (optional), strong sharp knife, medium-sized bowl, large bowl, wooden spoon

INGREDIENTS

- 900g/2lb potatoes
- 110g/3¾oz frozen peas
- 1–2 eating/dessert apples (your choice depending on sweetness preference)
- ⅓ celeriac/celery root
- 2 parsnips
- 2 carrots
- 1 small-medium onion
- 1½ teaspoons sea salt (the exact amount of salt will depend on the type of mayo), plus an extra pinch
- 2 tablespoons malt, apple cider or red wine vinegar
- 5 gherkins, drained
- 230g/8oz vegan mayonnaise or plain vegan yogurt (if using yogurt, the flavour will be more subtle)
- 2–3 tablespoons pickle juice from the gherkin jar
- 1 tablespoon yellow mustard
- ½ teaspoon black pepper
- 1 teaspoon white sugar

1. Cook the potatoes in their skins in a pan of boiling water for 15 minutes – you want them firm, not mushy – and then drain and leave them to cool completely at room temperature for 4 hours or preferably overnight. Once cooled, peel them.

2. Leave the frozen peas to defrost, or cook them briefly in a small pan of boiling water, but don't let them go mushy, then drain and cool.

3. Let's prep the fruit and veg.
- Peel and core the apples, then cut them into 1cm/½in cubes.
- Peel the celeriac/celery root, parsnips and carrots and chop them into 1cm/½in cubes. To peel the celeriac, cut it in half first, then use a sharp knife to cut off the skin.
- Finely chop the onion.

4. Place the celeriac and carrots in a pan of boiling water with a pinch of salt and the vinegar and cook for 5 minutes. The vegetables should be soft but not mushy.

5. While they're cooking, cut the potatoes and gherkins into 2cm/¾in cubes.

6. Drain, then cool the celeriac and carrots quickly by rinsing them under cold running water.

7. Put all the veggies, the apples and gherkins in a large bowl.

8. Combine the mayonnaise or vegan yogurt, pickle juice and yellow mustard in a separate bowl. Add the mayo/yogurt to the veg/apple mixture and stir.

9. Season with salt, pepper and sugar and mix. Cover and let it rest for 1 hour at room temperature or refrigerate for up to 24 hours.

SIX ESSENTIAL HERBS AND SPICES FOR CZECH CUISINE

1 FRESH DILL
Commonly used in Czech pickles, potato salads and soups, adding a tangy flavour.

2 FRESH MARJORAM
A key herb in Czech stews and soups like svíčková (creamy sauce).

3 CARAWAY SEEDS
Popular in rye bread and cabbage dishes like sauerkraut.

4 BAY LEAVES
Used in Czech soups and stews for a subtle, aromatic flavour.

5 ALLSPICE/ PIMENTO
Used in Czech marinades, pickles and some cookies, giving a warm, spicy flavour.

6 POPPY SEEDS
Used in Czech pastries, especially in koláče (sweet pastries), as well as in savoury dishes.

   use gluten-free Dijon mustard and gluten-free soy sauce or swap for tamari

SERVES: 4 GENEROUSLY | TIME: 20 MINUTES

ASA'S CAESAR-STYLE SALAD

"I've been making this salad at wellbeing retreats for years and it always gets compliments. The crispness of the lettuce with the creamy sauce and crouton sprinkles is yummy. You could add larger croutons made from sourdough bread or maple coconut bacon or tempeh."

EQUIPMENT

Sharp knife, large bowl, blender or glass jar, food processor or large pestle and mortar

INGREDIENTS

For The Salad

- 1 romaine lettuce
- ½ iceberg lettuce
- 1 spring onion/scallion
- 2 tablespoons (drained) capers
- Handful of rocket/arugula or baby spinach

For The Dressing

- 50ml/1¾fl oz/scant ¼ cup extra virgin olive oil
- 1 tablespoon apple cider vinegar
- 1 teaspoon Dijon mustard
- 2 tablespoons dark soy sauce
- 2 tablespoons tahini
- ½ teaspoon liquid sweetener of choice

For The Crouton Sprinkles

- 1 clove garlic
- 50g/1¾oz/1/3 cup sunflower seeds
- 1 teaspoon B12-enriched nutritional yeast
- Pinch of sea salt

1. Let's prep the ingredients.
- Slice the two types of lettuce into your preferred shape.
- Thinly slice the whole spring onion/scallion.
- Chop the capers.
- Mince the garlic for the crouton sprinkles.

2. Add all the salad vegetables to a bowl and mix them together. Add the capers last by sprinkling them on top, otherwise they will all end up at the bottom of the bowl.

3. Now let's make the dressing. Blend all the ingredients together or add them to a clean jam jar and stir well until combined into a smooth dressing. Set aside.

4. Now let's make the crouton sprinkles. Add all the ingredients into a food processor and pulse until mixed together. If you don't have a food processor, add the ingredients to a large pestle and mortar and grind to combine. You want a crumbly texture, so don't over-blend.

5. To assemble the salad, add the vegetables to a large, flat serving platter (or just leave them in the bowl), add the dressing and stir so it's all mixed in.

6. Sprinkle with the crouton sprinkles and serve. Simple, but delicious.

NN **PLANT-BASED OMEGA OILS**

Oils rich in omegas can be used in salad dressings or taken like a shot, a half to full tablespoon being the recommended amount. We recommend flax, hemp, pumpkin or black seed oils as they're high in fatty acids: omega-6, omega-3 and omega-9. These are important for heart and skin health and can help reduce inflammation. Ground and whole flaxseeds, chia, walnuts, hemp seeds, seaweed and edamame are also good sources of omegas and are cheaper than oils. ***Read about EPA & DHA algae derived oils on p 111.***

Flaxseed
VIRIDIAN

use gluten-free soy sauce or swap for tamari and use gluten-free oats.

SERVES: 4 | TIME: 10 MINUTES

SUKHIN'S SILKEN TOFU AND NATTO WITH OVERNIGHT OATS AND BERRIES

"Natto is a Japanese dish that can be eaten at lunch or dinner, as a side or for breakfast. This is one of my favourite ways to eat natto: for breakfast, paired with overnight oats and berries. Natto is a fermented soybean, with many health benefits that range from supporting bone and heart health and the immune system. The first time I tasted natto I vowed not to eat it again and did not for another fifteen years! It has a unique 'whiffy' smell, but the amount of hard-to-get nutrients for bone health and probiotics in it convinced me to try again. To preserve the live probiotics in natto, I do not add any hot ingredients or cook it. If you're going to replicate my East-meets-West breakfast, eat the tofu and natto first as it's savoury-umami, and follow with the overnight oats and berries to balance the flavours. A cup of green or matcha tea rounds off the palate with the five flavours of savoury/umami, salty, sweet, sour and bitter."

EQUIPMENT

2 bowls, sharp knife, small frying pan

INGREDIENTS (next page)

1. Prepare the overnight oats. Combine the oats and plant-based milk in a bowl, cover and leave to soak overnight in the refrigerator.

2. The next day, prepare the tofu and natto. Drain and slice the silken tofu and add it in equal portions to the 4 serving bowls.

3. Now let's prepare the other toppings.
   - Finely slice the spring onions/scallions.
   - Slice the cucumber into discs and set aside.

4. Lightly toast the sesame seeds in a small frying pan on a medium heat for 2 minutes, then set aside.

5. If using the nori sheet and not nori flakes/sprinkles, tear it up into slivers/small pieces and set aside in a dry bowl.

6. Remove the natto from its packaging into a small bowl and stir for about 50 seconds to generate more of the sticky strings.

7. Add the soy sauce, vinegar, sesame oil and nutritional yeast to the natto and mix together.

8. Pour the natto mixture over the sliced tofu ensuring to give everyone an equal share.

9. Sprinkle each bowl with the spring onions, toasted sesame seeds and the slivers/pieces of nori or the nori flakes/sprinkles.

INGREDIENTS

For The Tofu And Natto

200g/7oz silken tofu

1–2 spring onions/scallions

¼ cucumber

1 tablespoon sesame seeds

1 teaspoon nori (seaweed) flakes/sprinkles or ½ nori sheet, to sprinkle

100g/3½oz natto

4 teaspoons dark soy sauce

2 teaspoons apple cider vinegar

2 teaspoons sesame oil

4 teaspoons B12-enriched nutritional yeast

For The Overnight Oats And Berries

200g/7oz/2 cups rolled oats

200ml/7fl oz/scant 1 cup plant-based milk of choice

Handful of fresh berries (such as raspberries, blueberries or strawberries)

4 tablespoons mixed seeds – sunflower, pumpkin or hemp (optional)

K2 & the Magic of Natto p 370

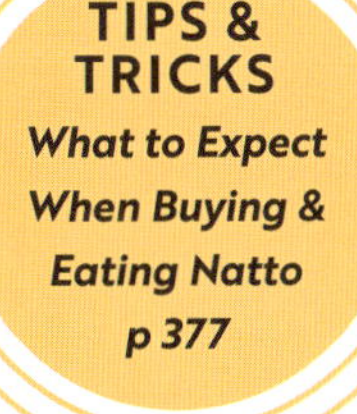

TIPS & TRICKS
What to Expect When Buying & Eating Natto p 377

10. Place the sliced cucumber around the tofu for extra crunch.

Serve alongside your main course or dinner, or as I do, for breakfast with the overnight oats, topped with the fresh berries and mixed seeds.

use gluten-free soy sauce or swap for tamari.

SERVES: 4 | TIME: 30 MINUTES

DR NITU'S TURMERIC SCRAMBLED TOFU

"Tofu is a minimally processed product made from soybeans and an excellent source of protein with good amounts of all nine essential amino acids. I made this recipe for my girls when they were growing up as a tasty, comforting alternative to scrambled eggs. Tofu is a great swap for eggs as it has roughly 3½ times less saturated fat than eggs, which is a huge difference. Saturated fat raises LDL cholesterol, which contributes to an increased risk of heart disease and stroke. We want to reduce our saturated fat intake, as in the UK, US and many parts of Europe, most of us have far too much. This recipe is rich in herbs and spices, which are the most antioxidant-rich of all food groups and they help reduce the desire for salt, oil and sugar. This scramble goes well on top of toast, inside a wrap or as part of a breakfast plate."

EQUIPMENT

Sharp knife, frying pan with lid, bowl

INGREDIENTS **(next page)**

Learn more about soy in our Thrive on Plants chapter p 29

1. First let's prep the chillies and veg.
- Finely slice the green chillies (deseed for less heat).
- Dice the onion and tomatoes.
- Slice or shred the spinach or kale. Remove stalks and save for a veg broth (recipe p 373). Baby spinach can be left whole.

2. In a dry frying pan on a medium heat, dry-roast the dried basil, turmeric and cumin for 2 minutes or until their smell becomes stronger – but avoid burning them.

3. Add the olive oil to the pan and heat for 1 minute. Add the onion and chillies and sauté on a medium heat for 5 minutes until the onion is translucent. For an oil-free dish, fry the onion and chillies in the hot water for 5 minutes.

4. Add the tomatoes to the frying pan and sauté for 3–4 minutes.

5. Add the frozen peas and, if using frozen spinach, add it now, but if using fresh you'll add it later. Cover and cook on a medium heat for 4–5 minutes.

6. Drain the tofu of liquid, then use your hands to crumble it into a bowl. If you don't like using your hands for sensory reasons you can grate it. **>>**

INGREDIENTS

1–2 fresh green chillies
1 large onion
2 tomatoes
32g/1oz/1 cup fresh spinach/kale or 1 small cube of frozen spinach
1 teaspoon dried basil
1 teaspoon ground turmeric
1 teaspoon cumin/jeera seeds or ground cumin/jeera
1 teaspoon olive oil or 1–2 tablespoons hot water
125g/4½oz/1 cup frozen green peas
1 x 400g/14oz block of calcium-set firm tofu
1–2 tablespoons dark soy sauce or tamari
Pinch of black salt (kala namak) for eggy sulphurous taste (optional but highly recommend)
Pinch of black pepper
½–1 tablespoon water (optional)
1 tablespoon tomato purée/paste, tomato ketchup or sriracha (optional)
Fresh basil or coriander/cilantro leaves, to garnish

7. Add the tofu to the frying pan and stir the ingredients together. Cover and cook on a medium heat for 2–3 minutes.

8. Add the soy sauce, black salt (if using) and pepper, mix thoroughly and cook for another 2–3 minutes with the lid on. It shouldn't be moist but also not so dry it catches. If it's catching, add a little water, 1 teaspoon at a time, to loosen.

9. Add the fresh spinach/kale and the tomato purée/paste, tomato ketchup or siracha and mix in.

Serve, sprinkled with a garnish of herb leaves. This recipe can be enjoyed on its own or as a side dish or in a wholemeal wrap.

The Low Down on Magnesium With Plant-Based Nutritionist Rohini Bajekal p 370

Dr Nitu leading a very popular Cooking For Hormone Health community class

SERVES: 4 | TIME: 45 MINUTES

ROSHNI'S MUTHIA

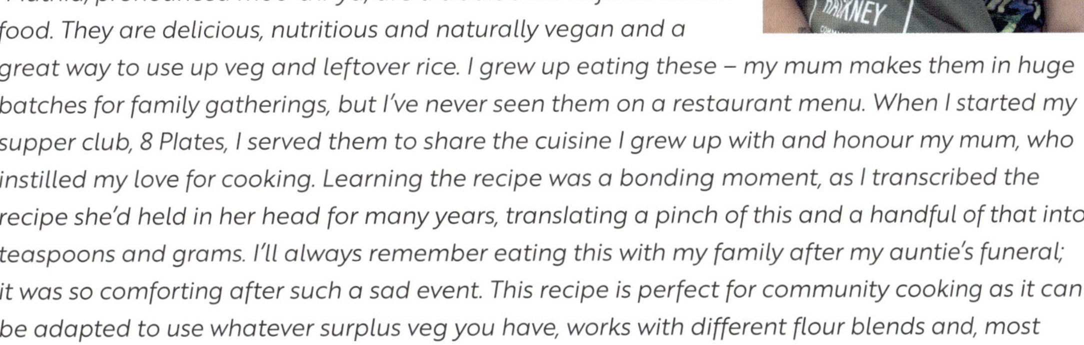

"Muthia, pronounced moo-thi-ya, are a traditional Gujarati snack food. They are delicious, nutritious and naturally vegan and a great way to use up veg and leftover rice. I grew up eating these – my mum makes them in huge batches for family gatherings, but I've never seen them on a restaurant menu. When I started my supper club, 8 Plates, I served them to share the cuisine I grew up with and honour my mum, who instilled my love for cooking. Learning the recipe was a bonding moment, as I transcribed the recipe she'd held in her head for many years, translating a pinch of this and a handful of that into teaspoons and grams. I'll always remember eating this with my family after my auntie's funeral; it was so comforting after such a sad event. This recipe is perfect for community cooking as it can be adapted to use whatever surplus veg you have, works with different flour blends and, most importantly, packs a flavour punch!"

EQUIPMENT

Bowl, hand grater or food processor, sharp knife, pestle and mortar, lemon juicer, steamer basket or a pan with lid and colander, frying pan, wooden spoon

INGREDIENTS **(next page)**

1. If using poha, rinse it, then soak it in enough cold water to cover in a bowl for 10 minutes or until the flakes are fluffy and separated.

2. Meanwhile, let's prepare the other ingredients.
- Coarsely grate the seasonal mixed veggies using a hand grater or in a food processor.
- Chop the spinach and coriander/cilantro into ribbons.
- Lightly crush the ajwain/carom seeds with a pestle and mortar.
- Finely chop the green chilli (deseed if you prefer less heat).
- Grate the ginger.
- Juice the lemons – you want 4–5 tablespoons of juice.

3. Mix all the ingredients for the muthia together in a bowl until you get a sticky batter mix.

4. Grease your hands with oil and then divide and shape the mixture into logs; you should get 8 logs.

5. Grease a stainless steel steamer basket, place the logs in it and then steam on a medium heat for 10–12 minutes. Depending on the size of your steamer basket, you may need to do this in 2–3 batches. If you don't have a steamer basket, improvise with a pan, colander and a pan lid. **>>**

INGREDIENTS

For The Muthia

- 80g/3oz poha (dried rice flakes) or 240g/8½oz cooked, leftover rice – I prefer poha
- 300g/10½oz prepped seasonal mixed veg such as dudhi/bottle gourd (traditional), carrots, courgettes/zucchini, butternut squash, kohlrabi, cabbage – use whatever you have
- 100g/3½oz spinach
- 20g/¾oz fresh coriander/cilantro
- 1 teaspoon ajwain/carom seeds (optional)
- 1 fresh green chilli (optional)
- 2 thumb-size pieces root ginger
- 2 lemons
- 3 tablespoons neutral oil, such as sunflower or rapeseed/canola oil, plus extra for greasing
- 2 teaspoons ground cumin/jeera
- 1 teaspoon ground turmeric
- 175g/6oz/1⅓ cups chickpea/gram flour
- ½ teaspoon bicarbonate of soda/baking soda
- 1–1½ teaspoons sea salt

For The Tempering

- 3 tablespoons neutral oil, such as sunflower or rapeseed/canola oil
- 2 teaspoons black or brown mustard seeds
- 4 teaspoons sesame seeds
- 5 fresh curry leaves (optional)
- ⅛ teaspoon asafoetida/hing (optional)

6. You will know they are ready when they have risen slightly and hold their shape. They may seem a little uncooked, but they will solidify as they cool.

7. Once the muthia have cooled, slice them into 2cm/¾in discs. You'll get about 6 discs per log.

8. You can enjoy them as they are, or for extra flavour, temper them. Serve hot.

To Temper

9. Heat the oil in a frying pan until hot and slightly simmering.

10. Add the mustard seeds and sesame seeds, then turn the heat down to medium and let them cook for a couple of minutes. The mustard seeds should be popping and the sesame seeds will start to turn golden brown.

11. Add the curry leaves and asafoetida/hing (if using).

12. Fry the muthia slices in the spiced oil on a medium-high heat until they are golden brown on both sides, about 8–10 minutes in total.

13. Enjoy with your favourite Indian chutney (although I prefer tomato ketchup!) and a cup of hot masala chai. Bliss.

TIP *You can experiment with other veg like beetroot/beets, swede/rutabaga, celeriac/celery root – anything that can be grated.*
For a stronger flavour, you can swap half the spinach with fresh methi (fenugreek) leaves. To change up the texture and nutrient mix, try blending the flour and adding juwar (sorghum) flour and magaz (coarse chickpea/gram flour).

IN CONVERSATION WITH...

Exploring Self-Care and Nourishment

A conversation with anti-racism activist, author and speaker Nova Reid

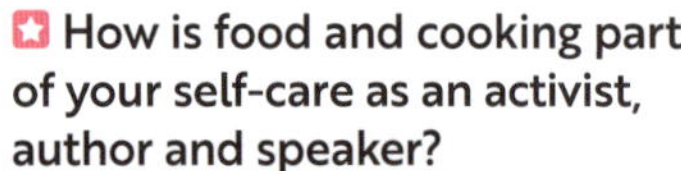

How is food and cooking part of your self-care as an activist, author and speaker?
Nova: There's an enmeshment between being human and being an activist. I do what I do because the environment I'm in impacts my health, and I want to do something about it. It's not just a job for me. It's a survival instinct. So making sure I'm nourished and being intentional with what I put in my body, because I'm often giving so much, makes a difference in my energy levels and how I'm able to sustain myself. Sometimes I just need comfort, and I find a lot of comfort in home-cooked food.

Do you feel a difference in home-cooked food, to food you buy on the go, even if it's quality food?
A homecooked meal is an act of love and care. When I'm on the go, I'm at risk of skipping meals, or eating things that are quick, that aren't what my body needs, and then I'll suffer for it. One of the things that helps is preparation. So if you or someone else is making a home-cooked meal, could you bulk-cook it to freeze? Then you're taking their love and care with you to nourish you during the day. Or when you get home at 7 or 8pm you can just heat it up. I love home-cooked meals, and I miss them when I'm travelling.

A lot of people struggle to put the same love and care into food they're preparing just for themselves, as opposed to food they're making for others. Do you find this?
I definitely prefer cooking for people rather than just me, yes. I get a lot of satisfaction seeing people enjoy my food. But that's only if I've got the energy to do it, because if I haven't got the energy, then there's resentment there, and no one wants a meal cooked with resentment. I need spaciousness to be able to enjoy cooking. And I need time, and energy, rather than me doing it because I need to eat something.

Given the capitalist system we're living in, spaciousness is incredibly hard to find.
We have to be intentional with how we create it. There will always be a bottleneck, because your schedule's changed, or somebody's ill, or something's happened in your personal life, which puts pressure on you. The spaciousness we create for ourselves is usually the first thing we sacrifice when these things happen.

You attended some of our online classes. Did these sessions nourish you and help fill your cup in any way?
Yeah, they did. I did classes with Betty and Sharon, Sierra Leone cuisine and a vegan take on Caribbean cuisine, which was new to me at the time. It was good vibes, very calming and some of the dishes I took on, me and my husband eat them regularly now.

Why is food such an important part of wellbeing for you?
I've not long come back from Jamaica, and we visited a Rastafarian village. They're

Digesting takes time and energy. We have to have the space to nourish and sustain ourselves.

eating an Ital, plant-based diet, very connected to source and land. They're very in tune with nature and how my ancestors used to live, but now, being born in Britain in the fast-paced, concrete jungle, we've become disconnected from the land, and therefore from food. We only see food packaged in plastic in a supermarket. We've lost the pipeline. Food is a way for us to better connect with ourselves. Not just being aware of what we're putting in our mouths, and what our body needs, but the whole ecosystem around it.

Your book, *The Good Ally*, and your work is about anti-racism. Is there such a thing as an anti-racist kitchen?
I don't accept this question as, to me, being anti-racist, the decolonizing of oneself, living a more honest and more liberated life: these are part of our humanity. It's not something separate. It's who you are. It can't be isolated to a kitchen or organization.

So an organization can't be anti-racist or embed anti-racist practice?
It's not about embedding. It's about living in more honesty, integrating the parts of ourselves that aren't pretty. It's about looking at: how do I perpetuate white supremacy? For example, if somebody comes into work and it's their birthday and they've brought in cuisine from their heritage for everyone to enjoy, and a week later that food hasn't been tried and gets thrown in the bin. There are so many ways racism or white supremacy manifests in our behaviour, that we don't accept as racism or white supremacy because that's "those problematic people over there doing the race riots", as opposed to reflecting on our own behaviours. Why haven't I tried my colleague's food? Let me get curious about that. What have I learned about Caribbean, West African, Indian or Pakistani food, or Caribbean, West African, Indian or Pakistani people, that is preventing me from wanting to engage? It's about looking at your behaviour and how you engage with people, culture and yourself, and what values you've learned that are harmful and need attention. It's a journey and a process.

Because there's an element of mindfulness for me when I eat. The silence, enjoying the taste, textures and how it warms my body.

Anything else you'd like to share about food and self-care?
Just that I really enjoy eating.

That is in itself important, as many people don't have, or aren't allowed, the time to enjoy their food.
I'm working on a project at the moment, and it's in my contract that my lunch breaks are a full hour.

That seems like quite a radical request, when it should be everyone's basic right.
It means I can take my time to eat and enjoy my food. Because there's an element of mindfulness for me when I eat. The silence, enjoying the taste, textures and how it warms my body. The peace, not having to talk. There's a whole mindfulness ritual going on. There's a lot of energy needed to eat and digest food. Because it's in my contract that I get a full hour, everyone else in the team has an hour for their lunch break too, rather than guzzling down their food and getting back to work.

How has this gone down?
There wasn't just this request. There are other requests as well, around rest, and it was very new for my employer. But if you want to work with me, these are the terms.

I'm stunned at how radical this sounds when it should be the norm.
I know. We're so used to getting something on a half an hour lunch break. Eating while walking, talking, on the phone, on Zoom, always eating while doing something else. I was like, no, eating is a ritual. Me and my body are having a moment. Digesting takes time and energy. We have to have the space to nourish and sustain ourselves.

A SWEET FINALE

We love a sweet treat at MIH. We imagine you do too!

As a health-conscious community organization, we've developed an approach to desserts we call nourishing sweet treats. These are delicious morsels packed with health-supporting ingredients but are still sweet enough to provide the comfort and joy everyone looks for in a good dessert.

Are these recipes sugar-free? No. But they do have a lot of fibre and other good stuff in them – root veg, nuts, seeds, herbs, spices, legumes, dried fruits, wild foods – which have a plethora of health benefits. You'll find the occasional recipe that's syrup- or sugar-heavy. This is because it's a veganized version of a cultural dish where authenticity and pleasure have been prioritized above all else, and that's all good with us.

If you have a health issue, go easy on the portion, scale down the sugar or just choose something else. There's plenty to try, from 'make in 5 minutes' mango sorbet to protein-packed black bean chocolate pudding to cake made with spinach, sweetcorn and nettles. So get stuck in.

Note to cooks – when we say sweetener, we're not suggesting an artificial sweetener, but whatever sweetening ingredient you choose, whether that's soft brown sugar, date syrup, maple syrup, rice syrup or whatever you have in your cupboard. We're not recommending artificial sweeteners.

MAKES: 16 COOKIES | TIME: 55 MINUTES, INCLUDING BAKING AND FIRMING UP TIME

SARAH'S CHOCOLATE, APRICOT & HAZELNUT COOKIES

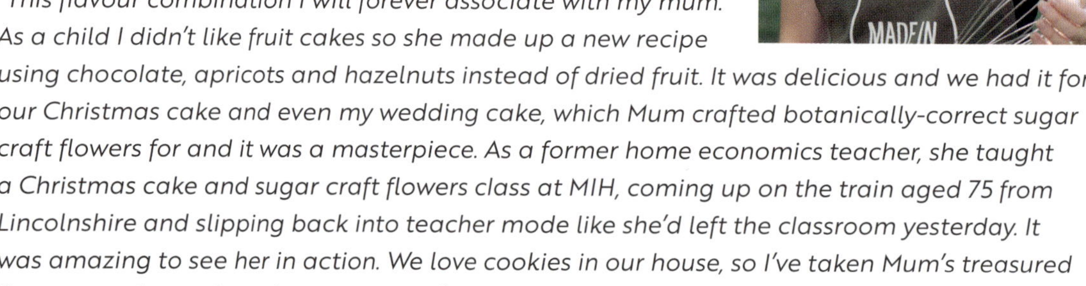

"This flavour combination I will forever associate with my mum. As a child I didn't like fruit cakes so she made up a new recipe using chocolate, apricots and hazelnuts instead of dried fruit. It was delicious and we had it for our Christmas cake and even my wedding cake, which Mum crafted botanically-correct sugar craft flowers for and it was a masterpiece. As a former home economics teacher, she taught a Christmas cake and sugar craft flowers class at MIH, coming up on the train aged 75 from Lincolnshire and slipping back into teacher mode like she'd left the classroom yesterday. It was amazing to see her in action. We love cookies in our house, so I've taken Mum's treasured flavour combo and used it in a cookie."

EQUIPMENT

2 baking trays lined with baking parchment, mixing bowl, wooden spoon, butter knife, weighing scales wire/cooling racks

INGREDIENTS

- 125g/4½oz/generous ½ cup vegan butter (I like Naturli vegan block)
- 100g/3½oz/⅔ cup dried apricots
- 1 teaspoon vanilla extract
- 150g/5½oz/¾ cup cane sugar
- 300g/10½oz/2¼ cups plain/all-purpose flour
- 1½ teaspoons bicarbonate of soda/baking soda
- ½ teaspoon sea salt
- 5 tablespoons soy or oat milk
- 100g/3½oz/¾ cup chopped hazelnuts
- 100g/3½oz/⅔ cup vegan chocolate chips of choice

1. Take the vegan butter out of the refrigerator and leave to soften for 30 minutes. Line 2 baking sheets (that will fit in your freezer or refrigerator) with baking parchment.

2. Chop the dried apricots into small pieces – at least 6 per apricot, depending on the size.

3. In a large bowl, add the vegan butter, vanilla extract and sugar and mix together until combined

4. Now add the flour, bicarbonate of soda/baking soda and salt. Mix together, then stir in the plant-based milk.

5. Add the hazelnuts, apricots and chocolate chips and evenly combine throughout the dough. I use my hands.

6. Break off pieces of dough (about 70–75g/2½–2¾oz per cookie) and roll into balls. Place, well spaced out, on the baking tray. Pop in the freezer for 20 minutes or refrigerate for 2 hours to firm up.

7. Preheat the oven to 200°C/400°F/gas 6.

8. Remove the baking sheets from the freezer/refrigerator and place in the oven (on the low and middle shelves) to bake for 12–15 minutes. Check after 10 minutes and if they're not flattening out (if you have a lively freezer, this could happen), remove from the oven, press down with a spoon or fingers if you can handle heat, then place back in the oven for 5 minutes.

9. Remove from the oven. Leave the cookies to rest on the baking sheets for 2 minutes, then transfer to wire/cooling racks.

10. The cookies will keep cooking and firming up for up to 30 minutes once out of the oven. They taste amazing when soft and gooey after 10 minutes out of the oven, or 2 hours later when they've firmed up and are fully cool.

These cookies will keep in an airtight container at room temperature for up to a week.

TIP ***Most cookie recipes call for 200g/7oz/1 cup-plus of sugar. This makes classic cookies with a cracked surface. The less sugar you use, the smoother, more dome-shaped the cookie will be. This recipe uses a little less sugar, but it's still sugar heavy. You can reduce more but the cookies will be softer and have less snap. You can make sweet treats with no refined sugar using a mix of apple purée, mashed bananas and syrups. They'll be yummy but they won't be cookies. Experiment and see what you and your household enjoy.***

use gluten-free oats.

MAKES: 16 SLICES | TIME: 45 MINUTES, PLUS 8 HOURS SETTING

AMY'S SALTED CARAMEL SLICES

"I haven't met anyone who hasn't enjoyed these Salted Caramel Slices. They're one of my favourite sweet treats. I made them in my Nourishing Sweet Treats classes and everyone made oohing and ahhing noises as they ate them, which is a good sign. I made them in a class for the Planet Organic team who get to sample some of the best treats in the world. They loved them and took the recipe sheets home to make again. Result! My approach to sweet treats is they should feel decadent and delicious but contain nourishing ingredients that lift our mood. You'll need a freezer to make these as they don't store at ambient temperatures."

EQUIPMENT

2 bowls, food processor (or high-speed blender), 20cm/8in square baking pan, spatula, medium saucepan, heatproof bowl (that can rest on top of your medium saucepan without going completely into it), sharp knife, big mug or saucepan

INGREDIENTS (next page)

1. Soak your dates for both the base and caramel layer (use separate bowls) in enough boiling water to cover for 10 minutes to soften them.

2. Now we'll start making the base. Add the oats to a food processor and process into a chunky flour.

3. Add the rest of the ingredients for the base – apart from the water – to the food processor, along with your drained dates, and process until you have a crumb texture which sticks together a bit when you press it between your fingers.

4. Now add the water and process until the mixture can be pressed into a dough. You don't want it to be too wet, but it needs to be sticky enough to be pressed into your baking pan.

5. Line a 20cm/8in square baking pan or something similar with baking parchment. Now press the base mixture down very firmly across the base of your baking pan so that it is even in height, compact and won't crumble when you cut it.

6. Place in the freezer.

7. To make the date caramel, drain your dates but don't squeeze them too much and then add all the caramel ingredients to the food processor or a high-speed blender.

8. Blend into a smooth caramel, stopping a few times to scrape down the sides with a spatula. If needed, add more milk, 1 tablespoon at a time. You want a thick gooey caramel, not a runny liquid.

INGREDIENTS

For The Base

36g/1¼oz/¼ cup dates

Boiling water, to cover (for soaking dates)

135g/4¾oz/1½ cups rolled oats

55g/2oz/¾ cup unsweetened desiccated/dried shredded coconut

1 tablespoon maple syrup (or use date syrup)

3 tablespoons almond butter or use tahini for nut-free version

Pinch of sea salt

3 tablespoons water

For The Caramel Layer

155g/5½oz/generous 1 cup dates

2 tablespoons maple syrup

2 tablespoons peanut or almond butter (use tahini for a nut-free version)

3 tablespoons coconut oil, melted

1 teaspoon vanilla extract

½ teaspoon sea salt

¼–½ teaspoon ground cinnamon

60ml/2fl oz/¼ cup plant-based milk* of choice (oat, soy and almond all work well) (you may need a little more)

*If using tahini in the caramel layer, you will only need 1–2 tablespoons plant-based milk

For The Chocolate Layer

170g/6oz vegan dark/bittersweet chocolate

2–3 tablespoons whole (skin-on) almonds

1 tablespoon coconut oil (optional)

9. Take the base out of the freezer and use a spatula to spread the caramel evenly over the oaty base. If you have time and you want perfect layers, leave in the freezer for 1–2 hours. If not a perfectionist, pop it back in the freezer while you're melting the chocolate – 10 minutes will firm it up enough to layer the melted chocolate on top.

10. Cut the chocolate into small 1–2cm/½–¾in pieces and place around two-thirds of it in a heatproof bowl.

11. Pour water into a medium saucepan so it is one-third full. Bring to the boil, then turn off the heat and place your bowl of chocolate over it. The bowl should not be touching the water. The steam alone will melt the chocolate. This is called a bain-marie.

12. Leave it for a few minutes, then with a spatula start to gently mix the chocolate to help it melt. While it is melting, roughly chop your almonds.

13. Once the chocolate is mostly melted, add the rest that you kept aside and stir until this melts as well. This process will help you to keep the chocolate shiny and smooth when it sets.

14. When completely melted, stir in the coconut oil and almonds.

15. Pour the chocolate over the caramel layer and even it out as best you can by tilting the baking pan and using a spatula or knife. Be careful not to disturb the caramel.

16. Return your caramel slices to the freezer for 5–10 minutes. When the chocolate is just setting (but not completely solid), gently score where you're going to cut the chocolate with a sharp knife. Place back into the freezer to completely set – ideally leave overnight.

17. If you're not precious about having perfect slices, you can cut into your caramel slices with a sharp knife now, but note the chocolate will probably crack a little.

TIP FOR PERFECTLY CUT SLICES

Boil some water and pour it into a large vessel such as an oversized mug. Place a sharp knife into the water and leave it for a few minutes to heat the metal. Wipe the knife dry and then carefully press down into your scored lines until your knife goes through just the chocolate layer. Put it back in the freezer for 5 minutes, then take it out and cut the rest of the way through. There's no need to heat the knife for this.

Store in an airtight container in the freezer. You can eat these straight out of the freezer but I recommend giving them at 5 minutes to soften up.

SERVES: 4 | TIME: 20 MINUTES + 15 MINUTES FOR THE CUSTARD

AMY'S STEWED DATE CARAMEL APPLES & SPICED CUSTARD

"This delicious, warming dessert is sweetened only with dates and dried apricots, which when heated create a wonderful sticky caramel syrup! It's lovely with the spiced custard. I made hundreds of portions of this for the Hackney Winter Warmer – an event I lovingly described as Glastonbury for Hackney elders. It was always packed and I had amazing conversations with so many great characters. This dessert went down a treat and many people took the recipe home. These events are a treasured memory for me – I hope you feel the warmth and community connection when you make this dish at home."

EQUIPMENT

Sharp knife, grater, saucepan, wooden spoon

INGREDIENTS

150g/5½oz/generous 1 cup dates
6 dried apricots
2 large apples (eating/dessert or cooking/baking – your choice)
2.5cm/1in piece root ginger
180ml/6fl oz/¾ cup water (plus a little extra if needed)
¼ teaspoons ground cinnamon
Juice of ½ lime

1. First let's prepare the ingredients.
- Chop the dates and the apricots into small chunks.
- Peel (if desired), core and chop the apples into small chunks or slices – your preference.
- Grate the ginger.

2. Put the water and dates in a saucepan on a medium heat and cook gently for a few minutes until the dates start to become soft.

3. Add the apples, apricots, ginger and cinnamon to the pan.

4. Keep stirring as the ingredients cook for 7–10 minutes. The liquid will begin to thicken into a caramel-y sauce and the apples will soften. If the liquid bubbles and catches on the edge on the bottom of the pan before the apples are soft, add ½ tablespoon of water.

5. When you have soft apples and a thick sticky sauce, remove from the heat and stir in the lime juice, which stops the apples from browning. Now make the custard (see next page). >>

SERVES: 4 | TIME: 15 MINUTES

AMY'S SPICED CUSTARD

"This delicious, comforting custard is made with nourishing ingredients and features festive spices cardamom, cinnamon and nutmeg. It gets its colour from turmeric, which is loaded with healing properties. This is great with a crumble, stewed fruit or on its own."

EQUIPMENT

Pestle and mortar, cup, measuring spoons, whisk, saucepan, wooden spoon, serving jug/pitcher

INGREDIENTS

- 2 green cardamom pods
- 450ml/15½fl oz/1¾ cups plant-based milk such as oat, soy or coconut
- 3 tablespoons cornflour/cornstarch
- 2 tablespoons sweetener, such as maple syrup, rice syrup, date syrup, coconut sugar or soft brown sugar (your choice)
- 1 teaspoon vanilla extract
- Pinch of sea salt
- ¼ teaspoon ground cinnamon
- ¼ teaspoon ground nutmeg
- Pinch of ground turmeric

1. First crush the cardamom pods using a pestle and mortar. Remove the pods and lightly crush the seeds.

2. Take roughly 100ml/3½fl oz/scant ½ cup of the milk and pour it into a cup. Whisk in the cornflour/cornstarch until there are no lumps and it has fully dissolved. Set aside.

3. Add the rest of the milk to a saucepan with the sweetener, vanilla, salt, crushed cardamom seeds, cinnamon, nutmeg and turmeric. Add the milk and cornflour mixture.

4. Heat on a medium heat, stirring continuously with a wooden spoon to ensure it does not burn on the bottom of the pan. As it heats, the custard will thicken.

5. When the custard starts to boil, turn off the heat and continue to stir for a few seconds before pouring into a serving jug/pitcher.

6. If the custard is not as thick as you'd like, add 1 teaspoon cornflour and 1 teaspoon water into a small ramekin, stir to combine, then add to the custard. Bring to a gentle boil again (just a few bubbles) to cook the cornflour.

7. Add your stewed apples to serving bowls or glasses, drizzle with the custard and enjoy as is, or sprinkle with 2-3 tablespoons of granola, a small handful of chopped nuts, or desiccated/dried shredded coconut. Enjoy.

NN **THE WHITE STUFF**

If you can swap sugar for something more nourishing then why not? Try using apple sauce or purée; fresh and frozen fruits like bananas, mango, berries; dates and other dried fruits; and sweet potatoes. Brown sugar contains slightly more minerals than white sugar but not enough to give any health benefits. We tend to avoid agave syrup/nectar, golden syrup/light treacle and white sugar as they have a high glycaemic index, which means a sugar crash (after the initial high) is more likely after eating.

SERVES: 4 | TIME: 5 MINUTES

SARA'S MANGO SORBET

"I can usually feel – and hear – the excitement in the class when I say we're making ice cream/sorbet and this recipe never disappoints. Sweet mango plus the sour lime is a guaranteed winner – and you can swap mango for other seasonal soft fruits if you like. Children usually ask me if they can suck the limes before they've even tried the sorbet – so do keep the lime quarters for serving."

EQUIPMENT

Food processor, fine grater/Microplane

INGREDIENTS

- 300g/10½oz frozen mango chunks
- 1 tablespoon water (optional)
- 9 tablespoons coconut or soy yogurt
- Juice of 1–2 limes (depending on how tart and zingy you want it)
- 1 whole lime (optional)
- Finely grated zest of 1 lime
- 6 squares of vegan dark/bittersweet chocolate

1. In a food processor, pulse the frozen mango to a fine crumble. If you have a processor that needs some liquid to pulse, add 1–2 teaspoons of water.

2. Add the yogurt and lime juice and pulse until it becomes smooth, but stop before it all melts from the heat of the blender and becomes a smoothie.

3. Cut the whole lime (if using) into quarters.

4. Serve the sorbet in small bowls or serving glasses with a grating of lime zest and chocolate over the top, and with a lime quarter wedged onto the side of each bowl/glass. So simple, so delicious.

TIP *Rolling, Rolling, Rolling*

Before squeezing citrus fruit, roll them back and forth on a flat surface with the palm of your hand for 10–30 seconds. When you squeeze it the fruit will release a lot more juice than had you not rolled it. Cool hey.

 use gluten-free oats.

SERVES: 8–12, DEPENDING ON HOW THICK YOU CUT THE SLICES
TIME: 40 MINUTES, PLUS 4–6 HOURS FREEZING

SARA'S TROPICAL BERRY RAW CAKE

"I have an artisan raw cake and chocolate business and this is one of my most popular cakes, with both adults and children. It's best made in the summer, with any fresh berries you can find. A version of this cake was presented to Sami Tamimi when MIH hosted him for a thank you dinner and he likened it to a plant-based semifreddo. You can substitute the oats in the crust for any other nut or seed, but the oats are lower cost. This cake is one to impress but it's really not hard to make. Enjoy."

EQUIPMENT

20cm/8in round cake pan, baking parchment, small saucepan, high-speed blender, food processor, spatula, wooden spoons, sharp knife, several small bowls, cocktail stick/ toothpick (optional)

INGREDIENTS (next page)

1. Line a 20cm/8in round cake pan with baking parchment.

2. Let's start with the coconut and lime layer. Chop up the creamed coconut and place in a small saucepan on a low heat to melt with the water and coconut oil. Keep an eye on it so it doesn't burn! Once melted, remove from the heat and set aside.

3. Moving on to the crust. Place the oats and seeds in a food processor and pulse until it resembles coarse breadcrumbs.

4. Add the rest of the crust ingredients into the food processor and pulse until they begin to combine. Stop pulsing once the ingredients begin to stick together. If your dates are on the dry side, you may need to add a few extra to get the mix to start sticking.

5. Add the crust mixture to the lined cake pan. Use clean hands or the back of a spoon to press down the mixture until it fills the cake pan in an even layer.

6. For added finesse slice 5 fresh strawberries (if using) and slide them into the edges of your cake pan evenly spaced out. (See photo.)

7. Place all the ingredients for the coconut lime layer – including the melted creamed coconut mix – in a blender and blend until combined. Reserve 2 tablespoons of this coconut lime mix in a small bowl to use at the end for decoration.

8. Using a spatula, scoop the rest of the mix into the cake pan and spread out in an even layer (being careful not to displace the strawberry slices around the edge, if used). Place in the freezer and freeze for about 20–30 minutes – until it's just firm enough to spoon another layer on top.

INGREDIENTS

For The Coconut Lime Layer

- 140g/5oz creamed coconut (that you buy in a block in cardboard packaging)
- 150ml/5fl oz/⅔ cup water
- 2 tablespoons coconut oil
- Juice of 3 limes
- 2 tablespoons syrup (date, maple, rice or whatever you have) (optional)

For The Crust

- 80g/3oz/scant 1 cup rolled oats
- 50g/1¾oz/⅓ cup sunflower seeds
- 180g/6¼oz/1⅓ cups dates (you may need a few extra)
- 1 tablespoon coconut oil
- Pinch of sea salt (optional)

For The Berry Layer

- 300g/10½oz fresh or frozen mixed berries (strawberries or raspberries work well), plus (optional) extra to decorate/top
- 60g/2¼oz creamed coconut (see above)
- 50g/1¾oz coconut oil
- 1 tablespoon liquid sweetener of choice (date, maple, fruit)
- 1–2 tablespoons water (optional)

To Serve

- 30g/1oz vegan dark/bittersweet chocolate (optional)

TIP

Instead of topping the cake with berries before freezing (step 12), sprinkle over some seeds or chopped/crushed nuts of choice.

9. For the berry layer, chop up the creamed coconut, then using the same pan as before, melt it with the coconut oil on a low heat. If using frozen berries, toss them into the pan while the mix melts to help them defrost. Once melted, remove from the heat and pour into the blender.

10. Add the fresh berries and syrup to the blender and blend. If the blender is struggling, add the water, 1 tablespoon at a time, to the mix to blend into a smooth paste. Taste to see if it needs a bit more sweetness for your liking.

11. Remove the cake pan from the freezer and evenly pour/spread the berry mixture over the coconut lime layer.

12. This is when the reserved coconut lime mix can be used to drizzle or dot specks in a pattern on top of the cake. Be creative! Top the cake with extra berries or nuts (see Tip), before placing it back in the freezer for 8 hours or overnight.

13. Once frozen, the cake will need defrosting at room temperature for 20 minutes before you remove it from the cake pan to ensure it doesn't crack. Place the cake on a serving plate.

14. While the cake is semi-frozen like this, melt the chocolate, broken into pieces, in a heatproof bowl set over a small pan of simmering water. I then love to drizzle the melted chocolate over the cake (and berry/seed/nut topping, if used), letting it run down the sides for an extra decadent look. Because the cake is cold it hardens like magic, adds a pop of colour, a crunch and some semi-bitter decadence!

15. Defrost for a final 1 hour or so at room temperature or defrost in the refrigerator overnight before slicing. Enjoy.

SERVES: 4 | TIME: 25 MINUTES

SARETA'S PISTACHIO & CARDAMOM KHEER

"Kheer is rice pudding – but not anything like British school dinners! This is a fragrant, warming pudding that will instantly transport you to an Indian household. It's served at all times of day but I particularly like it for breakfast. It's reminiscent of my childhood and more recent travels to my ancestral village. If you want, you could infuse it with saffron or rosewater."

EQUIPMENT

Sieve/fine-mesh strainer, saucepan, wooden spoon

INGREDIENTS

- 200g/7oz/generous 1 cup uncooked white basmati rice or pudding rice
- 6 green cardamom pods or 1 teaspoon ground cardamom
- 500ml/17fl oz/2 cups plant-based milk (oat, coconut and soy work well)
- 4 tablespoons date or maple syrup or brown sugar, plus (optional) extra for drizzling
- 30g/1oz raisins or other dried fruit of choice
- 2 drops of vanilla extract (optional)
- Pinch of sea salt
- 2–3 tablespoons shelled pistachios or another nut of choice (optional)

1. Rinse your rice in a sieve/fine-mesh strainer under cold running water until the water runs clear and then put it in a saucepan.

2. If using cardamom pods, bash them in a pestle and mortar or with the back of a spoon to slightly break them open. This will help release the flavour.

3. Add 300ml/10½fl oz/1¼ cups of the milk and all the rest of the ingredients – apart from the nuts – to the pan. I recommend adding 1 tablespoon of the syrup first and then adjusting to taste.

4. Bring the mixture to the boil, then reduce to a simmer. Gently stir it occasionally – you want it to become like a porridge. This will take about 3–4 minutes.

5. Stir in the rest of the milk, then continue to cook gently for about 7–8 minutes, stirring occasionally – the mixture will thicken further as the rice continues to cook and absorb the liquid.

6. Meanwhile, chop the nuts.

7. The pudding is ready when the rice is soft and fluffy but not dry. If it becomes too dry, you can add a tablespoon more of plant-based milk or water at a time to achieve the desired consistency. Using a fork or spoon, remove any hard bits of cardamom pods.

8. Serve the kheer in bowls with the chopped nuts and an extra drizzle of syrup, if you like.

 use gluten-free oats.

SERVES: 4 (3 SMALL PIECES EACH)
TIME: 20 MINUTES PREP; 20 MINUTES COOKING; 1–3 HOURS TO FIRM UP

SARETA'S MANGO BURFI

"Burfi (or barfi) are small, square fudge-like sweets usually made with dairy, ghee and sugar. They can be plain or flavoured with coconut, mango or whatever else you love! These are traditionally served at weddings, festivals and parties. I never used to like burfi as a child as I didn't like anything milky. But when I held my first supper club in 2015, a fundraiser for the Nepal earthquake, I made a vegan version and thought wow, I actually really like this. It's now a regular in my repertoire and people really enjoy it."

EQUIPMENT

Bowl, blender or pestle and mortar, frying pan, mixing bowl, 15cm/6in square non-stick baking pan or a non-stick baking sheet, wooden spoon, rolling pin or spatula

INGREDIENTS

120g/4¼oz/1 cup raw cashews, plus 6 raw cashews to decorate

Boiling water, to cover (for soaking cashews)

100g/3½oz/1 cup rolled oats

Pinch of sea salt

1 teaspoon ground cardamom or ground cinnamon

2 teaspoons date, maple or rice syrup (or other liquid sweetener of choice)

125g/4½oz canned mango pulp/purée (available in south Asian stores or world food aisles)

1. First soak all the cashews. Place them in a bowl, cover with ample boiling water and leave to soak for 20 minutes, then drain and rinse.

2. In a blender or pestle and mortar, grind the oats to a fine powder. Do the same with the 120g/4¼oz/1 cup of cashews, then cut the extra 6 cashews for the decoration in half and set aside.

3. Heat a dry frying pan on a low-medium heat, then add the ground oats and salt. Toast gently for about 3 minutes, stirring continuously, until a nutty aroma is released.

4. Add the ground cashews and cardamom or cinnamon. Continue to stir for another 1–2 minutes until it lightly browns.

5. Turn off the heat and transfer to a mixing bowl.

6. Slowly stir in the syrup and half the mango pulp/purée – as it comes together slowly add the rest; you might not use it all. Combine until it forms a thick dough-like texture. If it gets too wet, add extra soaked and ground cashews (see above), a teaspoon at a time.

7. Transfer the mixture to a 15cm/6in square non-stick baking pan or a non-stick baking sheet and gently press down with a rolling pin or spatula to about 1cm/½in thick, to either fill the baking pan or to an approx. 15cm/6in square if using a baking sheet.

8. Chill in the refrigerator for at least an hour (and up to 3 hours) to firm up. It should have a slightly sticky, fudgy texture when served.

9. Slice into 12 squares or rectangles and place half a cashew on the top of each piece to serve.

Store in an airtight container in the refrigerator for up to a week.

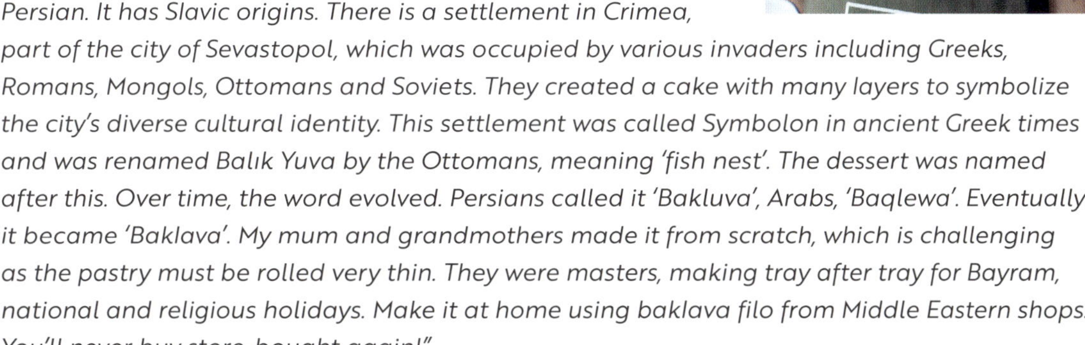

SERVES: MANY! UP TO 48 PIECES DEPENDING ON THE SIZE YOU CUT THE PIECES. TIME: 45 MINUTES

EMEL'S BAKLAVA

"Baklava is not Arabic, Greek, Armenian, Turkish, Assyrian or Persian. It has Slavic origins. There is a settlement in Crimea, part of the city of Sevastopol, which was occupied by various invaders including Greeks, Romans, Mongols, Ottomans and Soviets. They created a cake with many layers to symbolize the city's diverse cultural identity. This settlement was called Symbolon in ancient Greek times and was renamed Balık Yuva by the Ottomans, meaning 'fish nest'. The dessert was named after this. Over time, the word evolved. Persians called it 'Bakluva', Arabs, 'Baqlewa'. Eventually it became 'Baklava'. My mum and grandmothers made it from scratch, which is challenging as the pastry must be rolled very thin. They were masters, making tray after tray for Bayram, national and religious holidays. Make it at home using baklava filo from Middle Eastern shops. You'll never buy store-bought again!"

TIP ***It's important to have all the elements of your baklava ready before you start assembling because you need to move quickly in order for your pastry not to dry up. Follow this method and timings and you won't go wrong!***

EQUIPMENT

Medium saucepan, wooden spoon, pestle and mortar or food processor, pastry brush, 40 x 30cm/16 x 12in (4cm/1½in deep) baking pan, long thin oklava – rolling pin (available from Middle Eastern Shops or just buy a thin wooden pole from a DIY store cut to the length of a rolling pin), ladle

INGREDIENTS (next page)

1. Pop your sugar and water into a medium saucepan. Give it a gentle stir on a low heat until the sugar dissolves. Crank up the heat to bring it to a lively boil, then reduce to a simmer for 15 minutes, stirring occasionally.

2. Add the lemon juice, simmer for another 5 minutes, then take off the heat and set it aside to cool down. This is your syrup.

3. While the syrup cools, prep your nuts. You don't want them too big or they will break your filo sheets. Crush with a pestle and mortar or blitz them in a food processor. For a variety in texture, have some fine and some nice and chunky!

4. Preheat the oven to 180°C/350°F/gas 4.

5. Melt your vegan butter (if using). Using a pastry brush, brush the bottom of a 40 x 30cm/16 x 12in (4cm/1½in deep) baking pan with melted butter or oil.

6. Open your package of filo and cover with a clean dish towel to stop it from drying while you're working. >>

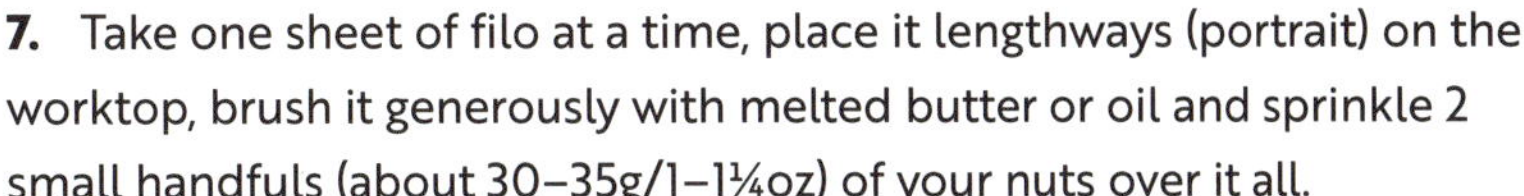

INGREDIENTS

400g/14oz/2 cups soft brown sugar

475ml/16fl oz/2 cups water

1 teaspoon lemon juice

400g/14oz/3 cups walnuts or hazelnuts

250g/9oz/generous 1 cup vegan butter or sunflower oil

500g/1lb 2oz baklava filo pastry (about 12 sheets)

7. Take one sheet of filo at a time, place it lengthways (portrait) on the worktop, brush it generously with melted butter or oil and sprinkle 2 small handfuls (about 30–35g/1–1¼oz) of your nuts over it all.

8. Using your oklava (or thin wooden pole), start from the bottom of the sheet and roll up the pastry sheet tightly around it like a Swiss roll, with the oklava still inside.

9. Once you've rolled the whole thing it should be the thickness of a vegan sausage!

10. Holding both ends of your oklava, scrunch your pastry together like an accordion and then carefully slide the baklava into the baking pan, still scrunched up. Place it lengthways into the baking pan, seam-side down, so the open ends are facing sideways, and the top of the scrunched roll is uppermost.

11. Repeat this process until you have filled up the whole baking pan (around 12 rolls).

12. Brush each roll generously with your melted butter or oil. You can slice the baklava into pieces now, or wait until after baking. Some people find it easier to do now.

13. Bake on the middle shelf for 15–20 minutes. Check after 12 minutes and turn the baking pan around. Aim for golden perfection!

14. Have your syrup ready with a ladle. When you take your baklava out of the oven, pour over 3–4 ladlefuls of the syrup. You should hear an intense sizzle – this is the sign of a good baklava. Any leftover syrup can be used in another recipe.

15. Set aside to cool and absorb the syrup. Cut into portions and enjoy!

TIPS FOR BAKLAVA MAKING

Search for filo in Middle Eastern stores or online with baklava on the packaging so it's thin enough. In my opinion, the best is Belgian brand Bazachi's Au Ble D'or product.

Make your syrup first and set it aside to cool. Your baklava must be hot straight out of the oven and the syrup must be at room temperature. This will ensure the syrup is absorbed but the pastry remains crispy.

Due to its high sugar content, baklava keeps for up to 2 weeks. Store in an airtight container at room temperature or in the refrigerator. It will be slightly chewier if stored in the refrigerator.

MAKES: 1 LOAF CAKE | TIME: 20 MINUTES, PLUS 1½ HOURS BAKING AND COOLING

HANNAH'S NETTLE, LEMON & ELDERFLOWER CAKE

"This is my most popular cake recipe. I'm a complete nettle head so I love it. A friend even asked me to make it for their wedding cake. I did a whole presentation about the nutritional properties of nettles at a festival called 'Nettle Fest'. There was no shortage of things for me to discuss! Nettles are a true British superfood (see Nutrition Nugget on p 294) – and I encourage everyone to add them to their diet. And what better way to get started than with a delicious cake? The cake tastes best eaten fresh out of the oven and still warm as a lemon drizzle, or frosted with cashew cream and eaten on the same day or day after. It's not a keeper."

EQUIPMENT

Bowl, 900g/2lb loaf pan, baking parchment, colander, large bowl, wooden spoon, blender, small offset spatula or knife, fine skewer, zester, wire/cooling rack

INGREDIENTS (next page)

1. If making the cashew cream frosting, soak your cashews in a bowl of cold water overnight, or in boiling water for an hour, drain and set aside.

2. Preheat the oven to 200°C/400°F/gas 6. Grease and line a 900g/2lb loaf pan with baking parchment.

3. Trim any tough stalks off the nettles and give the nettle tops a good wash under cold running water in a colander, then drain and pat dry.

4. Place the nettle tops in a food processor or blender along with the sunflower oil, plant-based milk or water, lemon zest and juice and elderflower cordial. Process until it looks like a green smoothie.

5. Now sift your flour and baking powder into a large mixing bowl and then add the sugar, ground ginger (if using) and salt.

6. Add the nettle mix to the bowl and stir gently to combine into a smooth green batter. Transfer the mix to your prepared loaf pan. Bake for 35–45 minutes. Set a timer.

7. While the cake is baking, you can prepare the frosting or drizzle – see methods on next page.

8. After the baking time, check the loaf cake to see if it's ready using a fine skewer. If the skewer comes out clean, it's ready; if it's still sticky, bake for another 5 minutes before checking again. Times vary depending on your oven and loaf pan used so it may take up to an hour (if using a silicone loaf pan). Once cooked, remove from the oven. Baking bit nailed. **>>**

INGREDIENTS

For The Cake

- 60–80g/2¼–3oz fresh young nettle tops
- 100ml/3½fl oz/scant ½ cup sunflower oil, plus extra for greasing
- 160ml/5½fl oz/⅔ cup plant-based milk or water
- Finely grated zest and juice of ½ lemon (save the other half for the decoration)
- 1 tablespoon elderflower cordial
- 275g/9¾oz/2 cups self-raising/self-rising flour
- 1 teaspoon baking powder
- 200g/7oz/1 cup cane sugar
- ½–1 teaspoon ground ginger (optional)
- Pinch of sea salt

For The Elderflower And Rose Cashew Cream Frosting

- 120g/4¼oz/1 cup raw cashews
- 80ml/2¾fl oz/⅓ cup plant-based milk of choice
- 2–3 tablespoons elderflower cordial
- 1 tablespoon rose water

For The Elderflower And Lemon Drizzle

- 2 tablespoons elderflower cordial
- 1 tablespoon lemon juice

To Decorate

- Finely grated zest of the (leftover) ½ lemon
- Edible wild flowers, wild blackberries or a string of redcurrants would really pop

FOR THE ELDERFLOWER AND ROSE CASHEW CREAM FROSTING

1. Add your drained soaked cashews to a high-speed blender along with the plant milk, elderflower cordial and rose water.

2. Blend until you reach a creamy, silky-smooth consistency. Scrape down the sides of the blender with a spatula in between blending. Cover and pop in the refrigerator.

3. Leave your cake to cool in the loaf pan for 20 minutes, then turn out onto a wire/cooling rack and leave for 30–40 minutes. Once completely cool, spread the cashew cheese all over using a small offset spatula or a blunt knife.

4. Decorate with lemon zest and edible wild flowers, or with blackberries or red currants.

FOR THE ELDERFLOWER AND LEMON DRIZZLE

1. Combine the two ingredients in a bowl and set aside.

2. While the cake is still hot in the loaf pan, pierce holes all over the cake using a skewer and pour the drizzle mixture all over. It will coat the cake and seep into the holes. Yum. Leave to cool completely in the loaf pan before turning out to decorate and serve.

3. Decorate with lemon zest and edible wild flowers, or with blackberries or red currants.

THE WONDER OF NETTLES WITH HANNAH WALKER

"Nettles are one of the most nutrient-dense greens available in the UK and across the US. They're high in iron, calcium, magnesium, vitamins A, C and K and a range of polyphenols – which are plant compounds with antioxidant properties that help to keep us healthy. If you keep pinching the tops off nettles you can get an almost year-round supply. You can use nettles in soups, stews, pesto and other sauces.You can use them raw if blended into a smoothie. The seeds are nutrition powerhouses as well, full of vitamin C, essential fatty acids and neurotransmitters such as acetylcholine and serotonin, which give you energy. Harvesting nettle seeds requires a bit of knowledge because you want to be harvesting from a female plant as male plants only produce flowers not seeds. To harvest the seeds, pick the whole end of the nettle, then when you get home brush them with your gloved hands to break the seeds off into a bowl. Dry them out – either by gently roasting them in a warm oven (switched off but after it's been used) for 10 minutes, or by hanging them in brown paper bags somewhere warm. Store them in a glass jar and sprinkle them on your food as an energy booster, add them to smoothies, or my favourite way to enjoy them is in my wild seed za'atar mix – you could add them to any spice mix!"

SERVES: 12 | TIME: 25 MINUTES

STEVE'S CHOCOLATE TORTE

"Rich and delicious, this cake goes down very well at a gathering. It is also very simple to make. You can make the tart with a biscuit or a nut base. This seed-based version of the recipe is delicious, as well as being nutritious, and cheaper to make than a nut version."

EQUIPMENT

2 saucepans, blender or food processor, 2 bowls, 22cm/8½in round springform cake pan, wooden spoon, whisk

INGREDIENTS

For The Base

- 50g/1¾oz coconut oil
- 120g/4¼oz/scant 1 cup sunflower seeds
- 120g/4¼oz/scant 1 cup dates

For The Filling

- 400ml/14fl oz/1⅔ cups oat or soy milk
- 1½–2 tablespoons cornflour/cornstarch
- 2 teaspoons cold water
- 2 teaspoons vanilla extract
- 270g/9¾oz vegan dark/bittersweet chocolate (at least 55 per cent cocoa solids)

TIP *This will keep in an airtight container in the refrigerator for up to a week, or can be frozen for up to 1 month. Scatter with berries, shredded coconut, chopped pistachios or dried rose petals.*

1. Let's make the base. Melt the coconut oil in a saucepan. Blend the sunflower seeds into a rough crumb using a blender or food processor.
2. Tip the blended sunflower seeds into a bowl. Add the dates to the blender and blend into a paste.
3. Add the seeds back into the blender with the date paste, then add the melted coconut oil and blend together.
4. Press the mixture into the base of a 22cm/8½in round springform cake pan to cover the whole base. No need to take it up the sides.
5. Now let's make the filling. Warm up the plant-based milk in a saucepan on a medium heat – it should be warm but not boiling, so no bubbles.
6. In a bowl, mix the cornflour/cornstarch with the cold water and whisk to make a paste, then stir into the warm milk in the saucepan.
7. Heat the mixture until it's boiling, stirring continuously with a whisk to thicken. Simmer for about 2 minutes to cook out the cornflour.
8. Now add the vanilla extract, stir, then turn off the heat.
9. Break the chocolate into pieces into another saucepan or a heatproof bowl. Pour your hot milk mixture over the chocolate and leave to melt for 15 seconds, then stir gently with a whisk. The chocolate will melt and combine with the thickened milk.
10. Pour this mix on top of your sunflower seed base. It will look runny, but once the mixture cools to room temperature it will set.
11. The torte can only be cut into portions when set at room temperature, or if you want the slices really neat, after being frozen for 2 hours. Use a hot knife. Defrost for 1–2 hours before serving.

SERVES: 4 GENEROUSLY | TIME: 30 MINUTES; PLUS OPTIONAL OVERNIGHT REFRIGERATION AND SOAKING

DR LEGUMES' GREEN PANCAKES

"We developed this recipe to meet a growing demand for tasty gluten-free options that are nutritious but also affordable to make. The main ingredient is green pea flour, which can be swapped for moong bean flour and is a good alternative to a gluten-free flour blend. We serve these with fresh berries and coconut yogurt. The response to this dish is excellent, some customers finishing a plate and ordering another straight away – so we know it's good!"

EQUIPMENT

2 large mixing bowls or blender, whisk, wooden spoon, large heavy non-stick frying pan with lid

INGREDIENTS (next page)

1. Weigh out the dry ingredients into a large mixing bowl or blender and mix or blend together. You get a smoother result using a blender, but you'll need to wash it out between blending the dry and the wet ingredients and combining them.

2. In a separate large mixing bowl or a clean, empty blender jug/pitcher, whisk or blend the silken tofu to a fine scramble, then slowly add the soy milk and aquafaba until you get a consistent lump-free texture. Now add the vanilla extract and whisk or blend again.

3. Add the wet ingredients to the dry ingredients and whisk or blend together until you create a smooth batter. For best results, store the batter in an airtight container in the refrigerator overnight or for as many hours as you can practically wait. This will improve the rise.

4. Preheat a heavy, non-stick frying pan on a high heat until hot.

INGREDIENTS

For The Dry Ingredients

200g/7oz/1½ cups green pea flour or moong bean flour

150g/5½oz/generous 1 cup chickpea/gram flour

2 tablespoons spirulina powder, or 1 tablespoon ground turmeric and a grind of black pepper (optional)

1 heaped tablespoon baking powder

100g/3½oz/½ cup soft brown sugar

For The Wet Ingredients

100g/3½oz silken tofu

250ml/9fl oz/1 cup soy milk

100ml/3½fl oz/scant ½ cup aquafaba (chickpea/garbanzo bean water from a can) (see p 376 for more info)

1 teaspoon vanilla extract

For Cooking The Pancakes

About 2 tablespoons vegetable oil

100g/3½oz fresh blueberries

To Serve

Plant-based yogurt (soya/oat/coconut)

Maple syrup

Fresh blueberries

Nut butter of choice (optional)

TIP *These pancakes also go beautifully with stewed seasonal fruit and almond cream.*

5. Reduce the heat to medium and add 1 teaspoon of vegetable oil. Using a tablespoon, carefully spoon the batter into three even spaces in the pan. Gently use the back of the spoon to spread the mixture into a round shape about 6cm/2½in in diameter, without pushing it flat. The pancakes should be about 1–2cm/½–¾in thick.

6. Carefully place 3 blueberries into the top of each pancake and gently press them into the batter so they are semi-submerged. Place a lid on top of the pan and leave to cook for 4½ minutes.

7. Remove the lid and use a heatproof utensil to flip over the pancakes. Replace the lid and cook for a further 4½ minutes. Once cooked, they should be lightly browned.

8. Transfer the cooked pancakes to a plate and keep warm in a low oven while you cook the rest in the same way, adding ⅓ teaspoon extra oil to the pan to cook each batch.

Serve the warm pancakes with a spoonful of plant-based yogurt, a drizzle of maple syrup and a few blueberries. For an extra boost of protein, add a spoonful of nut butter, if you like.

SERVES: 4 | TIME: 25 – 30 MINUTES, PLUS 3–4 HOURS FREEZING

RACHEL'S CHOC AVO NICE CREAM WITH STRAWBERRY SAUCE

For years, chef Rachel de Thample was a MIH ambassador, leading exciting foraging walks and wild food cookery classes. She's worked in the kitchens of Marco Pierre White, Heston Blumenthal and Peter Gordon and has published seven cookbooks including Less Meat, More Veg. *"The smooth, luxurious texture and the roasted strawberry sauce is a dreamy match. The sauce is a classy and delicious upgrade on the squeezy sundae sauce you can buy pre-made."*

EQUIPMENT

Blender, shallow freezer-proof container with a lid, ice-cream maker (optional), small roasting pan, sieve/fine-mesh strainer, bowl, wooden spoon

INGREDIENTS

- 2 ripe avocados
- 200ml/7fl oz/scant 1 cup almond, cashew or coconut milk
- 4 tablespoons unsweetened cocoa powder or raw cacao powder
- 4 tablespoons maple syrup, coconut sugar or soft light brown sugar (plus a little extra for the strawberry sauce, if needed)
- Pinch of sea salt
- 450g/1lb fresh strawberries

1. Halve the avocados, remove the stones and spoon the flesh into a blender.

2. Add the milk, cocoa or cacao powder, maple syrup or sugar and the salt. Blend until smooth.

3. Spoon into a shallow, freezer-proof container, cover with the lid and pop into the freezer, or churn in an ice-cream maker if you have one. The nice cream will take 3–4 hours to freeze to a suitable consistency, but check after 1–2 hours as you might prefer a softer-serve style.

4. While the nice cream freezes, you can roast the strawberries for your sauce. Reserve 4 strawberries for serving.

5. Preheat the oven to 180°C/350°F/gas 4. Tumble the strawberries into a small roasting pan, one where they'll fit in a single layer – you can leave the tops on.

6. Roast on the top shelf of the oven for 15–20 minutes, or until the strawberries have released their juices and started to thicken and caramelize. You want the berries to collapse and darken a bit.

7. Spoon the berries and juices into a sieve/fine-mesh strainer set over a bowl and use a wooden spoon to push the berries through. This will make a smooth sauce. It's already sweet but you can sweeten it with maple syrup or sugar to taste. The sauce can be served warm or cold.

8. Turn the reserved 4 strawberries into little fans by making 4 slices across each strawberry but not taking the cut all the way to the top.

9. To serve, add 1–2 scoops of nice cream to each bowl, top with a fanned strawberry and drizzle with the strawberry sauce. Gorgeous.

SERVES: 8 | TIME: NICE CREAM: 5 MINUTES, PLUS 3–5 HOURS FREEZING; TART TATIN: 15 MINUTES, PLUS 30 MINUTES BAKING

JOEL'S BANANA TARTE TATIN WITH NICE CREAM

"Having West African and Caribbean heritage, there are certain flavours I've come to expect as part of my cuisine even as a Londoner. Bananas, plantain and green bananas are staples that I try to incorporate in either my breakfast, lunch or dinner. One of the truly special examples of a banana dish that reminds me of my childhood, in particular dessert after lunch on special church days, is my late mum's Banana Tarte Tatin, which we grew up calling flan. It's a sweet taste of tropical heaven and a mouth party you won't forget. I'm sure Mum would be very happy I've continued her legacy by veganizing her delicious dish."

EQUIPMENT

Pestle and mortar, mixing bowl, shallow freezer-proof container with a lid, 23cm/9in round pie dish (or cake pan), rolling pin, heavy pan, wooden spoon, large bowl, large serving plate

INGREDIENTS (next page)

1. Let's start by prepping the bananas and hazelnuts for the tarte tatin.
- Peel and slice the bananas into thick circles (about 1cm/½in thick).
- Crush the hazelnuts into small pieces with a pestle and mortar.

2. We're now going to make the nice cream. Peel the three overripe bananas and put them in a mixing bowl. Use a fork to smush them up until it is like a thick mushy porridge. Add the vanilla extract and continue to smush until infused.

3. Decant the banana mixture into a shallow, freezer-proof container with a lid and pop it in the freezer.

4. Leave to freeze for 3–5 hours until frozen to an ice cream consistency. If you're feeling extra, you can stir it every 30 minutes to reduce the ice crystals, but it's not necessary.

5. When you're nice cream is 30 minutes or so away from being ready, you can start making your tarte.

6. Preheat the oven to 180°C/350°F/gas 4. Select a 23cm/9in round pie dish (or cake pan) that you are going to use for your tarte.

7. Roll out your puff pastry on a clean, flat work surface to about 0.5cm/¼in thickness and a little larger than the pie dish in size.

8. In a heavy pan on a medium heat, add the sugar and vegan butter. Stir it around continuously until melted and let the mixture get **>>**

INGREDIENTS

For The Tarte Tatin

- 3 bananas
- 50g/1¾oz/scant ½ cup hazelnuts
- 1 x 320g/11¼oz sheet of ready-rolled vegan puff pastry
- 100g/3½oz/½ cup coconut sugar or soft brown sugar
- 75g/2¾oz/⅓ cup vegan butter (we love Naturli)

For The Nice Cream

- 3 over-ripe or very ripe bananas
- ½ teaspoon vanilla extract

If using puff pastry from frozen, get it out of the freezer and leave to defrost for 4 hours before you want to use it.

If you're not making the banana nice cream, we suggest serving with either whipped coconut cream, a scoop of vegan vanilla ice cream or pourable oat cream.

darker and thicken. It will burn quickly, but you can smell when it is becoming fragrant and is caramelizing. This takes 1–2 minutes, but watch it carefully and remove from the heat when it's done.

9. Pour the caramel mixture into your pie dish and sprinkle the hazelnuts on top.

10. Place the banana slices side-by-side on top of the hazelnuts, covering the entire pie dish in one layer of banana slices.

11. Take the pastry round and place it on top of the pie dish. Lift the overhanging edges and gently tuck them in all around the inside of the dish so the pastry will puff up in the oven. Cut a 2–3cm/¾–1¼in slit on top to allow steam to escape.

12. Bake on the middle shelf for 30 minutes until the pastry has risen and turned golden and crispy. Take the tarte out of the oven and let it sit for 3–4 minutes to cool slightly, but no longer than 5 minutes otherwise the caramelized bananas will stick to the pie dish.

13. Using oven gloves or a clean dish towel to protect your hands, take a plate that's bigger than the pie dish, place it on top of the dish, then flip it upside down. Tap the bottom of the dish to allow the tarte tatin to fall neatly upside down onto the plate.

Cut the tarte into 8 slices and serve warm with a scoop of the banana nice cream, or serve with whipped coconut cream, vegan vanilla ice cream or vegan pourable cream. Enjoy.

Joel Bravette, our youth ambassador, performing Vegan Shut Up at our summer party and with Kate Magic, Sarah and his little one at Plant Powered Expo.

use gluten-free oats.

SERVES: 4 (MAKE 8 BARS/2 BARS EACH)
TIME: 20 MINUTES; 20 MINUTES SOAKING; 2 HOURS FIRMING UP

MELISSA'S TROPICAL BARS

"I created this quick recipe as a lover of dried fruit, which allows for a snack full of healthy fats and fibre whilst satisfying the desire for something sweet. A great addition to any lunchbox."

EQUIPMENT

Bowl, pastry brush (optional), blender, sharp knife, 20 x 10cm/ 8 x 4in loaf pan, baking parchment, small bowl, large mixing bowl, wooden spoon

INGREDIENTS

- 150g/5½oz/generous 1 cup dates
- Boiling water, to cover
- ½ teaspoon any oil, to grease the loaf pan
- 100g/3½oz/1 cup rolled oats
- 150g/5½oz dried tropical fruit trail mix (or any fruit and nut mix works)
- 1–2 teaspoons ground ginger
- ½ teaspoon ground nutmeg
- ½ teaspoon sea salt

1. Soak the dates in enough boiling water to cover for about 20 minutes.
2. While the dates are soaking, use a pastry brush to lightly grease a 20 x 10cm/8 x 4in loaf pan with the oil and line it with baking parchment.
3. Blend the oats into a flour in a blender.
4. Using a sharp knife, cut any chunkier elements of the trail mix into smaller pieces and then scatter about 2 tablespoons of it across the bottom of the loaf pan to decorate the bottom. Set the rest aside.
5. After 20 minutes, the dates will have softened. Drain, reserving 2 tablespoons of the date soaking water, then add the dates, ginger, nutmeg and salt to the oat flour in the blender.
6. On a slow-medium speed, blend the ingredients together until a dough has formed. If the mixture is crumbly, add 1–2 tablespoons of the reserved date soaking water and blend again to form a dough.
7. Now add the dough and trail mix ingredients to a mixing bowl and mix thoroughly until combined and the trail mix is evenly distributed.
8. Transfer to the loaf pan, then using either the excess baking parchment or cling film/plastic wrap, cover the mix and with the back of a spoon firmly press the mixture into the loaf pan ensuring it gets into all the corners and is packed in tightly. I press the mixture down with a spoon in a circular motion on top of the baking parchment.
9. Leave to refrigerate for a couple of hours until the block has firmed up. This step is crucial for cutting it into neat bars.
10. Remove from the loaf pan and turn it the right-side-up so the dried fruit trail mix is facing upwards. Using a sharp knife, cut it into bars.

Store in an airtight container in the refrigerator for up to a week.

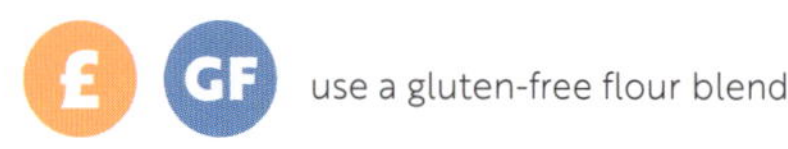

SERVES: 8 | TIME: 45 MINUTES

ZOE'S PUMPKIN AND GINGER STICKY TOFFEE PUDDING

"This dessert used to be a big hit when I cooked at the Bonnington Café, a collectively run vegetarian restaurant in Vauxhall, South London. Working for Made In Hackney inspired me to become more focused on the health benefits of food, and I've learned so many creative ways of using less sugar. I adapted this recipe by replacing most of the added sugar with natural sugar from the pumpkin. It is now also one of my go-to desserts when cooking on retreats as it is a healthy but indulgent dessert! You can get creative with this recipe and switch the pumpkin for different kinds of fruit or veg, depending on the season, such as apple or pear purée. It is also a great way of getting more veg into your food."

EQUIPMENT

Bowl, peeler, sharp knife, colander, large saucepan, 23cm/9in round cake pan (or cupcake tray), 2 medium-sized saucepans, wooden spoon, large bowl, blender, cocktail stick/toothpick

INGREDIENTS (next page)

1. First put your dates for the toffee sauce in a bowl, cover with the boiling water and leave to soak for 20–30 minutes. If they're left for up to an hour this is fine.

2. Peel and deseed the pumpkin or squash, chop it into 1–2cm/½–¾in cubes, place in a large pan, cover with boiling water from the kettle and boil for about 10–15 minutes until soft. Once soft, drain and set aside.

3. Preheat the oven to 180°C/350°F/gas 4.

4. Grease a 23cm/9in round cake pan and lightly dust with flour. The exact tin size doesn't matter, but the smaller the tin the deeper the pudding will be. You can also use a greased and flour-dusted cupcake tray – this mix makes 12 cupcakes.

5. Now let's make the pudding. Chop the dates, then add the dates and soy milk to a medium saucepan, bring to a simmer and cook for 5 minutes until the dates are soft. Turn off the heat and stir in the bicarbonate of soda/baking soda – it will fizz up!

6. Blend the cooked pumpkin/squash into a purée. In a large bowl or blender, mix together the sunflower oil, maple syrup and pumpkin/squash purée.

7. Add the date/milk mixture and stir it through. In a separate bowl, mix together the flour, ginger, cinnamon and baking powder.

8. Now pour the wet pumpkin/squash mixture into the dry mix and

INGREDIENTS

For The Toffee Sauce

- 100g/3½oz/¾ cup dates
- 150ml/5fl oz/⅔ cup boiling water
- 1 tablespoon plus ½ teaspoon coconut oil
- 3 tablespoons maple syrup
- ½ teaspoon sea salt
- 100ml/3½fl oz/scant ½ cup soy milk (or other plant-based milk)

For The Pudding

- 350g/12oz pumpkin or squash (you need 250g/9oz once peeled and deseeded)
- 200g/7oz/1½ cups dates
- 250ml/9fl oz/1 cup soy milk (or other plant-based milk)
- 1 teaspoon bicarbonate of soda/baking soda
- 100ml/3½fl oz/scant ½ cup sunflower or any neutral oil, plus extra for greasing
- 120ml/4fl oz/½ cup maple syrup
- 200g/7oz/1½ cups self-raising/self-rising flour (or spelt flour for a more nutritious version, but it will not rise as much!), plus extra for dusting
- 2 teaspoons ground ginger
- 1 teaspoon ground cinnamon
- 1 teaspoon baking powder

stir until everything is incorporated, but do not overdo it.

9. Pour the mixture into the cake pan (or cupcake tray) and bake on the middle shelf for 25–30 minutes (reduce to 15–20 minutes if making cupcakes) until the edges have set but the middle is still soft. Do the cocktail stick/toothpick test. If it comes out clean, it's ready.

10. While the pudding is baking, finish the toffee sauce. Drain the soaked dates, reserving the water.

11. Place the dates in a saucepan with the coconut oil on a low-medium heat. Leave them to melt for about 5 minutes, or until the dates are nice and soft. Leave to cool for 5 minutes.

12. Pour into a blender with the maple syrup, salt, soy milk and half the reserved soaking water. Blend until a smooth sauce forms. It should be a pouring consistency. Discard the leftover soaking water.

13. Remove the pudding from the oven and set aside to cool in the cake pan for 10–15 minutes (for cupcakes, cool for 5–10 minutes). Remove from the cake pan (or cupcake tray) to a serving plate and serve straight away while it's still warm.

14. Just before serving, gently heat the toffee sauce in a small saucepan for 3 minutes, then once bubbling, remove from the heat.

15. Cut the pudding into portions (or serve the cupcakes), then pour the toffee sauce over the warm pudding. For an extra treat, serve with plant-based ice cream, custard or yogurt.

MAKES: 12 SLICES | TIME: 25–30 MINUTES, PLUS 1–1½ HOURS BAKING

SANDRA'S CARIBBEAN SWEET POTATO PUDDING

"Sweet potato pudding is a cherished dessert in the Caribbean, holding great cultural significance, and is prepared for special occasions and celebrations. Its African influence is rooted in culinary traditions that use root vegetables and tubers. The European influence introduced new cooking methods and ingredients such as sugar and spices now integral to Caribbean cuisine. The concept of pudding that existed in Europe was adapted to local ingredients like sweet potatoes. For me, sweet potato pudding is nostalgic and evokes fond memories of my childhood. My mum made this dish often. Many times she requested my help in grating the sweet potatoes and coconut by hand. As a child, I sat in quiet anticipation for the pudding to be baked, cooled and consumed."

EQUIPMENT

Small bowl, 25cm/10in square baking pan, peeler or blender, grater or Microplane with a fine setting, skewer, 2 large bowls, sieve/fine-mesh strainer, pastry brush, wooden spoon

INGREDIENTS (next page)

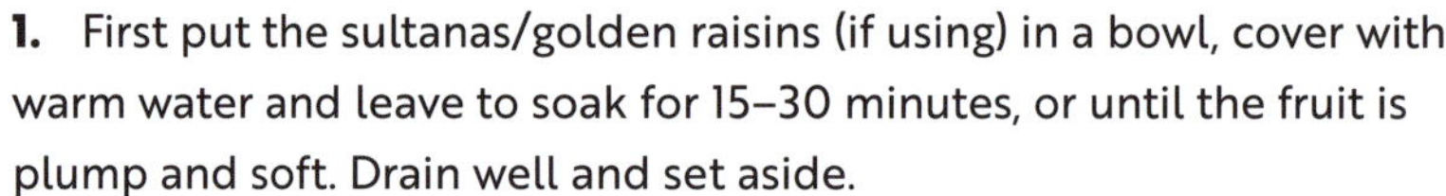

1. First put the sultanas/golden raisins (if using) in a bowl, cover with warm water and leave to soak for 15–30 minutes, or until the fruit is plump and soft. Drain well and set aside.

2. Preheat the oven to 180°C/350°F/gas 4. Lightly grease a 25cm/10in square baking pan with neutral oil and set aside.

3. Peel and finely grate the sweet potatoes, fresh coconut and root ginger. If grating coconut is too much effort see Tip, or use dessicated coconut, hydrating it in boiling water for 20 minutes before use.

4. Add the grated sweet potatoes and coconut (grated fresh or dried) to a large bowl along with the soaked sultanas/golden raisins (if using) and sifted flour and mix – add enough flour to make a thick, slightly sticky consistency that's still pourable.

5. In a separate large bowl, combine the coconut milk, sugar and vanilla extract. Mix well until the sugar is dissolved.

6. Next add the ground spices and root ginger to the wet mixture. Stir well to incorporate the spices evenly.

7. Add the spiced wet mixture to the sweet potato mixture and mix until well combined.

8. Pour the mixture into the prepared baking pan and spread out evenly. >>

INGREDIENTS

100g/3½oz/¾ cup sultanas/golden raisins (optional)

Warm water, to cover (for soaking dried fruit, if using)

Neutral oil, such as rapeseed/canola or sunflower oil, for greasing

900g/32oz sweet potatoes (white or orange sweet potatoes both work)

80g/3oz/1 cup fresh coconut flesh or unsweetened desiccated/dried shredded coconut

Thumb-size piece root ginger

60g–120g/2¼–4½oz/½–scant 1 cup self-raising/self-rising wholemeal/whole-wheat flour (depends on how wet or dry your potatoes are)

240ml/8½fl oz/1 cup coconut milk

85g/3oz/scant ½ cup coconut sugar or soft brown sugar

1 teaspoon vanilla extract

½ teaspoon ground mixed spice (that includes allspice/pimento)

¼ teaspoon ground cinnamon

¼ teaspoon ground nutmeg

9. Bake on the middle shelf for about 1 hour, or until the pudding is set (looks firm) and the top is golden brown. Depending on your oven, it may need as long as 1½ hours, especially if you used desiccated coconut. You can use a skewer to test if it's baked – it should come out clean if cooked.

10. Remove from the oven and leave the pudding to cool in the baking pan for 2–3 hours so it can develop its full flavour and texture. Slice the pudding into squares and serve (at room temperature) from the baking pan. It's not traditionally served with anything, but if you wanted to serve with oat cream or plant-based yogurt, this would be nice.

Store any leftovers in an airtight container in the refrigerator for 2–3 days and eat chilled straight form the fridge. Leftovers can also be frozen for up to 1 month; defrost in the refrigerator before eating.

Nourishing sweet treats going down a storm at the end of class

use gluten-free oats.

SERVES: MAKES 12 FLAPJACK BARS | TIME: 25–30 MINUTES

V'S BANANA CHOCOLATE FLAPJACKS

"I developed this one-bowl recipe as a healthy-ish packed lunch staple for my kids, which you can have in the oven in around 5 – 10 mins with hardly any washing up – result! The combination of chocolate and banana is pure comfort food and these beauties have been a firm family favourite for years – either eaten warm as a pudding with a drizzle of vegan cream, or enjoyed as a snack once cooled."

EQUIPMENT

Medium-sized rectangular baking sheet, large mixing bowl, wooden spoon, palette knife/spatula

INGREDIENTS

- 5 tablespoons coconut oil or vegan butter
- 3 ripe bananas
- 180g/6¼oz mixed dried fruit and seeds or roughly chopped nuts of choice (I use dried apricots, sunflower seeds, pumpkin seeds and cashews)
- 180g/6¼oz/scant 2 cups rolled or jumbo oats
- 2 tablespoons sweetener of your choice (maple/date syrup/brown sugar)
- Handful of dried coconut flakes (optional)
- 2 teaspoons vanilla extract (optional)
- 150g/5½oz vegan dark/bittersweet chocolate

TIP ***You can eat the uncoated flapjacks as they are. If not adding the chocolate topping, cool the flapjack mix slightly, then cut into bars. Remove from the baking pan once they have firmed up a bit.***

1. Preheat the oven to 180°C/350°F/gas 4.

2. Put the coconut oil or vegan butter in a medium rectangular baking pan – mine measures 17 x 22cm/6½ x 8½in. Place in the oven on the middle shelf for about 3 minutes until melted.

3. While the oil/butter is melting, peel and mash the bananas using a fork. Chop any larger pieces of dried fruit (if using) into small pieces.

4. Once the oil/butter is melted, take the baking pan out of the oven and swirl the contents around the baking pan getting into all the corners, then leave to cool a little.

5. Mix the rest of the ingredients – except the chocolate – into the mashed banana. Scrape the melted oil/butter into the mixture (leaving a coating to create the greased baking pan you need) and stir to combine.

6. Transfer the mix into the baking pan and spread evenly. Bake for 15–20 minutes until golden, then remove from the oven (see Tip).

7. To add the chocolate coating, break the chocolate into squares and place evenly on top of the flapjacks when they come out of the oven. Pop back into the turned-off oven leaving the door ajar – the chocolate will melt in 5 minutes. Spread the chocolate using a palette knife/spatula. Leave to cool in the baking pan, then cut into bars to serve. Enjoy!

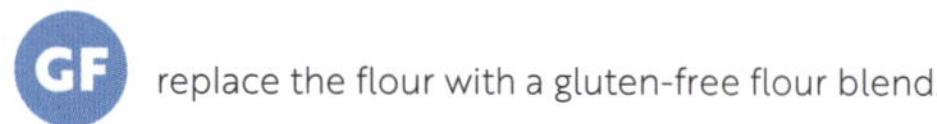

GF replace the flour with a gluten-free flour blend.

SERVES: 4 GENEROUSLY | TIME: 45 MINUTES

JORDAN'S SWEETCORN CAKE WITH MANGO CUSTARD

"This recipe was from a Mexican-themed cookery class I led with an amazing group of people from Micro Rainbow. It's inspired by a delicious sweet cornbread I tried in a Mexican restaurant. With the mango custard, I wanted to make something light and acidic to cut through the density of the cake and also remind the participants of their home food cultures. It got a big thumbs-up."

EQUIPMENT

Approx. 27 x 11cm/10¾ x 4¼in loaf pan, baking parchment, 2 large mixing bowls, whisk, cocktail stick/toothpick, wire/cooling rack, sharp knife, blender/food processor, saucepan, wooden spoon

INGREDIENTS (next page)

MAKE THE CAKE

1. Preheat the oven to 190°C/375°F/gas 5. Grease a 27 x 11cm/10¾ x 4¼in loaf pan by lightly brushing it with vegetable oil (if using) or line it with baking parchment.

2. In a large mixing bowl, whisk together the polenta/cornmeal, flour, sugar, baking powder, bicarbonate of soda/baking soda and salt until well combined.

3. In a separate bowl, combine the plant-based milk, coconut oil and apple cider vinegar. Whisk until smooth.

4. Pour the wet ingredients into the dry ingredients and stir until just combined. Gently fold in the sweetcorn until evenly distributed throughout the batter.

5. Pour the batter into the prepared loaf pan and spread it out evenly.

6. Bake on the middle shelf for 25–30 minutes until the top is golden brown and a cocktail stick/toothpick inserted into the middle comes out clean. Set a timer.

7. While the cake is baking, you can make your mango custard.

8. When you take your loaf cake out of the oven, leave to cool in the loaf pan for 10 minutes, then tip it out onto a wire/cooling rack and leave to cool for a further 30 minutes before slicing to serve (don't be scared to cut the warm cake, it will tolerate it). Enjoy the warm cake with the mango custard.

INGREDIENTS

Vegetable oil, for greasing (optional)

For The Cake

120g/4¼oz/scant 1 cup polenta/cornmeal

60g/2¼oz/scant ½ cup plain/all-purpose flour

100g/3½oz/½ cup soft brown sugar

1 teaspoon baking powder

½ teaspoon bicarbonate of soda/baking soda

¼ teaspoon sea salt

240ml/8½fl oz/1 cup plant-based milk (such as almond or soy milk)

60ml/2fl oz/¼ cup melted coconut oil

1 tablespoon apple cider vinegar

140g/5oz/1 cup canned (drained) sweetcorn kernels

For The Mango Custard

2 large ripe mangoes (you need 260g/9¼oz mango purée)

100g/3½oz/½ cup caster/granulated sugar

Finely grated zest of 1 lime

60ml/2fl oz/¼ cup lime juice (from about 2–3 limes)

30g/1oz/¼ cup cornflour/cornstarch

1 x 400ml/14fl oz can full-fat coconut milk

Pinch of sea salt

2 tablespoons vegan butter or coconut oil

MAKE THE CUSTARD

1. Peel and pit the mangoes, then chop the flesh into chunks.

2. Place the mango chunks in a blender or food processor and blend until smooth. Set aside.

3. In a saucepan on a medium heat, whisk together the mango purée, sugar, lime zest, lime juice, cornflour/cornstarch, coconut milk and salt until well combined and smooth. Bring the mixture to a simmer, stirring constantly to prevent lumps.

4. Once the mixture starts to bubble and thicken, reduce the heat to low and continue to cook, stirring constantly, for 2–3 minutes until the mixture has thickened to a custard-like consistency.

5. Remove from the heat and stir in the vegan butter or coconut oil until melted and fully incorporated into the custard.

6. Serve the custard warm or cold – it's delicious both ways – poured over the sweetcorn cake. Yum.

TIP *You can slice the cold loaf cake and freeze to eat it portion by portion. Wrap each slice individually in baking parchment, then pop them in a reuseable freezer bag and freeze for up to 1 month. Defrost the slice(s) as required, then warm up gently in a pan, in a moderate oven or in a toaster before serving. You can store the custard in a clean glass jar or airtight container in the refrigerator but it will need eating within 2 days, which isn't usually a problem!*

HELP – MY CAKES HAVE SUNK!

There's nothing more annoying than cupcakes or muffins coming out of the oven all lovely and puffed up only for them to sink 5 minutes later. Your domestic god/goddess takes a real ego hit. What's caused this baking outrage could be a number of things, but usually it's one of these three:

1 ***Your oven temperature was inconsistent and they haven't evenly baked.***

2 ***The cakes are underbaked and so the crumb structure couldn't sustain the initial height it had risen to.***

3 ***The recipe called for too much raising agent e.g. baking powder or bicarbonate of soda/baking soda – which caused the cakes to rise too quickly and, once out of the oven and cooling, the crumb structure wasn't able to sustain the height.***

May your muffins be high and your cakes stay risen!

GF use gluten-free miso (if using white miso).

SERVES: 4 | TIME: 20 MINUTES

VIVIANNE'S PROTEIN-RICH BLACK BEAN CHOCOLATE PUDDING

"This dessert was always a winner in my Vegan Meatz masterclasses. The black beans were a surprising element and opened people's minds to the possibilities of using legumes in desserts. The earthy tones of dark chocolate are the perfect match for an umami-rich miso and roasted nuts dessert pairing."

EQUIPMENT

Blender, colander, spatula, small bowl, pestle and mortar, frying pan

INGREDIENTS

1½ x 400g/14oz cans black beans

60–80ml/2–2¾fl oz/¼–⅓ cup sweetener of choice (date syrup, maple syrup, soft brown sugar or coconut sugar)

50g/1¾oz/½ cup unsweetened cocoa powder or raw cacao powder

1 teaspoon vanilla extract

2 tablespoons (shelled) pistachios or other nuts of choice

Pinch or two of sea salt flakes

For The Tahini-Miso Salted Caramel

100ml/3½fl oz/scant ½ cup tahini

100ml/3½fl oz/scant ½ cup date or maple syrup

1 teaspoon brown rice or white miso paste

1. Drain the black beans but reserve the bean juice, aka the aquafaba, as we will use this.

2. Rinse the black beans and then add them to a blender along with 60ml/2fl oz/¼ cup of your sweetener of choice.

3. Start blending, adding the aquafaba bit by bit – use about a third to a half of the aquafaba (depending on the power of your blender). Save the rest in the refrigerator for another recipe.

4. Blend until almost smooth, stopping to scrape down the sides of the blender with a spatula, as needed.

5. Add the cocoa or raw cacao powder, blend, then add the vanilla extract and blend again.

6. Now you should have a pretty thick spread. Taste and add the remaining sweetener, if needed. Decant into a bowl and set aside.

7. In a separate bowl or blender, mix together/blend all the tahini-miso salted caramel ingredients until combined. Set aside.

8. Using a pestle and mortar, crush the pistachios into small pieces. Add to a dry frying pan and roast on a medium heat for 1–2 minutes. Set aside to cool.

9. To serve, add 1–2 scoops of the chocolate bean cream to each serving bowl, drizzle with the tahini-miso salted caramel and finish with a scattering of the roasted pistachios and a small pinch of salt flakes.

Store the chocolate bean cream and caramel in separate airtight containers in the refrigerator for up to 3 days. Both can also be frozen for up to 3 months – defrost in the refrigerator overnight before serving.

IN CONVERSATION WITH...

How to Talk About Your Food Choices

Earthling Ed's Top Tips For Talking About Your Food Choices

At many points on your plant-based journey, it is common to find yourself needing to explain your dietary choices to friends, family, colleagues or serving staff in restaurants. These conversations are not always easy, and yet the value of being able to calmly and emphatically talk about your food choices cannot be overstated, especially when someone has commented or asked about them in a way that feels derogatory or accusatory.

Meet Ed Winters, aka Earthling Ed, a vegan activist and educator famous for setting up tables at universities and events with signs saying, "Give me your best argument for not being vegan", inviting people to debate him. He's the author of two books: *This Is Vegan Propaganda* and *How To Argue With A Meat Eater And Win Every Time*. He's renowned for his compassion, patience and respectful interactions, so what better person to give us his top five tips on having conversations about vegan food choices. Over to Ed.

TIP 1
Ask Questions

Get people to talk about themselves and their beliefs. Rather than think, I need to convince someone of the things I believe, approach a conversation thinking, I want them to reflect on the things that they believe. I think the majority of people, on some level, agree with the core principles of veganism, because everyone wants a food system that's healthier, more equitable, affordable, sustainable, ethical. So rather than impart your wisdom, interrogate what they believe with questions. We create a stronger conversation when we meet people where they're at. Encouraging introspection is a really powerful thing to do, and asking lots of questions invites people to go deeper in their thought process. I'm also mindful not to overload people with statistics and complex terms, at least not in an informal conversation. It's like peeling an onion. There's a core belief somewhere in there, you've just got to get down to it. And that core belief is probably one that aligns with veganism. It's just trying to help people see that for themselves, rather than thinking we're forcing what we think onto them, which is never going to work.

TIP 2
Body Language

It's not just the verbal language we use, it's how we present ourselves physically. If we're having a conversation and someone's telling us about their beliefs, and we're scowling, shaking our heads or showing signs of irritation, then we're not creating a space where people can be vulnerable and honest. People don't want to feel like they're being judged. You need to create an atmosphere of openness and curiosity. Smile or laugh when it's appropriate. People need to feel it's okay to be vulnerable. Body language can calm things down if the conversation is starting to spiral or is getting heated. Try sitting back and opening up your body to show your own vulnerability.

TIP 3
Be Mindful of Language

Make sure we're not using accusatory words. Your fault. You're this. You, you, you. I like to use "we" instead. So I'd say, "When we eat animal products," even though, obviously, I don't, but I'd say, "When we eat animal products, we are paying for these things to happen to animals." It shows that this isn't just them. It's a collective thing, and you understand, and you're part of this system too. Inclusive language can be really helpful.

We also need to be mindful of emotive language. Sometimes we want to be as emotive as possible but that might not be helpful for the person we're conversing with. You might use a phrase like meat is murder, but end up arguing about the semantics of that instead of talking about the issue. Read the room. Try to understand the people you're speaking with and gauge what language might be most effective.

TIP 4
Validation & Relatability

Validating people is important. People may say things that are wrong. But we have to understand why people think the things they do. It's frustrating to hear vegans don't get enough protein, but I can understand why people think that. Validating people is not the same as agreeing. You can fundamentally disagree with someone, but still understand why they think the way they do. This moves us on to relatability. Most of us weren't born vegan or plant-based. We have a story about why we've become vegan. We can use this to show we've been where that person is, we see ourselves in them and we've changed, and as a consequence of us changing, hopefully they can see themselves in us, and they can change as well if they want to. So being relatable and not being afraid to dip into personal stories is important. It's not two opposing ends of the spectrum, debating or arguing, but two people with different life experiences that have a lot of crossover having a conversation about something important.

Most of us weren't born vegan or plant-based. We have a story about why we've become vegan.

TIP 5
Listening

We often overlook the value of listening but it's important for two reasons. Firstly, we want the person to feel heard. We want them to know that what they're saying is being absorbed. There's nothing worse than trying to express yourself and knowing that what you're saying is falling on deaf ears. It's so frustrating when you say something and the person either hasn't listened properly, or is just not listening, and, as a consequence, hasn't understood what you're trying to say. And often with arguments, what you realize is that you're both arguing about different things, and that makes it even worse, because no one's listening. So listening is good because it makes the person feel heard and that they can express themselves more openly. It's also good because it means you're responding to what someone's actually saying. Sometimes we get in our own heads and we're thinking, what am I going to say next? And because we're so wrapped up in our own thoughts, we forget listening is what guides us into deciding what to say next.

I think the majority of people, on some level, agree with the core principles of veganism.

DRINK TO THAT

There's nothing quite like a nice drink.

Hot or cold, they not only provide refreshment but a moment of pause and calm. Drinks are the cornerstone of hospitality and the fuel of social gatherings: cuppas and catch ups, party punchbowls, mocktails to toast to life's milestones – they're an essential ingredient of holidays, celebrations and festive occasions. Drinks also provide comfort during life's more challenging moments – nursing us during sickness, helping us to process shocks and to heal heartaches.

For health and inclusivity, all the drinks at MIH are alcohol-free and are packed with body- and soul-nourishing ingredients such as fresh fruits, herbs and spices. We love to start our masterclasses by serving herbal teas, golden milks or power smoothies, and at community events we've served herbal cocktails, fruit punch and spiced hot chocolate to hundreds of thirsty folk.

You'll find a few of our favourite drinks here. We hope they bring the same comfort, joy and nourishment to you, as they do for us.

SERVES: 4 TIME: 5 MINUTES

BABA'S FLU BUSTER SHOT

"When I start to feel run down and can feel the twinges of a sore throat and cold coming on, I hit it with one of these shots for a few days in a row. I vary the ingredients and quantities depending on what I have in, but the base is more or less the same. Most often it does the job and I keep whatever was lurking in my immune system at bay. If you want to make this a long drink, add more water. I make it like a shot."

EQUIPMENT

Sharp knife, high-speed blender, sieve/fine-mesh strainer

INGREDIENTS

- 2 oranges
- 2 lemons
- 2 thumb-size pieces root ginger
- 5cm/2in piece turmeric
- Generous pinch of black pepper
- 240ml/8½fl oz/1 cup water

1. Peel the oranges and lemons and save the peels to preserve or use in a tea or to zest onto another dish.

2. Add all the ingredients to a high-speed blender and blend until smooth.

3. You can drink it as is or strain it through a fine sieve/fine-mesh strainer for a smoother drink.

The Bentley-Lafene family – plus Sky – line up for the Veg Dash fundraising event.

SERVES: 4 TIME: 5 MINUTES

SARAH'S BEGINNER GREEN SMOOTHIE

"This recipe is a hit with both my pda (pathological demand avoidant) autistic son, who hates anything too earthy-tasting, and my oldest, bestest friend Kim, who also doesn't enjoy green smoothies. I think she's more triggered by the compulsion people feel to need to like them because it's the right and healthy thing to do, than actually not liking them. She's a rebel heart. Either way, this smoothie is very yummy and can be dialled up for more advanced green smoothie drinkers and kept simple for those starting their green smoothie journey. Enjoy."

EQUIPMENT

Sharp knife, high-speed blender

INGREDIENTS

- 3–4 bananas
- 2 ripe mangoes
- 200g/7oz spinach
- 200ml/7fl oz/scant 1 cup room-temperature water
- 100g/3½oz kale (optional)
- 1–2 teaspoons spirulina, chlorella or greens blend powder (optional)

1. Peel the bananas and roughly chop them. Save the skins to make carnitas (see p 240).
2. Peel the mangoes and cut the flesh away from the pits.
3. Add the bananas, mangoes, spinach and water to a high-speed blender and blend until smooth.
4. If you're good with a bit more earthy-tasting smoothies and you want to up the goodness hit, add the kale, the spirulina, chlorella or green powder and then blend again.

Serve in glasses at room temperature.

Chlorella, Spirulina and B12 p 368

ORGANIC
Super
Greens
POWDER
VIRIDIAN

SERVES: 4 TIME: 2 MINUTES

SARAH'S COMFORT SMOOTHIES

MONKEY MONKEY

use gluten-free oats.

EQUIPMENT

High-speed blender

INGREDIENTS

4 bananas

2 tablespoons peanut butter (crunchy or smooth)

2–4 teaspoons raw cacao/ unsweetened cocoa/ carob powder (optional)

25–50g/1–1¾oz/¼–½ cup rolled oats

2–4 pitted dates

450ml/15½fl oz/1¾ cups room-temperature water

Pinch of sea salt (optional)

CHERRY CHOC DREAMS

use gluten-free oats.

EQUIPMENT

High-speed blender

INGREDIENTS

440g/15½oz/2 cups frozen or fresh cherries

2 bananas

25–50g/1–1¾oz/¼–½ cup rolled oats

2–4 teaspoons raw cacao/ unsweetened cocoa/ carob powder

2–4 pitted dates

450ml/15½fl oz/1¾ cups room-temperature water

Pinch of sea salt (optional)

Cacao Versus Cocoa p 368

PINK POWER

use gluten-free oats.

EQUIPMENT

High-speed blender

INGREDIENTS

3 bananas

250g/9oz/2 cups frozen raspberries

1 tablespoon ground flaxseed

1–2 tablespoons goji berries

65g/2¼oz/½ cup whole (skin-on) almonds (ideally soaked in cold water for 4–6 hours first, then rinsed, but not essential)

2 tablespoons peanut butter (crunchy or smooth)

3 dates

½ teaspoon maca powder (optional)

450ml/15½fl oz/1¾ cups room-temperature water

1. Peel the bananas and break into pieces with your hands, then add to a high-speed blender.

2. Add the rest of the ingredients to the blender and blend until smooth.

Sit down, take 5 minutes, and enjoy.

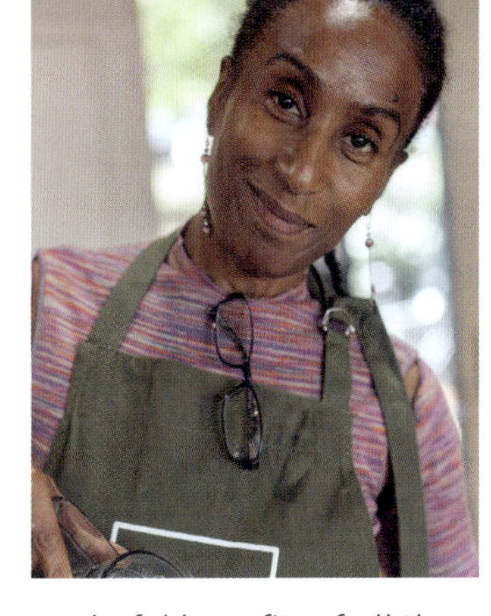

SERVES: 4 TIME: 5 MINUTES

FREDDIE'S POST-WORKOUT SMOOTHIE

"This is a super-refreshing and revitalizing smoothie that's perfect to drink post-workout. It's a great reward because of the wonderful benefits of all the ingredients. You've got ginger, which is anti-inflammatory and can be used to ward off colds; kale, which helps with eye, heart and bone health; turmeric, which is an anti-inflammatory powerhouse; Himalayan salt, which is packed with minerals and replaces the salts you've just lost; and of course cucumber, the ultimate hydrator. I love it and I hope you do too."

EQUIPMENT

Bowl, high-speed blender, sieve/fine-mesh strainer, measuring jug/pitcher

INGREDIENTS

2 thumb-size pieces root ginger
1 cucumber
1–2 lemons
600ml/20fl oz/2½ cups room-temperature water or coconut water
Medium handful of kale
1 teaspoon ground turmeric
½ teaspoon black pepper
Generous pinch of sea salt

1. Let's get the ingredients ready. Roughly chop the ginger and cucumber.

2. Roll the lemons to activate the juices and then squeeze out 2 tablespoons of juice into a bowl.

3. Add the water or coconut water and ginger to a high-speed blender and blend until smooth.

4. Pour the liquid through a sieve/fine-mesh strainer over a bowl and press with a spoon until all the fibre is separated from the water.

5. Pour the liquid back into the blender, then add the cucumber and all the other ingredients and blend until smooth. You can add the kale stalks and all.

6. Pour into your favourite glasses, sit down, breathe deeply and enjoy. Post-workout drinks are best consumed at room temperature so reframe from putting ice or ice-cold water in it.

SERVES: 4 TIME: 15–20 MINUTES

WOIN'S SPICED TEA

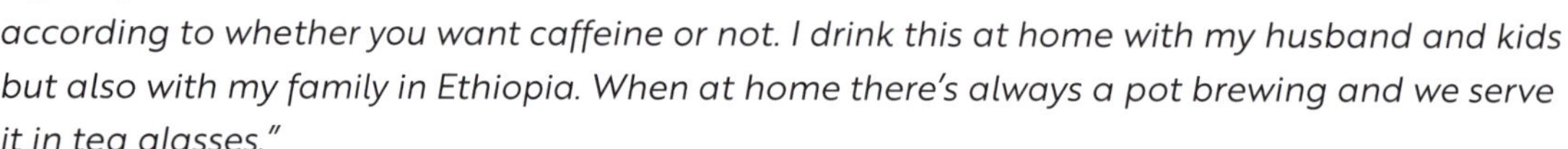

"Ethiopia is known for its coffee but spiced tea is also a staple drink. This version is refreshing and warming on a cold London night after dinner. You can drink it with or without black tea according to whether you want caffeine or not. I drink this at home with my husband and kids but also with my family in Ethiopia. When at home there's always a pot brewing and we serve it in tea glasses."

EQUIPMENT

Pestle and mortar, saucepan, tea strainer or fine sieve/fine-mesh strainer

INGREDIENTS

Thumb-size piece root ginger
4–5 green cardamom pods
2 cinnamon sticks
½ teaspoon whole cloves
1.25 litres/44fl oz/5 cups water

1. Slice the ginger into thin ribbons.

2. Mix all the spices – except the ginger – together in a mortar, then lightly crush them using a pestle.

3. Bring the water to the boil in a saucepan.

4. Add the spice mixture and ginger and simmer the infusion on a medium heat for 10–15 minutes.

5. Pour the spiced tea through a tea strainer or a fine sieve/fine-mesh strainer into teacups. Serve hot.

TIP ***If you wish, add a black tea bag (or up to 4 tea bags) to the pan, or keep it as is for a caffeine-free drink.***

SERVES: 4 (GENEROUSLY) TIME: 30 MINUTES

NENA'S ZOBO

*"Zobo is a Nigerian drink made from the dried red petals of the roselle plant (*Hibiscus sabdariffa*) and a mix of spices. Roselle is native to West Africa but has spread to parts of Asia and the West Indies. You buy it dried under different names – zobo, hibiscus flowers, hibiscus or sorrel – but it has different local names. Do not confuse it with the leafy salad green sorrel with the tangy taste. Zobo has a refreshing taste and health benefits such as aiding digestion, reducing high blood pressure and being packed with antioxidants that boost immunity."*

EQUIPMENT

Sharp knife, medium-large saucepan with lid, wooden spoon, high-speed blender or masher, sieve/fine-mesh strainer, a large jug/pitcher

INGREDIENTS

- 50g/1¾oz/1 cup dried zobo/hibiscus flowers/sorrel
- 1 whole pineapple
- 1 orange
- 2 litres/70fl oz/8½ cups water
- Thumb-size piece root ginger
- 1 tablespoon whole cloves
- 1 cinnamon stick
- 1 teaspoon sweetener for the zobo drink (ideally date or maple syrup, Xylitol, or soft brown sugar) (optional)

1. First let's prepare the ingredients.
- Rinse the zobo/hibiscus flowers and pat dry.
- Slice the skin off the pineapple and set aside to use later.
- Cut the pineapple into chunks of a size your blender can manage.
- Cut the orange into slices.

2. Add the water to a saucepan, then add the zobo/hibiscus and cook on a low heat for 1–2 minutes.

3. Add the pineapple and ginger to a high-speed blender and blend until smooth. If you don't own a blender, mash the pineapple chunks down and finely slice the ginger.

4. Add the pineapple and ginger to the saucepan and stir. If you mashed the pineapple, ensure to add the juice and mashed chunks to the saucepan.

5. Add the cloves, cinnamon stick and orange slices. You can also add the pieces of pineapple skin to the pan. If using non-organic pineapple, wash the skin well.

6. Cover and cook on a low heat for 20 minutes until it is a deep red.

7. It doesn't need extra sweetener but if you want to add the teaspoon of sweetener, do so now and stir in.

8. Remove from the heat and pour through a sieve/fine-mesh strainer into a large jug/pitcher. You might wish to keep the orange slices in the drink when serving for visual appeal. It's your call.

Enjoy your zobo warm or cold. To store, cover and keep in the refrigerator for up to 3 days.

IN CONVERSATION WITH…

Exploring Why People Go Vegan

A conversation with activist, author and organizer Sean O'Callaghan aka FatGayVegan

Sean: Compassion is a spectrum or a range of behaviours that you can keep expanding. You might buy ethically produced clothing, eat organic food or vote in a way that aligns with your beliefs. A natural extension of those choices is to go vegan, as it's a fair and just thing to do for people, planet and the animals.

I decided to go vegan after a series of events made me realize my choices related to how animals are commodified, and so I decided I didn't want to be complicit in that anymore. For you and me to exist in the modern world, somebody or something is suffering due to us, but going vegan is a way to minimize that – at least when it comes to animal suffering and our impact on the planet.

There's a lot of misinformation, misleading marketing spin and cultural norms that take people away from being vegan. I'm not here to judge anyone's choices. But I'm very happy to answer any questions. Here are some we've been repeatedly asked in the MIH kitchen.

I eat a lot of plants and buy high welfare meat, dairy and eggs. Isn't that enough?

I'd say that animals, high welfare or not, have still had to die earlier than their natural life cycle because you wanted to eat them when you could have eaten something else. And it's not just meat. Dairy cows and egg-laying hens die much sooner than if they were left to live out their lives because they're depleted from constantly producing milk and eggs. And even if an animal has had a better life, the end is the same. They're taken to a slaughterhouse where they're electrocuted, shot in the head or gassed. When animals are in slaughterhouses they are deeply distressed, fearful and try to escape. They fight for their life. If more people saw inside slaughterhouses, I believe many more people would go vegan.

But hens lay eggs anyway. Surely it's wasteful not to eat them.

It's a supply and demand situation. A chicken will lay an egg and roost on it until it starts growing another chicken inside of it. If that egg doesn't become another chicken, it will be cracked open by other chickens and they'll eat the contents to replenish the nutrients expelled by laying the egg. If you keep taking the egg away, it will lay another, and it gets into a cycle of continually laying eggs. Each egg depletes the nutrients it needs to stay healthy, and that's why chickens used for egg production get old, sick and frail before their time. And let's not forget most people aren't buying higher welfare eggs but eggs from industrial farming. Male chicks get lobbed into incinerators on factory production lines and laying chickens are kept in horrendous cramped spaces. Look up videos of this and see how you feel afterwards. As a compassionate person, I imagine it won't sit well with you.

But humans have always eaten animals products.

Just because something has been done in the past isn't a good reason for it to continue. I think the natural order is for humans to be adaptive, and that we need to evolve to survive. The way we've exploited animals for the last 50 plus years is unsustainable. It's not the natural order. Capitalism swept in and found you could make cheap mass protein for people and it could be commodified. So if you want to talk about the natural order of things, it's for humans to change when we need to. If we go on like this, the planet will become uninhabitable. If we follow the natural order of that, it's extinction of humankind.

I don't like to ask people to make me special food or feel uncomfortable about what they're eating because of my choices. How do you manage that?
I think people who love me or care about me will understand, be interested and it won't hurt their feelings. They'll understand I'm doing this because I believe it's the right thing to do, it's not to judge them. It's okay for us to have choices and to assert those choices to our friends and family. If we do it kindly, most people accept it.

I don't like to stand out or explain myself to people. How will I cope in social situations if I go vegan?
A lot of it comes from confidence and belief. Once you have a good idea why veganism matters and your head and heart match up, you'll be more relaxed talking to people about your choices. There are social events all over the planet designed for vegans where you can gather with like-minded people, which can be very affirming.

My grandma has been making me the same cake since I was a child. It was also my granddad's, who's now passed away, favourite cake. Giving that up feels like too much of a sacrifice.
If Grandma loves you, which it sounds like she does, you and she could have a beautiful bonding moment recreating the cake recipe in a veganized form. It doesn't take away your memories of your grandfather. It's an evolution of a family tradition.

What about when you travel – isn't it difficult?
It can be but it depends where you travel. If you can't speak the language and keep going to non-vegan restaurants then yes it will be challenging. Do your research – find out what dishes are vegan from the local cuisine. Write up a card explaining your dietary needs in the local language for serving staff to read. There are also great online resources such as Happy Cow that list vegan and vegan friendly restaurants around the world. Or why not book self-catering so you can prepare your own meals? Travel was more of a challenge when I went vegan 25 years ago – but it's easier these days. If you want to be vegan, you'll make it work.

I've heard the term speciesism. What's that about?
That term refers to giving preference to one species of animal over another. So you might give care, love and protection to a dog or cat, but not extend those same feelings of protection and care to other animals. It's a way to succinctly describe the difference between how you act towards a pet to a farm animal or an animal in the wild you don't have a relationship with.

But surely I can still eat fish. They don't feel pain and we need them for omega oils?
Fish do feel pain, and from a vegan perspective, any sentient creature that feels pain and exhibits fear is worth saving. There are many amazing resources online about the creative, unique and complex world of fish societies. But because most people don't know about this, it's easier to think fish don't feel pain. It's not just about an individual fish, but the industrial fishing and farming practices that have stripped the sea of life and polluted the oceans with fishing tackle. It's not good for the planet, it's not good for the workers and it's not good for human health. You can get your omegas from algae – see p 262.

So you think everyone should go vegan – even indigenous communities like Inuit and Maasai?
That's a conversation to have with people who live that reality. I can only speak with any authority on the world that I grew up in – which is probably similar to most readers of this book who live in built-up urban environments, or towns and villages in rural communities who source their food from stores, markets and supermarkets. Do you consider what indigenous communities do when you make other choices? If not, it's probably not relevant to your decision to go vegan or not.

There's a lot of misinformation, misleading marketing spin and cultural norms that take people away from being vegan.

MAKES: 10 X 20ML SERVINGS .
YOU THEN ADD STILL OR SPARKLING WATER TO DILUTE.
TIME: 1 HOUR, PLUS COOLING; 15 MINUTES ACTIVE COOKING; 50 MINUTES SIMMERING; 1–2 HOURS COOLING DOWN

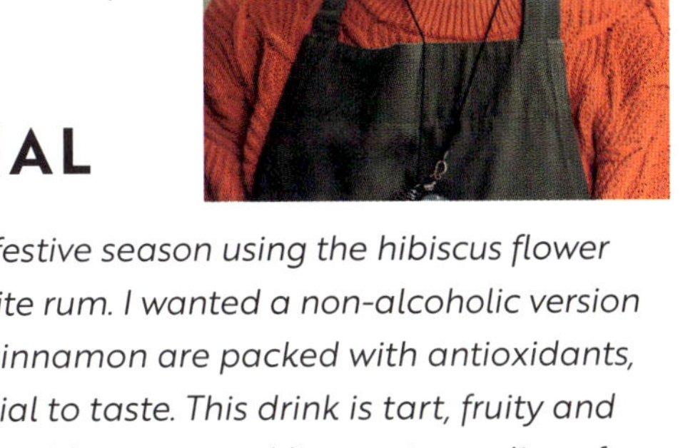

SHARON'S SORREL CORDIAL

"This is a traditional Caribbean drink made during the festive season using the hibiscus flower to create a fruity yet spicy drink typically laced with white rum. I wanted a non-alcoholic version so created this low sugar cordial. Sorrel, pimento and cinnamon are packed with antioxidants, which have many therapeutic benefits. Dilute this cordial to taste. This drink is tart, fruity and spicy rather than very sweet. Serve it in a cocktail glass with some sparkling water, a slice of lime and fresh mint and you've got yourself a mocktail."

EQUIPMENT

Colander, pestle and mortar, measuring jug/pitcher, medium-large saucepan, fine sieve/fine-mesh strainer, sterilized 200ml/7fl oz glass bottle with a lid

INGREDIENTS

50g/1¾oz/1 cup dried hibiscus flowers/sorrel
5 allspice (pimento) berries
4 whole cloves
Thumb-size piece root ginger
1 litre/35fl oz/4¼ cups water
125–150g/4½–5½oz/2/3–¾ cup cane sugar
1 cinnamon stick
Slices of lime or sprigs of fresh mint, to serve (optional)

1. Rinse the hibiscus flowers/sorrel in a colander under cold water to remove any debris, then pat dry.

2. Crush the allspice berries, slightly crush the cloves and slice or grate your root ginger.

3. Pour the water into a medium-large saucepan and bring to a rolling boil.

4. Now add the sugar and stir well, followed by the cinnamon, allspice, cloves and ginger.

5. Mix well, then add the hibiscus flowers/sorrel and boil constantly for 10 minutes.

6. Reduce the heat to low-medium so it's gently simmering and leave the mixture to reduce to a third of its original volume to form a syrup. This takes between 45–60 minutes.

7. Once it has reached the syrup stage, leave to cool, then when it's warm and comfortable to handle, strain the contents through a sieve/fine-mesh strainer and pour the cordial into your sterilized bottle.

Keep in the refrigerator. It will keep for up to 1 month. To serve, pour 20ml/¾fl oz/4 teaspoons of the cordial into a glass and top up with still or sparkling water. Adjust the sweetness and thickness by adding more cordial to your preference. You might like to add a slice of lime or a sprig of fresh mint to serve. If you like, you can warm it up and enjoy as a hot drink.

SERVES: 4 TIME: 5 MINUTES

ROWAN'S WATERMELON MOCKTAIL

"Watermelon is so good. It's refreshing on a hot day and honestly it's just tasty. The lime and mint additions were inspired by non-alcoholic mojitos and I've used mint from my mum's garden. I enjoy mocktails because they're sweet, fruity and feel special."

EQUIPMENT

Sharp knife, high-speed blender, fine sieve/fine-mesh strainer, large jug/pitcher, cocktail stirrer or metal spoon, ice-cube tray, 4 long glasses, 4 reuseable metal straws (optional)

INGREDIENTS

1 medium-size watermelon
2 lemons
4 limes
800ml/28fl oz/scant 3½ cups sparkling water
4 teaspoons rice syrup (optional)

To Serve/Decorate
1 lime
Ice cubes
4 small watermelon slices
4 sprigs of fresh mint

1. Chop the watermelon into chunks and remove the skin so that the chunks will fit easily into a high-speed blender. Add to the blender and liquidize.

2. Pour the watermelon juice through a fine sieve/fine-mesh strainer into a large jug to remove the bits.

3. Roll the lemons and limes backwards and forwards with medium pressure for 10 seconds. This helps to release the juice from the fruit.

4. Cut the lemons and limes for the mocktail in half and squeeze the juice into the jug.

5. Cut the lime to serve/decorate into quarters and set aside.

6. Add the sparkling water and rice syrup (if using) to the jug. Stir.

7. Add 3–4 ice cubes to each glass and pour the mocktail over.

8. Decorate each glass with a slice of watermelon and a lime quarter poked on the rim of the glass, plus a sprig of mint. To get the mint to stand up, wedge it between the watermelon and lime. Cheers.

AMANDEEP'S INDIAN HOT DRINKS

SERVES: 4 TIME: 10 MINUTES

MASALA CHAI

"There is debate about where chai originated but many stories tell of an Indian Royal Court over 5,000–9,000 years ago, where the king crafted a drink from Ayurvedic spices to heal the body. Spiced, herbal teas have long been a part of India's culinary and medicinal heritage. British colonizers introduced the black tea plant to India in the 1850s to compete with China in tea production. Tea is still grown in cooler parts of India and Sri Lanka. A masala chai is a blend of aromatic spices, herbs and black tea boiled together with water and milk. This is my version."

EQUIPMENT

Pestle and mortar, saucepan, fine sieve/fine-mesh strainer

INGREDIENTS

- 4 green cardamom pods
- 2 cinnamon sticks
- 800ml/28fl oz/scant 3½ cups water
- 4 whole cloves
- Pinch of fennel seeds
- 2 teaspoons loose black tea or 1 tea bag
- 140ml/4¾fl oz/scant ⅔ cup plant-based milk of choice
- Sugar/maple syrup/date syrup/stevia, to sweeten to taste (optional)

1. Slightly crush the cardamom pods and cinnamon sticks so that they release their flavours more.

2. Put the water in a saucepan. Add all the spices and start to warm on a low heat for 2 minutes.

3. Add the loose tea or tea bag and bring to the boil. Let it boil for 2 minutes, then reduce the heat a little.

4. Add the milk and turn up the heat. Once it boils (ensure it doesn't boil over), reduce the heat and let it simmer for about 6 minutes.

5. If you want to sweeten the tea (it's not necessary), add sugar/maple syrup/date syrup/stevia to taste now.

6. Switch off the heat and pour through a fine sieve/fine-mesh strainer into mugs. Sit back and enjoy.

SERVES: 4 TIME: 5 MINUTES

AMANDEEP'S GOLDEN MILK

"You can now find expensive turmeric lattes on trendy coffee bar menus, which I find quite funny and refuse to pay for because they're actually so cheap to make yourself. Most Indian people have grown up drinking them or being fed them by parents and grandparents when they're sick as part of Ayurvedic health practices. Turmeric, or curcumin, has anti-inflammatory properties and is said to have a huge range of health benefits. You need to have it with black pepper to ensure your body can get the most from it. Traditionally, golden milk was sweetened with jaggery but I use maple syrup. This is a comforting drink without caffeine so it's nice to have in the evening."

EQUIPMENT

Pestle and mortar, saucepan, fine sieve/fine-mesh strainer

INGREDIENTS

4 green cardamom pods
140ml/4¾fl oz/scant ⅔ cup water
1 teaspoon ground turmeric
Pinch of black pepper
800ml/28fl oz/scant 3½ cups plant-based milk of choice
2 teaspoons maple syrup or other sweetener of choice (date syrup/stevia/sugar), to taste (optional)

1. Slightly crush the cardamom pods so that they release their flavour more.

2. Put the water in a saucepan, add the cardamom pods, turmeric and black pepper and warm on a low heat for a minute.

3. Add the milk and turn up the heat to medium. Once it comes to the boil (watch out it doesn't boil over), reduce the heat and let it simmer for a minute.

4. Add the maple syrup or other sweetener to taste (if using).

5. Switch off the heat and pour through a fine sieve/fine-mesh strainer into mugs. Sit back and enjoy!

Activate Your Turmeric p 369

SERVES: 4 TIME: 10 MINUTES

AMY'S SPICED HOT CHOCOLATE

"This cosy drink is a lovely twist on regular hot chocolate. It's simple to make and bursting with warming spices. I made a huge vat of spiced hot chocolate and served it at the Winter Warmer event for over 55s held annually by Hackney Council and it went down a treat with people coming back for seconds and thirds."

EQUIPMENT

Saucepan, wooden spoon, small bowl, whisk

INGREDIENTS

- 1 teaspoon ground cardamom or 2 green cardamom pods (optional)
- 1 litre/35fl oz/4¼ cups plant-based milk of choice, plus 2–3 teaspoons extra milk or water
- 2 cinnamon sticks or 1 teaspoon ground cinnamon
- 1 teaspoon vanilla extract or ½ teaspoon vanilla powder
- Tiny pinch of grated/ ground nutmeg
- 4 tablespoons raw cacao powder or unsweetened cocoa powder
- 1 teaspoon tapioca flour (for a thicker hot chocolate) (optional)
- 2 tablespoons sweetener of your choice
- Tiny pinch of sea salt (optional)

1. Lightly crush the cardamom pods (if using).

2. Combine the 1 litre/35fl oz/4¼ cups of milk and all the spices in a pan and warm on a medium heat until it starts to simmer.

3. To a small bowl, add the cacao or cocoa powder, along with the tapioca flour (if using) and 2–3 teaspoons of extra milk or water. Mix with a spoon until it forms a smooth paste, then add to the hot milk.

4. Whisk everything together well and simmer for around 5 minutes.

5. Add your sweetener of choice (I like coconut sugar) and salt and stir gently. For a longer drink, you can add a little hot water – this will loosen the hot chocolate but it will still taste delicious.

6. Pour into your favourite mugs and enjoy. If you want to be really decadent, a melted chocolate drizzle or whipped coconut cream make great toppings!

GF use gluten-free oats and oat milk.

SERVES: 4 TIME: 5 MINUTES

SHARON'S FRONT END LIFTER

"Irish moss is a traditional Caribbean drink with a variety of health benefits, one of which is supporting men's reproductive health, hence the cheeky name of this drink. Today, sea moss (the main ingredient in Irish moss) has become a sought-after health food. It contains zinc – which supports reproductive health (so the old folk knew what they were talking about) – as well as nutrients that support the immune system, magnesium and calcium for muscle health, iodine for thyroid, and prebiotic and probiotic properties for gut health. Traditionally, this drink would have been made on the hob/stovetop, boiling the sea moss to extract the properties. Modern knowledge says it's best to create a raw sea moss gel using no heat. You can buy raw sea moss gel or make it yourself (see how below) from dried sea moss. Making your own gel is cheaper but requires more time."

EQUIPMENT

High-speed blender

INGREDIENTS

- 6 tablespoons rolled oats (preferably soaked in just enough cold water to cover them for 1 hour in advance, but this is not essential)
- Small thumb-size piece root ginger or ¼ teaspoon ground ginger
- 500ml/17fl oz/2 cups oat milk
- 6 tablespoons raw Irish moss gel
- 6 dates
- ½–1 teaspoon ground cinnamon
- Pinch of ground nutmeg

1. If you have soaked the oats, drain off any excess soaking water before use.

2. Grate the root ginger (if using).

3. Add all the ingredients to a high-speed blender and blend until well combined and smooth. Pour into glasses and enjoy.

NN *The 411 On Sea Moss p 369*

TIP *How To Prepare A Raw Irish Moss Gel p 379*

IT'S ALIVE!

We absolutely love fermented food and drinks at MIH. For plant-based eaters they're an incredible way to boost the variety and health of your gut microbiome and they contain crucial vitamins such as K2. Once you become accustomed to fermented foods, they add a phenomenal depth of flavour to your creations.

Fermentation is a way of preserving and enhancing the nutritional profile of food and drinks that is centuries old and is an integral part of global food culture. Developed originally out of necessity as a way of preserving food before refrigeration, the fact that the process boosts the nutritional profile of food and makes it taste amazing is fortuitous indeed!

At the cookery school, we regard fermentation as a core skill. It's one of those things that's easy when you've done it a few times, but can be nerve-wracking to get started with, especially if you've not eaten fermented food before and it conjures up ideas of gone-off food. Ferments are pricey to buy (we get it artisan producers: it takes time and love to make), but making your own can literally take a single piece of veg, salt, filtered water, a recycled jar, a bit of effort and some patience.

Fermented food and drinks you might have already encountered include sourdough bread, sauerkraut (unpasteurized), kimchi, fermented nut and seed cheeses, atchike, miso, soy sauce, tempeh, natto, apple cider vinegar, dosa, kombucha, rejuvelac and kefir. But there's many more.

We're lucky to have some amazing fermentation teachers at Made In Hackney and we're proud to say we've inspired thousands of folk to get their ferment on. If you still need more inspiration, here are six reasons to start making and eating fermented foods today.

* 6 REASONS TO START EATING FERMENTED FOODS

1 **Flavour –** fermented foods have complex umami flavours unmatched by other types of food preparation.

2 **Fun and Cheap to Make –** fermented foods are generally quite expensive to buy but usually very fun and affordable to make at home. It seems like a faff at first, but then you get into it and it becomes easy.

3 **Boost Nutritional Profile –** fermentation boosts the nutritional profile, in particular B vitamins and K2, of some foods and enhances the bioavailability (your body's ability to absorb and use nutrients) of calcium, phosphorus and iron. Cool.

4 **Healthy Gut Microbiome –** say what? This is the balance of healthy bacteria in your intestinal tract. A diverse array of bacteria in your gut has been associated with better mood, immune responses and improved bodily functions.

5 **Blood Pressure –** eating fermented foods can reduce your chance of having high blood pressure as they help to block an enzyme connected to raised blood pressure.

6 **Ease Digestive Issues –** Fermented foods can help reduce inflammation in the gut and be part of dietary protocol to support irritable bowel syndrome and Crohn's disease.

Feeling inspired? Get stuck into these recipes to see how diverse and delicious fermented foods and drinks can be. But first, some commonly asked questions.

Fermentation FAQs by fermentation teacher Asa Simonsson

▶ **Are fermented foods suitable for kids?**
Yes absolutely, and the younger they start to eat them the more likely they are to enjoy their unique flavour. Once you start weaning your baby, you can add a few drops of liquid from a sauerkraut to their meals and build from there. It's worth noting that fermented drinks such as kombucha, kvass, kefir and ginger beer can contain residue alcohol. Every batch is different and you can tell when you taste it. Moderation and common sense are key.

▶ **Is beer a fermented drink?**
Yes it is but it's fermented using yeast. The health-supporting ferments we're focusing on in this chapter are lactic acid, bacterial ferments, quite different to yeast. Sorry!

▶ **Can pregnant people eat ferments?**
Yes, especially if they were eating them pre-pregnancy. If they weren't, they may want to wait to introduce them until after baby has arrived, as for some people ferments can initially be quite taxing on the digestion. Also be mindful of the potential for alcohol residue in some fermented drinks, so exercise common sense. Consult

a naturopath, dietician or health practitioner to discuss this in more detail.

▶ Does it matter what probiotic you buy when making vegan cheese?

For the simple recipes in this chapter, it doesn't matter. Any vegan probiotic powder will work fine. If you get deep into vegan cheese-making, you can buy specific bacterias and culture strains to create funky-smelling, blue cheese-esque delights with rinds and everything. But for now, any vegan probiotic will do.

▶ My ferment went mouldy – what happened?

Fermented foods are far less likely to go mouldy than most other foods. If the top of your kimchi, kraut or cheese has gone mouldy, it means the batch was contaminated by either an unsterilized jar or unclean fingers, gloves or fermentation stone. If your ferments repeatedly go mouldy, it's likely you have mould spores in your house. To stop this happening, you need to get rid of the source of the mould. We know, we know. You go to make a jar of sauerkraut and now you've fallen down an extraction and damp investigation hole. Long-term exposure to mould is bad for your health, so you'll thank us in the long run even if you're cursing us now.

▶ Why do I always need to leave a space at the top of my ferments?

As food and drinks ferment they get gassy and start to contain air bubbles, which will cause them to rise and expand. A 2cm/¾in gap between the top of your ferment and your bottle or container lid leaves room for this expansion.

▶ I've heard about exploding ferments. I'm scared.

People love to share exploding ferment stories – but really it's very rare. Explosions can happen during the fermentation process if you use a bottle with an airtight lid, and then forget to burp it while it's fermenting. "Burping" is where you undo the lid to release the air and it makes a satisfying popping noise and the gases fizz up to the top, then you put the lid back on. If you forget to do this for multiple days, the build-up of gases can become so powerful the bottle can, in theory, explode. This all sounds highly dramatic but you just need a little sign on your counter saying BURP FERMENTS. If you're the sort of person that starts a project then forgets all about it, don't use an airtight lid. A clean, porous cloth works fine. See, no drama.

All rightee. Prepare to have your culinary mind blown as you enter the magical world of fermentation.

Happy folk get their ferment on in one of our many fermentation classes. Ferments are pricey to buy in stores but so cheap to make yourself at home.

ASA ON FERMENTATION

"My aunty was a cookery teacher in the late 1960s. She had a non-malignant growth on her finger and the doctor wanted to remove it, but someone suggested eating more raw and fermented foods. She did, and the growth disappeared. She was so amazed she bought an organic farm and started making sauerkraut for restaurants and spas. Because of her I've grown up eating ferments, but I became particularly interested in them when I studied nutrition. Allopathic medicine is good for conditions that need medicating or for surgeries, but it can't do much for treating chronic disease – that's where food and lifestyle come in. Improving your gut health with fermented foods is a fantastic place for people to start."

use gluten-free soy sauce

MAKES: 350–400ML/12–14FL OZ
TIME: 10 MINUTES PREP; 1–2 DAYS FERMENTATION

ASA'S FERMENTED KETCHUP

"This is a much healthier version than your average store-bought ketchup. It's much nicer tasting too. I created it for my kids when they were young as they loved ketchup and I wanted to make something a bit healthier that they still enjoyed. They loved it and I used it on pasta and when they had vegan sausages. They're young adults now and they still enjoy it."

EQUIPMENT

Measuring jug/pitcher, large mixing bowl, wooden spoon, sterilized 350–400ml/12–14fl oz Mason jar with lid

INGREDIENTS

- 200ml/7fl oz/scant 1 cup tomato purée/paste
- 5 tablespoons maple syrup
- 1 tablespoon extra virgin olive oil
- 1½ tablespoons apple cider vinegar
- 2 tablespoons dark soy sauce
- Pinch of sea salt (optional)
- Pinch of ground cloves
- Pinch of ground cinnamon
- Pinch of smoked paprika
- 1 capsule of vegan probiotic powder
- Cold filtered water, to preferred consistency (optional)

1. Add all the ingredients to a bowl – except the probiotic powder and water – and mix with a wooden spoon until everything is blended together. Break open the probiotic capsule, tip in the powder and mix it in well.

2. If you want a runnier texture, add a little cold filtered water until you reach the desired consistency, but be mindful that adding water means the ketchup may go off quicker.

3. Add to the sterilized jar, leaving a 2cm/¾in gap between the top of the sauce and top of the jar to give space for the fermentation gases.

4. Let it ferment for 1–2 days at room temperature. If it's warm in the room it's fermenting in, burp the ketchup on the second day by opening the jar to let the gases out, then put the lid back on.

5. Store in the refrigerator and it will keep for a couple of weeks.

Make this to go with the Vegan Phish Supper (see p 107) or MIH burgers (see p 88). Yum.

MAKES: 1 X 1–1.5-LITRE/35–52FL OZ JAR; A SERVING IS 1–2 TABLESPOONS
TIME: 30 MINUTES PREP; 1–3 WEEKS FERMENTATION

ASA'S GOLDEN KRAUT

"This sauerkraut is seriously delicious and also anti-inflammatory, with turmeric, black pepper, ginger, onion, garlic and cruciferous veggies. Make it in a 1–1.5-litre/35–52fl oz/4¼–6½-cup jar and top your meals with 1–2 tablespoons a day to boost your gut microbiome. Cauliflower is a really healthy cruciferous vegetable – one of the vegetables Dr Michael Gregor recommends eating every day."

EQUIPMENT

Sharp knife, grater, food processor (optional), large mixing bowl, rubber/food hygiene gloves, sterilized 1–1.5-litre/35–52fl oz/4¼–6½-cup jar with lid, fermentation stone/ clean stone or small glass ramekin, sterilized smaller jars (for storing)

INGREDIENTS

½ medium white cabbage (about 500g/1lb 2oz)
2 small white onions
1–2 cloves garlic
2 carrots
2cm/¾in piece root ginger
2cm/¾in piece turmeric
¼ small-medium cauliflower (about 200g/7oz)
1–1½ tablespoons sea salt
1 teaspoon black pepper

1. Let's prepare the vegetables.
- Remove the outer leaves of the cabbage if they are damaged or dirty-looking.
- Cut the cabbage and onions into thin ribbons.
- Finely slice the garlic.
- Finely grate the carrots, ginger and turmeric.
- Rice the cauliflower by pulsing it in a food processor until it looks like rice, or cut it into small pieces with a sharp knife.

2. Put all the vegetables in a mixing bowl and add the turmeric, ginger, salt and pepper. It will look like a lot but it will fit into the jar after working with it.

3. Mix everything together with your hands. Wear rubber or food hygiene gloves if you don't want to end up with yellow-tinged hands. Leave it standing for 15 minutes for the salt to draw out some of the water in the vegetables – this is called osmosis.

4. Now firmly massage the vegetables with your fingers for 5–10 minutes. As you do this, the vegetables will start to release liquid.

5. When enough water releases from the vegetables that they drip when you pick up a handful and they start to look soft, it is ready to be packed into your jar. Fresh cabbage will produce a lot of water very quickly. Older cabbage can take longer and you may have to add 1–2 teaspoons of cold filtered water to it.

6. Now pack the massaged vegetables tightly into the sterilized jar ensuring they are fully submerged under the water with no air bubbles. Leave a 5cm/2in gap between the surface of the water to the top of the jar for the gases to come out. This is important.

7. Pop a weight on the vegetables to keep them under the water surface. You could use a fermentation weight, a clean stone or a small glass ramekin. Make sure it's clean. >>

8. Leave to ferment at room temperature for 1–3 weeks. The longer you leave it, the deeper the flavour and the more fermented it will be.

9. Check regularly that the cabbage is under the water and push it down (with clean hands!) if not. If you don't use a proper fermentation pot, you will need to burp the jar once a day to let the gases out by opening the lid and putting it back on. Sometimes it spits juicy liquid so wrap a dish towel around it.

When fermented to your taste preference, transfer to smaller sterilized jars and store in the refrigerator. It will keep for months if unopened. Once opened, use within 1 month. Enjoy a tablespoon or 2 on top of a salad, with steamed or stir-fried veggies, in a sandwich filler or as an accompaniment to Linda's Czech recipes (see p 256).

MAKES: 1 X 1–1.5-LITRE/35–52FL OZ JAR; A SERVING IS 1–2 TABLESPOONS
TIME: 20 MINUTES PREP; 1–3 WEEKS FERMENTATION

ASA'S BEETROOT KRAUT

"Beetroots are not only tasty and super high in antioxidants but they're also excellent for heart health as they lower blood pressure and increase nitric oxide. Adding beetroot to your diet daily is super good for your heart. You can roast it, use it in soups or eat it raw in a salad. It's also seriously delicious in a ferment."

EQUIPMENT

Sharp knife, grater, large mixing bowl, rubber/food hygiene gloves, sterilized 1-litre/35fl oz jar with lid, fermentation stone/clean stone or small glass ramekin, sterilized smaller jars (for storing)

INGREDIENTS

1 medium purple cabbage (about 800g/1lb 12oz)
2 beetroots/beets (about 250g/9oz)
1 tablespoon chopped fresh herbs, such as dill, mint, lemon balm and/or parsley (optional)
1½–2 tablespoons sea salt

1. Let's prepare the vegetables.
- Remove the outer leaves of the cabbage if they are damaged or dirty-looking. Peel the beetroots/beets.
- Chop the herbs, if using.
- Thinly slice the cabbage, and coarsely grate the beetroots.

2. Put all the vegetables in a mixing bowl and add the herbs and salt.

3. Mix everything together with your hands. Wear food hygiene gloves or rubber gloves if you don't want purple hands for a day or two. Leave it to stand for 15 minutes for the salt to draw out some of the water in the vegetables – this is called osmosis.

4. Go to step 4 of Asa's Golden Kraut method (see p 342) for the remaining steps as they are the same.

SERVES: 12 | TIME: DAY 1: 8 HOURS OR OVERNIGHT SOAKING; 10 MINUTES PREP; DAYS 2–3: 12–24 HOURS FERMENTING; DAY 4: 25 MINUTES PREP, PLUS 2–4 HOURS SETTING TIME IN FREEZER OR OVERNIGHT IN REFRIGERATOR

ASA'S FERMENTED CHOCOLATE CHEEZECAKE

"I got into raw food about 18 years ago when my dad was ill with cancer and I wanted him to adopt the diet. Alas he didn't, but I fell in love with it, in particular the incredible possibilities of raw cakes and chocolate. I started making them for people who had health issues and were choosing to avoid sugar and dairy, and they loved them. This recipe may seem like a faff as you have to do bits over three to four days, but each step takes under ten minutes, so once you've made it a few times, you can do it on autopilot and it's far simpler than baking. It's decadent and rich and the depth of flavour the ferment gives is quite incredible."

EQUIPMENT

Mixing bowl, colander, high-speed blender, spatula, glass/ceramic bowl with lid (or dish towel), food processor, sharp knife, 20–25cm/8–10in round cake tin (or silicone dish), baking parchment, small saucepan, wooden spoon, sieve/fine-mesh strainer, serving plate

INGREDIENTS (next page)

1. First, make the fermented cashew cheeze. Soak the nuts in the room-temperature filtered water for 8 hours or overnight.

2. Drain the nuts in a colander and rinse them well in cold filtered water. Using a high-speed blender, blend the nuts, adding as little of the measured cold filtered water as possible, but enough just so that the blender will keep going. Depending on the quality of your blender, it might take you some time to get it silky smooth and you may need to stop quite often to scrape the mixture down from the sides.

3. When it's smooth and lump-free, scoop the mixture out into a glass or ceramic bowl.

4. Break open the probiotic capsule, tip the powder into the mixture and stir well to make sure it's well blended. Cover the bowl with a lid or a dish towel.

5. Leave to ferment at room temperature for 12–24 hours. Preferably it should be slightly warmer than your room, for example, in an airing cupboard or on the floor if you have underfloor heating, or on top of a radiator. It should have some bubbles and smell a little like bread when done and be slightly acidic in flavour. It is now ready to use in your cake recipe. >>

INGREDIENTS

For The Fermented Cashew Cheeze

250g/9oz/2 cups raw cashew nuts

1 litre/35fl oz/4¼ cups room-temperature filtered water

5 tablespoons cold filtered water, or as needed to assist in blending

1 capsule of vegan probiotic powder

For The Cake Base

250g/9oz/3 cups unsweetened desiccated/dried shredded coconut

200g/7oz/1¼ cups dates

For The Filling

100g/3½oz coconut oil

80ml/2¾fl oz/⅓ cup maple syrup

50g/1¾oz/½ cup raw cacao powder or 30g/1oz/scant ⅓ cup carob powder (for a caffeine-free option), OR 150g/5½oz fresh strawberries, OR 150g/5½oz mango flesh

To Decorate (optional)

20–30g/¾–1oz carob bar

Fresh berries

Orange slices

Crushed roasted nuts of your choice

6. Make the cake base by putting the coconut in a food processor and processing it just a little. Chop up the dates slightly before adding them to the coconut, then process again until a sticky dough-like texture forms.

7. Line the cake tin with baking parchment, or use a silicone dish. Press the dough into the lined tin to make the crust base for your cheesecake, then put in the refrigerator or freezer while you make the filling.

8. For the filling, melt the coconut oil in a small saucepan on a medium heat. If making the chocolate version, pour the melted coconut oil into a bowl, add the maple syrup and stir until completely smooth.

9. Sift in the cacao or carob powder and stir to combine. Add the chocolate and cashew cheese to a blender or food processor and blitz briefly to combine. If making the strawberry or mango version, add the melted coconut oil, the maple syrup and the strawberries or the mango flesh to the blender/food processor and blend until completely smooth.

10. Pour the filling on top of the crust base and smooth out with a spatula.

11. Place the cake in the freezer for 2–4 hours so the coconut oil sets. Or chill in the refrigerator overnight.

Take the cake out of the tin/dish and place on a serving plate. Serve as is or decorate with grated carob, fresh berries, orange slices, crushed roasted nuts or whatever else you fancy that complements your cheezecake. If not eaten straight away, store it (undecorated) in the refrigerator. It will keep for at least a week in the refrigerator, or it can be frozen (undecorated) for up to 3 months (defrost before eating).

SERVES: 4 | TIME: 6–8 HOURS OR OVERNIGHT SOAKING; 20 MINUTES PREP; 2 DAYS FERMENTATION

ANGELA'S NACHO-AVERAGE DIP

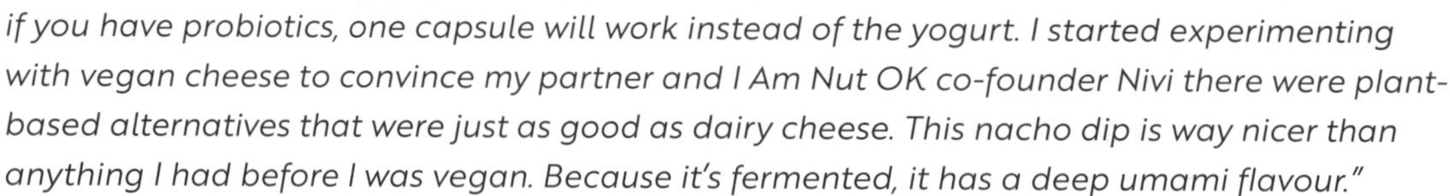

"Who doesn't love nachos and dip? This is a simple but delicious sauce you ferment using yogurt as opposed to a probiotic. But if you have probiotics, one capsule will work instead of the yogurt. I started experimenting with vegan cheese to convince my partner and I Am Nut OK co-founder Nivi there were plant-based alternatives that were just as good as dairy cheese. This nacho dip is way nicer than anything I had before I was vegan. Because it's fermented, it has a deep umami flavour."

EQUIPMENT

Mixing bowl, colander or sieve/fine-mesh strainer, measuring jug/pitcher, high-speed blender, airtight container, large serving platter/2 large plates, small bowl (optional)

INGREDIENTS

- 300g/10½oz/2½ cups raw cashews
- 1 litre/35fl oz/4¼ cups room-temperature filtered water
- 150ml/5fl oz/⅔ cup cold filtered water (you may need more if your yogurt is very thick)
- 200g/7oz/1 cup live plain vegan yogurt or 1 capsule of vegan probiotic powder
- 2 teaspoons sea salt
- 3 teaspoons paprika
- 1–2 cloves garlic
- 20g/¾oz B12-enriched nutritional yeast aka Nooch (see more on p 377)
- 1–2 pickled jalapeños or 1–2 tablespoons sliced pickled jalapeños, drained, or 1 fresh red chilli and 1 fresh green chilli (optional)
- ½ red or white onion (optional)
- 2 tomatoes (optional)
- 2 x 200g/7oz bags of plain tortilla chips

1. Cover the cashews in the room-temperature filtered water in a bowl and leave to soak for 6–8 hours or overnight.

2. The next day, drain and rinse the cashews in a colander or sieve/fine-mesh strainer using cold filtered water, then add the measured cold filtered water, the cashews and all the other ingredients – except the pickled jalapeños/chillies, onion, tomatoes and tortilla chips – to a high-speed blender. Blend until smooth.

3. Pour everything into an airtight container and cover with the lid. Leave out to ferment for up to 2 days at room temperature, then pop in the refrigerator for an hour to firm up before serving.

4. Slice the pickled jalapeños or fresh chillies into discs, finely slice your onion and finely dice the tomatoes, if using. You might wish to quick-pickle your sliced onion (see p 382) but this is optional.

5. To present, scatter your tortilla chips over a large serving platter or two large plates.

6. To serve, you can pour the dip into a bowl and place in the middle of the serving platter, or pour it over the tortilla chips.

7. Scatter the jalapeños, onion and tomatoes on top of the tortilla crisps and gentle toss through, or serve them on the side.

Serve as is or with an additional side of guacamole. Enjoy.

TIPS & TRICKS
Quick Pickled Onions
p 382

SERVES: 8 | TIME: 8 HOURS OR OVERNIGHT SOAKING; 20 MINUTES PREP; 2 DAYS FERMENTATION

BRUNA'S CULTURED CASHEW CREAM CHEESE

"This recipe is incredibly versatile. I recommend making a large batch and storing it in the refrigerator to use in risotto, creamy pasta, as a spread, or even as a substitute for sour cream. It's not only delicious but also rich in probiotics. It will keep well in the refrigerator for a month and if frozen will keep for up to three months."

EQUIPMENT

Weighing scales, large bowl, measuring jug/pitcher, colander, high-speed blender, airtight container, baking parchment, tea towel, spoon, paper towel

INGREDIENTS

- 300g/10½oz/2½ cups raw cashews
- 1 litre/35fl oz/4¼ cups room-temperature filtered water
- 100ml/3½fl oz/scant ½ cup cold filtered water, or a little more if needed
- 1 tablespoon lemon juice
- Pinch of sea salt, plus (optional) extra to taste
- 1 capsule of vegan probiotic powder
- Apple cider vinegar, to taste (optional)

1. Soak the cashews in the room-temperature filtered water for at least 8 hours (overnight is fine). For a quicker soak, you can immerse them in boiling water for 2 hours. The nuts are soaked so they blend easier but also because there are nutritional benefits – check out p 28 to find out more.

2. Drain the nuts in a colander in cold filtered water. Transfer to a high speed blender, add the measured cold filtered water, the lemon juice and salt.

3. Blend until smooth and creamy adding more water 1 teaspoon at a time if needed. You want a thick paste.

4. Once you've achieved a smooth consistency (non-high speed blenders might struggle with this), break open the probiotic capsule and add the powder to the blender. Pulse gently to mix. Instead of probiotic you could use 3 tablespoons of liquid from a lactic acid ferment like sauerkraut or water kefir.

5. Place the cheese in a clean airtight container. Cover with parchment, ensuring the paper touches the cheese to prevent a dry top layer.

6. Now cover with a dish towel and leave in a warm spot to ferment for 2 days. If your kitchen is warm (above 25°C/77°F), leave to ferment for 24–36 hours instead. Avoid fermenting in temperatures below 18°C/64°F, as it may hinder proper fermentation.

7. Monitor the cheese during fermentation. Look for air bubbles (easily seen through a transparent container) and notice a pleasant fermentation odour, similar to plain live yogurt. Taste it periodically with a clean spoon (do not double dip!) to understand the fermentation stages. It takes 2 days to develop some acidity and a fermented flavour.

8. Once fermented, adjust the acidity by adding more lemon juice or a little apple cider vinegar, along with additional salt to your taste.

Store in the same airtight container. Cover the surface with fresh baking parchment, ensuring it touches the cheese to prevent moisture loss. Place a paper towel on top of the baking parchment before sealing it with the lid. This helps absorb excess moisture and keeps the cheese fresh for longer, preventing mould growth.

Use as a spread or enhance its flavour with chopped fresh or dried herbs or ground spices such as oregano, basil or smoked paprika. It can also be used like yogurt if you make it a little thinner. Enjoy experimenting and eating your cream cheese! It's great served on a piece of toast, on top of a salad, with crudités or crackers.

TIPS & TRICKS

Choosing Your Probiotic p 382

NN CULTURED VEGAN CHEESE

Cultured cheese is any plant-based cheese made from seeds or nuts that has been fermented as part of its preparation. It is rich in probiotics and has many nutritional benefits. It has a deep umami taste and excellent nutritional profile. It's very different to the non-cultured vegan cheeses that are more commonly available in supermarkets, although these products have improved hugely over the last decade. You can make non-cultured homemade vegan cheese that is delicious and nutritious as well, it just doesn't have the probiotic benefits of a fermented cheese.

£

MAKES: 6 | TIME: FERMENTED VERSION: 1 HOUR, PLUS 8+ HOURS RESTING TIME, NON-FERMENTED VERSION: 1 HOUR

SHARON'S HOT CROSS BUNS

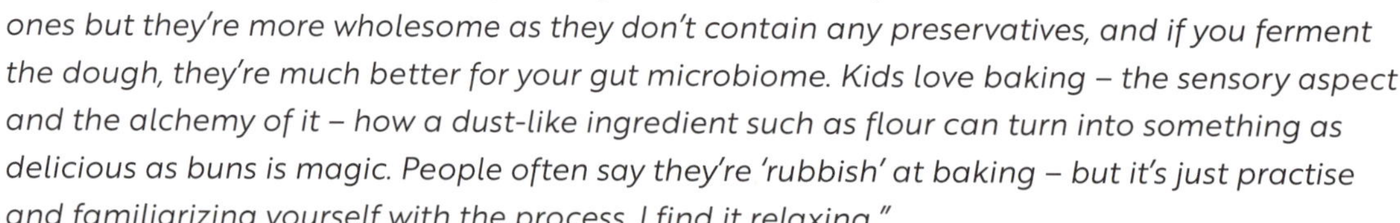

"I've made these buns with children many times and they've always been a delight. They look just as good as store-bought ones but they're more wholesome as they don't contain any preservatives, and if you ferment the dough, they're much better for your gut microbiome. Kids love baking – the sensory aspect and the alchemy of it – how a dust-like ingredient such as flour can turn into something as delicious as buns is magic. People often say they're 'rubbish' at baking – but it's just practise and familiarizing yourself with the process. I find it relaxing."

EQUIPMENT

2 medium-size bowls, zester, small saucepan, wooden spoon, spatula, 2 large mixing bowls, baking sheet, baking parchment, clean dish towel, pastry brush, piping/pastry bag or a small snadwich bag, wire/cooling rack

INGREDIENTS (next page)

1. In a medium-size bowl, combine the flour, yeast (¼ teaspoon if leaving overnight, or 2 teaspoons for the quicker version), sugar, salt, cinnamon, raisins and orange zest.

2. Make a well in the middle of the dry ingredients to add the liquid.

3. Put the plant-based milk and vegan butter into a small pan and heat gently until melted and lukewarm. To test that it's not too hot, you should be able to put a finger into the milk and it not feel hot nor cold. If using light oil, omit this step and just add the oil to room-temperature milk.

4. Pour the milk mixture into the flour and use a spatula/wooden spoon to gently mix to create a soft dough. If it's too dry, add a little more milk, a tablespoon at a time, until it is soft but not overly sticky.

5. Now knead the dough. Tip the dough out onto a clean floured surface, then push the dough away using the heel of your hand, then back over itself, turn, then repeat the process for about 4–5 minutes to create a smooth, elastic dough. If you're planning to make the buns straight away, lightly oil a clean bowl and place the dough in there, cover with a clean dish towel and leave to sit (away from a window) for about an hour, or until doubled in size.

6. If you're planning to make fermented buns (we recommend this for a deeper flavour), place the dough into a clean oiled bowl, cover with cling film/plastic wrap and, if making later the same day, leave out at room temperature for 8 hours. Or, if leaving overnight and making the next day, leave in the refrigerator. It's vital the seal is airtight so don't use a dish towel. If you don't buy

INGREDIENTS

250g/9oz/1¾ cups strong flour or a mix of strong wholemeal/whole-wheat flour and white flour, plus extra for dusting

¼ teaspoon fast-action/ instant active dried yeast for fermented version or 2 teaspoons for quick version

2 tablespoons sugar (preferably unrefined soft light brown sugar)

½ teaspoon sea salt

¼ teaspoon ground cinnamon

40g/1½oz/1/3 cup raisins

Finely grated zest of 1 large orange (optional)

180ml/6fl oz/¾ cup plant milk

2 tablespoons vegan butter or light oil (such as light olive oil or rice bran oil), plus extra oil for greasing

For The Flour Crosses

30g/1oz/3½ tablespoons plain/all-purpose flour

2 tablespoons plant-based milk of choice (you may need a little more)

For The Glaze

2 tablespoons plant milk of choice

½ tablespoon vegan butter or light oil (such as light olive oil or rice bran oil)

3 tablespoons unrefined soft light brown sugar or maple syrup

single-use kitchen items, use a plastic reuseable shower cap and only use it for baking.

7. If the dough has been in the refrigerator overnight, remove and leave on the side for an hour so it comes back to room temperature before working. In the meantime, line a baking sheet with baking parchment and lightly dust with flour.

8. Next, punch the dough down and knead for a minute to remove any air bubbles. See p 374 for info on kneading. Now divide the dough into 6 equal pieces, roll each piece into a ball and place each one onto the prepared baking sheet.

9. Cover with a clean tea towel and leave to rise at room temperature until doubled in size. Once the buns are nearly risen enough, preheat the oven to 200°C/400°F/gas 6.

10. To make the crosses, mix the flour and plant-based milk into a thick paste and place into a piping/pastry bag or a small sandwich bag, snip off a small end, then pipe crosses over the buns.

11. Bake the buns for 18–20 minutes until golden brown.

12. To make the glaze, gently heat the plant-based milk, vegan butter or oil and sugar or syrup in a small pan until melted and combined. Brush the glaze over the baked hot cross buns while still warm, then leave to cool completely on a wire/cooling rack. Enjoy whole or split open with your spread of choice.

TIP ***These hot cross buns are best eaten fresh on the day they are made, but any leftovers can be split, lightly toasted and enjoyed over the next day or so.***

MAKES: 1 X 1-LITRE/35FL OZ JAR;
A SERVING IS 1–2 TABLESPOONS
TIME: 30 MINUTES PREP
3 DAYS FERMENTATION
(BUT YOU CAN FERMENT IT FOR WEEKS OR EVEN MONTHS)

SANDOR'S BAECHU KIMCHI

Sandor Katz is a fermentation icon – his books all underground classics. He travels the world delivering workshops and learning about different fermentation techniques. When he agreed to teach for us we were elated. Over to Sandor. *"This is a basic kimchi, perfect if you've never made it before and need to learn the process. Once you've made it a few times experiment with different vegetables and proportions of chilli. I love kimchi for its deep umami flavour coupled with the spiciness. It elevates almost any meal and you can make it according to your heat preference. Traditional Korean kimchi is very spicy. Some store-bought kimchi is not vegan as it contains fish sauce – so if you're vegan or plant-based, do check before eating."*

EQUIPMENT

Sharp knife, large mixing bowl, measuring jug/pitcher, weighing scales, spoon, plate, full jar/weight, small saucepan, wooden spoon(s), small bowl, rubber/food hygiene gloves, sterilized 1-litre/35fl oz jar with lid

INGREDIENTS **(next page)**

1. Coarsely chop the cabbage into chunky ribbons and place in a large bowl along with any other prepped vegetables you like (see Tip).

2. Mix a strong brine with the 1 litre/35fl oz/4¼ cups of cold filtered water and the salt. Stir well to dissolve the salt. If you want to taste as a guide, think sea water salty.

3. Pour the brine over the cabbage/vegetables. Firmly press the vegetables down with your hands a few times to submerge. If there's not quite enough water to cover the veg, don't worry; the salt will pull more water out of the vegetables and there will be plenty.

4. Cover the vegetables with a plate, place a full jar or other weight on it and press firmly every few minutes until the vegetables are fully submerged. Leave the vegetables in their brine on the kitchen counter for at least 2 hours or overnight.

5. About 20 minutes before your vegetables have finished soaking in brine, you can make the paste. This gives the kimchi a lovely sauce.

6. In a small saucepan, mix the rice flour with the cold filtered water. Stir thoroughly to dissolve the flour and break up any clumps. Cook gently on a low heat, stirring constantly to prevent burning.

INGREDIENTS

1 napa/Chinese cabbage (about 1kg/2lb 4oz)

1 litre/35fl oz/4¼ cups cold filtered water

90g/3¼oz/⅓ cup sea salt, plus an extra (optional) 1–2 teaspoons

1 tablespoon rice flour (this can be replaced with the same quantity of wheat flour for a cost-saving option)

125ml/4fl oz/½ cup cold filtered water

2–4 tablespoons (or more) gochugaru Korean chilli powder (add to your taste preference)

5cm/2in piece root ginger

Bunch of spring onions/ scallions or 1 onion

3–4 cloves garlic

TIP

If you want to add some other veg with the cabbage, daikon, radishes and carrots work well. Add about 300g/10½oz in total of these extra coarsely grated veg (or cut them to the shape and thickness you want them to be).

7. Keep stirring as the flour starts to thicken. Cook for a few minutes until the mix achieves a gluey pastiness, but remains thin enough to pour. If too thick, add a teaspoon of hot filtered water and stir.

8. Remove from the heat. Once it's cooled to body temperature, during which time it will further thicken, mix this with the chilli powder into a bright red paste.

9. Now we're going to prepare the remaining ingredients.
- Grate the ginger.
- Slice the spring onions/scallions or onion and garlic to preferred size.

10. In a small bowl, mix the ginger, spring onions/onion and garlic together, then stir this into the cooled rice flour/chilli paste mixture.

11. Drain the water off the vegetables and press them lightly to force the water out. Taste the vegetables for saltiness. If you cannot taste salt, add 1–2 teaspoons of salt to the chilli paste mixture. In the unlikely event that the vegetables are too salty, rinse them.

12. Using a wooden spoon or your hands wearing rubber/food hygiene gloves, mix the vegetables with the chilli paste mixture until everything is well covered.

13. Now pack the kimchi into the sterilized jar. (See p 383 for how to sterilize jars.) Pack it as tight as you can, pressing down until paste or liquid rises and covers the vegetables. Fill the jar almost to the top, leaving a 1–2cm/½–¾in gap for expansion. Press down repeatedly to get the vegetables fully submerged, then screw the top on the jar.

14. Leave it to work it's fermentation magic. Every day wash your hands and undo the lid to release any built-up gases. This is called burping. Use your fingers to push any vegetables under the liquid that are peeking out. Once it tastes ripe and good to you (minimum 3 days), store in your refrigerator.

Once opened, use within a month. If you have a cool spot like a cellar (not if it has mould, as this can contaminate your ferment) or live in a very cold country, you can leave your kimchi to ferment more slowly, which enhances its depth of flavour.

Enjoy the kimchi with a salad, any Japanese or Korean meal or have it as part of a sandwich, burger or toastie filling.

SERVES: 6–8 | TIME: 15 MINUTES PREP; 2–5 DAYS FERMENTATION

SANDOR'S TEPACHE

"Tepache is a refreshing and delicious, lightly-fermented beverage made from the skins and cores of pineapples. It is effervescent and tangy, with almost no alcohol, enjoyed by children and adults alike. Tepache is from Mexico, where it is frequently made at home using the by-products of eating fresh pineapples. I love to make it whenever I eat a pineapple, and I love it as is, or as a cocktail base. I recommend sourcing organic pineapple if you can, as you're fermenting the skin."

EQUIPMENT

Sharp knife, weighing scales, measuring jug/pitcher, bowl, sterilized 2-litre/70fl oz/8½-cup wide-mouthed bottle or Kilner-type jar with lid, spoon, sieve/fine-mesh strainer, large cup or sterilized storage bottle

INGREDIENTS

1 large fresh pineapple

100g/3½oz/½ cup sugar (ideally an unrefined sugar like piloncillo, panela, muscovado or other soft brown sugar)

About 1.5 litres/52fl oz/6½ cups cold filtered water

1 cinnamon stick

2–4 cloves, according to taste preference

Other spices, such as root ginger or ground ginger (add to your taste preference) (optional)

1. Peel the skin from the pineapple with a sharp knife. Quarter the pineapple lengthways and remove the core from each quarter. Eat the pineapple flesh, and cut the skin and core into pieces.

2. Add the sugar to 250ml/9fl oz/1 cup of the cold filtered water in a bowl and stir so it dissolves.

3. Get your sterilized bottle or jar and add the pieces of pineapple skin, core and the spices.

4. Pour the sugar water over the pineapple skin/core and add more of the measured water to cover all the pineapple and mostly fill the bottle/jar, but leave a gap of about 2.5cm/1in at the top.

5. Cover with a loose lid and leave out on a shelf (don't put it in the refrigerator or it won't ferment). The fermentation creates carbon dioxide and the loose lid enables pressure to escape. Stir daily.

6. Ferment for anywhere between 2–5 days. The hotter the room you leave it in, the quicker it will ferment. The longer you leave it, the stronger the fermentation and flavour will be. During this time it will get fizzy and start to develop a sour taste.

7. Taste daily to get a sense of the developing flavour so you can stop fermenting it to your taste preference.

8. When ready, strain out the solids and drink straight away, or seal it in a sterilized bottle for another day for carbonation. Tepache is best stored in the refrigerator and used within 2 weeks.

TIP ***If it gets too sour, leave the strained liquid with the surface exposed and in a couple of weeks it will turn into pineapple vinegar. Delicious!***

MAKES: 1 X 1.5-LITRE/52FL OZ/6½-CUP JAR; SERVES 4–6 | TIME: 10 MINUTES PREP; STAGE 1: 7 DAYS FERMENTATION; STAGE 2: 2–4 DAYS FERMENTATION

SHARON'S CAFFEINE-FREE KOMBUCHA

"I began my kombucha-making journey over eight years ago after I was gifted a SCOBY by a friend. After doing my research and some experimenting, I came up with my method. I reduced the sugar, as many recipes call for almost double the amount, and used caffeine-free tea bags. Many people believe you need caffeine for kombucha to ferment, but this isn't true and was quite a revelation! I love making kombucha for myself and gifting it to family and friends. It might seem daunting at first, but once you've made your first batch, you'll be off."

EQUIPMENT

Kettle, ceramic jug/pitcher, spoon, sterilized 1.5-litre/52fl oz/6½-cup jar, muslin cloth/cheesecloth, string or an elastic band, sterilized 1.5-litre/52fl oz/6½-cup bottle with a stopper/lid or a few smaller bottles with stoppers/lids, sieve/fine-mesh strainer

INGREDIENTS (next page)

STAGE 1

1. Boil the kettle and place the tea bags into a clean ceramic jug/pitcher with the freshly boiled filtered water. Brew the tea for about 5 minutes. Discard the tea bags in your compost once brewed.

2. Add the sugar to the tea mix and stir until completely dissolved.

3. Top up the jug with the cold filtered water. Make sure it is cold or you'll kill your SCOBY.

4. Now pour the tea into your sterilized jar, add the SCOBY, cover with a breathable muslin cloth/cheesecloth and secure with string or an elastic band.

5. Leave to ferment at room temperature for at least 7 days before going on to stage 2, the second ferment, where we add flavouring.

STAGE 2

6. To flavour your kombucha, stir in either the juiced ginger, juiced turmeric, fruit juice or fresh fruit purée (to make the purée, blend your fruit of choice and push through a sieve/fine-mesh strainer). Experiment with your own flavours. I like mango-ginger.

7. Pour the flavoured kombucha ferment into your sterilized bottle(s), leaving a 2cm/¾in gap at the top as it will ferment and expand. >>

TIPS & TRICKS
411 on SCOBYs
p 383

INGREDIENTS

4 rooibos tea bags

300ml/10½fl oz/1¼ cups just-boiled filtered water

100g/3½oz/½ cup cane sugar

1.2 litres/40fl oz/5 cups cold filtered water

1 SCOBY

To Flavour

(quantities are for 500ml/17fl oz/2 cups, so you can create 3 different flavours of your choice with this batch)

1 tablespoon juiced root ginger

Or ½ tablespoon juiced turmeric

Or 1 tablespoon fruit juice of your choice

Or 50g/1¾oz fresh fruit purée (see method)

Traditionally, kombucha is made with black or green tea bags, which contain caffeine. If you're happy to make a caffeinated blend, you can swap the rooibos tea for 4 bags of green or black tea.

8. Tighten the lid(s) and leave the bottle(s) out on the side (at room temperature) to ferment for around 2–4 days, remembering to burp them every day to release any gases that have built up. To burp, simply open and close the lid(s) once a day. When ready, store in the refrigerator. Once opened, use within a week.

Enjoy straight from the refrigerator, or leave on the side to come to room temperature before consuming.

LET'S TALK ABOUT… KOMBUCHA
With fermentation guru Sandor Katz

Kombucha has a long history, probably originating in Northern China. Because it is delicious and easy to make and share, and the mother is easy to transport, kombucha has been popular in many different places. I first encountered kombucha in the mid-1990s. A friend of mine was sick with AIDS before effective treatments had been developed, and he was trying kombucha, hoping it would help stimulate his immune system. He was making and drinking a lot of it and encouraging friends to adopt his rapidly accumulating mothers. In those days commercial kombucha did not yet exist, and it was spread exclusively through grassroots channels. I liked kombucha from my first taste and have made it (though only sporadically) ever since.

One of the things I love about fermentation is how easy it is to do yourself at home, and kombucha is an especially accessible gateway into fermentation. I'm excited that more and more people are making and seeking out kombucha and other products of fermentation. I like kombucha, and sometimes I really love it, but over the course of my fermentation investigations, I have learned about many other incredibly delicious lightly fermented beverages, such as tepache, ginger beer, mauby and smreka, to name a few. I hope the interest in kombucha will diversify into a broader range of beverages and foods. I never buy kombucha – I recommend people make it themselves. But if you are buying it support small, local, artisan makers. Lots of the mass-produced products sold as kombucha are not made using anything resembling the traditional kombucha process. It should not be pasteurized. Any genuinely living kombucha sold in a store needs to be refrigerated, so if it isn't, don't buy it. When you start your fermentation journey don't be afraid. Fermentation makes food safer.

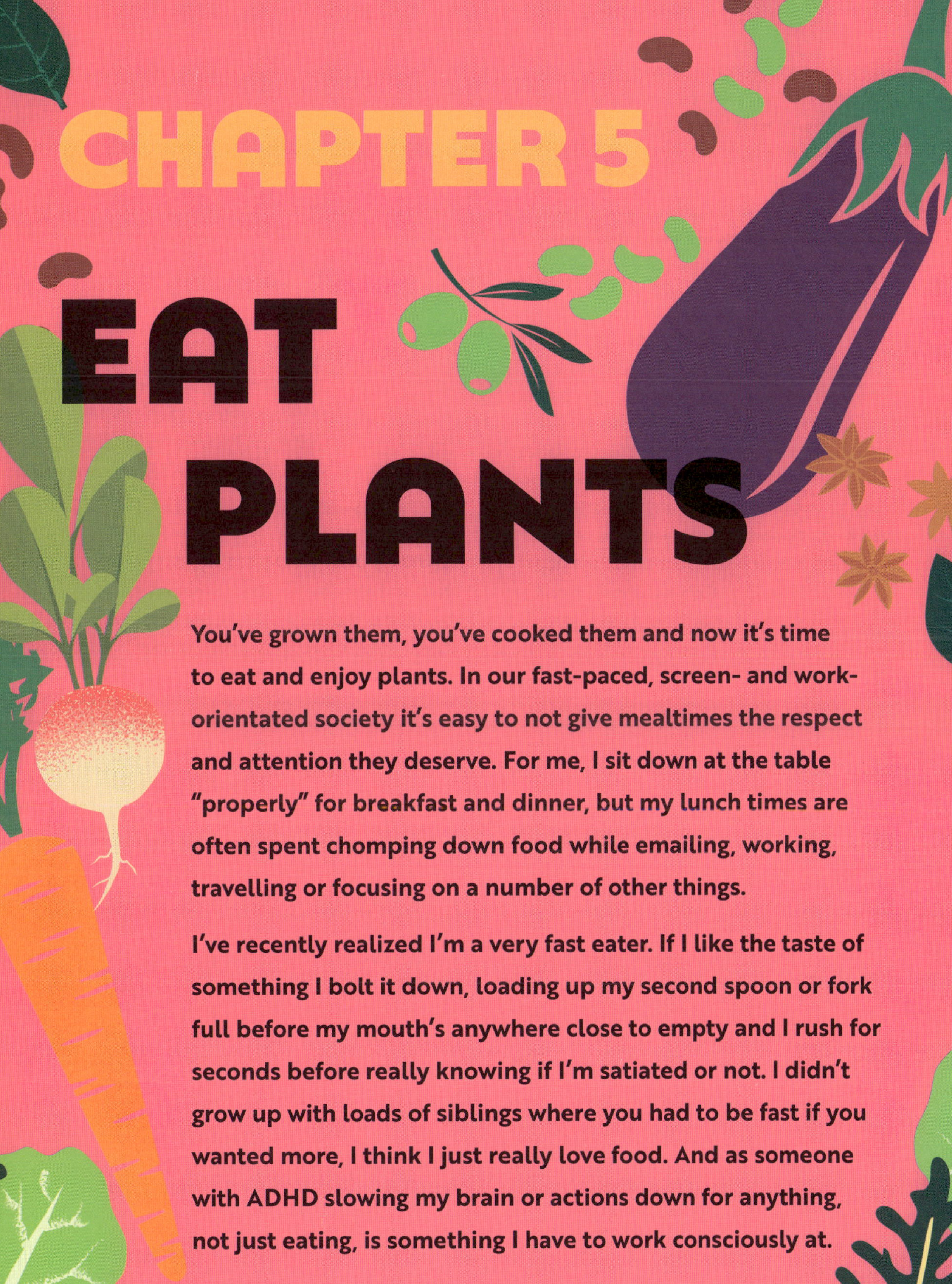

CHAPTER 5

EAT PLANTS

You've grown them, you've cooked them and now it's time to eat and enjoy plants. In our fast-paced, screen- and work-orientated society it's easy to not give mealtimes the respect and attention they deserve. For me, I sit down at the table "properly" for breakfast and dinner, but my lunch times are often spent chomping down food while emailing, working, travelling or focusing on a number of other things.

I've recently realized I'm a very fast eater. If I like the taste of something I bolt it down, loading up my second spoon or fork full before my mouth's anywhere close to empty and I rush for seconds before really knowing if I'm satiated or not. I didn't grow up with loads of siblings where you had to be fast if you wanted more, I think I just really love food. And as someone with ADHD slowing my brain or actions down for anything, not just eating, is something I have to work consciously at.

Here are some ways to respect and savour mealtimes. There will be many days when you will only have time to grab a sandwich to eat on the bus, or you only have the energy to flop in front of the TV and eat off a tray on your lap. These moments are an inevitable part of life. But let's not make them our every day. Let's try to give our bodies and our food a moment.

SET THE SCENE Give yourself a nice, calm space to eat. For me this means clearing the kitchen table of any toys, receipts, to-do lists, mugs and setting it with a placemat, utensils and a water glass. If I'm feeling fancy I might put some flowers in a vase. I don't do tablecloths or napkins or anything that creates work – but do whatever gives you a sense of occasion. Many cultures eat sat on the floor at low tables or on tablecloths spread on the ground. You know what feels good to you.

PRESENTATION My presentation skills are rudimentary, but I try and plate my food so it looks visually appealing. Again this means different things to different people but simple ways include using nice crockery (lovely bits can be found in charity shops); garnishing with herbs, nuts, seeds, splashes of colour like pomegranate seeds; and arrange it on your plate with thought. The fine-dining style of serving a little food on a huge plate makes me feel sad, so I never recreate this look at home, but use smaller plates and bowls that I amply fill. Abundance makes me feel happy.

SCREEN-FREE Eating dinner watching TV can be a bit of a treat but we don't recommend it. The story line will take you away from the sensory act of eating and it will block opportunity for conversation. We have a no phones rule during mealtimes in our house. Scrolling social media is worse than watching a show as your attention is diverted in so many different ways.

SLOW IT DOWN It's recommended we chew our food 32 times before swallowing! Forty times for harder food like nuts, and five to ten times for softer things like berries and watermelon. I eat way too fast, and this is probably why I suffer from bloating. Have a go at slowing yourself down and consciously chewing your food more. I realized I was swallowing after ten chews. It must be such a load on the digestion. It also takes 20 minutes for our brain to signal that we are full. So if we eat slower we're less likely to overeat.

The magic of chewing p368

ENJOY YOUR FOOD Eat without any guilt and remorse – states of mind created by the diet industry. If you're going to have a treat, thoroughly enjoy it. I love the phrase, "Everything in moderation, including moderation". To me this means: sure, moderation is important, but so is a blow out every now and then. The global dieting industry is anticipated to be worth $405.4 billion by 2030 – and it's this capitalist machine that plays on people's insecurities to create unhappiness, guilt, yo-yo dieting, unbalanced habits and skewed perceptions about realistic body shapes and sizes. A well-planned wholefoods plant-based diet will stand you in excellent stead for meeting your body's nutrition requirements, with lots of scope for treats and culturally varied food. Appreciate everything that's come together to put that food on your plate and enjoy it.

SOCIAL DINING Eating with others can be a great pleasure. Invite friends over, suggest a lunch potluck at work, or attend a community feast or lunch club.

IN CONVERSATION WITH...

The Transformative Power of Mindful Eating

A conversation with StillChill founder and mindfulness practitioner Rose Eskafi

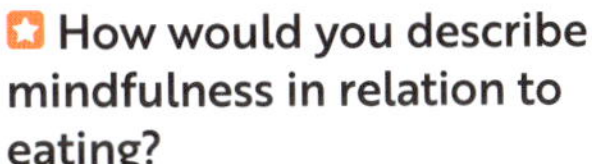

How would you describe mindfulness in relation to eating?

Rose: Mindfulness is about engaging your senses, and there's no better time for that than when you're eating or cooking, right? There are so many different colours, textures, flavours – so much for us to be aware of when it comes to eating. Unfortunately, most of us eat in front of devices, our phone or TV. So mindful eating encourages you to slow down and feel connected to your food and to yourself through your food. Recognizing what it's taken for that plate of food to be in front of you. How many people has it passed through? How many different climates has it gone through? What has it taken for you to be able to enjoy this meal? It's a way to remember our connection to the planet, to each other and also to ourselves.

Guide us through what we might think about when doing a mindful eating practice?

Become aware of how you're holding your body. Often, when we're in this autopilot state, we're holding ourselves tensely. That's the first step. How am I holding my body? Do I need to lengthen my spine? Relax my shoulders? What does it mean for me to be alert in front of this food? Then it engages your senses. Look at the plate of food: what are the colours? Shapes? Sizes? The textures you can see before you've even had a spoonful? Place the food in your mouth and hold it without chewing for a moment. Notice its weight, its temperature and how your body is naturally responding to it. Are you salivating? Is there joy? Is there disgust? Slow everything down to notice the little intricacies, all the different points of contact with the food. Once it's inside your mouth and you're noticing your response, start chewing. What does it feel like to chew? Is it soft? Crunchy? Wet? Dry? We're often already thinking about the next bite when there's still a bite in our mouth. Be present with that bite, chewing at least ten times, ideally double this or more, then swallow. Noticing. What does that journey feel like from my mouth all the way down to my stomach? Where can I feel this food? How is my body responding to it, am I warming up? Cooling down? What can you hear? Smell? Feel? So there is all this sensory stuff happening moment to moment that oftentimes we miss out on. Mindful eating is about tapping into that.

I have ADHD and eat as fast as I think. I have to really consciously work on slowing down to eat. Do you think mindful eating is more challenging for the neurodiverse community or is it too broad to say?

I would argue it's easier for neurodivergent people to tune into their senses. It may be more difficult to focus for prolonged periods at a specific time, but actually feeling the sensory act of eating comes naturally to us. It's a great way for us to notice and be present. Sometimes it's really difficult to pay attention to just one thing. This really allows us to move through all different types of senses. So it's not about clinging on to one thing, it's about moving through all the different senses. Sometimes thinking about it in that way can be helpful.

Given the paradigm of society that we're living in now, how is mindfulness a rebellious act, if you think it is at all?

I do think it is. Slowing down is an act of resistance in itself, in the very speedy, over-consumptive world we're living in. We're constantly encouraged to do more, be more, eat more of a certain thing, more, more, more. Mindfulness encourages us to do less and buy less, it means reconnecting to ourselves, but also to nature and the planet. This idea of more has led to so much greed and corruption and caused us to be in the position we're in today. Slowness encourages us to pause, reflect on whether we're living in our values, in the intentions that we want to be living in, and whether this is the path we want to continue on. It encourages us to be more intentional.

When did you start your mindfulness journey?
I started meditating during my psychology degree as a way to manage stress. It was so transformative for me that I was curious to continue after I graduated. Psychology focuses on mental health, the mind, thoughts and thinking. I was experiencing a lot of emotional turmoil and reactions I wasn't understanding through the Western lens, and I found myself drawn towards mind, body, somatic practices and learning more about my emotions. I went on a personal journey to understand myself better – mindfulness and self-compassion were game changers. I'd studied psychology since I was 16 years old. Nothing had ever been as impactful for me. I went on to study mindfulness and compassion at a Master's level to facilitate this for other people, and learn more about the science behind it. Even there, I felt there are things that don't fully align with my cultural background. So I learned about trauma and became trauma informed. I learned about cultural sensitivity and how to apply it to my work. And now the work I do is mindfulness, somatics, with a culturally sensitive lens. It centres indigenous practices and healing through heritage, which food is a huge part of. I'm Iranian; food and herbalism are such integral parts of our culture. I found reconnecting to that so healing, and I wanted to teach other people how to reconnect to themselves in this way.

What settings can mindfulness be really useful in that might surprise people?
Within organizing spaces. Mindfulness is really effective in settings where there are a lot of people interactions and teamwork, as a way of conflict resolution, coming together and connecting through a common cause, and as a way to regulate our nervous system. People who organize – whether it's climate or politics, all are interconnected at the end of the day – are often extremely stressed, burnt out, and suffer at the hands of their compassion and care. Mindfulness and self-compassion are powerful antidotes, or a soothing balm for people who are politically engaged, because they give respite, allowing people to relate to themselves and each other in a different way. It's the space I'm most interested in facilitating and I have seen massive transformations. How it's received, and how people mobilize themselves and show up for each other in that work.

Mindfulness has become a very mainstream idea. Is this great, or has the essence been lost along the way?
Oh, how long have you got? This is something I feel strongly about. I do think it's lost its essence. Mindfulness is seen as a tool for people to use as a way to feel better. A quick fix. But actually it's a way of life, and a philosophy in itself. Unless people fully understand where it comes from, which is Buddhist philosophy, I don't think we're going to move forward collectively in the way that we need to. The wellness industry is worth a few billion, possibly trillions of pounds globally. It's incredibly powerful, but the way it's often used and taught is on a quite superficial level. While it's still helpful and impactful, if we're looking at making real, meaningful change collectively, we need to engage with it on a deeper level.

Mindfulness is seen as a tool for people to use as a way to feel better. A quick fix. But actually it's a way of life, and a philosophy in itself.

So if someone thinks, "Oh, I thought mindfulness was just peeling the spuds and thinking, 'I'm peeling the spuds'", how would you suggest they go deeper to explore its roots?
If we stay with the example of the spuds, I'd say, the spud that's in front of me, where has it come from? How has it ended up in front of me? Could I make more conscious choices with the way I'm buying? Could I be buying more locally, or organic? What am I doing with this spud? How am I engaging with it? Am I just chopping it up? There are so many parts we automatically brush over. When it comes to the cooking process, what's the texture of the spud? Is it the same as every other spud in the bag? What's the size? Why have I picked this one? Be intricate about your experience with the spud. And that encourages us to slow down. It's bringing awareness to the process, and the sensory experience. And of course, taking a breath.

When I was having a really tough time with my health for a long period last year, I did a lot of different meditative, calming practices to try and get well. What eventually brought me back was accepting I love being busy and filling my life with high-energy exercise and other things that bring me joy.
I love that, and that's what mindfulness is about. It sometimes gets wrapped up with the idea of calming down or relaxing, but actually it's about being aware of where you're at and what your needs are. It's like hanging out with yourself, knowing something about what you're going through and what you need, rather than forcing ourselves to be this calm, relaxed person, when actually there is a lot going on in our lives, and some of us really thrive in a busy environment. So yeah, I think that's a really good example of what it means to be mindful.

Mindful eating encourages you to slow down and feel connected to your food and to yourself...

Is there anything about mindfulness that we've not touched upon that's important to say?
The main takeaway point for me is mindfulness is about being mindful of our consumption, whether it's what we take in media-wise, what we eat or buy. It's about becoming aware of what we're doing, how we're doing it and why we're doing it. It's not necessarily this tool that's going to transform you into a calm being. If we're drawing from its essence, which is Buddhist philosophy, it's about being aware of who you are and what we can do, personally and intentionally, to work towards collective liberation. **It's always about coming back to collective liberation.**

Neighbours share a laugh after eating together at one of our Community Feasts

WHY IT'S ABOUT SO MUCH MORE THAN BEING VEGAN

For me, going vegan is a way of living and being on this Earth that allows you to live with kindness and compassion. Some of the greatest ills of humankind – rampant unchecked capitalism, environmental degradation, colonialism and imperialism, racism, misogyny, gender violence – stem from people exerting their power, privilege and might over another, usually more marginalized, group or entity. If human society collectively reined in their desire to oppress, dominate, hoard and consume, rather than support, coexist and collaborate, what kind of a beautiful and alternative world might we be living in? I dream of this world, a world of peace, love, justice and equality. A world where resources are divided equally and everyone has enough to eat, safe shelter, a chance to fulfil their dreams, and have a fair chance at health and happiness regardless of where they live, their ethnicity, religion, culture, age, gender, sexuality or physicality. A world where the environment is preserved and exalted for the life-giving force it is. Where truth is sacred and not distorted for ill gains. A world where people and planet, as opposed to profit and power, are always prioritised. A world where joy is everyone's natural birthright.

Going vegan, for me, in my privileged urban life in the Global North, is one of many steps towards building that alternative world. For me, being vegan has never been motivated by a single issue or cause. I'm vegan because I care about people. I'm vegan because I care about racial justice. I'm vegan because I care about gender equality. I'm vegan because I care about tearing down the Euro-patriarchy. I'm vegan because I care about the planet, and all its magnificent ecosystems and every being that dwells within them whether they be human, animal, fish, bird or insect. I do not judge, disrespect or dislike people who are not vegan. Some of my greatest friends, loves and collaborators are not. But they support me unequivocally in my choice to be so, and in the process many of them are now going more plant-based. I do not expect or think it practical for the entire human population to go vegan. I'm being mindful of remote, food limited communities and people without jurisdiction over their food supply. But I know if everyone who could, did, (and that is a vast majority of the global population) so much more would change for the better in this world than just the food on our plates.

Thank you for growing, cooking and eating more plants with us.

THE
EXTRA
BITS

NUTRITION NUGGETS

Wherever you have seen the Nutrition Nuggets logo in our recipes, you can find extra information here about the health benefits of the ingredients used.

THE MAGIC OF CHEWING

Chewing your food for long enough is one of the most overlooked dietary interventions that could improve millions of people's health. Chewing breaks down food into small pieces making it easier for you to digest and for your body to absorb a greater number of vitamins, minerals and other nutrients. You might have noticed when you chew your mouth produces saliva. Saliva contains epidermal growth factor, a polypeptide that plays a critical role in oral health and wound healing. Food that is not broken down properly can cause bacterial overgrowth and increased fermentation in the gut, which can lead to conditions such as bloating, indigestion, flatulence and constipation.

AMINO ACIDS AND THE FOOD COMBINING MYTH

There was a book published fifty years ago that popularized the idea of food combining: it said for vegetarians to get a complete set of amino acids – the building blocks of protein – they needed to combine proteins. This isn't true. All plants contain all nine essential amino-acids in varying quantities – amazing right? Our bodies cycle through amino-acids on a daily basis, so as long as we are eating a variety of foods and meeting energy requirements, we will not run into major issues. For example, grains are rich in methionine but low in lysine. Seeds and beans are lower in methionine but rich in lysine. So although grains and beans do not need to be combined in a single meal, they are often prepared this way in various global food cultures. Rice and dhal, porridge/oatmeal with soy milk, a wholemeal peanut butter sandwich or black bean tacos – are all delicious and nutritious examples you can enjoy, but without being wedded to an out-of-date idea about getting a complete set of amino acids.

CACAO VERSUS COCOA

Cacao and cocoa come from the same plant and are often used interchangeably, but they are slightly different due to the way they are processed. Both are picked, dried and fermented but then cocoa is finely ground and roasted. Cacao on the other hand isn't roasted but kept raw and therefore contains more minerals and antioxidants. Cacao is often more expensive, which seems unjust given it's simpler to make. But often cacao is sold by smaller, artisan brands.

CHLORELLA, SPIRULINA AND B12

Chlorella and spirulina are types of green algae. They contain high amounts of minerals, vitamins and antioxidants. Chlorella is 50–60% protein and contains vitamins A, B, C and K, as well as calcium, iron, magnesium, phosphorus, zinc and lutein. Spirulina is high in iron and magnesium and also contains vitamin C and B6. It contains a mineral that mimics B12 and therefore inhibits absorption of actual B12. Consequently it's best to take spirulina at a different time to your B12 supplement. Chlorella on the other hand contains actual B12, so if you're going to invest in one, opt for chlorella. As with any new herb or supplement, be mindful when adding spirulina or chlorella to your diet. Research is still inconclusive as to whether pregnant women can use either safely and it can possibly worsen symptoms of some autoimmune diseases. This doesn't mean it isn't a great addition to everyone else's diets.

CITRUS SKINS

The peel of any fruit or vegetable has a higher concentration of nutrients, vitamins, antioxidants and fibre than the fruit itself. The zest of citrus has three times more vitamin C per tablespoon than a tablespoon of the flesh – 14% of your recommended daily allowance. Citrus peels are also incredible flavour components, really elevating a dish's flavour profile.

THE DEAL WITH COCONUT OIL

There was a time when coconut oil was hailed as the go-to oil from a health point of view. And then it kind of wasn't. Our learned and diverse teachers have differing views on it but the evidence-based recommendation from Plant Based Health Professionals UK is that it is not heart healthy and to go easy on it due to it being high in saturated fat. So by all means enjoy it as a treat and use it from time to time for the flavour profile of a dish or in vegan baking, but don't make it your go-to daily oil. Reach for extra virgin olive oil or rapeseed oil as general all-purpose oils.

MORE ON GARLIC

Garlic contains an enzyme called alliinase and a lot of essential oils with strong antimicrobial activity that can kill bacteria in the gut, a process that can make some people gassy. Alliinase is great for keeping away colds and sore throats. For some people garlic is quite stimulating – especially raw – and they need to avoid eating it close to bedtime. Also some people believe to maximize the medicinal benefits of garlic you should leave it to rest for ten minutes after cutting before cooking with it. Garlic breath? Eat some raw apple, lettuce or chicory to reduce the odour.

UP YOUR IRON

To increase your iron absorption when eating leafy greens, squeeze some citrus such as lemon, lime or orange onto them. When you eat iron-rich foods such as leafy greens alongside vitamin C your body absorbs more iron. You can also achieve this by eating a tangerine with some cashew nuts. Or having a stir fry with leafy greens and vitamin C-rich red pepper.

ACTIVATE YOUR TURMERIC

Turmeric, or curcumin, is a bright yellow wonder spice incredible at reducing inflammation and joint pain. You can eat the root raw or buy the spice ground and dry. To activate its beneficial compounds, it's important to combine turmeric with black pepper, which is why a good golden milk/turmeric latte should always have black pepper in it.

THE 411 ON SEA MOSS

Long a staple in Caribbean kitchens, sea moss has become a global nutritional superstar. There are a variety of sea mosses including Irish moss, gold sea moss, St Lucian sea moss, purple sea moss and Jamaican Irish sea moss. Confusingly Jamaican sea moss is often referred to as Irish moss but it is a different variety to the Irish sea moss that grows in cooler waters. It is thought that Irish immigrants to Jamaica adopted the local variety and referred to it by the same name as the moss that grows off Ireland's coast. Jamaican Irish moss (Chondrus crispus) is a nutritional powerhouse containing 92 of the 102 essential minerals and vitamins our bodies need and is the most potent sea moss variety. Wild crafted sea moss is believed to be nutritionally superior to farmed, pool-grown sea moss or what some people call "fake sea moss". To tell the two apart, farmed sea moss has thicker tentacles, is encrusted with more salt, and has an unpleasant smell. It's often not fully dehydrated or fully air sealed and looks plumper than wild crafted sea moss. Both green sea moss and purple sea moss are nutrient dense (green higher in chlorophyll, purple higher in antioxidants, but neither are as nutritionally dense as the Chondrus crispus *variety). Both are dried in the dark. Golden sea moss is dried out in the sun, which bleaches out the colour, but regardless is still very nutrient dense, so don't worry if your sea moss product is clear/golden. Of all the forms, dried sea moss is the cheapest, but you then need to make it into a gel. If you don't want to prepare it, invest in your health and support an artisan supplier and buy the gel.*

**Although advice varies some experts believe you should avoid eating sea moss if you have a thyroid disorder, have a heavy-metal load, are on blood thinners or have a shellfish allergy. Some people find sea moss gives them bloating and gas. These symptoms usually alleviate as your body gets used to it after one to two weeks. If these symptoms don't go away reduce or stop taking it.*

K2 & THE MAGIC OF NATTO

Did you know this ancient Japanese fermented soy bean dish is the best plant-based source of K2? Yep. It's fermented with a bacteria called* Bacillus subtilis*, the strain essential for the creation of K2. Vitamin K (both K1 and K2) is needed for proper blood clotting and bone health. One tablespoon of natto contains 150mcg of K2, almost twice the recommended daily amount. Compare this to sauerkraut, which has 2.75mg per ½ cup. Other fermented foods like tempeh and kombucha contain K2, and in the gut the body converts K1 into K2. K1 is an easier nutrient to find, in things like dark leafy veg, broccoli and blueberries. A high-quality supplement such as Viridian's Vegan Essential (**see p 5**) contains K2, as do many other (but certainly not all) vegan supplements. However both Veganhealth.org and Plant Based Health Professionals UK don't think there's enough evidence to suggest it's essential vegans supplement with K2. So what's the take away? Eat dark leafy greens, broccoli and blueberries, and if you can access natto – great, add that in too.

THE LOW DOWN ON MAGNESIUM

With plant-based nutritionist Rohini Bajekal

Magnesium is an essential mineral that supports your heart, blood sugar levels, muscle and nerve function, immune system and mood. While a true magnesium deficiency is rare, many people in the UK have low levels, particularly young women. Chronically high stress levels as well as a diet high in ultra-processed foods are common causes of low magnesium. I recommend consuming plenty of tofu, dark leafy green vegetables, chickpeas/garbanzo beans and whole grains such as oats, nuts and seeds. While there is limited evidence to support magnesium supplements for insomnia, magnesium has been found to support restful and restorative deep sleep.

DAIRY CHEESE & HEALTH

Although high in protein, dairy cheese is high in saturated fats and salt, which can contribute to high blood pressure and cholesterol levels and increase your risk of cardiovascular disease. Global nutrition guidelines recommend a maximum 30g/1oz portion of dairy cheese a day – the size of a matchbox. Cultured nut and seed cheeses are packed with beneficial probiotics and healthy fats and are an excellent way of boosting the health of your gut microbiome.

OUR MEAT BAGS!

The NHS recommends people eat no more than 70g/2½oz of red meat a day. That's one and a half small sausages. When we started MIH in 2012 this wasn't widely known, so to illustrate it we tasked a crafty volunteer to whizz up some "meat bags" – pink bean bags with screen printed pictures of steak and sausages sewn on the front. They were hilarious. These bags ranged in weight from 70g/2½oz to 250g/8¾oz. We'd toss them in a frying pan, let people hold them, and ask people to guess which one represented the maximum daily intake of red meat. 95% of the time people didn't choose the tiny 70g/2½oz bag.

THE GUT MICROBIOME

With Dr Sunni Patel

When we talk about the gut, we are talking about the digestive tract all the way from where it enters the mouth to where it leaves the body. We're describing 9m/30ft of digestive tract that houses trillions of microorganisms. Gut health is all about how we can maintain a healthy balance of gut microbiome, mainly bacteria, so we can get the best of our physiological bodies. It's critical for immune response, mental wellbeing and digestion. Gut bacteria alone have 150 times more genetic material than our own human genome. It outweighs our number of human cells by trillions. So you can see how important the gut is. The gut is coined the second brain because it is so intricately linked via the central nervous system and endocrine systems, which are symbiotically connected to our gut microbiome. Stress, diet and lifestyle are known to create imbalances between the gut and the brain. This intimate relationship is often referred to as the gut–brain axis. The gut microbiome, if not balanced, thriving and diverse, can be responsible for certain inflammatory mental health conditions. There are several nutrients like glutamine, glutamate and sucrose that are known to help improve our emotional state and help our mucus lining and intestinal lining function, which helps to maintain mental and gut health. Beyond that we also know if we hit our 30g/1oz of fibre intake a day, we'll be fuelling good gut bacteria, which will help maintain the gut–brain axis.

DATES ARE CLEVER

Dates, medjool or otherwise are super sweet. But they have a low to medium GI (glycaemic index) and contain chromium, an essential trace mineral believed to help the way the body uses insulin. Insulin helps blood sugar enter the body's cells so it can be used for energy. Thanks nature, you're really cool.

BROWN VS WHITE RICE

Brown rice means you're eating the rice as a whole grain. That's important because the less processed the grain, the more nutrients you get. The bran and germ, the two outer layers of brown rice, contain most of the vitamins and minerals in the grain. It contains iron, calcium, magnesium, phosphorus, selenium, B vitamins, fibre and protein. Remember white rice isn't "bad", it's just that brown has more beneficial nutrients.

The community meal service dream team of kitchen and meal delivery volunteers.

TIPS & TRICKS

Throughout our recipes you'll spot little badges guiding you to this section where you'll find advice for shopping and working with ingredients that might be new to you. If you're an old timer with this ingredient just pass the badge by and cook on. If you're not, flick back here and get the knowledge.

▶ SHOPPING ETIQUETTE

When shopping in stores and markets serving a community that's not your own, be mindful that your enthusiasm to learn should not generate additional labour for the staff. These spaces are not there to serve you so don't expect extensive help from the already busy staff to navigate the store and its products. Therefore, if visiting a cultural store for the first time, allow yourself an appropriate amount of time to get to know it and familiarize yourself with the layout and products. Don't go in a rush. Google Lens is a great tool to point at labels for translation if needed.

As with any other store, asking where you can find one product is no biggie, but don't request explanations of what's suitable for what dish or other culinary insights. And like if you were a guest in someone's home, don't express shock, surprise or disdain at any smells or ingredients that are new to you.

▶ WHAT'S THE DEAL WITH BEST BEFORE DATES?

Best before dates are a suggestion and recommendation for when to consume food by to ensure the best quality, which is totally different to a use by date where the food will most likely be off. To check food is still good to eat use your senses. Ask yourself does it smell and look ok? If something is slightly past its best there's no need to throw it, just chop it up and whizz it into a pesto, soup or smoothie.

▶ EATING ETIQUETTE: USING OUR HANDS

Eating with our hands is the oldest way of eating. Despite their central place today, forks were not widely used in Europe until 1500 – although they existed centuries before, they were viewed as an unnecessary luxury. Across Africa, Asia and the Middle East consuming entire meals – including stews and soups – with your hands is still commonplace and many people remark how much better the experience is. Although customs vary region to region, there are a few general rules. Wash your hands thoroughly before eating and scrub your nails clean. Handle food with your right hand not your left. This is because in Islamic countries the left hand is reserved for unclean activities, such as using the toilet, and the right hand for clean activities, such as eating. Traditionally you eat using your thumb, index and middle finger and you only lick your fingers right at the end of the meal. In West and East Africa soups and stews are common and they are usually served with a carbohydrate such as fufu, ugali, injera or garri. Rip pieces off and dunk into the food using them as you would cutlery to lift the food to your mouth. The food goes inside your mouth, but your fingers don't. It's a very hygienic and sociable way of eating.

If you're only used to eating with cutlery this can all take a little practice, but you'll soon begin to enjoy it.

▶ Zero-Waste Cooking With Hannah Walker

Many people feel intimidated by the idea of attempting to live a zero-waste lifestyle, particularly with regards to cooking and eating. Plastic packaging is rife and non-plastic products are ironically often more expensive. A more approachable starting point is to focus on making the most of what we have with "root-to-stalk" cooking, which saves us money and also helps to fight food waste. It's about utilizing all the bits of fresh produce – the peels, tops, stalks and other usually discarded bits – and processing them into edibles – or drinkables! This might be in a dish like with the carnitas that use up banana skins on p 240, or fermenting, preserving or making pestos and dips. There's no rocket science involved – it's more about planning and being a bit bold and creative. And it can be great fun! Here are my top tips to getting started.

▶ Make time for meal planning. Consider the quantities of fresh ingredients you need and how any extras can be used later in the week.

▶ Cook in bulk. If you don't want to eat the same thing day after day, freeze individual portions to defrost as you want them. If you want to avoid plastic, freeze in glass jars – just be sure to leave a 2½cm/1in gap at the top. This will prevent the glass breaking when the food/fluid expands when frozen.

▶ Get creative with trimmings! Beet leaves, carrot tops, broccoli stalks, green tops of leeks are perfectly edible and extremely nutritious. These can be used in pestos, soups and stir-fries to name just a few ideas.

▶ Keep a ziplock bag in the fridge or freezer to add veggie scraps. When the bag is full, use to make a veggie stock (p 167 for a recipe). This is a particularly good use for onion and garlic peels, as well as the ends of carrots, celery and cores of peppers. I avoid using too many cruciferous vegetables as they can make your stock bitter. The core and stalks of these vegetables I chop up finely, stir fry and eat!

▶ Get familiar with the different ways of preserving produce. Fermenting, pickling and dehydrating are all excellent ways to extend the shelf life of your produce and add different flavours to meals.

Leo and Hannah at a community outreach day with our plant-based Eat Well Guides.

Most Commonly Thrown Ingredients Hannah Loves To Cook With

1: Banana Peels – use as a pulled pork replacer (see p 240), in curries or candy to make a crunchy sweet treat.

2: Citrus Peels – use in teas, to make preserves (see p 246 for a preserved lemon recipe), or the zests to enhance flavour and nutritional profile.

3: Brassica Stalks – use in ferments, pickles and finely sliced in stir fries.

4: Aquafaba (chickpea/garbanzo bean juice and other bean juices) – an egg replacer in vegan baking and cooking.

5: Carrot and Beetroot Tops – great to use in pestos, dips, soups and stews.

6: Stale Bread – turn into breadcrumbs, herby croutons or use to make bread casseroles or puddings.

7: Wilted Salad – blend into pesto, soups or even green smoothies.

8: Potato Peels – use to make sweet or savoury crisps.

I Knead You

Kneading is the process of working a dough mixture into a smooth, elastic mass. You knead the dough so that it will keep its shape and rise as it's baked. If you're not sure you're kneading properly, start by pushing the heel of your palm into the ball of dough, stretching it away from you. Lift the far side of the dough up and slightly stretch it up, then fold in half back towards you. Keep doing this rolling and folding motion and it will start to feel very natural.

Garlic

There are lots of different ways to peel and cut garlic. We have two favourites. Lie a single clove down flat and with the flat side of your knife slightly crush it so the skin pops off. Then peel it off with your hands. Many chefs cut a clove in half lengthways and then peel off the skin – they say this is the fastest method. Crushing garlic with a crusher makes it more potent and flavoursome, but if you find garlic repeats on you opt for slicing instead.

Lid On, Lid Off

Keep the lid on saucepans when making sauces where you want the flavours to infuse and the sauce to cook faster – the lid is trapping in the heat and ensuring it warms up quickly. When you want sauces to reduce and thicken up it's good to remove the lid as the water cooks out of the sauce. When cooking grains and pseudo grains like quinoa and brown rice it's good to turn the heat off and keep the lid on at the end of cooking for the grains to steam for the last ten minutes.

All Rise – The Magic Of Proving

Proving is essential to get bouncy, delicious doughs – whether they be breads or pizza bases. It refers to the last step before baking when you leave a dough made with yeast to rest and rise for an hour-plus before baking. With bread this is sometimes called the second ferment or the final rise and, unlike with pizza dough, it's done after the bread is in its final shape. During proving the yeast eats the sugars and ferments the dough and produces gas, which makes the dough rise to give it a light, springy feel. You can over-proof and under-proof breads by leaving dough for too long or short a time, but you don't need to worry about that when making pizza dough. Leave it for an hour and you should be good. If your room is blazing hot or very cold you may need a slightly shorter or slightly longer proving time.

Cooking Onions

Chef Yasmin Khan says in Asia onions are usually cooked for at least 15 minutes to get them sweet and soft. It takes an additional ten minutes to caramelize them. This is longer than many European cuisine practices, which tend to fry onions for between 5–8 minutes.

The Right Rice

Golden Sella is a type of basmati rice found in supermarkets or Afro-Caribbean shops. If you cannot find it, buy long grain easy cook rice. Golden Sella is preferred as it doesn't turn to pottage when cooking – it maintains its structure well.

Getting To Know Saffron

Saffron – or *Zafron* in Arabic and Hebrew, and *Za'afaran* in Farsi – is a spice collected from the *Crocus sativus* or saffron crocus. Due to its value it is referred to as red gold and is a treasured delicacy in Persian, Indian and North African cookery. Saffron is the most expensive spice in the world due to a short harvesting period (between late October and November) and the fact each crocus only produces three stigmas, or threads, which have to be harvested individually by hand. It takes 75,000 saffron flowers to make 450g/16oz of saffron. It is grown in Iran, Kashmir, Spain, China, France and Italy. Although more cost-effective to buy in larger quantities, due to its price many people buy saffron by the gram/ounce and only use a small quantity in each dish.

Roasted Fenugreek Seeds

In Sri Lanka fenugreek (*uluhal* in Sinhala) is a staple spice used in dhals and curries – but it's used lightly roasted and is sold like that. This gives an incredible depth of flavour to the dish. Roasted fenugreek is hard to find in the UK – even online – so we recommend roasting fenugreek seeds on a medium heat until their colour deepens and then storing in a glass jar. Next time you make dhal experiment by adding 1½ teaspoons of roasted fenugreek after it's been cooking for 10–15 minutes.

Cooking Gyoza

Dumplings can be steamed, boiled or fried. Experiment with each method and see which you prefer. The steaming method is the healthiest choice as it uses no oil and the veg maintain more of their vitamins and minerals. When steaming it's important to ensure your stainless steel steamer basket base doesn't touch the water and your water isn't too high. Gyoza need between 12–15 minutes to steam. If boiling bring a pot of water to the boil then add six to eight dumplings at a time to the water. They are cooked when they rise to the surface, which will take 3–4 minutes. Experiment to see which cooking method you prefer. And have fun.

Where to Buy Textured Soy Protein

We love Clearspring's organic soy chunks – they plump up beautifully and are lovely and chewy. You can buy soy chunks online, in health food stores, East Asian grocery stores and in some mainstream supermarkets. Unlike tofu and tempeh they don't need refrigerating so you find them stored ambiently on a store shelf. See p 156 for why this amazing plant protein is particularly helpful for high altitude communities in Peru.

Sourcing Cashew Nuts

Over the last few years the price of cashew nuts has skyrocketed. You can often find non-organic cashews for a cheaper price in the world food aisle of many supermarkets and some stores have deals on organic ones – so look out for bargains.

Just Freeze It

Dishes like homemade plant-based haggis, burgers, falafel and sausages may seem like quite a lot of effort and faff, but the beauty of them is you can make a big batch and freeze them for future, quick and nourishing dinners. Making them can be excellent Sunday afternoon projects. The haggis freezes well and you can portion it up in slices ready for future meals. If budget allows, double up the recipe and make two: one for now, one for later.

* INGREDIENTS

▶ All Purpose Seasoning

APS can be found in most major supermarkets in the herbs and spices section or the world food aisle (problematic term, we know). It is commonly a blend of salt, paprika, coriander/cilantro, chilli, onion, pepper, garlic, nutmeg and allspice/pimento – but different brands have different blends. It's used to give dishes a fantastic depth of flavour and umami quality. If you don't want to eat MSG look out for this on the label as some do contain it.

▶ Amchoor Powder

Amchoor powder is a delicious, powdered seasoning made from dried, unripe green mangos. It has a zesty, citrus taste and is used in marinades, sauces, curries and more. It's also sometimes used as a thickener. It is commonly used in South Asian cuisine. You can buy amchoor powder from South Asian grocery stores, the world food aisle in supermarkets in cities with diverse populations and online.

▶ AQUAFABA

With Bruna Oliveira

Aquafaba is a cooking liquid derived from legumes such as peas, lentils, beans and chickpeas. Typically, we opt for aquafaba from chickpeas/garbanzo beans, butter beans and cannellini for their lighter colour and mild, salty flavour. It serves multiple functions in cooking, acting as a binder, emulsifier and firming agent. When whipped, aquafaba mimics the foaming properties of egg whites, thanks to its soluble proteins. These proteins form minuscule bubbles within a foam, imparting structure and a delightful, airy texture to various culinary creations like omelette, mousse, pavlova, waffles, pancakes and sponge cakes.

Unlike eggs, which contain fat, protein and water, aquafaba primarily consists of carbohydrates, proteins and water. However, its unique composition, including saponins that help form stable foams, make it a versatile ingredient for enhancing many delicious plant-based recipes.

▶ Asafoetida/Hing

Hing or asafoetida is a natural flavour enhancer. Its common name is "stinking gum". It grows in Northern India, Afghanistan, Iran and Northwest China. It comes from the dried sap of the ferula plant roots and has a strong odour. For people following a vegetarian sentient diet (a diet often followed by monks/nuns and spiritual meditation practitioners that avoids any stimulating foods such as alliums), hing is used to enrich the flavour profile of dishes instead of garlic, onion and chives.

▶ Chipotle Paste

Chipotle paste is a Mexican condiment made from ripened chipotle chillies that have been dried and smoked. Different chefs have different recipes, but the main ingredients are onion, garlic, vinegar, sugar, spices such as cumin or paprika, dried herbs and tomato purée. Some recipes include other Mexican chillies and chilli preparations such as Ancho, Pasilla, Chiles de Arbol and chillies in adobo. You can make your own and freeze in batches or it's widely available in food stores including supermarkets. Depending on your heat tolerance you will need to adjust the amount of chipotle you use and different brands vary in heat level. So test before using it.

▶ Coconut, How to Choose and How to Grate

Before we begin talking about grating, let's just clarify what type of coconut we're talking about, which is the coconut with a brown shell, hard white flesh and coconut milk in the middle, not the green coconuts you buy for drinking with a green outer shell, delicious jelly-like flesh (if you're lucky and get a good one!) and super hydrating coconut water in the middle.

If you plan on using grated coconut regularly, investing in a coconut scraper would be a good idea. You can buy them online or at stores that sell Caribbean or East Asian utensils. You have two models – a hand cranked scraper, which you bolt on to a table and is quite easy and enjoyable to use, or a more rudimentary coconut scraper disc that you attach to a chair or table and use to manually grate the coconut, which is much harder work. We've found folk who like gadgets really enjoy the hand crank model.

To crack open a coconut hit it repeatedly at its widest point with the back of a cleaver or rolling pin until it cracks and you can pull it apart, ensuring to have a bowl ready to catch any milk. Next boil a pan of water with a steamer basket placed inside. Add the coconut to the steamer and steam for ten minutes with a lid on. Remove from the water and use a dinner knife to work around the edges to remove the flesh from the shell. Next use a peeler to remove any brown skin. Now grate with whatever grater you have on the fine setting. Alternatively, you can buy unsweetened desiccated coconut in a supermarket baking section and leave to soak in boiling water for 20 minutes to rehydrate.

▶ Cornmeal Vs Cornstarch

Cornmeal and cornstarch (also known as cornflour) are made from different parts of the corn kernel. Cornmeal is made from dried and ground whole corn kernels, whereas cornstarch is made from just the endosperm – the starchy middle – and is ground into a fine powder. Cornstarch/cornflour is mainly used to thicken sauces. Cornmeal is good for a range of baking projects – cakes, loaves, tortilla and breads.

▶ Garlic Purée – How to Make Your Own

Garlic purée can be expensive to buy and varies in quality. To make your own, peel 400g/14oz of garlic cloves and add to a high-speed blender. Blend into a paste. Add 1 teaspoon salt and 60ml/2fl oz neutral oil like rapeseed oil and blend again. Decant into a jar and store in the fridge.

▶ Green Split Pea Or Moong Bean Flour (different beans, same preparation)

If you have a high-speed blender you can make this flour yourself. Take 200g/7oz of dried green split peas and soak them overnight. Drain and dry the peas thoroughly (the drying step is important) and blend them into a fine flour. Green pea flour can be bought online from UK protein company Hodmedod's or various wholefood stores, and moong bean flour is a low-cost flour available in South Asian grocery stores. Note: you're not buying pea protein powder – this is a nutrition supplement and costs four to five times more.

▶ Liquid Smoke

Liquid smoke is an amazing ingredient that gives plant-based dishes a deep, smoky taste. As the name suggests, it comes in liquid form in a bottle, and you use it sparingly as it's very strong. To create liquid smoke hardwood chips or sawdust from trees such as hickory, mesquite and apple wood are burned at high temperatures and then the smoke is captured in condensers. This turns to water droplets, which are then concentrated and filtered to get that deep smoky flavour. Some liquid smoke purists think it should only be made with smoke and water, but you won't find a brand that sells such a minimalist product, and it usually contains ingredients such as chicory, molasses, caramel colouring and vinegar. Not all liquid smoke is created equal. Some contain colourings and E numbers, so do check the label.

▶ Natto

Natto is available online or in East Asian supermarkets. It usually comes in a multipack of 50g/1¾oz serving size packets, but a few brands sell it in one container. It can be hard to find organic natto with no additives and flavourings – you can buy online or from the Japan Centre in the UK. Natto is sticky and has a strong, whiffy smell. When you spoon up the soy beans you'll see long stretchy fibres, which can be quite disconcerting if you've never had it before. These sticky strings are a form of glutamic acid and contain the nattokinase and are what make natto so unique. Natto is an acquired taste but once you've tried it a few times your palate adjusts and you start to crave it.

▶ Nutritional Yeast aka Nooch

Nutritional yeast, or nooch as it is lovingly referred to by the vegan community, is an essential ingredient for creating cheesy tastes and textures in a plant-based kitchen. It looks weirdly like flaky fish food. Not all nooch is vegan because of the source of some of the supplements added so ensure you buy one labelled vegan. We recommend buying one enriched with B12. Nooch isn't a new thing but has been around for decades – sold since the 1950s largely in independent health food stores. The science behind its creation dates back to 1916. Nooch is made from a living strain of *Saccharomyces cerevisiae* yeast – the same type of yeast you find in bread and beer. Inside a fermentation chamber it's fed a glucose-rich carbohydrate such as molasses or sugar, and it grows cell by cell by forming proteins that make up its cell walls. It takes up to two weeks for the yeast to mature and then it's heated, pasteurized and dried, which kills it. Eating active yeast unlike other live ferments would give us a tummy ache. As the cells die, the proteins in the cells break down and amino acids like glutamic acid are released, and these give it that deep, cheesy flavour. The drying process toasts it and turns it into wafer-thin, flaky pieces. Genius! There's a longtime joke in the British vegan community about calling nooch Gary. This happened after an irate person online ranted about vegans calling vegan cheese, cheese, despite it not being made from cow's milk. He suggested it may as well be called Gary, and the name stuck.

▶ PALM OIL AND WHERE TO BUY IT

With Duchess Nena

Palm oil comes in two forms – palm kernel oil, which is for cosmetic use, and palm oil made from the fruit flesh, which is culinary. When buying palm oil for cooking it should be a rich orangey red colour. Like coconut oil it's solid when it's cold and when it's very hot it can be very liquid. When shopping for palm oil in Nigeria in the market, sellers put a little of the oil on your hand so you can taste and smell the freshness. Fresh palm oil tastes so delicious. When you have a good oil, you just rub a yam with it and a little salt and that's all you need for a tasty dish. When buying in the UK and elsewhere you can't do that as it's sealed so you need to make sure you're not buying old palm oil that has gone rancid. Off palm oil goes brownish but it can be hard to check without opening it and smelling – so I recommend opening it straight after buying so if it's bad you can show the vendor and get it swapped. It should smell rich and nutty as opposed to fermented and rancid. It should be stored in a cool cupboard.

When cutting Nigerian yam and cassava, or green plantain, rub a little palm oil onto your hands to stop the liquid from their skin getting on your hands as it can cause them to become itchy. Palm oil has medicinal uses in Nigeria. It's used to bring down fevers and sometimes it's mixed with onion, garlic, herbs and spices, left for a week to infuse and then given medicinally. Palm kernel oil is very good for the skin and locks in moisture. You can rub it onto small burns with a little salt instead of running under cold water and you won't get a scar.

▶ Plantain For Newbies

If you're not a regular plantain eater, shopping for this much-loved produce for the first time might be a little bewildering. If you're not of African or Afro-Caribbean heritage, kindly shop keepers may inform you "That is not a banana, you know", regardless of the fact that it may be the hundredth time you've purchased it. Unlike when buying bananas, the skin being black is not a bad thing. In fact the blacker the skin the riper and sweeter the plantain will be. Choosing plantain is really about how firm you'd like it for your dish. For kelewele (see p 184) you want them to hold their structure when you cut them (so perhaps not an entirely black skin) but you do want them to be ripe and sweet so the skin will need to have a lot of black on it. They should feel firm but have a little give to them. Buy them often and you'll soon get to know your preference. While we're talking about plantain, they're not to be confused with green bananas, which are usually smaller in size to plantain and have an elongated end. West African folk like our teacher Nena Ubani tend to pronounce plantain "plaarn-tain", while Caribbean heritage folk like our teacher Sharon Gardner usually say "plaarn-tin". For jokes Sharon will only allow her class participants to say "plaarn-tin" – so now you're ready for her.

▶ Poona Yam

If you live in a multicultural city like London, Paris or New York you'll have no problem sourcing fresh poona yam from an Afro-Caribbean or South Asian grocery store. If you don't live in a place likely to sell yam you could buy some online for the full authentic experience or swap it out for white potato. Potato tastes completely different to yam but it will still make a delicious Ital stew. A good poona yam is firm to the touch with no soft spots, splits or cracks in the skin. Poona yam skin has ridges but a fresh yam should not be shrivelled up or deeply wrinkled.

▶ Pulses, Tinned Versus Dried

From a budget point of view, dried pulses and lentils are more cost-effective than tinned, even if you factor in the energy cost of cooking them. We appreciate we don't always have the time to leave bowls of things soaking (especially folk living in shared accommodation), so in that case you'll be using tinned and that's fine. People used to worry about tins leeching a chemical called BPA (Bisphenol A) into food stuffs, but in the UK 90%, and in the US 95% of tins, are now BPA-free. BPA was used (and still is) to stop aluminium can linings from corroding. BPA has all the molecular characteristics of an obesogenic, a term created in 2006 to describe chemicals that potentially cause us to put on weight more easily. To find out if the tin has BPA in it check the label. Unjustly, budget lines are more likely to have BPA – but this doesn't always ring true, with *Ethical Consumer* finding in 2023 some organic lines were still using the chemical in their tins.

▶ Raw Irish Moss Gel

To prepare Irish Moss gel yourself, soak the sea moss for 12–24 hours in cold, filtered water. The water will become gooey and the sea moss will expand. Wash the sea moss until the water runs clear. Now blend the sea moss with water in a high-speed blender until it turns into a gel. The ratios are three parts sea moss to one part filtered water. Store overnight in the fridge and it will firm up to a gel-like consistency. It will keep in the fridge for up to three weeks or you can decant it into an ice cube tray and store it in the freezer. This is useful as you can pop it out a few cubes at a time.

▶ Scotch Bonnet For Newbies

If you're new to this divine heat-giving pepper, listen up. Heat preference is individual. Chefs Duchess Nena and Michael Ninvalle both like their dishes extra hot so use three whole scotch bonnets with seeds. Wow. Apparently this is hot even by Nigerian/Caribbean standards so we recommend anyone new to eating this pepper use a quarter to a half with the seeds removed and build up from there.

Be careful handling the scotch bonnet as the skin is hot. Hold the stem and make sure to wash your knife and board properly after use. Do not rub your eyes or anywhere else on your body after handling scotch bonnet. You've been warned! In multicultural cities across the UK, Europe and US you often see scotch bonnets for sale on market stalls with 10–20 peppers in a bowl for £1/$2. For households that like their dishes low to medium heat pop two to four peppers in the fridge for use in the short-term and the rest in the freezer whole.

It's hard to find organic scotch bonnets, so if this is important to you, grow your own on a sunny window ledge.

▶ Shichimi Togarashi or Japanese Seven Spice

This is a traditional Japanese seasoning of seven components – black and white sesame seeds, nori sprinkles, chilli flakes, black pepper, ginger powder and orange peel. It is believed to have originated in the 17th century created by a merchant called Tokuemon in Edo, a fishing village that is now Tokyo. The name comes from the Japanese word *shichi* meaning seven and *mi* meaning flavours. It's available in some supermarkets and East Asian grocery stores. We love Clearspring's as it is excellent quality and they source from artisan growers in Japan. If you don't have access to shichimi togarashi or nori sprinkles you can improvise by adding ¼ teaspoon chilli, ¼ teaspoon ginger, a pinch of black pepper, ½ teaspoon sesame seeds and ¼ teaspoon of freshly zested orange peel into a small ramekin and mixing. It's not exactly the same, but it's not a bad improvisation.

▶ Shiitake Mushrooms & Seaweed

If shiitake mushrooms and seaweed aren't in your regular shop these can seem like pricey new additions. Shiitake mushrooms are more cost-effective to buy dried as you can buy smaller quantities and they keep for months in a store cupboard. Budget supermarkets in the UK have just started stocking dried shiitake so depending on where you live you might be surprised to find them in your nearby supermarket.

Seaweed is another ingredient that, thanks to the popularity of Japanese cuisine, is appearing in more stores. This tends to start and end with nori sheets and seaweed crispies so you might still need to visit a health food shop, East Asian grocery store or shop online for kelp/kombu. Both shiitake and kelp/kombu are nutrient-rich, deep flavour enhancers for making plant-based phish dishes so are excellent new additions to your plant-based store cupboard staples.

▶ Spring Roll Sheets

If buying dried spring roll sheets stored ambiently you usually get between 13–15 in a pack. If buying frozen, these packets usually contain 30-plus sheets. Weird, we know! Frozen sheets need taking out the freezer and leaving to defrost for 30–60 minutes before use. Frozen wrappers are often cheaper than non-frozen and you can buy them in bulk from supermarkets with world food aisles (a problematic term, we know) and East Asian grocery stores. Top tip – some ingredients are cheaper in the world food aisle than the same product (just a different brand) in other aisles.

▶ UZIZA

With Duchess Nena

If you live in a place with a West African diaspora you should be able to buy fresh uziza leaf. If you haven't bought it before, go on a culinary adventure and seek it out! The fresh, organic leaves – the real stuff because they have travelled from Nigeria – don't tend to look too good visually when you're buying them, but to tell if they're good tear one leaf and see if there's a strong minty, floral scent to them. If there is, they're good.

You can buy dried uziza leaf online and also the seeds, which are sometimes referred to as piper guineense. These seed pods look a bit like grain of selim but don't confuse the two. Out of the two I would always choose the seeds over the dried leaf, as they retain the flavour and scent better. If you can't find fresh uziza, buy the seeds instead and use them in the same quantities in recipes. If you have got your hands on fresh, store them in your freezer wrapped in baking parchment otherwise they go off rapidly.

Duchess Nena and Sarah in class.

FORAGING TIPS

Foraging and The Honourable Harvest With Hannah Walker

I was taught how to forage responsibly, but I read about the beautiful idea of the honourable harvest in Robin Wall Kimmerer's amazing book *Braiding Sweetgrass* where she discusses her botany profession against the backdrop of her indigenous knowledge. It's very moving, and teaches you to only take what you need. Always leave enough for wildlife and other foragers. Only pick from vibrant, thriving populations that look healthy enough to sustain themselves.

You also need to make sure you're allowed to forage from the land. In the UK you can't forage in the Royal Parks, and in the US some national parks have banned foraging or have daily limits. On common land you can't dig up plants by the roots.

Always make sure you're 100% sure you can identify what you're picking. Cross-reference with different books and plant ID apps – but warning, plant ID apps do make mistakes. Unless you're an extremely seasoned forager, avoid harvesting anything that remotely resembles poisonous plants such as Lords and Ladies, Poison Hemlock and Giant Hogweed.

Finally, know about the land you're on. Is it polluted, sprayed with agricultural chemicals, was there an industrial site there before? These are important questions to ask before you start picking.

Foraging For Dandelions

If you aren't 100% sure what a dandelion is, use a plant ID app or book to confirm what you're picking. There are many wild plants with yellow flowers that are toxic such as ragwort and lantana, and daffodils are also poisonous to humans. Dandelions look nothing like these plants, but I've seen beginner foragers confuse plants that don't look alike. To fine tune your ID skills take note of the shape of the petals and leaves, the plant's structure, where the flowers and leaves are positioned and the plant's location. If in doubt, leave it.

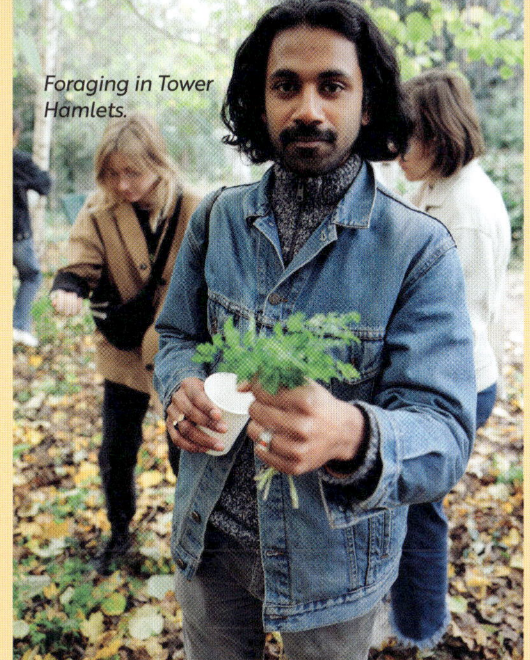
Foraging in Tower Hamlets.

Harvesting Nettles

Harvest from the middle of a patch to avoid any dog wee. Harvest nettles when they're young and before they've flowered or gone to seed. After that, they contain high levels of oxalate which is taxing on the kidneys. You can however harvest and eat the seeds at this stage – and they're packed with nutrients.

I pick with my hands by pinching upwards – or "grasping the nettle" – to squash the stinging needles rather than letting them penetrate my skin. You might want to wear rubber gloves and build up to this. You can make so many things with nettles – soups, stews, pestos, breads – so I hope that this is just the beginning of a great nettle adventure.

Do not confuse stinging nettles with dead nettles, which have white and pink flowers. They look similar but are entirely different plants and although they have medicinal uses you don't eat them in culinary quantities.

* Trouble Shooting Bacterial Fermentation With Asa Simonsson

If you're new to eating fermented foods the smell and taste might be quite an experience. A sauerkraut or other good bacterial ferment should taste sour and smell deep and tangy, but not off. The vegetables should have a crunch. If there is mould (a fungus) on the top of your ferment then the batch has been contaminated either by your fingers, the jar, or the vegetables not being fully submerged under the water. You will need to throw this away and start again. This is more likely to happen if you have mould in your house – so if this is a reoccurring issue you need to address the mould in your home.

Sauerkraut is a bacterial fermentation – so you're much less likely to get mould on it than many other types of commonly eaten food. Not leaving a large enough gap between the top of the water and the top of the jar is a common beginner issue. This gap is essential for the gases to get out otherwise when you burp it, it might spurt liquid. Wrap your jar in a tea towel and open it in the sink to stop any spurts hitting your wall or kitchen cupboards.

Quick Pickled Onions

Quick pickled onions will elevate many dishes, and especially your nacho plate (see p 348). To quick pickle, finely slice a red or white onion – I prefer red as they go a great pink colour – and stuff them into a 600ml/20fl oz-plus size jar. Some quick pickles use cold vinegars, but I like to heat them up as it speeds up the pickling process and softens the onions. Add one part water to one part vinegar, two tablespoons of maple syrup or other liquid sweetener and one teaspoon sea salt into a small saucepan. Simmer for 3–5 minutes on a low to medium heat. Let it cool for one minute (so the hot liquid doesn't crack your jar), then pour it on top of the onions. Press the onions down with a spoon to ensure they're fully covered by the liquid. Leave to cool for 20–30 minutes then pick out with a fork (so they're not too wet) and serve mixed through your nachos. Without the vinegar they will last a week in the fridge. In the vinegar they will last up to two weeks in the fridge. Quick pickling is more for the taste and crunch than a long-term preserving method.

Choosing Your Probiotic

To make the simple cheeses in this recipe book any vegan probiotic capsule will work. Non-vegan probiotics contain cultures from dairy, so it is important you look for a vegan one. We like using capsules as they give you a neat portion, but some probiotics can be bought as powder. If you get deeply into vegan cheesemaking, you'll start working with specific strains such as *acidophilus* or mesophilic cultures – which can be bought online from specialist vendors. You can even buy strains of penicillium to create rinds on firm vegan cheeses and to create the effect of a blue cheese. For the recipes in this book you don't need to get into all that, but it's a fascinating subject if these recipes spark your interest. We recommend books by vegan cheese OG Miyoko Schinner. Her class for us was legendary not only for the awesome cheeses she made, but the fact she knocked her blender over and broke it and had to improvise for the rest of the class. Total legend!

What's A SCOBY and Where Do You Get One?
SCOBY stands for Symbiotic Culture of Bacteria and Yeast. It's a thick, gelatinous mass of cellulose that at first glance can look like an ear or a lobe of skin that's been lopped off and left to go weird inside a jar! Your SCOBY is alive, although don't worry, it isn't sentient, but it does grow and it can die if you don't look after it. We like to name our SCOBYs at MIH – the best name a class participant gave being Voldemort. Ha. Back in the day SCOBYs could only be sourced by being passed from home fermenter to home fermenter. Nowadays you can buy them online. Keep your SCOBY in a SCOBY hotel – a glass jar with the SCOBY submerged in a small amount of kombucha covered with breathable cloth. If you're not using it for a few weeks feed it with some cool, sweet tea. Make a brew with one tea bag and a teaspoon of sugar then wait for it to cool before pouring it over the SCOBY to cover. Your SCOBY will grow in size. To share your SCOBY, peel it in half so it reduces in thickness. Pop in a jar covered with kombucha or sweet tea and gift to a friend.

How To Sterilize Jars

ON THE HOB/STOVETOP – Add the clean jars and lids (and rubber seals, if the jars have them) to a large saucepan, cover with water (2.5cm/1in above the top of the jars), bring to the boil and boil for ten minutes. Carefully drain/remove from the boiling water, turn upside-down, place on a clean wire/cooling rack and leave to dry and cool naturally.

IN THE OVEN – Preheat the oven to 160°C/325°F/gas 3. Wash the jars and lids thoroughly in soapy water, rinse well, then put them on a baking sheet and place in the oven for 15–20 minutes. Remove from the oven and leave to cool down naturally. If the jars have a rubber seal, use the hob/stovetop method.

INDEX

Mr

THANK YOU

THE COMMUNITY

To all the incredible people who got stuck in at our events/classes. Your wiliness to try something new and connect with your community over good food and good times is what makes MIH special. Thankyou for trusting us. We see you and appreciate you. .

THE CHEFS

There would be no MIH without our amazing chefs. Your skills, dedication, talent and energy are an inspiration. You've nourished, upskilled and evolved the diets of hundreds of thousands of folk. You're not just chefs, but food and community activists. Respect.

THE VOLUNTEERS

You give your time, heart and soul to MIH and do it with good vibes. You've cooked, tested recipes, cycled, hosted, managed logistics, led outreach stalls, crunched data, mopped floors, been hand models, shot photography and everything in between. No words can thank you enough.

THE TEAM

To the beautiful souls past and present who've been part of the MIH team – I bow down. Your can-do attitude, dedication, commitment, sense of humour, innovation and patience to put up with me (at least for the first 12 years) is astounding. It's hard graft, but you show up, get it done and make magic happen. My deepest respect to you all.

OUR SUPPORTERS

To all the people, funders, donors, organisations, collectives, restaurants, fellow charities and community groups who support our work and mission, I offer my sincerest gratitude. We look forward to continuing to work with you and the new supporters we hope this book brings.

THE MOVEMENT

To the movement, present and ancestral, building a world with justice, compassion, collectivism and plant-based food at its core, my deepest respect. I hope this book gives you joy and nourishment to sustain you during these rough times. Better days are coming.

MY FAMILY & FRIENDS

To my heart – Baba, Rowan, Gigi. Thank you for putting up with me and my endless book drama (and all the other dramas). To big sister Carol, Nana Julia, Uncle Adam, Aunty Joyce, oldest friend Kim, dearest Nynke and my Ibandla sister-queens for your unending love. To Mum and Dad. I miss you. I love you. I wish you could read this book.

THE BOOK TEAM

To everyone at Watkins who believed in this book and poured their talent into making it happen. Editor Ella, head of design Karen, food photographer Sarah, food stylist Bianca and assistant Susannah, prop stylist Megan, shoot volunteers Peter and Leo, photographer Marcus, photography assistant Katja, the team at Clearspring, Mr Organic and Viridian. We did it! And it's beautiful.

If you'd like to get involved or make a donation to support our work visit www.madeinhackney.org

MADE IN HACKNEY
MADE IN HACKNEY
MADE IN HACKNEY

MADE IN HACKNEY